People everywhere are hungry for meaning and purpose, wanting to make a difference, and be of service to something larger than themselves. *The Better World Handbook* provides valuable information and resources to manifest these intentions into practical reality. Keep a copy on your desk or reference shelf, and use it!

— MICHAEL TOMS, CEO, New Dimensions Radio, and co-author of *True Work: Doing What You Love and Loving What You Do*

We can make the world a better place and this book shows you how easy it is to really make a difference. I highly recommend that you buy it, use it and enjoy what you can do to help create positive change.

— JEFFREY HOLLENDER, President, Seventh Generation, and author of *Naturally Clean: The Seventh Generation Guide to Safe and Healthy Non-Toxic Cleaning*

The Better World Handbook provides a wealth of practical ideas for transforming our everyday activities of shopping, living, and working into an artful way of life that is more sustainable, just, and meaningful.

— DUANE ELGIN, author of *Voluntary Simplicity: Toward a Way of Life That is Outwardly Simple, Inwardly Rich* and *Promise Ahead: A Vision of Hope and Action for Humanity's Future*

The Revolution is not just around the corner, it's around every corner. I love this old saying because it captures the important truth highlighted in this inspiring book: The world can be changed through action in our everyday lives — where we spend our money, how we help out in our community, the ways we travel. This practical, enjoyable handbook shows how small improvements can add up to a big difference in the world.

— JAY WALLJASPER, editor *Ode* Magazine and co-author of *Visionaries: People and Ideas to Change Your Life* and *The Great Neighborhood Book: A Do-it-Yourself Guide to Placemaking*

the
better
world
HANDBOOK

SMALL CHANGES THAT MAKE A BIG DIFFERENCE

the
better
world
HANDBOOK

Ellis Jones · Ross Haenfler · Brett Johnson

NEW SOCIETY PUBLISHERS

Cataloging in Publication Data:
A catalog record for this publication is available from the National Library of Canada.

Copyright © 2007 by Ellis Jones, Ross Haenfler and Brett Johnson.
All rights reserved.

The authors will use their profits from the sale of this book to help maintain and develop The Better World Network, a nonprofit organization created to carry on the work this book has begun. Contact the authors by visiting: www.betterworldhandbook.com or www.betterworldnetwork.org.

Cover concept: Ellis Jones. Design: Diane McIntosh.
Image: iStock, Jan Stadelmyer.
Printed in Canada.
First printing January 2007.

Paperback ISBN 13: 978-086571-575-2

Inquiries regarding requests to reprint all or part of *The Better World Handbook* should be addressed to New Society Publishers at the address below.

To order directly from the publishers, please call toll-free (North America) 1-800-567-6772, or order online at: www.newsociety.com

Any other inquiries can be directed by mail to:
New Society Publishers
P.O. Box 189, Gabriola Island, BC V0R 1X0, Canada
1-800-567-6772

New Society Publishers' mission is to publish books that contribute in fundamental ways to building an ecologically sustainable and just society, and to do so with the least possible impact on the environment, in a manner that models this vision. We are committed to doing this not just through education, but through action. We are acting on our commitment to the world's remaining ancient forests by phasing out our paper supply from ancient forests worldwide. This book is one step toward ending global deforestation and climate change. It is printed on acid-free paper that is 100% old growth forest-free (100% post-consumer recycled), processed chlorine free, and printed with vegetable-based, low-VOC inks. For further information, or to browse our full list of books and purchase securely, visit our website at: www.newsociety.com

NEW SOCIETY PUBLISHERS   www.newsociety.com

CONTENTS

PREFACE TO
THE SECOND EDITION

SINCE THE FIRST EDITION of *The Better World Handbook* came out in 2001, we've been on a book tour, spoken to university students, community groups, and churches, participated in the Better World Handbook Festival, and read hundreds of supportive emails from people all over the world. Through each of these wonderful interactions, one consistent theme emerges again and again: people are *hungry* for ways to make a real difference in the world while leading meaningful, fulfilling lives. Many of you have inspired us with stories of how you and others in your communities are taking positive steps toward a more just and sustainable world — your feedback, commitment, and hopeful vision has driven us to write an updated and improved *Better World Handbook*. Thank you.

Your optimism, creativity, and passion are needed now more than ever. In the five years since the first edition, we've faced challenging times: the 9/11 attacks, the invasion of Iraq, the Abu Ghraib torture scandal, and Hurricane Katrina and the bungled relief effort that followed. We know how difficult it can be to maintain hope when so much seems to be heading in the wrong direction, so here's something you should know. A growing body of evidence points to the recent emergence of what could be called a Better World Movement. Millions of people in the US and around the world are starting to see the profound connections between their own daily choices and the potential for social change spanning a wide spectrum of global issues. They are taking action in their everyday lives, and making their collective impact felt across the social, economic, cultural, and political spheres. Many of the participants in this movement are not formally organized, nor does it seem likely that they will ever meet. But they are a powerful force to be reckoned with. So we are here to tell you that you are not alone. And to thank you, though we may never meet, for the incredible contribution you are making to the world.

The book focuses on answering four basic questions (1) How do we overcome those things that stop us from making a difference in the world? (2) What kind of vision of a better world do we want to work toward? (3) What are the major challenges we currently face as a global society? (4) What can we do in everyday lives to make the world better?

Whether you're passionate about the environment, human rights, social justice, democratic reform, global community, independent media, nonviolence, women's rights, local business, peace building, simple living, wildlife conservation, civil rights, fair trade, renewable energy, cultural diversity, sustainable growth, personal empowerment, animal rights or just living with integrity by "walking your talk," this book will help you bring that ideal into reality. We like to call it practical idealism.

We know that you're busy, which is why we've done thousands of hours of research for you and compiled it into a single, compact, readable, easy-to-use, action-packed handbook. This was no small task, but it has been a true labor of love. This edition features new actions, updated research and resources, and a new chapter called Spirituality and Religion. Our hope is that it will help you recognize the profound impact you have on your local, national and global communities and inspire you to turn your good intentions into everyday actions that will make a powerful difference across the entire spectrum of the world's problems. Welcome to The Better World Movement!

ACKNOWLEDGMENTS

THE THREE OF US WOULD LIKE TO THANK: All of our readers for their invaluable support and feedback that made this new edition possible. The many gracious people who hosted us on our original book tour. Gillian O'Brien and all of the amazing volunteers that helped create The Better World Handbook Festival in Vancouver, BC. Brian Klocke for his contributions to the first edition. Darin Johnson, Tom Lindsley and Bethel Erickson for their feedback on the Spirituality and Religion chapter.

Ellis: Ara Francis, my wonderful partner. Paul Todisco, my best friend. Joel Federman, my longtime mentor. Carl McKinney, my greatest teacher. Erik and Garda Persson, my Swedish grandparents. Harold and Opal Jones, my American grandparents. The Puengprasith's, my Thai family. The Ramirez's, my Panamanian family. My AFS and Peace Corps friends. All of the students in my classes who wrote their own books to build a better world. Brett, Ross and my parents, especially my mother, Anita.

Ross: My amazing partner Jennifer (Skadi) Snook; my mother Ruth and brother Brad. My father Duane and step-mom Carolyn. Grandpa and Grandma Burfeindt; Grandpa and Grandma Haenfler; and the rest of my family. Nate Miller, Collin Ahrens, Jimmy Beam, and Matt Ramirez for their loyalty and friendship. Positive XStraightEdgeX and hardcore kids everywhere. Boulder Mennonite Church; all of my students; Brett and Ellis; and God.

Brett: My partner Jen for her love, companionship, and willingness to put up with my long hours and distracted mind; my parents and brothers for their unconditional love and support; Ross, for being an unstoppable force for good; Ellis, for being a one-of-a-kind visionary. To all who go out of their way to nurture love and justice.

INTRODUCTION

Our Mission For This Book

O UR MISSION IS TO HAVE A POSITIVE IMPACT on the world by encouraging you to:

- *rediscover your relationship with the world*
- *understand your power to make the world better*
- *turn your values into effective actions*

Many people care about making the world a better place but feel they don't have the time or the energy to really make a difference. If you fit into this category, then this is the book for you. *The Better World Handbook* is the definitive guide for people who care about creating a better world but are not sure where to begin. It will help you to recognize the profound impact that you have upon your local and global communities and will inspire you to put your values into action.

The Better World Handbook has three major sections.

BUILDING A BETTER WORLD begins by uncovering the vicious cycle of cynicism most of us are caught up in, and then details how this cycle can be transformed into a powerful cycle of hope that moves us back into a powerfully positive direction. This section continues by covering the ten most common "thought traps" that stop people from making a difference in the world, and then lays out strategies that will allow you to move freely beyond each of them so that you maximize your ability to create a better world.

THE SEVEN FOUNDATIONS OF A BETTER WORLD provide a global vision of a better world that is worth fighting for. In addition, this section summarizes the main challenges that humanity faces in the 21st century, provides viable alternative solutions that we can implement, and shares examples of what thousands of people around the globe are already doing.

ACTIONS FOR A BETTER WORLD makes up the bulk of the book and is divided into 14 chapters. In this section, we've sifted through an overwhelming amount of information and focused on the most practical, effective actions that you can take to create a better world. Read the action chapters in whatever order best suits your curiosity and desire to act. We hope that you find actions applicable to every area of your life — actions that you can take to make a positive difference in the world.

You may begin reading this book and become so inspired that you want to change everything in your life all at once. Or you may find yourself so overwhelmed by all of the changes mentioned that you shut down completely. Avoid both of these pitfalls — find a balance within yourself. No one changes his or her life overnight. Take on more than you can handle, and you'll almost certainly burn yourself out very quickly. A few changes that last for the rest of your life are far more powerful in their impact than dozens of changes that you can only sustain for six months or a year. The trick to changing your daily actions permanently lies in your finding a way of living that integrates your desire to make the world better with your desire to pursue your own personal dreams.

While reading, you will undoubtedly come across values, issues, and actions that you don't agree with. Don't let that stop you from making a difference. The beauty of this book is that it includes a vast array of actions based upon many different values. Some will interest you more than others. Identify those actions that you truly believe in and can commit to integrating into your life right now. Act on those issues that inspire you, and find out how you can act on the values that we don't cover here. You must decide for yourself how you can contribute to making the world a better place.

We encourage you to make this book your own. As actions excite you, dog-ear the page or scribble notes in the margin. And be sure to check off actions as you implement them in your life. We want this book to be an essential resource that will inspire you for years to come.

HOW YOU CAN HELP

If the ideas and actions presented in this book encourage you, please visit our websites at BetterWorldHandbook.com and BetterWorldNetwork.org, where you can find updated information on all kinds of ways to make a difference. If you have any suggestions to improve the next edition of the book, please don't hesitate to email us at contact@betterworldhandbook.com, or write to us at The Better World Network, 1280 Olive Drive #122, Davis, CA 95616, USA. We'd love to hear from you! Really.

For those of you who would like to learn more, we are available for lectures and workshops worldwide. For speaking engagements, email us at speaking@betterworldhandbook.com.

If this book truly inspires you, you can help build the nonprofit organization we've created to carry on what we've begun with this book. You can find out more about this work and even help support it from our website at BetterWorldNetwork.org.

BUILDING A BETTER WORLD

The Cycle of Cynicism
The Cycle of Hope
The Ten Thought Traps

You must be the change you wish to see in the world.
— M.K. Gandhi

WE HAVE BECOME A NATION OF SLEEPWALKERS. We look around at the world's problems and wish they would go away, but they stubbornly persist despite our most heartfelt desires. So we end up living in a kind of ethical haze. It's not that we are bad or that evil is winning some kind of eternal battle. The vast majority of us have good intentions when we go about our daily lives. It's that we have been lulled into a sense of complacency about the world's problems, as if they are less-than-real occurrences. We react similarly to how we might normalize the strange events that occur while we're in the middle of a dream. People starve, communities fall apart, violence thrives, families fade, and nature disappears, and we continue on with our lives as if nothing is wrong. We are stuck in our daily patterns, living on auto-pilot when it comes to the rest of the world.

But like a whisper in the back of our minds that stays with us always, we have the feeling that something has gone awry. We have lost our faith in each other. Politicians are corrupt, corporations seek to make a profit at any cost, and even our democratic election process is called into question! It seems that everything and everyone is for sale. Nothing remains sacred. We feel that perhaps we can only truly rely on ourselves. When these negative beliefs become widespread, we disengage from the outer world, recoiling into our own personal lives. As we withdraw, we see our society rushing aimlessly toward an unknown future, without any sense of morality or conscious purpose to direct it. Awash in a sea of information, we lack the wisdom to guide our own destiny.

How did we end up here? Many people point the finger at a culture that breeds apathy. In fact, beneath apathy there lies an even bigger culprit: cynicism.

1

Cynicism is the deeply ingrained belief that human beings are, and have always been, inherently selfish. Cynicism in this form is not just a long-term emotional state or an adopted intellectual philosophy, it is a way of relating to the world.

Cynicism fundamentally destroys hope. We begin to see the world as a place that will always be filled with social problems, because we are convinced that people look out for their own best interests above all else. The pursuit of happiness becomes little more than an attempt to accumulate material wealth, increase social status and indulge any desire. Helping others, giving something back, and making a difference in the world no longer show up in popular culture.

Indeed, people who decide to help, give back or make a difference are often labeled as odd, naive, overly sentimental, unrealistic or simply irrational. The most you can strive for under this cynical worldview is to come out somewhere nearer the top than the bottom.

In a world of constantly increasing complexity, cynicism becomes the safest, most strategic position to adopt. It involves no action and thus no risk. Cynics can portray their inaction as more rational, objective, and more realistic than people who are trying to change the world. Apathy becomes an accepted state of being.

So what happened? How did we become this cynical? Simply put, our modern society manufactures cynicism. Every day we are bombarded with media reports of crime, disaster, conflict and scandal, in our communities and from around the globe. The stories are usually too brief for us to gain any meaningful understanding of the problems and lack any options for us to contribute significantly to their resolution. Waves of negative imagery relentlessly wash over us as we try to keep up with what's happening in the world around us. Like sponges, we absorb the negativity; it spills over into how we look at the world and affects how we act or fail to act.

The Cycle of Cynicism begins when we first find out about society's problems. When we recognize that others are suffering, we want the suffering to stop. We even wonder if there is anything we could do to help. When no viable avenues for action are presented, and we fail to generate any ourselves, we do nothing. We end up feeling powerless and sad. We may become angry and blame people in positions of power for not doing anything to stop it either. We feel that we are good people, we see an injustice, but we don't do anything about it. In the end we reconcile this dissonance by accepting that perhaps nothing can be done. And we initiate a process of slowly numbing ourselves to the suffering. We subtly begin to avoid finding out about the suffering in the first place, since knowing only makes us feel bad. Over time we shut out our awareness of most social problems and retreat further and further into our insular, personal lives. We become apathetic.

How do we break out of the Cycle of Cynicism? We must stop blaming others for not doing anything and begin to take personal responsibility for being good

THE CYCLE OF CYNICISM

1. Finding out about a problem.
2. Wanting to do something to help.
3. Not seeing how you can help.
4. Not doing anything about it.
5. Feeling sad, powerless, angry.
6. Deciding that nothing can be done.
7. Beginning to shut down.
8. Wanting to know less about problems.

Repeat until apathy results.

people in the world. We need to seek out information that provides us with a basic understanding of our world's problems and a variety of options for action. We have to generate a form of practical idealism based on well-informed actions that actually make a difference in the world. Each of us must decide what we want our life to stand for and how we can uniquely contribute to a better world. We must learn to think about what we can provide for the next generations rather than about what we can take for ourselves in this lifetime. By doing this, we can choose to create our own society's destiny instead of leaving our children's future up for grabs. Finally, throughout it all, we need to recognize that we can't do everything.

THE CYCLE OF HOPE

1. Taking personal responsibility for being a good person.
2. Creating a vision of a better world based on your values.
3. Seeking out quality information about the world's problems.
4. Discovering practical options for action.
5. Acting in line with your values.
6. Recognizing you can't do everything.

Repeat until a better world results.

We must reconnect with a set of core values that every one of us can embrace despite our many differences — values like compassion, freedom, equality, justice, sustainability, democracy, community, and tolerance. No society — especially one as powerful and rapidly changing as ours — survives for very long without a moral compass to guide its evolution and progress. We have to deliberately build our society to increasingly reflect and nurture the growth of these values in the world.

Think about the world that you would like to live in. Let yourself imagine a world that you could be proud to leave for your children — a world where peace, justice, compassion, and tolerance prevail and where each person has more than enough food, shelter, meaningful work and close friends. What would a more loving, accepting, patient, understanding and egalitarian world look like? Your vision of a better future will provide you with an inspiring goal to work toward and will keep your passion alive for the journey ahead. As we start out, we must be aware of the many traps that can stop us from making a difference in the world.

THE TEN THOUGHT TRAPS

Trap #1: "That's just the way the world is"

If you look back through history, you'll discover that the world has always faced seemingly insurmountable challenges: slavery, hunger, warfare and intolerance. But can you imagine how the world would be different if all people throughout history had resigned themselves to just accepting the troubles of their time? Can you imagine the cynics of the day saying that:

- America will always be an British colony
- slavery will always exist
- women will never be allowed to vote
- whites and blacks will never share the same classrooms
- people in wheelchairs will never have access to public buildings
- free public schooling is an unrealistic dream.

. . . so there's no point trying to change anything.

For every social problem that has existed there have been people dedicated to solving it and creating positive social change. Every situation that has been created by humans can be changed by humans. A better world is always a possibility. Although current problems may seem overwhelming, to surrender hope only ensures that nothing will change. Embrace your vision for a better world and you'll find all the hope you will ever need.

Once you let yourself envision a better world, you can then consider where you fit into this whole picture. Our culture teaches us that we are each autonomous individuals who are only responsible for our own well-being. We end up believing that we are independent creatures who should make our own way in life without depending on others. In reality, we all rely on each other for our daily existence. We eat food that grows in soil nurtured by microscopic organisms. We drink water that has vaporized from the oceans. We breathe oxygen respired by the trees and wear clothing made by people across the planet whom we will never meet. We rely on our friends and family for support and create a sense of belonging and meaning within our communities. Our personal well-being is inextricably linked to the well-being of our families, our friends, our communities and our planet. And the well-being of others, in turn, is shaped by our own well-being.

When you truly understand the interconnected nature of the world, you realize that you are both very powerful and yet very small — you influence everything around you, yet there is so much more to life than just you. When you validate the clear connections that bind us all together, you gain awareness of how each of your actions affects other people and the planet around you.

Trap #2: "It's not my responsibility"

You may be saying, I didn't cause the world's problems so why should I be responsible for fixing them? That may seem true on the surface, until you realize that the problems that our world faces are created by the daily actions of millions and millions of people. The CEO of a company may be the person who should be held most responsible for the pollution created by her/his company. But don't the shareholders bear some responsibility, and the people who purchase its products, and the local television station that covers car crashes and celebrity weddings instead of investigating local water quality?

All of us hold some measure of responsibility for the challenges that our society faces, even if it's only because we have not taken the time to become informed about our world and about the well-being of others. We don't like to take responsibility for other people's messes, and we like to think that our own messes are very small. But our impact on the world is much larger than we think. For example, try to answer the following questions:

- Whose car causes smog?
- Whose use of energy causes global warming and climate change?
- Whose apathy leads to some of the lowest voter turnouts in history?
- Whose frown makes people think that your city is not a friendly place?
- Whose purchases keep an unethical company in business?
- Whose lack of support for a community group causes it to close its doors?

The answer to these questions is, all of us together. The responsibility lies with the group as a whole and with each individual. How you spend and invest your money, the career you choose, the car you drive, your participation or non-participation in our democracy and countless other decisions all have an impact on our planet and its people. This book offers many concrete suggestions on how you can take responsibility for your part by creating forward-looking solutions to today's problems.

Trap #3: "One person can't make a difference"

Even if you are willing to take responsibility and do your part to make the world a better place, you may be thinking, But I'm only one person on a planet of six billion people. I can't possibly make a difference!

Problems such as racism, hunger, and inequality seem so big that it's easy to feel small and powerless. You might be surprised to realize the myriad ways your actions can contribute to a better world.

- ✓ Your money invested in the right bank can help create wealth for poor communities.
- ✓ Your letter can be the one that changes the behavior of an entire corporation.
- ✓ Your vote can elect government officials that really make a difference.
- ✓ Your timely call to a friend can change their outlook for the day.
- ✓ Your donation can help a social change organization meet its lofty goals.
- ✓ Your purchase can allow a locally owned business to thrive in your community.
- ✓ Your participation can transform a small group of people into the beginnings of a social movement.

Your actions have this potential to create a better world, but when we act we are never guaranteed the results that we hope for. We will never have access to a "time-line" of when poverty and war will be eradicated from our society. We also can't control how and if others will act. We only have control over our own intentions and actions. We must be willing to act and have faith that it will make a difference. We must be willing to act and risk failure. We must be willing to create a project of which we may never see the end results. We must have the faith and determination to plant seedlings even though they will not provide shade for years to come.

As citizens, consumers, and individuals we must realize that we are the lifeblood of the political, economic, and social spheres that make the world go round. On a daily basis, you not only have the power to perpetuate the world's problems, you have the opportunity to stand up for the creation of a world based on your own deeply held values.

Trap #4 "I can't make enough of a difference to matter"

You may be thinking, sure, one person can make a difference, in theory, but it's not *enough* of a difference to really matter. Our seemingly small actions appear to be meager drops of water in a vast ocean. No one wants to be the next Don Quixote, being seen as foolish and ineffective, stuck in a world of idealistic dreams and delusions of grandeur. How much of a difference can you actually make anyway? In truth, you can make one person's difference — no more, no less.

The reality is that the world's problems are the end result of decades of actions by governments, corporations, and individuals just like you. This means that no one person will ever be able to snap his or her fingers and change the world. It also means that problems cannot be solved without individuals taking action to change their own behavior. It is the basic contradiction that is integral to our own democracy — no one person can control the outcome, yet if every individual decides that his or her own vote is therefore pointless, then the whole democratic system fails.

If you decide to boycott a product, your decision won't bankrupt the company. But if you and a significant number of others stop buying for a period of time, this powerful company will soon come running to figure out how they can change their behavior or product to get you back. There are many instances of governments and corporations being brought to their knees because of the actions of "ordinary people." A small network of activists shamed Nike for allowing low pay and oppressive working conditions in its "sweatshops."

Often, we become so caught up in our own immediate, personal lives that we forget what kind of massive impact we have as a collective. We must begin to think long-term and think of the big picture. From the vantage point of one human being, it is difficult to grasp the progress of social movements and large-scale changes. Only when we look back with the luxury of hindsight can we determine how much of a difference we made.

It's important to remember that not only do each of your actions have a direct impact on the world, but also every choice you make sends a message to those around you. Your choice to use your bicycle instead of your car, support a political candidate or sell fair trade coffee at your church can inspire others to do their part. We create momentum for each other. At the same time, we support each other to live in a manner that creates possibilities for a better future.

Don't ever let anyone convince you that you have no power — together we have the power to change the world. All significant changes in the world start slowly, at a single time and place, with a single action. One man, one woman, one child stands up and commits to creating a better world. Their courage inspires others, who begin to stand up themselves. You can be that person. When you act, you are tapping into a lifeline of others who have gone out of their way to improve the world.

Once you become aware of how your actions affect others and accept responsibility for your role in creating a better world, your values will come to the forefront of your life. In what ways do you want to change the world? What do you value most in life? What would the world be like if everyone was taking responsibility for how their life creates and shapes the world?

Trap #5: "This seems totally overwhelming"

Wanting the world to be a better place is one thing, but being willing to personally take on bringing that world into being is another. As you more fully integrate your values with your actions, you are bound to become frustrated. The first thing you may notice is that we all live in contradiction with many of our values.

- You wish people were friendlier, but you realize that you are often too busy to smile and say hello to the cashier at the place where you go every day for lunch.

- You detest the thought of children slaving away in a sweatshop, yet you find out that the new pair of shoes you just bought at a bargain price were made by workers paid only a fraction of their living expenses.

Your realizations may leave you feeling frustrated, guilty, or even hypocritical. But remember we don't have to be perfect people, have perfect knowledge, wait until the perfect time, or know the perfect action to take before we begin making the world better. Those are all just ways that we keep ourselves from making a difference.

In fact, instead of thinking of the integration of your values and actions in terms of black and white (either you're perfect or you're a hypocrite), consider reframing the issue in terms of a continuum. Just as we now know that every little bit of exercise helps maintain our overall health, every one of these decisions makes a difference for the planet.

Take recycling, for example (something many of us would ideally like to do more often but don't always have the energy), and take a look at the diagram below. On this continuum, the farther you move to the right the larger your contribution to a healthier environment. Starting a recycling program at your work will make an impact for years to come and have a much bigger impact than just recycling yourself. But remember any progress along this continuum is a positive and important contribution to a better world.

Keep in mind that the goal is a better world and not a perfect world. It is not an all-or-nothing commitment. That's why this book is called *The Better World Handbook* not The Perfect World Handbook. You take those actions that are sustainable for your unique life. Once you start, you'll gain better knowledge, better timing and better actions and ultimately become a better person for it.

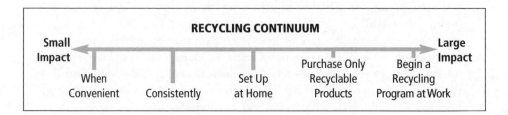

RECYCLING CONTINUUM

Small Impact ← → Large Impact

When Convenient — Consistently — Set Up at Home — Purchase Only Recyclable Products — Begin a Recycling Program at Work

Learn to live with your imperfections; embrace them — they are what make us human. And consider this: If you were somehow able to manage to be perfect, who would be able to live up to your standards? Who would want to join you in making a difference? Who would be able to do what you do? No one.

With each conscious choice you make to create a better world, you take responsibility for your existence. You increasingly become the director of your life as you more fully integrate your values with your actions. You create a stronger and healthier society and planet. Now is the time to commit to transforming your good intentions into action.

Trap #6: "I don't have the time or the energy"

The last thing most of us want is to add even more responsibilities to our already busy schedules. Not only do we not have the physical energy for more activities, we don't have the psychic energy to worry about the world's problems. We fill our daily schedules with paying bills, returning messages, making meals, keeping appointments, writing notes, cleaning our houses and fixing our appearances.

- We surround ourselves with more and more technology to save ourselves time and then often find ourselves at the mercy of it. In the end, it seems that we have even less time and more to get done.

- When you take the time to reschedule your life based on your most deeply held values, you will find all of the time necessary to live a fulfilling life that contributes to others.

- Upon examining your priorities, you may discover that although you value spending time with your family, you actually spend most of your free time watching TV. Why not shift your energies?

Many of the actions in this book take very little time to complete yet make a real contribution to the world. Some, such as installing a low-flow showerhead or setting up an account at a socially responsible bank, you only have to do once. Others, such as buying less stuff, will actually save you time that you would otherwise spend in traffic, in lines, and on working to pay for the stuff you bought. In fact, we expect you to find that living out your values and engaging in meaningful daily action actually gives you energy! And there's no better feeling than the feeling that you're making a positive difference in the lives of others.

Trap #7: "I'm not a saint"

You don't have to be a saint to make a difference in the world. Many people stereotype individuals committed to social change as people who have put aside families, convenience, and pleasure for a cause they deem to be of greater importance. Images of Mother Teresa, Cesar Chavez, Martin Luther King Jr. and Mahatma Gandhi come to mind. We see these individuals living in poverty, fasting, or protesting and we label them as self-proclaimed martyrs. We can't imagine doing the things they do, and we think, I'm not someone who can change the world, I don't want to sacrifice everything, or I'm not that good.

This book is not about giving up your whole life for a cause, nor is it about good deeds that you do twice a year when you finally get all of your chores done. It is about living a life full of passion and power — one that will enrich you and the world around you. The point is to balance your personal needs, your family's needs and your community's needs. The goal is not to live the perfect life but to make improvements in your life so that your actions are increasingly in line with your values. And be sure to forgive yourself when you don't live up to your own ideals.

Committing yourself to making a difference can be fulfilling, meaningful and fun. You don't have to move to a cabin in the woods, read dense political theory all day, live in poverty, or walk around with a frown because of the heaviness of the world's problems. Rather than being a sacrifice, working for a better world can help you create a deep happiness beyond your imagination.

Once you have committed to living out your values, the next step is to learn about and take the most practical, effective actions available to bring about the better world you envision. Without adequate information, it's difficult to take effective actions and easy to take actions that unintentionally work against what you're trying to accomplish.

Trap #8: "I don't know enough about the issues"

None of us wants to feel like we're leaping into action uninformed. Because the world's problems are so complex, it's easy to think we will never know enough to act in ways that will really help solve these problems. Make an effort to get quality information about the world so that your actions will actually be effective (see the MEDIA chapter for tips). At times you will just know in your heart which actions you should take.

In our ever-changing world there will always be more to know, but taking action can actually help inform you about the issues you care about. When you become involved, it connects you with others who care about the same issues and creates numerous opportunities for learning. Don't worry, you don't have to start from scratch. This book provides you with plenty of information to get started, and you can seek out further information as you get inspired.

Trap #9: "I don't know where to begin"

In fact, you have already begun. You already act in ways that take others' well-being into account, whether you lend your mower to a neighbor, jump-start a co-worker's car, or let a car change lanes in front of you on the freeway. You have probably already taken some of the actions in this book. Go ahead and check them off.

Just start where you feel the most comfortable. Maybe pick an area in your life where you are already taking some actions. Then work up to actions that will be more challenging. Or start with the action that would be the most fun, the one you could do with a friend, or one that will give you the most fulfillment.

Throughout the book, we suggest that you focus your energies. Identify actions that are important to you and that are realistic for you to take on. Be open to challenging yourself, but don't overwhelm yourself with unrealistic expectations. If making the world better isn't fulfilling for you, you won't keep it up very long.

Trap #10: "I'm not an activist"

When many of us think of social change, we imagine environmentalists in tie-dyed shirts blocking logging trucks or gas-masked rebels facing off with lines of riot police. Not wanting to get involved in such intense actions or to be associated with what the media portray as irrational or radical protesters, we don't get involved. In reality, people of all professions, backgrounds, interests, and lifestyles are involved in social change. Lawyers, teachers, autoworkers, computer programmers, cashiers and clerical workers are among the many making a difference in the streets, in the office, in their communities, and at home.

You can be yourself and fulfill your commitment to a better world. You don't have to follow some pre-designed path for making the world better. You don't have to change who you are in order to live out your values. In fact, with your values at the forefront of your life, you're actually being more true to yourself. This book provides you a range of actions with which to carve out your own niche. Be creative, forge your own unique path, and translate commitment into action in your own way.

People all over the world are living out their vision for a better world. Many people are simplifying their lives, buying less stuff, working less, and giving back more to their community. Concern and knowledge about the environment has been spreading for the last 30 years, and recycling has become a widespread habit. People are taking time to learn about other cultures and appreciate diversity. No matter where you turn, you see individuals doing their part. You are not alone in building a better world. In fact, you are part of a growing movement that is changing the face of the world!

A WORD OF CAUTION

Beware! When you start living your life more in line with your values, some conflicts may arise. Your actions will sometimes threaten others who haven't put as much thought into how they want to live their lives. They may even try to stop you from making changes in your life because they do not want to examine their own existence in the world. Accept this — it comes with the territory.

It is also common to take on a self-righteous attitude when you have strongly held values. This attitude is destructive to the goal of a better world. People do not want to be around someone who lives life to show others how wrong they are.

If you have an understanding of the beauty and the complexity of life, then you will always attract people who are yearning for peace and fulfillment. Understand that you are no better than anyone else; you are just someone trying to live life the best way you know how.

THE SEVEN FOUNDATIONS OF A BETTER WORLD

Economic Fairness
Comprehensive Peace
Ecological Sustainability
Deep Democracy
Social Justice
Simple Living
Revitalized Community

The arc of the universe is long but it bends towards justice.
— Martin Luther King, Jr.

MAKING THE WORLD A BETTER PLACE is a lifelong journey. If we plan and prepare for this journey as we would for any other, it will make the trip less frustrating and more gratifying. When we learn a bit about where we have been and consider where we are going, it helps us to understand our current place in the voyage. An understanding of the scope of the world's problems and their potential solutions will help you realize the importance of your everyday actions and will inspire you to create meaningful change.

This section outlines seven essential foundations upon which we can build a better world. We begin our exploration of each foundation by describing the challenges that face us at home and around the world. Then we launch into concrete goals — viable alternatives that can confront the challenges and help us construct the foundation. We also give inspiring examples of dedicated people around the world who are already making a positive difference. We end with some of the best, most accessible resources from which you can learn more about each issue.

CHALLENGES	GOALS
Economic Inequality	End of Global Poverty
Debt Crisis and Unfair Trade	Fair Trade
Sweatshops	Ethical Economics
War and Genocide	International Cooperation
Militarization	Nonviolent Culture
Unilateralism	
Culture of Violence	
Resource Overconsumption	Clean Energy Sources
Pollution	Sustainable Resource Use
Global Warming	Stable Population Growth
Overpopulation	Global Ecological Cooperation
Lack of Democracy	Open and Honest Politics
Money in Politics	Democratic Media
Media Control	Civic Participation
Gender Inequality	Equal Rights For All
Racism	Universal Health Care and Education
Heterosexism	
Inadequate Health Care	
Prisons	
Advertising Overload	Reclaimed Consciousness
Commercialization of Childhood	A Culture of Simplicity
Hyper-Consumerism	
Loss of Connection	Revolution of Caring
Lack of Compassion	Smart Growth
	Strong Local Institutions

FOUNDATION #1: ECONOMIC FAIRNESS

A world dedicated to economic fairness would strive to meet every person's basic needs so that no one would lack food, shelter, clothing, or meaningful work. People's strength of character and passion should determine their opportunities rather than the economic circumstances into which they were born. Everyone would benefit from economic prosperity.

CHALLENGES
Economic Inequality — Debt Crisis and Unfair Trade — Sweatshops

Economic Inequality

As each year passes, the immense gap between the rich and the very poor grows. While recent economic development in China and India has pulled millions out of poverty, about one billion people around the world still live in extreme poverty — living on less than one dollar a day.[1] 2.5 billion people (40% of the world's population) live on less than $2 a day.[2] Much of the world's poor is caught in a "poverty trap." Their daily struggle against hunger and disease is an overwhelming challenge for those without education, financial resources, or modern technology. This poverty is not caused by absolute scarcity. There is more than enough wealth in the world to meet everyone's needs — poverty is caused by an unfair system of distribution. In 2005, the richest 10% of humanity made more money than the remaining 90% of the world's population combined![3] The poorest 40% of humanity only received 5% of the world's income.[4] Citizens and leaders of wealthy nations should not be able to sleep at night knowing that 850 million people are chronically hungry![5]

This cycle of inequality does not bode well for the 1.3 billion people — over one-fifth of the world's population — who lack access to clean water and the 24,000 people who die from hunger-related causes every day. That's one person dying every 4 seconds![6] And 6.5 million children under five years of age die every year from hunger-related causes — that's 18,000 a day, every day of the year.[7] As global economic inequality grows, the developing world's voice in the global economy decreases — leaving the world's poor in even a more powerless position.

In the rich countries huge corporate mergers further concentrate the world's wealth by generating millions of dollars in profits for wealthy stockholders and executives, often while laying off (downsizing) tens of thousands of workers. In 1980, the average American CEO earned 42 times as much as the average worker they employed. By 2003, the gap had grown to over 300 times.[8] In 2004, the CEO of Yahoo brought home a salary of $60 million in addition to cashing out $230 million in stock options — that's almost $800,000 per day (including weekends).[9]

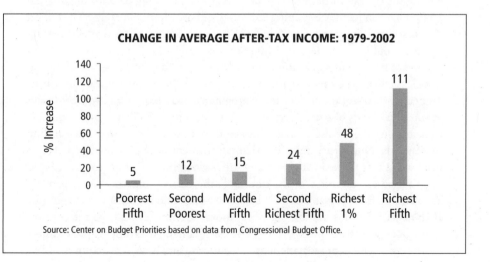

CHANGE IN AVERAGE AFTER-TAX INCOME: 1979-2002

Source: Center on Budget Priorities based on data from Congressional Budget Office.

Since the 1970s, the US economy has increasingly become top heavy — with the privileged gaining huge amounts of wealth and the middle and lower classes often struggling to make it, let alone move ahead. The richest 1% of Americans owns over 33% of the country's wealth—with the richest 10% owning a staggering 71%.[10] Currently, the richest 1% of Americans owns as much wealth as the entire bottom 90% of the US population combined![11] Stock ownership is even more skewed. The richest 1% owns 44% of all value in stocks and mutual funds—three times the share of the poorest 90% of Americans.[12] While a privileged few wield fortunes in the billions, others live in disempowering poverty. Despite great progress in the 1960s, the official poverty rate in 2004 is higher than in 1973.[13] In fact, more than 11 million US children live in poverty.[14]

Compared to 19 other rich, industrialized countries, the US has more inequality, less mobility out of poverty, and more child poverty.[15] This inequality has even affected average life expectancy. According to the latest CIA estimates, the US ranks 48th in overall life expectancy, behind Bosnia and Herzegovina![16]

Debt Crisis and Unfair Trade

Most developing countries owe staggering amounts of money to wealthier nations and global financial institutions. Interest payments on these debts further exacerbate the hardships poor people suffer. International aid often doesn't work or doesn't make it to the people who need it most. Despite their claims to the contrary, the world's major international lending institutions, the International Monetary Fund (IMF) and the World Bank, have consistently favored First World corporations and are widely acknowledged to have increased poverty among the world's most desperate peoples. Despite having paid off the original $540 billion in loans, developing countries still owe approximately $520 billion in accumulated interest.[17] The Jubilee Debt Coalition estimates that eliminating this debt could save the lives of 19,000 children every day.[18]

Once poor countries acquire so much debt that they have no hope of paying it back, the IMF bails them out on the condition they accept "structural adjustment programs" (SAPs, also called austerity programs). SAPs require government budget cuts in all kinds of social programs in favor of programs that focus on quickly transforming the countries' assets into cash that can be paid directly to lending institutions. Not surprisingly, the rich government officials who accepted this debt in the first place don't personally suffer when it comes time to pay it back. Food subsidies, education, health care, and other services that the poor depend on are often the first programs to go.[19] In 2000, Mozambique's debt payments on its IMF loans were $1.4 million per week, more than four times what the country spent weekly on basic health care.[20] The Nicaraguan government spent almost twice as much on debt repayment as on education and health care combined.[21]

While many of the rich countries preach the ideology of "free trade" to get their products into poor countries, they highly subsidize their own industries (especially agriculture) and put tariffs on products coming from poorer countries. When poor countries export products to the richer world they face tariffs that are four times higher than when the trading relationship is reversed—to the sum of $100 billion a year.[22] These "rigged rules and double standards" benefit rich countries and undermine the poverty-fighting potential of global trade.[23] As corporate interests have dominated trade negotiations, corporate profits demand priority over labor standards, environmental protection, and any other social considerations.

Sweatshops

When companies create jobs in poor countries, they often force workers to endure sweatshop conditions — unsafe work environments, forced overtime, and pitiful wages. Profit-hungry businesses and corrupt governments keep wages low by firing workers who try to organize unions and failing to enforce labor laws. A US Department of Labor investigation found that workers in an American Samoa factory were often beaten, deprived of food, and forced to work without pay — a modern form of slavery. The factory sold its clothing to J.C. Penney's, Kohl's, Sears, Target, and Wal-Mart.[24] Thousands of miles away, children as young as ten work on banana plantations for half the legal minimum wage while being exposed to enormous amounts of toxic pesticides.[25] Forced overtime, 16-hour work days, beatings, child labor, toxic fumes, and mandatory pregnancy tests for women are commonplace.[26]

Sweatshop labor is a major reason we North Americans can walk into gargantuan department stores and find aisle after aisle of inexpensive goods. In effect, cheap goods often come at the expense of workers' well-being. Sweatshop workers make athletic shoes, electronic components, clothes, toys, trinkets and more. Sweatshops are not just problems in faraway lands, either. The US has its share of sweatshops, particularly in large cities like Los Angeles and New York. In addition, large fruit and vegetable growers across the US have hired Latino migrant farm workers as a source of inexpensive labor for decades. Mistreated workers are afraid to speak out due to the threat of deportation.[27]

GOALS
End of Global Poverty — Fair Trade — Ethical Economics

The fight to end world poverty is not a lost cause. There has been significant progress in the last three decades in many parts of the world. For example, average life expectancy has significantly increased in many areas of the "developing" world, including the Arab States, South Asia, East Asia and Latin America.[28] There are three key factors in creating economic fairness around the globe: ending global poverty, fair trade, and ethical economics.

End of Global Poverty

Citizens around the world are pressuring their local and national governments to create and implement foreign policies that are both practical and ethical. In the late 1990s, the Jubilee Coalition put its commitment to the world's poor into action by lobbying for the cancellation of international debt for the world's 41 poorest countries. Largely because of this public pressure, in 1999, the US, Canada and United Kingdom agreed to cancel $100 billion in Third World debt.[29] In 2000, leaders of over 180 governments adopted the Millennium Declaration, which identifies priorities and goals to cut extreme poverty and hunger in half, and cut infant mortality by two-thirds between 1990 and 2015. More recently, the global Live 8 concerts and the "ONE" campaign (www.one.org) ignited public support for debt relief and aid to the world's most disadvantaged. In 2005, the World Bank and IMF agreed to 100% debt cancellation for the world's 38 most-indebted nations — freeing up over $1.5 billion annually for these countries to spend on healthcare and education.[30]

In 2002, the US and other wealthy countries agreed to "urge all developed countries that have not done so to make concrete efforts toward the goal of 0.7% of Gross Domestic Product as official development assistance."[31] Five countries have already met this goal (Netherlands, Norway, Denmark, Sweden and Belgium).[32] Unfortunately, the US is not living up to its obligation. Currently the US gives a meager .15%.[33]

The world community has achieved great things when it has acted as a unified force. For example, through a massive vaccination effort coordinated by the World Health Organization (WHO), smallpox, a virulent disease that had killed millions of people, was eradicated from the planet. That same type of resolve is needed to end global poverty as we know it!

Fair Trade

International trade holds enormous potential to liberate those who live in deep poverty. This potential can only be fulfilled if those who are committed to equality put pressure upon corporations and governments. Tens of thousands of protestors at the 1999 World Trade Organization meeting in Seattle ignited a global movement committed to economic justice. This movement can transform trade negotiations so that the needs of the poor and of workers around the globe are primary concerns.

Fair trade is an alternative economic model rooted in empowering rather than exploiting workers. The Fair Trade movement, now 50 years old, supports fair prices and working conditions in poor nations that produce goods for consumers in wealthier nations. Yearly North American sales of almost $400 million of fairly traded coffee, art, and clothing have created sustainable jobs in countries needing economic development.[34]

Fair trade is based on five principles: directly trading with producers (cutting out middle-men to ensure a better price to workers), fair minimum prices, access to credit, support of sustainable agriculture and a rigorous certification process to ensure compliance with these principles.[35] Fair trade coffee is the most successful example of this model. The world price of coffee hovers around $1 per pound but most farmers only receive around 50 cents per pound. With fair trade certified coffee, producers are guaranteed $1.26 per pound with the vast majority of the proceeds going directly to the farmer.[36] Over 30 million pounds of fairly traded coffee are sold each year.[37] Even McDonald's is trying to capitalize on the great PR of selling fair trade coffee.[38] In addition to coffee, TransFair has started certifying bananas, pineapples, mangoes and grapes. Fair trade bananas control half of the market in some European countries.[39] Fair trade is on the march! Consumers committed to fair trade are unleashing the full potential of trade to fight poverty.

Ethical Economics

Throughout our history, ordinary people have had to organize, struggle and fight for safe working conditions and economic security. Victories happen everyday across the world. Within the last decade, local workers and activists across the US have enacted "living wage" laws in over 120 cities and counties to increase the minimum wage up to double the federal level — some ordinances also include health insurance and vacation time.[40] In 2003, Milwaukee's city council unanimously passed a resolution requiring the city to purchase clothing (such as uniforms) made with fair labor practices rather than in sweatshops.[41] In 2005, a three-year boycott led by migrant farmers ended in success as Taco Bell agreed to exclusively buy tomatoes from companies with better wages and labor standards.[42] College students around the country have also joined the struggle. United Students Against Sweatshops (USAS) has almost 200 affiliated groups at colleges and universities across the country.[43] Students have convinced many of their schools to stand for just wages and working conditions in the apparel industry through a number of creative actions, including sit-ins, hunger strikes, and shantytowns.[44]

An economically just future must include businesses and financial institutions that are committed to community development and a just distribution of the world's wealth. Community development banks, credit unions, loan funds and land trusts are committed to creating wealth among the economically disadvantaged. These institutions create strong, vibrant local economies that large corporate banks and state governments often leave behind. More than 450 Community Development Financial Institutions (CDFIs) provide capital to the US poor for home ownership and small business growth.[45] In the last 30 years, ShoreBank of Chicago has invested over $1.7 billion in businesses and individuals in its mission to promote community development in the South Side of Chicago.[46] Internationally, the practice of "micro-lending" (loans as little as $10) has been perfected by myriad financial institutions to help the impoverished start their own businesses and become self-sufficient. Most famously, Grameen Bank has lent over $5 billion since its inception and lends $64 million each month to impoverished Bangladeshi villagers.[47] In 2006, the Nobel Peace Prize was awarded to Muhammed Yanus and Grameen Bank for their pioneering work with micro-credit.

RESOURCES

Sachs, Jeffrey. *The End of Poverty: Economic Possibilities For Our Time.* Penguin Press, 2006. Renowned economist Sachs recounts his experiences in global development work and outlines his plan to end global poverty by 2025. In addition, he provides one of the best primers on the inner workings of the modern global economy.

United Nations Development Programme. *Human Development Report.* Annual. www.hdr.undp.org. Addresses trends in global poverty, development assistance, and assesses progress toward humanitarian goals.

Korten, David. *The Post-Corporate World.* Berrett-Koehler and Kumarian Press, 1999. Korten supplies a well-researched, thorough criticism of a corporate-dominated economy, proposes new ways of structuring our economy and society to support humanity and the environment, and then gives inspiring examples of what's already working in the creation of a post-corporate world.

Anderson, Sarah, John Cavanagh, and Thea Lee. *Field Guide to the Global Economy,* revised edition. The New Press, 2005. This visually appealing and very readable account of corporate-led globalization introduces the reader to progressive economic analysis backed up by high quality statistical research. Includes the forces behind globalization, the ten claims of globalization, and examples of grassroots resistance.

Collins, Chuck and Felice Yeskel. *Economic Apartheid in America.* The New Press, 2005. Engaging, accessible summary of economic inequality in the United States, including taxes, wealth, income, and political corruption. The second half thoroughly discusses the policies and actions that are necessary to more equitably share our economic gains.

FOUNDATION #2: COMPREHENSIVE PEACE

A world committed to comprehensive peace would shift its creative energies toward cooperating rather than competing, resolving conflict rather than escalating it, seeking justice rather than enacting revenge, and creating peace rather than preparing for war.

CHALLENGES
War and Genocide — Militarization — Unilateralism — Culture of Violence

War and Genocide

We live in the age of total war. War has always been humanity's most destructive invention, and over time we have become increasingly effective at harnessing its power. Scholars estimate that at least 10 million people lost their lives in World War I.[48] Despite cries of "never again," by the time we finished World War II, the number of dead had increased fivefold to over 54 million.[49] Since World World II over 20 million people have been killed in 150 wars.[50] In the 1990s alone, wars and internal conflicts forced 50 million people from their homes, while civil wars claimed 5 million lives worldwide.[51] Two decades of Sudanese civil war have left 1.5 million dead.[52]

Far too often, combatants deem civilians to be legitimate military targets. During World War II, the Allies firebombed Dresden and Tokyo and dropped two atomic bombs on Japanese cities killing 120,000 people immediately (and another 120,000 over time).[53] Saddam Hussein used chemical weapons against ethnic minorities in Iraq. Whether it is the horror of the 9/11 attacks or the over 30,000 Iraqi civilian deaths since the US invasion — the killing of innocent civilians can be written off as collateral damage in a war of good vs. evil.[54] At the core of these acts is the dehumanization of those who are different — whether by ethnicity, race, religion, or nationality.

Ethnic hatred and desire for power has led to mass killings in the former Yugoslavia, Rwanda, and Darfur. In 1994, close to one million Tutsis were slaughtered in three months of brutal hand-to-hand attacks in Rwanda. The world community, with the exception of Ghana, sat on its hands and watched the tragedy.[55] A researcher for Human Rights Watch stated that global inaction occurred because "Americans were interested in saving money, the Belgians were interested in saving face, and the French were interested in saving their ally, the genocidal government."[56] History repeated itself in 2003 when upwards of 300,000 civilians in Darfur, Sudan were either killed by paramilitaries or died from chaos-related hunger and disease. An additional two million people were displaced from their homes.[57]

While the Rwandan genocide involved the brutality of the machete, for technologically advanced nations war has become easier and less personal. We can fire missiles or drop bombs without ever having to see the face of our faraway enemy or the horrific consequences of our actions. Perhaps the most disturbing trend, however, is that massive bloodshed and civilian casualties no longer shock us — we've become accustomed to slaughter.

Militarization

In the 20th century, we created a military arsenal so powerful that it is finally capable of destroying all human life on the planet. As you are reading this sentence, there are at least 20,000 nuclear weapons in nine countries.[58] The nuclear club now includes the US, Russia, China, the UK, France, Israel, Pakistan, India, and North Korea with Iran urgently wanting to join. The US alone controls over 10,000 of these weapons and spends over $5 billion every year just to maintain its nuclear arsenal.[59]

With approximately $1 trillion in military and arms expenditures, war has become one of the most lucrative businesses in the world.[60] The US is the world's number one arms dealer, exporting 40% of all the arms sold to any country, including corrupt dictatorships and human rights violators.[61] Even before the start of the Iraq War, the US government spent seven times as much money on their military than any other country, accounting for nearly half of all military expenditures on the planet.[62] For 2006, the Bush Administration requested $441.6 billion for the military.[63] In comparison, all agencies of the United Nations use about $10 billion each year.[64] Every dollar governments

Rank	Country	Dollars (billions)	% of Total
1	United States	522	48%
2	China	63	6%
3	Russia	62	6%
4	United Kingdom	51	5%
5	Japan	45	4%
6	France	42	4%
7	Germany	30	3%
8	India	22	2%
9	Saudi Arabia	21	2%
10	South Korea	21	2%

MILITARY SPENDING IN 2005 ($ Billions and Percent of World Total)

Source: Center for Arms Control and Non-Proliferation. "US Military Spending vs. the World". February 6, 2006, www.armscontrolcenter.org/archives/002244.php

US: "ROGUE STATE"?

The US government talks a good game about the need for international cooperation to enhance human rights, democracy, and peace, but many of its actions illustrate a more self-interested approach:

- Invasion of Iraq (US defies vast majority of United Nations members).
- Antiballistic Missile Treaty (US withdraws after 30 years).
- Kyoto Protocol On Climate Change (US refuses to sign).
- International Treaty To Ban The Use Of Land Mines (US defies 122 countries).
- International Criminal Court (US is one of only 7 to refuse to sign along with Libya, China, Qatar).
- Convention on the Rights of the Child, (US refuses to sign; the only other holdout country was Somalia.[66]).
- Comprehensive Nuclear Test Ban Treaty (US refuses to ratify).
- Convention On The Elimination Of All Forms Of Discrimination Against Women (US is the only developed nation that opposes it).

spend on the military is one less dollar available for education, health care, assistance to the poor, and environmental protection.

Unilateralism

We live in a time when the US is the last remaining superpower, able to impose its will upon less powerful nations. The Bush Administration made it clear with the invasion of Iraq that it will use the United Nations when convenient and subvert its authority when it appears that it will be an obstacle to furthering US interests. The Charter of the United Nations clearly prohibits the invasion of a sovereign country except in the case of self-defense. In order to ensure military dominance, the US maintains over 700 military bases and has over 250,000 troops spread all over the world in Europe, East Asia, North Africa and the Middle East (and that was before the invasion of Iraq).[65] A foreign policy based on arrogance and bullying strains relations with both allies and foes.

Culture of Violence

The arena of violence is unfortunately not confined to the military battlefield. Millions of homes around the world are battlegrounds instead of sanctuaries. In the US approximately 1.5 million women are raped or sexually assaulted by their intimate partner every year.[67] The problem is even worse in parts of Africa. One in three Nigerian women and nearly one in two Zambian women report being beaten by their male partner.[68]

Much violence is driven by men's attempts to live up to the cultural ideal of being a "real man." This "tough guise" glorifies power and control while disdaining vulnerability and weakness. The desire to be "tough" is just as prevalent in the Oval Office as it is in the schoolyard scuffle or the bar room brawl.

Children get multiple messages everyday that violence is an appropriate means to settle conflict—from war and criminal executions to TV "heros" exacting revenge upon their enemies. More than 1000 studies, including a Surgeon General's report and a National Institute of Mental Health report, show a cause-and-effect relationship between media violence and aggressive behavior in some children.[69] This exposure to violent media also may desensitize children to the pain and suffering of others and make them become more fearful of the world around them.[70] This culture of fear is especially pronounced in the US where people commit much more gun violence than in other industrialized nations. In 2001, handguns were used to murder 6 people in New Zealand, 56 in Japan, 96 in Great Britain, 168 in Canada, 338 in Germany and 11,348 in the US.[71]

Despite the lack of evidence that the death penalty acts as a criminal deterrent, governments across the world continue to execute criminals in acts of revenge. In 2004, at least 3,800 people were executed in 25 countries. Ninety percent were carried out by the Chinese government, followed by Iran, Vietnam and the US.[72] Only eight countries since 1990 are known to have executed people who were under 18 at the time they committed their crime — Iran, Nigeria, Pakistan, Saudi Arabia, Yemen, China, the Congo and the US. Out of that group, the US has executed the most child offenders.[73] In addition, 116 people sentenced to death in the US since 1973 have later been proven not guilty and released.[74]

GOALS
International Cooperation — Nonviolent Culture
International Cooperation

With an increasingly interconnected world, the well-being of one nation increasingly impacts the well-being of others. The world community can no longer walk away from regions of the world that are torn apart by violence and chaos. In the past, privileged countries could wash their hands of international "hotspots" if their immediate self-interest was not in jeopardy—as the world did with Rwanda. Humanitarianism used to be the only argument for providing aid to countries in need. Now fighting poverty and supporting human rights has become an absolute necessity in order to prevent the conditions that lead to the rise of extremist ideologies.

"Failed states" such as Afghanistan in the 1980s and the Sudan in the 1990s provided fertile recruiting grounds for radical Islam. As a global community, we need to embrace *all* members of the human family, promote human rights, encourage tolerance, and do what we can to empower the disenfranchised. The "West" cannot fight extremist ideologies with missiles and threats. War and aggression create a cycle of violence where the dynamic of revenge spreads hatred and retaliation. We must break the cycle of violence through cooperation and constructive engagement across ethnic, religious and national divides. Christians, Jews, and Muslims need to realize that their futures are inextricably linked to each other. For example, it is crucial that these communities make a concerted effort to ensure a two-state solution in Israel/Palestine.

The invasion of Iraq has highlighted the principle that a war cannot bring reconciliation between peoples. It is time that we start to build bridges globally with all nations instead of constantly preparing for war. A peaceful world will not come about through fearing each other. It will only come from citizens around the world standing up to their governments and demanding alternatives to militarism. The enormous economic savings of having an economy that does not revolve around the military would also create the opportunity to fight disease, poverty, and bring justice to millions around the world.

The foreign policies of all nations around the world need to better reflect the peaceful values of the majority of their citizens. The US must take a leadership role in reducing and eliminating weapons of mass destruction. At the very least, this includes signing the international treaties that we have not signed, including bans on chemical and biological weapons, the production and sale of landmines and the reduction of nuclear weapons stockpiles. The US should not sell arms to non-democratic governments or ones that persistently violate human rights.

Our international aid should include more resources to help stop conflict before it starts and fewer tools for perpetuating it. We need to fund non-military conflict resolution and channel more of our defense spending into conflict prevention efforts and the advancement of practical, nonviolent resolutions. If we paid off our debt to the United Nations, it would help the UN effectively use its resources to resolve conflicts, and if we took a more active role in the UN's workings (outside of just the Security Council), we would strengthen its accountability. A standing global peacekeeping force, under the auspices of the United Nations, could be mobilized at a moment's notice to stop spiraling violence in war-torn countries—protecting hundreds of thousands of people at a time.

Ordinary people have been challenging the status quo and facilitating the transition to a more enlightened, cooperative approach to foreign policy. For almost 20 years, Witness For Peace has sent over 7,000 US citizens to troubled parts of Latin America and the Caribbean to document the destructive impacts of misguided US foreign policy and to support efforts for nonviolent social change. In 2005, 16,000 people stood up to protest the School of the Americas (SOA), a US government military training facility that has produced some of Latin America's most brutal dictators and generals. Thousands risked arrest and jail, committing civil disobedience and speaking out on behalf of Latin American citizens. On a grander scale, tens of millions of people from cities in over 60 countries across the globe, protested the invasion of Iraq before it ever happened, including Washington, DC (200,000), Rome (2-3 million), London (1 million), Barcelona (1.3 million),

Sydney (200,000) and Damascus (200,000).[75] At no time before in human history have there been mass global protests to prevent a war. We are building a global culture every day that is demanding an end to war in our lifetime!

Nonviolent Culture

We must create a culture that values compassion, tolerance, and cooperation instead of domination, arrogance and greed. This transformation needs to occur throughout all of our social institutions. While there are legitimate uses for guns in our society, we urgently need to pass and enforce an assault weapons ban, increased gun show accountability and stricter child safety provisions. The US needs to join every other industrialized country in ending the use of the death penalty. In 1997, the American Bar Association called for a nationwide moratorium on executions. In January 2000, Illinois became the first state to agree to stop executing people until more research can conclusively prove that the system works.

We need to reclaim the media and the images it presents to us about violence, reconciliation, and masculinity. Television networks ought to move violent programming out of those time slots when our youngest children are most likely to watch TV. Each of us needs to make a commitment to teach nonviolent conflict resolution skills to the children in our lives — especially to young boys.

It is essential that we integrate conflict resolution into our schools' curriculum. Our children need to grow up with a wide range of skills and tools they can draw on to solve problems when they become adults. A number of organizations have cropped up to make conflict resolution education a reality for every child. In the US, Educators for Social Responsibility have been extremely successful with getting their Resolving Conflict Creatively Program (RCCP) adopted at K-12 schools across the nation. In 2000, 6,000 teachers and 175,000 young people participated in their program, learning a comprehensive strategy for nonviolent conflict resolution and how to build caring, peaceful communities.

⇨ RESOURCES

Fog of War directed by Errol Morris. Sony Pictures Classics, 2003.

Why We Fight directed by Eugene Jarecki. Sony Pictures Classics, 2005. These two excellent documentaries explore the roles of war and the military in US foreign policy and the American psyche.

Grossman, Lt. Col. Dave. *On Killing: The Psychological Cost of Learning to Kill in War and Society.* Little Brown & Co., 1996. Grossman takes us through a history of wars to explain the socio-psychological techniques used to make it possible for soldiers to kill other human beings. He then shows how this same dehumanization process is taking place in our society through television, movies, and video games.

📖 Hedges, Christopher. *War Is A Force That Gives Us Meaning*. Anchor, 2003. Hedges, a former New York Times war correspondent, draws upon his experiences in Kosovo and other war zones to explore the intoxicating psychic appeal of war — including a sense of moral clarity and a powerful national unity of purpose.

📖 King, Jr., Martin Luther. *Strength to Love*. Fortress Press. 1986. A fantastic collection of Martin Luther King's sermons on peace, nonviolence, love, and hope. Check out Dr. King's other books as well, *Trumpet of Conscience* and *Why We Can't Wait* are outstanding.

📖 Kinzer, Stephen. *Overthrow: America's Century of Regime Change from Hawaii to Iraq*. Times Books, 2006. A provocative history of 14 US-led coups, revolutions, and invasions that have toppled foreign governments, including Iran, South Vietnam, Chile, and Iraq. Kinzer uncovers US political and economic motives and analyzes the unintended long-term consequences for each regime change.

📖 Power, Samantha. *A Problem From Hell: America and the Age of Genocide*. HarperPerennial, 2003. Power, the executive director of Harvard's Carr Center for Human Rights, writes a thoroughly researched and powerfully written account of 20th-century acts of genocide and the US's often anemic responses.

FOUNDATION #3: ECOLOGICAL SUSTAINABILITY

A world committed to ecological sustainability would create a new vision of progress that recognizes that the future of humanity depends upon our ability to live in harmony and balance with our natural world.

CHALLENGES
Resource Overconsumption — Pollution — Global Warming — Overpopulation

Resource Overconsumption

Historically unprecedented levels of resource consumption are impacting every corner of the globe, permanently extinguishing unique species and threatening much of the biodiversity upon which all life depends. A 2000 report by the World Resources Institute found that increasing demands for natural resources are causing a rapid decline in many of the world's ecosystems.[76] The Living Planet Index, which measures the trends in wild species, found that from 1970 to 2000 land and marine populations dropped by 30% while populations of freshwater species decreased by a whopping 50%.[77]

We have cut or otherwise destroyed nearly 80% of the world's ancient forests.[78] World demand for paper and lumber along with local demand for firewood is causing developing nations to lose 6% of their forests every decade.[79] The results are increased global warming, species extinction and loss of potential medicines. Natural forests contain about 50% of all life forms on the planet—with tropical forests containing the most biodiversity.[80] Many consider that we are causing an "extinction crisis" as we are causing species extinction at approximately 1000 times the natural rate.[81]

Unsustainable resource use threatens our way of life. Overfishing of ocean fisheries has created widespread alarm around the world. Globally, 75% of marine fisheries are being fished at or beyond their sustainable capacity.[82] The quest for hefty profits rather than sustainable fishing has created a shortage that now threatens the entire industry's ability to feed the world's population. In addition, many countries, including the US, China and India, overpump their aquifers to irrigate their grain harvest. Falling water tables indicate that many aquifers will run dry in the near future—causing declines in food production.[83] Many experts also agree that the era of cheap oil is coming to an end.[84]

The vast majority of the demand for natural resources comes from the rich industrialized nations of the world — especially the United States. This is no surprise, since the US lifestyle demands 120 pounds (54 kilograms) of natural resources per person per day.[85] The average American consumes as much energy as:

2   Germans
5   Mexicans
9   Chinese
15   Indians
54   Bangladeshi.[86]

Since 1940, Americans alone have used up as large a share of the Earth's mineral resources as all previous humans put together.[87] In fact, it would require four additional Earths to support the human race if all people on the planet lived the extremely wasteful lifestyles of North Americans.[88]

Pollution

Have you ever noticed a brown cloud hanging over big cities? Or inhaled the crisp, clean air when you camp in a remote wilderness area? Unfortunately, air pollution is more than just a smelly annoyance; it kills about 70,000 Americans each year (more people than die from breast and prostate cancers combined)[89] and an estimated 3 million deaths worldwide every year.[90] Air quality is especially dangerous in rapidly industrializing countries such as China and India. Twelve of the fifteen cities with the worst air quality are in Asia (including Beijing, Jakarta, New Delhi, Shanghai and Calcutta).[91] The main causes of air pollution are energy production (especially from coal), industrial processes and transportation.[92]

According to the World Commission on Water, more than half of the world's major rivers are "seriously depleted and polluted, degrading and poisoning the surrounding ecosystems, threatening the health and livelihood of people who depend on them."[93] Our oceans also bear our toxic burden. The US Justice Department found a fleet-wide conspiracy within Royal Caribbean cruise lines to save millions of dollars in disposal fees by covering up the dumping of oily waste into the ocean off of Puerto Rico.[94]

Global Warming

According to the Intergovernmental Panel on Climate Change, the earth's average temperature will increase between 2.5-10.4 degrees Fahrenheit (1.4-5.8 degrees Celsius) during this century.[95] Global warming threatens our future. Even modest warming could significantly impact agricultural yields, habitat integrity and vulnerable coastal populations around the globe. Even a one or two degree variation in temperature could shrink the grain harvest in major food-producing regions.[96]

Emissions of greenhouse gases from burning of fossil fuels, especially coal and oil, have substantially contributed to global warming.[97] The US is the biggest culprit — emitting more than twice as much carbon dioxide (the primary global warming gas) per capita as the average rich industrialized nation (U.K., Japan, Germany).[98] Contributing to the problem, US federal automobile fuel efficiency standards have not been raised since 1985 — that's over 20 years ago![99] Even as the oil and automobile industries are admitting that precautionary action is warranted to halt global warming, the US and Australia (the world's largest per capita emitters of greenhouse gases) have refused to join the 160 nations that have publicly committed to emission reductions.

Overpopulation

In October of 1999, the world's population surpassed 6 billion people, doubling its size since 1960. In 2005, the human population grew by over 205,000 people per day or 75 million per year.[100] The United Nations projects that the world's population will increase to over 9 billion by 2050—a 50% increase from 1999 — with the entire 3 billion added to the developing world.[101] We might like to think that overpopulation is India's and Africa's problem, not ours, but when population strains lead to deforestation, global warming, war, malnutrition, starvation, and epidemics, the problem becomes a global one.

Overpopulation is a complex issue with a multitude of causes. The majority of women in the developing world want to control their fertility but currently don't have access to birth control options. Amazingly, the US exacerbates this problem by refusing to pay its share of the United Nations Population Fund, the primary international family planning resource. Poverty, coupled with limited educational and occupational opportunities for women, further exacerbate rapid population growth. As the developing world increasingly adopts a consumer lifestyle, the potential for ecological damage greatly multiplies.

GOALS
Clean Energy Sources — Sustainable Resource Use — Stable Population Growth — Global Cooperation

Clean Energy Sources

One of the most important changes we can make is to shift from fossil fuels to our most powerful and abundant natural resources: sun, wind and hydrogen. We already have environmentally sound, energy-efficient technologies to harness these renewable energy sources — we just need to use them. In 1997, the United Nations sponsored a global climate conference in Kyoto, Japan emphasizing the seriousness of global warming. The meetings produced a commitment from over 160 countries to significantly reduce greenhouse emissions by 2012 (the US was not among them). As a consequence, the demand for non-polluting energy sources is increasing worldwide, and the costs of using these technologies is steadily declining. Local US leaders have not let the feet-dragging of the federal government keep them from taking action. The mayors of "146 cities in 36 states, representing over 10 percent of the US population, pledged to enforce Kyoto's US targets in their own cities."[102] At the same time, sales of hybrid electric vehicles in the US have exploded from fewer than 10,000 in 2000 to over 200,000 in 2005.[103]

Renewable energy is not some naïve idealistic dream. It is technologically sound, affordable and spreading around the globe today. Global production of wind energy increased ninefold from 1995-2004 and continues to grow at almost 30% per year.[104] Global sales of photovoltaic solar cells (these are the ones that generate electricity from your rooftop) increased by 57% in 2004 and ten-fold over the past 10 years.[105]

Creative, inspiring uses of "green" energy abound. Iceland has launched pioneering efforts to harness geothermal and hydropower to produce hydrogen for use in cars and boats.[106] In the Spring of 1999, Santa Monica became the first major city to meet its municipal energy needs entirely with non-polluting energy (geothermal).[107] In 2001, San Francisco voters overwhelmingly approved a landmark $100 million initiative that pays for solar panels, energy efficiency and wind turbines for public facilities. And get this: the money is paid back through energy savings — at no cost to taxpayers![108]

Sustainable Resource Use

If we are to live in balance with our surrounding environment, we must learn from the principles of nature. The concept of waste, for example, does not exist in the forest. A fallen tree becomes a home for animals and insects, and helps to fertilize the soil for surrounding plant life. We must also learn to "close the loop" and use resources wisely. In order to combat pollution, Germany, Sweden, Spain, the U.K., and other countries are adopting "green" taxes — they lower income taxes and tax energy use, thereby encouraging energy efficiency and investments in wind and solar power.[109] Many activists, consumers, and governments around the world are also holding industry to a higher standard of resource efficiency.

Encouraging examples of this kind of conservation ethic are happening all over the world. The world's largest producer of commercial floor coverings (Interface, Inc.) is on the cutting edge of environmentally sustainable business-es. They have implemented the principle of producer responsibility by using fewer materials, creating 100% recyclable carpets, and implementing customer leases that make Interface responsible for reclaiming the floor covering.[110] Many European Union countries already have "Extended Producer Responsibility" programs whereby product manufacturers are required to take responsibility for the environmental impacts of their products. Car manufacturers must reuse or recycle 85% of the materials used to make their vehicles.[111]

The creation of an economy where goods are produced, used, and remade into new products in the most environmentally responsible manner is a challenge that must involve every sector of our society — businesses, all levels of govern-ment, and citizens from around the world. Governments must stop subsidizing environmentally destructive industries, such as logging and oil, with corporate tax breaks. Switching from a pesticide- and fertilizer-based agricultural system to sustainable, organic farming will maintain soil integrity and preserve our health. Relying more on tree plantations and sustainable aquaculture will relieve pressure to cut down old-growth forests and overfish our oceans.

Fortunately, many people are already stepping up to the challenge. Twenty-six communities in New Zealand are pioneering a national Zero Waste pilot program to significantly reduce the amount of materials headed for the landfill.[112] Canberra, Australia and Toronto, Canada have even aimed to eliminate waste completely by 2010.[113] Even consider this book. It is made of 100% post-con-sumer recycled paper, meaning that not one tree was cut down to produce it.

Stable Population Growth

Annual world population growth hit its peak in 1989 at 87 million people (that's births minus deaths). Since then, many industrialized countries have stabilized their populations, while developing countries still struggle with massive population growth. Wealthier nations must provide developing nations with the resources they need to curb their ballooning populations. These efforts need to be focused on improving the status of women, increasing access to family planning services, and bringing economic opportunity to poverty-stricken rural areas.

There have already been some amazing successes around the globe. Bangladesh, the most densely populated country in the world, has actually decreased its fertility rate from approximately 6.4 to 3.4 children per woman. Much of the decline is attributed to the regular use of contraceptives by 45% of

Bangladeshis in 1996, up from less than 8% in 1975.[114] Empowerment of women is essential to stabilizing population. In Brazil, literate women average only two children while illiterate women average more than six children.[115]

Global Ecological Cooperation

To effectively address the challenges of climate change, resource depletion, and the breakdown of ecosystems, the nations of the world must act collectively and cooperatively. One only needs to look at the ozone layer to see the great potential of concerted global action. Scientists during the 1980s discovered a "hole" in a protective layer of the upper atmosphere. Based on their research, the Montreal Protocol, signed in 1990, phased out the production of ozone-damaging chemicals, such as chlorofluorocarbons (CFCs). This regulation slowed down the growth of the hole and eventually reversed the trend. Scientists now predict that the hole will be repaired by 2050.[116]

We must remember that public action can turn the tide and give us hope for the future. Public pressure for more stringent environmental regulation has led to technological progress that has significantly improved automotive and industrial emissions. Air quality in most of the developed world has been improving for the last thirty years because of this pressure.[117] The foundations for a new "eco-society" are being built everyday with each hybrid-electric vehicle, wind turbine, recycling center and roof topped with solar panels.

⇨ RESOURCES

📖 Brown, Lester. *Plan B 2.0: Rescuing A Planet Under Stress And A Civilization In Trouble.* W.W. Norton, 2006. Written by one of the great environmental thinkers of all time, this award-winning book provides a readable analysis of our greatest social and environmental challenges. It details global problems and presents a realistic plan of action for ending poverty and nourishing our natural systems.

📖 Brower, Michael, and The Union of Concerned Scientists. *Consumer's Guide to Effective Environmental Choices.* Three Rivers Press, 1999. A well-researched book that evaluates which of our actions make the most impact on the environment (and which ones you shouldn't worry too much about).

📖 Hawken, Paul, Amory Lovins, and R. Hunter Lovins. *Natural Capitalism: Creating the Next Industrial Revolution.* Back Bay Books, 2000. The authors strike an unusual middle ground between capitalism and environmentalism. They use a number of current examples to illustrate a trend toward more eco-friendly, better technologies and more practical, sustainably-run businesses.

📖 McDonough, William and Michael Braungart. *Cradle to Cradle: Remaking the Way We Make Things.* North Point Press. 2002. True sustainability can be achieved only by thinking way outside the box — cars that actually clean the air, edible grocery bags, and 100% recyclable books. The book itself is printed on a polymer (rather than paper) that can be cleaned, melted and re-formed into a completely new book.

📖 Ryan, John C. and Alan Thein Durning. *Stuff: The Secret Lives Of Everyday Things.* Northwest Environment Watch, 1997. This fascinating, concise book traces the environmental impacts of everyday objects including a cup of coffee, a pair of sneakers, an aluminum can and a hamburger.

📖 The World Watch Institute. *State of the World* and *Vital Signs: The Environmental Trends That Are Shaping Our Future.* W.W. Norton. Annual publications. Provides up-to-date research on pressing global environmental problems, their causes, and their potential solutions. Great resources for assessing environmental trends.

FOUNDATION #4: DEEP DEMOCRACY
A world built on deep democracy would empower citizens to participate in shaping their futures every day (not just on election day), provide broad access to quality information, and democratize our most powerful institutions.

CHALLENGES
Lack of Democracy — Money in Politics — Media Control

Lack of Democracy
In 1989, 100,000 Chinese students and workers marched peacefully to protest government corruption in Tiananmen Square. Millions around the globe witnessed the Chinese government's violent crackdown that killed hundreds and injured additional thousands. Scenes of government repression and corruption happen around the globe every year. When the "bullet" triumphs over the "ballot box," the hope of future generations for prosperity and freedom is stolen.

A government is democratic to the extent that average people have the ability to influence decisions that affect their daily lives and the future of their society. Unfortunately, dictatorships of military or wealthy elites rule much of the world without the consent of the people. Government of, by, and for these elites has created tremendous suffering for the average person. Unaccountable leaders in the developing world have often squandered their countries' wealth while leaving their people deeply indebted to international institutions.

Here in the US, we like to think that we're immune to rule by the few, when in fact, despite our historically groundbreaking beginnings, we are slowly moving back to that kind of government. Over the last 100 years, voter turnout has steadily declined. In 1996, for the first time in US history, less than 50% of the voting age population came out to the polls for the presidential election. In

2002, only 37% showed up to the polls, making it the second lowest turnout for a non-presidential national election in modern US history.[118]

This is a saddening state of affairs when the foundations of democracy are eroding in what many people consider to be the greatest democracy in the world. The US has one of the lowest voting rates of any democratic country. While around half the US population participates in presidential elections, countries like Azerbaijan, Uganda, Slovakia and Sri Lanka have over 70% of their people turn out.[119] The 2000 presidential election also highlighted a number of obstacles to fair elections. Communities of color were more likely to have long voting lines, outdated voting equipment (causing higher rates of disqualified votes) and residents who were wrongly credited with felonies and prevented from voting.[120] We need to face up to the fact that our democracy is in crisis. Without the participation of average people in government, by definition the government cannot represent the interests of average people.

Money In Politics

It's no wonder that Americans have become cynical about the influence of money on politics when a donation of $100,000 to a national party will get you: (1) access to congressional golf tournaments, (2) admission to retreats with leading party members and/or (3) photo opportunities with Hollywood legends.[121] Explaining the etiquette of influence peddling, one Washington lobbyist explains, "We always prefer to give the money directly to the guy, or the woman, that you're going to support. You like to walk in, you like to give them the check, you like to look in their eye and say 'I'm here to help you.'"[122] This kind of system works well for those who have tens of thousands of dollars to purchase seats at fundraising dinners, but it leaves the rest of us behind.

Where does all that money come from?

- One-quarter of 1% of the US population gives 80% of all the private money in our elections.[123]
- Total spending from Political Action Committees (PACs) grew from $19 million in 1973 to almost $900 million in 1999-2000. Over 40% of all campaign finances for 2002 House candidates came from PACs.[124]
- In 2004, PACs linked to corporations spent four times as much as PACs linked to labor unions.[125]

Almost $900 million dollars was donated to presidential candidates for the 2004 election — a 66% increase from the 2000 election.[126] Elections have become so expensive that the candidates have to look to the most wealthy to finance their campaign, particularly rich individuals and corporations. Such an extreme funding imbalance creates a situation in which the wealthy and powerful gain access, influence, and political clout at the expense of the poor, people of color, workers and the environment.

Executives of Exxon-Mobil and Wal-Mart gave $750,000 and $1.3 million, respectively, to Republican candidates in the 2004 election.[127] Many people consider the Republican Party to be the party of big business, but the Democrats increasingly provide some stiff competition for that title. Some of the top donor corporations, like Microsoft, gave roughly $500,000 to each of the two major parties in the 2004 elections.[128] The emergence of political commercials by "527" organizations has provided another avenue for big money to dominate political debate ($400 million dollars was spent by 527s to influence the 2004 federal election).[129]

So does money really matter? In the information age, candidates need more and more money for advertising. Politicians have turned to massive and misleading TV ad campaigns that have proven effective in gaining voter support. For 2004 federal and state elections, candidates and parties spent $1.6 billion on TV ads — a sixfold increase since 1972 (controlled for inflation).[130] The escalating cost of ads makes candidates even more beholden to their big-money sponsors. Without millions of dollars, they can't run TV ads and they don't get elected. This big money stranglehold on our government far too often sabotages our efforts to make government effectively work for the people.

Media Control

In non-democratic countries the biggest threat to a free and independent press is government censorship. In authoritarian countries, media outlets are either owned outright or supervised by the government. Only 22% of the world's population lives in countries with a press free from government control.[131]

In democracies, the main threat to good journalism is not the government but the almighty dollar. The obsession for ratings leads to shock journalism and puff pieces aimed at grabbing viewers' attention instead of informing them. At other times journalists shirk their responsibility to ask tough questions to those in power. The media's failure to fully investigate the Bush administration's claims of Iraqi weapons of mass destruction and the purported link between al-Qaeda and Saddam Hussein blinded the American public from the truth.

The integrity of a democracy relies heavily upon the quality of information available to its citizenry. We Americans believe in the First Amendment because our democracy flourishes when we can hear a diversity of voices, and we trust citizens to make up their own minds. The media industry, under the control of fewer and fewer corporations, is eroding the freedom and diversity that make our democracy great. Corporate mergers have left fewer than five corporations in control of the majority of our information.[132] The rash of mergers in the past decade has increased the pressure to maximize profits in the media industry.

Devotion to stock prices and advertising revenues often sacrifices quality journalism. Corporate decision makers commonly sweep professional standards aside and fill the news with sensationalized stories and programs that will raise their ratings — gruesome tales of murder, celebrity divorces, sex scandals; or Jerry Springer, COPS, and When Animals Attack. From 1993 to 1996, network news coverage of homicide increased 721% while the national homicide rate decreased by 20%.[133] Viewers did not ask for more detailed coverage of violence. But TV executives know that if they spend more time examining stories about violent crimes, more people will tune in to their news broadcasts. Instead of providing a vibrant forum for discussing pressing social issues, election coverage often focuses on superficial characteristics of the candidates.

GOALS
Open and Honest Politics — Democratic Media — Civic Participation

Open and Honest Politics

Creating governments that are responsive to their citizens and not beholden to powerful interests is one of the most important challenges we face. The fall of the Berlin Wall in 1989 and the dissolution of the Soviet Union in 1991 helped bring about a major democratic transition in Eastern Europe. Shifts toward democracy are also occurring in sub-Saharan Africa and Latin America. In 2002, 44% of the world's population lived in established democracies—that's the highest percentage in human history![134]

When democracy is established, we need to create and enforce strict limits on political contributions and lobbying so that large amounts of money do not distort the "one person, one vote" philosophy. One important way to decrease the need for large political contributions is to restrict political advertisements (which usually contain half-truths at best) and give sensible amounts of free TV time to any candidate who is running for office. These changes would substantially lower the costs of campaigns, increase outreach to the public, and raise the overall level of political discourse — the 30-second TV advertisement could give way to a serious consideration of the issues that distinguish the candidates.

Publicly financing campaigns may seem counter-intuitive at first glance. Why should we want to pay for mudslinging, misleading campaign ads? Well, with public financing, we could lay down guidelines for what are appropriate uses of our money and take back control of how parties run campaigns. Wealthy interest groups would no longer be able to hold millions of dollars over the heads of our government officials, the vast majority of whom plan to run for reelection. It may even be cheaper in the long run for taxpayers, because the representatives that we elect have fewer favors to grant after the election — which mean less corporate tax giveaways and pork barrel projects. Public financing also encourages citizens to run for office — those who are currently scared away by the thought of having to use slimy fundraising tactics or those who wouldn't be able to attract big-money donors.

In fact, a growing number of states have already begun taking steps in this direction. Citizens in Maine, Vermont, Arizona, North Carolina, New Mexico and Connecticut have some form of "clean" elections with strict limits on contributions and significant public financing. To access public funds, candidates have to get donations from a substantial number of citizens, and the maximum donation allowed is $5 to $50 (that's not a typo!).[135] Consequently, the average person has as much influence as the millionaire across town. Now that's democracy! Eighty percent of Maine's state legislature were elected as "clean money" candidates.[136]

Another important way to open up politics is to increase the participation of alternative political voices. Smaller political parties, often called third parties, have played a vital role in our country's history. They articulate ideas that the two major parties are not addressing and often influence one or both of them in the process. Minor party candidates who can demonstrate that they represent a significant number of people should have easier access to ballots, participation in debates, and media coverage. These kinds of changes will provide a much more comprehensive discussion of ideas throughout our society.

The 2000 presidential election debacle has led to many positive reforms. The National Association for the Advancement of Colored People's (NAACP) election reform efforts significantly minimized problems at polling places for the 2004 election. The "Help America Vote Act" increased funding to improve accessibility of polling places for the disabled, standardize procedures for provisional ballots, and improve training for poll workers to ensure non-discriminatory treatment of citizens. It is now time to allow voters to register to vote on Election Day and join many other democratic nations by making Election Day a national holiday!

Independent Media

A well-functioning democracy requires a media system that provides diverse sources of information and encourages civic participation. The government once considered the airwaves such an integral part of our democracy that politicians decided the public should own and control them. It is time for the public to reclaim the responsibility of producing quality media from the corporate conglomerates. The first step is to break up the concentration of media power. Let's give control to a greater number of smaller companies that could legitimately compete with a broader range of information. Also we must create and maintain a non-commercial public media system (PBS, NPR) as well as independent alternative media that exist outside the control of transnational corporations and advertisers. The rise of independent political blogs, alternative podcasts, radio networks like Air America, and television channels such as Link TV and Current TV are all examples of citizens rising up to take back control of our media.

Civic Participation

True democracy involves much more than just an election every few years. Legal protections from government abuses must be extended to all citizens. Freedom to openly disagree with the actions and ideas of the powerful is central to the democratic ethos. The light of open government needs to drive out political corruption and cronyism. As we have seen in post-invasion Iraq though, the transition toward democracy is an arduous one that takes decades and cannot be imposed from the outside.

Regardless of the structure of the political system and the media, the overall health of a democracy rests firmly on the backs of its citizens. Civic participation is the soul of a democracy. For a democracy to flourish, average people must choose to educate themselves on the issues of the day, seek solutions to the problems they see, and implement these solutions on a daily basis in their communities. Daily civic participation is essential to creating a just government and a just society. Without adequate citizen participation, corporations and special interests tend to get their way — their voices become louder when fewer and fewer of us are speaking up.

Civic involvement includes educating ourselves through a variety of media, joining community groups, participating in boycotts, volunteering for good causes, demonstrating when important social concerns arise and even talking with your neighbors about issues you care about. In 2004, door-to-door get-out-the-vote efforts in the US led to a surge in voter registration and voter turnout, especially among young people and people of color.[137] In Eastern Europe, Ukraine's "Orange" Revolution organized nationwide protests, sit-ins, and strikes to protest corruption and fraudulent national elections resulting in a clear victory for the opposition candidate. The "Rose" revolution in Georgia, the "Tulip" revolution in Kyrgyzstan, and the "Cedar" revolution in Lebanon showed that "people power" can break the chains of political oppression!

Our country has a great history of people's movements pushing our government towards a peaceful and just future: the populist movement that fought inequality and the Robber Barons, the Civil Rights movement, the Gay and Lesbian Rights movement, the Women's movements (including the Suffragettes), the Chicano Farmworkers' movement, the Environmental movement and the anti-Vietnam War movement. More recently citizens have successfully halted every attempt to drill for oil in the Arctic National Wildlife Refuge (ANWR).

⮕ RESOURCES

📖 Glassner, Barry. *The Culture Of Fear: Why Americans Are Afraid Of The Wrong Things.* Basic Books, 2000. Barry Glassner systematically breaks down our current media environment and demonstrates how our perception of an ultra-violent world is a product of a media system addicted to hype and politicians obsessed with control.

📖 Hazen, Don, and Julie Winokur, eds. *We the Media.* New Press, 1997. Hazen and Winokur's book uses an engaging format (and excerpts from the most eloquent media critics) to discuss the issues of corporate ownership of the media, media literacy, and the numerous alternative sources of information on TV, radio, and the Web.

📖 Hightower, Jim. *If The Gods Had Meant Us To Vote, They'd Have Given Us Candidates.* HarperPerennial, 2001. Jim Hightower delivers a common sense, populist message to everyone that is fed up with politics as usual. He explores how the little guy is being squeezed out of a system of democracy that gives us candidates all of whom support big corporate·interests and government fat cats.

📖 Loeb, Paul Rogat. *Soul of a Citizen: Living With Conviction in a Cynical Time.* St. Martin's Press, 1999. www.soulofacitizen.org. Encourages us to challenge the cynicism of our time by creating sustainable social change in our everyday lives. Read this book — it will make you feel like getting involved in your community.

📖 McChesney, Robert W., Russell Newman, and Ben Scott. *The Future of the Media: Resistance and Reform in the 21st Century.* Seven Stories Press, 2005. This edited volume illustrates how corporate control of the media threatens our democratic ideals. When a handful of corporations control the vast majority of the media, they inevitably pursue their own interests over the interests of citizens.

📖 Sifry, Micah L. and Nancy Watzman. *Is That a Politician in Your Pocket? Washington on $2 Million a Day.* John Wiley and Sons, 2004. Exposé on how big money brings influence in Washington. Wealthy individuals, business groups and other "special interests" drive politics through campaign contributions and lobbying.

📖 Moore Lappe, Frances, and Paul Martin Dubois. *The Quickening of America: Rebuilding Our Nation, Remaking Our Lives.* Jossey-Bass, 1994. This powerful book illustrates through examples how we can create meaningful communities by living democracy. It challenges our preconceptions about community and offers suggestions on how we might "create the lives we want."

FOUNDATION #5: SOCIAL JUSTICE

A world dedicated to social justice is a place where everyone receives respect and equal access to jobs, education, and health care regardless of race, gender, ethnicity, sexual orientation, age, physical or mental abilities, or economic background.

CHALLENGES
Gender Inequality — Racism — Heterosexism — Inadequate Health Care — Prisons

Gender Inequality

Discrimination and violence against women are still deeply rooted in many cultures around the world. In their lifetime an estimated one in three women in the world will be subjected to violence in an intimate relationship and one in five women will be a victim of rape or attempted rape.[138] To make matters worse, this violence is often shrouded by a culture of silence. In Thailand and other countries, sexual slavery is common, with over 2 million girls aged 5 to15 trapped in the sex trade every year.[139]

Nations often systematically deny women education, economic opportunities, health care, birth control, and equal legal protections.[140] Worldwide, women are twice as likely to be illiterate, and they earn 25% less than men earn.[141] Lack of voting rights and women in government positions perpetuate a male-oriented world where women have little power. Worldwide, women only occupy 16% of national legislative seats.[142]

Unfortunately, women's reproductive health is a low priority worldwide. Every minute a woman unnecessarily dies of pregnancy-related causes—more than half a million each year. Poor reproductive health conditions are the leading causes of illness and death among women ages 15-44.[143] The International Women's Health Coalition reports that, "One in 13 women in sub-Saharan Africa and 1 in 35 in South Asia die unnecessarily from causes related to pregnancy, unsafe abortion, and childbirth."[144] Hundreds of millions of women still have inadequate access to birth control, leading to 80 million unwanted pregnancies each year and 20 million unsafe abortions, which in turn result in an estimated 78,000 deaths annually.[145]

While most of the US abortion debate is focused on the federal level with Roe *v.* Wade, many of the battles to maintain reproductive freedom for women are being lost at the state level. Currently, 87% of US counties have no abortion provider.[146] While South Dakota voters recently overturned their legislature's ban on abortion, many other states are attempting to pass similar legislation.

Despite making tremendous strides, US women still experience numerous injustices. Only 14 out of 100 US senators are women (and that is the highest number ever), while only 66 women are among the 435 members of the US House of Representatives — ranking 66th in the world in gender equality.[147]

Sexual harassment, domestic violence, and sexual violence are still pervasive, with 900,000 reports to police of women assaulted by their male partners in 1998 alone. Single women head 55% of all families living in poverty.[148] And, although women have entered the workforce by the millions, they still perform considerably more housework and childcare than men do.

Racism

Racism is still having devastating effects in the US and around the world. Many racial and ethnic minorities are prevented from fully participating in their societies. Stereotyping and prejudice lead to exclusion and discrimination. The effects of racism vary from genocide and hate-crimes to segregation and fear. Recent events highlight the continuing significance of race and ethnicity in human relations. Tensions between Sunni and Shia muslims in Iraq have led to waves of violence. Riots in Paris uncover a segregated, disenfranchised immigrant population without economic opportunities. Hurricane Katrina hit the gulf coast of the US and revealed an African-American underclass that bore the full brunt of the disaster. Ultra-nationalist political parties gain strength in Europe, blaming economic and social problems on recent immigrants from Africa and the Middle East. A lack of political representation and economic resources perpetuates the marginalization of minorities.

Despite many decades of struggle, prejudice and discrimination live on in our racially segregated schools, neighborhoods, churches and workplaces. The staggering wealth inequality throughout the world hits people of color especially hard, even in the US. Our society creates significant inequalities in income, education, home ownership, treatment by police, treatment by the courts, access to health care, corporate America and the halls of government. In 2004, African-Americans (24.7%) and Hispanics (21.9%) were over twice as likely to live in poverty as Whites (8.6%).[149] In 2002, the US median household wealth for African-Americans was $6,000, for Hispanics it was $7,900 and for Whites it was $88,000—that's over 11 times the wealth of Hispanics and 14 times that of African-Americans.[150] Today, 33% of African-American and 29% of Hispanic children live below the poverty line in the US.[151] These injustices are then perpetuated by an unequal educational system. Schools attended by predominantly African-American and Latino students tend to be poorly maintained, have more unqualified teachers, and few up-to-date textbooks.[152]

People of color around the globe disproportionately bear the brunt of our society's creation of toxic chemicals and pollution. This fact did not seem to phase D.F. Goldsmith when they wanted to ship 118 metric tons of mercury (one of the largest stockpiles of toxic metals in the US) to India.[153] Mexican authorities estimate that less than one-third of the toxic waste created by American companies in Mexico is returned to the United States as mandated by

Mexican law.[154] The predominately black residents of "Cancer Alley," a stretch of land along the Mississippi in Louisiana, are exposed to 4,517 pounds (2,049 kilograms) of chemical releases each year; the average American is exposed to 10 pounds (4.5 kilograms).[155] These cases are not unusual. Naturally, exposure to such toxins increases rates of illness and mortality.

Heterosexism

Homosexuals are perhaps the last group still culturally acceptable to slander. Around the world gays and lesbians are discriminated against and often forced to live in the shadows of their societies. Homosexual acts are even punishable by death in nine nations including Saudi Arabia and Pakistan.[156] Gay men attempting to marry in the United Arab Emirates face "government-ordered hormone treatments, five years in jail, and lashings."[157]

In the US, heterosexuals continue to benefit from many privileges that lesbians and gays do not have. Heterosexuals can legally marry, show affection in public, be with their partner during severe illness and receive tax benefits — while not needing to worry about hate crimes, discrimination, slurs or violence. Reflecting the intense heterosexism still prevalent around the nation, by 2006, 26 states had passed constitutional amendments restricting marriage to heterosexual couples, and 12 more are currently considering such legislation.[158] Kids continue to torment young lesbians and gays at school, reflecting our society's deeply rooted homophobia.

Inadequate Health Care

Billions of poor people have inadequate access to basic health care. The World Health Organization states, "The poor are treated with less respect, given less choice of service providers, and offered lower-quality amenities. In trying to buy health care from their own pockets, they pay and become poorer."[159] Infant mortality in sub-Saharan Africa is 36 times higher than in Sweden.[160] Due mostly to the AIDS epidemic, the average life expectancy in Zambia has fallen from 54 in 1991 to 32.[161] For the same reason, Zimbabwe's life expectancy fell from 65 to 33.[162] There are enough resources and pharmaceuticals to significantly reduce the AIDS crisis, but the people who need them the most, the poor, can't afford them.

Despite being the richest country in the world, the US is the ONLY industrialized country that does not have universal health insurance—16% of Americans (46 million people) have no health insurance.[163] In fact, the World Health Organization ranked the United States health care system 37th in the world because it is enormously expensive and excludes tens of millions of people from quality care.[164]

Prisons

While prisons are necessary to protect the general population from dangerous criminals, authorities often misuse prisons to control their populations. In non-democratic nations, prisons are often used to silence political opponents and to send a message that dissent is not allowed. Family members disappear in the middle of the night, never to be seen again.

The US is quickly becoming the prison capital of the world, incarcerating a higher percentage of its citizens than any other country. In 2000, over 2 million people called US prisons and jails "home"—the majority for non-violent drug offenses.[165] An astounding increase in imprisonment took place during the 1990s. We had fewer than 200,000 adults behind bars in 1970; 315,974 in 1980; and 739,980 in 1990.[166]

Despite widely acknowledged statistics showing that the national crime rate (including violent crime) has been going down for years, politicians continue to be rewarded for appearing "tough on crime."[167] Since few dollars end up focused on reintegration and rehabilitation, the prison system has become merely a place to lock up our societal problems and hope they go away.

GOALS
Equal Rights For All — Universal Health Care and Education

Equal Rights For All
We need to ensure that no one faces discrimination due to their personal characteristics or background. People of color and ethnic minorities deserve non-stereotypical cultural images, equal access to education and jobs, fair political representation, and just treatment in the legal system. The Association of Community Organizations for Reform Now (ACORN) has empowered communities of color by registering over 1 million new voters in the 2004 election alone. They have also organized successful living wage campaigns in Chicago, Boston, Oakland, Detroit, Minneapolis and St. Paul, forced companies to clean up toxic dumps, and successfully pressured banks to reinvest in their communities.[168]

Women worldwide should be guaranteed equal pay for equal work, as well as proportional representation in their respective governments and strengthened legislation protecting them from sexual assault. The United Nations' Gender Development Index indicates that gender equality has improved in almost all countries over the past three decades.[169] These gains are directly tied to the growth of the global women's movement. In protests to gain the right to vote and hold elective office, scores of Kuwaiti women have marched into local election offices and registered to vote, arguing that the voting ban violates their constitution's gender non-discrimination clause.[170] In 1980, US women employed full-time only earned 60 cents for every dollar their male counterparts earned. By 2004, that number had risen to 77 cents.[171] V-day, a movement to end violence against women, has spread to 81 countries and raised over $30 millions dollars for local organizations.[172]

Over the last two decades, the global movement for gay and lesbian equality has achieved great successes. In 1994, South Africa became the first country to protect gay and lesbian equality in its constitution. In 2001, the Netherlands became the first country to grant gay and lesbian marriage equality, and Belgium, Spain, Canada and South Africa soon followed. More than fifteen other countries offer some form of legal recognition and rights for same-sex couples.[173] In addition, the US Supreme Court ruled as unconstitutional the remaining state laws that criminalized sexual relations for gays and lesbians. In 2004, fifteen US states that include almost 1/2 of the US population, had laws banning discrimination on the basis of sexual orientation.[174] Until lesbians and gays have equal rights and protections as individuals, couples, and parents, our society is not truly free. As a global society, we now have the opportunity to stand up and support equal rights and to nurture all loving relationships.

Universal Health Care and Education

The world community needs to commit itself to providing quality education for all of the human family. Studies in the developing world have found that the simple act of providing a free lunch to students leads to huge gains in attendance, educational performance, and how long students stay in school.[175] Increased education has a number of positive societal benefits — especially for women. Education leads to improved economic prospects, better reproductive health, smaller family size, and improved HIV awareness.[176]

Significant gains in human well-being could be easily made with targeted investments in human health. Providing full access to family planning services could prevent millions of unplanned pregnancies, reduce the incidence of abortion, and cut maternal deaths by 20 to 35%![177] In the late 1990s, Bangladesh committed to improving the health of women, children, and the poor. Between 1998 and 2002, maternal and child mortality decreased by over 20%.[178] In addition, the World Health Organization led a international coalition to eradicate polio from the globe[179] The global number of polio cases decreased from 350,000 per year in 1988 to only 800 in 2003!

The world has more than enough resources to provide universal health care and education to everyone. Experts estimate that primary education for all children, the eradication of adult illiteracy, school lunch programs for the 44 poorest countries, assistance to preschool children and pregnant women in the 44 poorest countries, and universal basic health care and family planning would cost the world community an additional $68 billion in international aid.[180] That may seem like an overwhelming amount of money. But that figure, equivalent to roughly 15% of the annual Pentagon budget, totals less than one-fifth of one percent of the world's income.[181] Americans spent more on cosmetics ($8 billion) in 1998 than it would have cost ($6 billion) to provide basic education for all people in the world who did not have it.[182] Extending access to basic health care and nutrition to those without would cost $13 billion annually — that's $4 billion less than US and European pet owners spend on pet food.[183]

⇨ RESOURCES

📖 Cole, Luke, and Sheila Foster. *From the Ground Up: Environmental Racism and the Rise of the Environmental Justice Movement.* New York University Press, 2000. A fascinating history of the environmental justice movement and the factors that lead toxic facilities to be placed in poor communities of color in the United States. Their work documents how thousands of people are now fighting for their children, their health, and their communities.

📖 Hallinan, Joseph T. *Going Up the River: Travels in a Prison Nation.* Random House, 2003. Portrays the causes and effects of the "prison boom" that has incarcerated two million people in the US. Tells the stories of wardens, inmates, guards, prison planners, townspeople, and others.

📖 Kivel, Paul. *Uprooting Racism: How White People Can Work for Racial Justice.* New Society Publishers, 2002. Provides an understanding of white privilege and racism and offers concrete suggestions on how to resist oppression.

📖 Kozol, Jonathan. *Amazing Grace: Lives of Children and the Conscience of a Nation.* HarperPerennial Library, 1996. Kozol describes the impacts of poverty and community breakdown in New York City's South Bronx. Drugs, inadequate housing, rampant unemployment and overcrowded schools make a clarion call for justice for those living on the margins of our society. Also check out: *Savage Inequalities: Children in America's Schools* (HarperPerennial Library, 1992), and *Ordinary Resurrections: Children in the Years of Hope* (HarperPerennial, 2001), also by Kozol.

📖 Marcus, Eric. *Is It a Choice?: Answers to 300 of the Most Frequently Asked Questions About Gay and Lesbian People.* Harper San Francisco, 1999. Answers the questions about homosexuality that most people feel they can't ask. A very readable, helpful book that leaves no topic untouched.

📖 Zinn, Howard. *A People's History of the United States: 1492 to the Present.* HarperCollins, 1999. This classic presents history from the people's point of view — those who have been made invisible in our national mythology — the oppressed, the enslaved, the impoverished. A gripping historical overview that you won't find in conventional history books.

FOUNDATION #6: SIMPLE LIVING

A society that embraces simple living would encourage each person to find meaning and fulfillment by pursuing their true passions, fostering loving relationships, and living authentic, reflective lives rather than by seeking status and material possessions.

CHALLENGES
Advertising Overload — Commercialization of Childhood — Hyper-Consumerism

Advertising Overload

Our consciousness is under assault. Advertising saturates every aspect of our lives. Ever since the advent of modern advertising in the 1920s, corporations have utilized carefully chosen, powerful, and emotion-laden images and slogans to forever imprint their brands on our minds. And the assault is working.

We take in more than 3600 commercial impressions every day.[184] Much of this bombardment has come from "ad creep": commercialism that has moved into previously ad-free parts of our society — even schools. Telemarketers encroach on our homes and personal time. TV monitors show continuous commercials in elevators. Commercials precede movies in the theaters and on video. Spammers clog up our email in-boxes.

Advertisements, called product placements, have even snuck into the scripts and scenery of our television programs, movies, and video games. Unbelievably, the ABC television network agreed to promote Campbell's Soup on its talk-show program "The View" by having hosts "weave a soup message into their regular on-air banter."[185] The next time you hear somebody expressing a rave review of a new movie or product, consider that it might be a new kind of advertising — "buzz" marketing. Some corporations even pay people to enter "chat rooms" on the internet (or hang outside bars or movie theaters) and talk up their products.[186]

Commercialism is even undermining the integrity of our public institutions. The Chevrolet Suburban has purchased the label "official vehicle of Texas state parks," even though it has been rated the "meanest vehicle for the environment."[187] In professional sports, ads are placed behind home plate, on outfield walls, and in the ice. Increasingly the stadiums, once named after honored citizens or local communities, are now named after corporations: Petco Park, Network Associates Coliseum, Minute Maid Park, SBC Park, Citizens Bank Ballpark. One college has even named its arena, the Dunkin' Donuts Center, and The Peach Bowl is now officially known as the Chick-fil-A Bowl. Excessive commercialism is not only an annoyance but it often undermines many of our deeply held values and sacred institutions that transcend the desire for material possessions.

Commercialization of Childhood

Parents and citizens ought to be especially concerned about the increasing commercial pressures on children. Corporations are becoming increasingly excited about the opportunity to "brand" children with products as early as 1-$^1/_2$ to 2 years of age.[188] Currently, corporations target over $12 billion of advertising at children.[189] An especially cherished demographic for many advertisers are "tweens"—children who are not yet teenagers (8-12 year olds). The "tweens" are thought to influence billions of dollars in parents' spending and are at an opportune developmental stage where advertising can have long-lasting effects.[190] The average 8-13 year-old watches over 3 1/2 hours of television every day.[191] Even 25% of all preschoolers have a TV in their bedroom and spend two hours a day watching it.[192] The average child sees between 20,000 and 40,000 television commercials every year.[193] Children are also spending 60% more time watching television than they spend in school.[194]

This brings us to one of the most worrisome examples of the commercialization of childhood, the immense increase in advertisements aimed at children while they are at school. For most of our history, we have protected our schools as commercial-free havens for children. Corporations and administrators are now violating this principle. School districts have become strapped for funding, and corporations have come asking for commercial access into the classroom. Corporate advertisements are now pervasive in school hallways, on sides of school buses, on book covers and within corporate-sponsored educational materials. Some schools even distribute free product samples. Our kids are being seen as "consumers-in-training." Consider these examples:

- In Evans, Georgia, high school senior Mike Cameron was suspended for wearing a Pepsi T-shirt during a school photo-op that had been arranged to win a contest for promoting Coca-Cola products.[195]
- Channel One is a corporate-sponsored, 12-minute in-class "news" program that is light on news and big on fluff. Two minutes of commercials bring junk-food ads right into the classroom every day, reaching eight million school kids.[196] Channel One warns advertisers, "If you're not targeting teens, you may be missing out on a relationship that could last a lifetime."[197]
- In order to reach a Coca-Cola contract quota, a Colorado education official encouraged teachers and administrators to increase student use of school vending machines by allowing soft drinks in classes.[198]

Hyper-Consumerism

Why would the most profit-savvy members of our society spend billions of their hard-won dollars to create fleeting images in our minds? Because ads work. Commercialism is the engine that drives our cultural obsession with material possessions. Although we hate to admit what market research has shown over and over again for decades, each of us is consciously and unconsciously influenced by the advertisements we see. Many advertisements encourage us to have self-conscious feelings of inadequacy and dissatisfaction. Advertisers want us to obsess about our appearance, our image, our smell, our car — to worry about whether we are "cool" or "sophisticated." The collective impact of the advertising barrage sells us the idea that satisfying each of our fleeting desires is more important than contributing to the welfare of others — a very destructive message that ads convey 24 hours a day, 7 days a week.

The quest to "have it all" has programmed us to have overscheduled, frazzled, harried lives where we run from place-to-place without much sense of where we are going. Stretching ourselves too thinly sucks out the meaning of daily experiences. Long hours at work lead us to eating fast food meals while driving. Rushed cell phone calls provide our only lifeline to friends and family. Time-starved parents use "guilt money" to buy their kids happiness. Our material abundance has created serious levels of time poverty.

Hyper-consumerism has become a way of life. Good consumers attempt to meet every need, solve problems, enhance their lives, and find their identity by purchasing products ("Exercise in a Bottle" is an actual name of a product). Consumption surpasses other more socially beneficial goals, such as having sound character, contributing to the well-being of others, or becoming a good citizen. Consumerism's exclusive focus on satisfying fleeting individual desires systematically undermines the civic culture necessary for a healthy democracy.

While much of the world suffers from epidemic levels of hunger and poverty, the world's affluent continue unabated in their pursuit of material possessions. On a global level, advertisers encourage people to leave behind their distinctive cultural practices in favor of this new form of materialism. Unfortunately, the global media do not portray to these countries the downside of adopting consumerism (an increase in debt, higher stress levels, environmental destruction, a rise in selfishness, etc.). It seems that the only thing in the world safe from commercialism is religion. Well . . . maybe not. A group of corporations sponsored one of Pope John Paul's last visits to Mexico. As part of the arrangements, select packages of Sabritas potato chips (made by Frito-Lay) contained complimentary pictures of the Pope — a deal approved by the Vatican.[199]

GOALS
Reclaimed Consciousness — A Culture of Simplicity

Reclaimed Consciousness
We must learn to think, feel, communicate, and experience the world beyond the confines of material possessions. We must commit to leading lives fueled by compassion and love rather than by consumption and personal gain. We have begun to realize the seriousness of the problem — more than 80% of the

American public is concerned about the pervasiveness of greed and selfishness in our society.[200] If we want to replace materialism as our cultural blueprint, we must start scaling back the march of commercialism. Alaska, Hawaii, Maine and Vermont have even banned billboards in many public places.[201] As a society, we must demand that our public institutions and values retain their integrity instead of being sold off to the highest bidder.

A great place to start is by reclaiming our shared holidays from Madison Avenue. In recent years, Christmas has become more a celebration of materialism than of the values of generosity, strong families, and spiritual connection. Moreover, believe it or not, in 1939 Thanksgiving was specifically moved one week earlier in order to lengthen the Christmas shopping season.[202]

Another important step would be to return to an ad-free school environment. Revenues from advertisements are minor compared to overall school budgets. A school free from corporate slogans and logos would send a strong message to our children that we value their learning environment and independent development. Some countries, such as Norway, have begun to protect their children (even outside the schools) by banning all TV advertisements aimed at children under 12 years old. The American Psychological Association advocates restricting all advertising directed to children eight years old and younger.[203]

A Culture of Simplicity

A culture of simplicity is a viable alternative to the culture of hyper-consumerism. Voluntary simplicity provides people with a more balanced way of living, based on their most deeply held values. It involves recognizing the trap of consumerism and unplugging (at least partially) from the commercial culture that perpetuates it. Living simply involves:

- living more frugally
- working less
- slowing down
- spending more time with loved ones
- developing your passions and creativity
- building strong communities
- focusing on inner growth instead of on outward appearances
- engaging in meaningful and satisfying work that contributes to others

Time, energy, and money, currently swallowed by the "more is better" philosophy, are freed up to pursue more important endeavors. We can return to living as multidimensional human beings.

Currently, just to make ends meet, many two-parent families feel compelled to have both parents work full-time while their children are in daycare or school. For a culture of simplicity to flourish, it must be possible for people to have the freedom to work less while still earning enough to live on so that their lives can be about more than just "making a living."

Many of our grandparents fought for the 40-hour work week, and we've all benefited from their struggles. But in our current economy, the issue of over-working has arisen once again. We must create a culture that says — "enough!" More is not always better. Work and "success" should not always be our number one priority. The time is ripe for a change. Sixty-five% of Americans think that a movement to shorten the work week is a good idea.[204] It's time to consider the benefits of a shorter and more flexible work week: an improved quality of life, stronger relationships, more volunteerism, more authentic lives, higher worker morale, less traffic congestion and more jobs.

A culture based on simplicity may seem out of reach for our country of die-hard consumers, but simple living is becoming one of the fastest-growing trends around the world.[205] One in five Americans has already taken important steps toward a simpler life and has reported very worthwhile results.[206] Simplicity study groups are also popping up all over the country, providing an opportunity for individuals to transform their lives while finding support and sharing results. As we limit commercialism and create a culture of simplicity, we will create stronger families and communities, help nurture our natural environment and foster more meaningful lives.

⇨ RESOURCES

📖 Andrews, Cecile. *The Circle of Simplicity.* HarperCollins, 1997. Andrews uses a critique of consumer culture to offer a more creative, community-oriented, spiritually full alternative to consumerism. Individual strategies for simple living complement suggestions for society-wide changes that promote a culture of simplicity.

📖 Klein, Naomi. *No Logo: Taking Aim at the Brand Bullies.* Knopf Canada, 2000. Written by a journalist, this book examines the pervasiveness of corporate images in our culture and its effect upon our children and our identities.

📖 Lasn, Kalle. *Culture Jam: How to Reverse America's Suicidal Consumer Binge — And Why We Must.* Quill Publishers, 1999. The founder of *Adbusters Magazine* provides a scathing look at how corporations brand us and, through the media, set the agenda for our culture. Luckily, Lasn also gives us suggestions for strategies we can use to put control back in the hands of common folk.

📖 Schor, Juliet. *The Overspent American.* Basic Books, 1998. Schor is an engaging economist who analyzes the immensity of American consumer debt, its historical causes and solutions for escaping consumerism.

📖 Schor, Juliet. *Born To Buy: The Commercialized Child And The New Consumer Culture.* Scribner, 2004. Schor uncovers how companies use movies, magazines, video games, and TV to target kids of all ages, training them to become the consumers of the future. Her in-depth research, including interviews with advertising executives and kids, leads to a better understanding of the problem and some potential solutions.

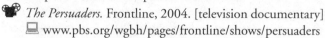 *The Persuaders.* Frontline, 2004. [television documentary]

www.pbs.org/wgbh/pages/frontline/shows/persuaders

A behind the scenes look into the marketing industry, this great Frontline episode demonstrates how corporations and politicians use marketing techniques to shape our perceptions and manipulate our desires.

FOUNDATION #7: REVITALIZED COMMUNITY

A revitalized community would create a healthy and caring environment for people to celebrate their many shared values while embracing individual differences, and would provide support for each person's physical, emotional, and spiritual needs.

CHALLENGES
Loss of Connection — Lack of Compassion

Loss of Connection

Many of us are losing our sense of being connected to people and place. We feel increasingly alienated from each other, so we've chosen to retreat into insular lives that revolve around our families and friends. We've closed ourselves off to the larger outside world and, in the process, have eroded our own ability to create positive social change. This trend has led us to abandon our sense of responsibility for the well-being of our communities, our country, and our fellow human beings around the world.

Americans have become much more mobile than they were even 50 years ago. Being able to move to a different city or state provides us with the opportunity to go where our best job prospects may lie. But our sense of connection, our roots, in any one area or group of people withers away. When we move frequently, there is little reason to invest in making our temporary community more beautiful, more livable, or safer. There may not be enough time, or you may not have the energy to develop deep, meaningful friendships. As a society, we are losing our ability to plant roots.

In addition, many communities are no longer the vibrant, nurturing places that they used to be. Housing developers have designed spaces that maximize building efficiency while unintentionally creating communities that lack character, uniqueness, and heart. Community after community becomes McDonaldized, duplicating generic versions of themselves all over the country. Warehouse-sized retailers, fast food outlets, and other corporate chains move in to replace small, community-rooted businesses, and soon you have created a place called Anywhere, USA.

Equally alarming, urban planners and developers increasingly design communities for our automobiles at the expense of walking, bicycling and safe areas for children to play. We spend more and more time in our cars (often in gridlock) — commuting back and forth to work, driving to the store, taking the kids to school and running errands. We spend thousands of hours working just to pay for our cars and millions of dollars of our taxes to pay for new roads. We build extra-wide streets to accommodate cars instead of people, and we increase speed limits so that we can work further away from home without losing more time. Current urban planning models leave us with no pedestrian-friendly public spaces or businesses within five miles of our houses. It's no wonder we are in our cars all the time. We shop in one community, work in another, and sleep in another. Many of us spend so much time at work and in our cars that our home is little more than a bedroom oasis between hour-long commutes.

Lack of Compassion

From an early age, society teaches us to look out for number one. The US, perhaps more than any other country in the world, values the individual. Taking personal responsibility for one's life has become an essential part of what it is to be American. Unfortunately, we generally accept selfishness as both natural and, to a certain extent, desirable. Our exclusive self-interest has left many of us lonely, isolated and empty. And we cannot survive on selfishness alone. Selfishness lacks the one thing we desire more than anything else — meaning.

Material objects have gained meaning and value at the expense of human relationships. We have stopped valuing such desirable human qualities as being nurturing and caring and replaced them with an emphasis on the ability to acquire marketable skills and achieve material success. Our culture's glorification of material progress also teaches each subsequent generation that success is about what you have acquired rather than who you have become. When doing what you want trumps spending time with others, it's not surprising that our kids grow up short on love and human contact, and long on television and video games.

Many of us have also become quite calloused to the suffering of others. The media and politicians represent the poor as lazy and irresponsible rather than as lacking the same opportunities the majority enjoy. The poor are rarely portrayed as needing a helping hand to overcome economic and social obstacles. Crime reports on television stimulate our instincts of fear and self-preservation, instead of motivating us to make our communities safer. Wars and disasters that take the lives of tens of thousands no longer faze us for more than a few hours as we numb ourselves in order to carry out the rest of our day. As we neglect the value of our fellow human beings in times of need, we slowly chip away at our own sense of being valued by others.

GOALS
Revolution of Caring — Smart Growth — Strong Local Institutions

Revolution of Caring

We need a revolution of the heart in this country — a revolution that would throw out selfishness and empower compassion. Our challenge is to create a society that encourages loving relationships and strong communities where people can count on each other for support and mutual well-being. To do that, we need people who are willing to act in ways that reflect caring for others' well-being.

We must look into the eyes of the homeless, the poor, the elderly, children, and the disenfranchised and see their humanity as our shared bond. We must embrace those that live beyond our borders and consider everyone as equal members of the human family — a family that values all people regardless of their social or economic status.

We must recognize that our own well-being is inextricably linked to the well-being of our community and that it is valuable to be a part of a healthy and loving community that cherishes shared values and embraces individual differences. We must reassert that contributing to the common good is a worthy calling for every one of us and not just the lifelong vocation of saints and dreamers.

Smart Growth

To create communities worth living in, we must work together to intentionally plan them. We must bring back the town squares, parks, pedestrian-only streets and other gathering places that bring a community to life. We must intentionally plan our housing and business developments to encourage community building by creating safe, open areas where we can walk, bike, talk to each other and play with our children. Many US cities are rejecting more suburban sprawl in favor of walkable "mixed-use" neighborhoods that combine residential and business areas and attract people of varying incomes. As we begin to reclaim our own sense of community, we will rediscover the value of developing a deep relationship with the place and people around us.

People around the globe have already begun taking back their communities. On September 22, 2000, residents in 800 European cities and towns from 27 countries participated in the European Union's annual "Car-free Day," where they banned automobiles from the city centers.[207] Fifty-seven percent of the population of Groningen, a city in the Netherlands of almost 200,000 people, travel around their city by bicycle![208] In Curitoba, Brazil, 75% of commuters ride the local buses rather than taking their cars to work — that's more than 800,000 people every day.[209] Public transit has a proven track record — when it is properly planned and funded, people use it.

Strong Local Institutions

We must work together to create a society where justice and harmony prevail. When we revitalize our community institutions, including religious groups, locally owned businesses, parent-involved schools, community centers, homeless shelters, and other social and political groups, it will strengthen our commitment to one another. To make this happen, we must be personally willing to integrate ourselves in our communities. This could involve volunteering for a local organization, keeping up on local events, getting involved in local schools, supporting local businesses, or just getting to know our neighbors by their first names.

As we strengthen community institutions, we can also reevaluate their purposes and how they work. For instance, you could add community service to your local school's curriculum. Community service would more fully integrate the next generation into your community and help instill an ethic of service that will carry on for years to come. Your community could start a locally owned business alliance to help maintain your area's distinct character. Locally owned businesses help create and perpetuate your community's economic wealth, because your dollars stay within the community instead of being siphoned off to distant corporate headquarters. A locally owned business in a locally owned building reinvests 85% of its profits in the local economy, as compared to a typical fast food franchise that invests only 20% of its profits in the local economy.[210]

Citizens have started using their own community institutions to support the common good for their neighborhood or town. In Greenfield, Massachusetts, citizens convinced Wal-Mart to pay for a study that would examine the economic impacts of building a superstore in their community. When they found out that 60% of local businesses would be negatively affected, they rejected Wal-Mart's building proposal.[211]

⇨ RESOURCES

🎥 *Independent America.* Tom Powers, executive producer, 2005.

🎥 *Wal-Mart: The High Cost Of Low Prices.* Robert Greenwald, executive producer/director, 2005.

These provocative documentaries encourage us to stand up and fight for independent businesses and the uniqueness of our communities by keeping out big-box retailers.

📖 Etzioni, Amitai. *The Spirit Of Community: Rights, Responsibilities, and The Communitarian Agenda.* Crown Publishers, 1993. A very engaging discussion regarding the balance between individual freedom and social responsibility. Proposes solutions to individualism that will strengthen our sense of community while preserving each person's unique character.

📖 Kunstler, James Howard. *Home From Nowhere: Remaking Our Everyday*

World for the 21st Century. Free Press, 1998. Kunstler's book is a rousing polemic aimed at creating alternatives to heartless sprawling communities. Advocates "new urbanism" principles such as multi-use zoning districts, car-free urban cores, revised tax codes, and designes that encourage human interaction.

📖 Lerner, Michael. *The Politics of Meaning: Restoring Hope and Possibility in an Age of Cynicism.* Perseus Publishing, 1996. Michael Lerner puts out a powerful call for us to bring meaning back into our lives by rebuilding our communities in such a way that people once again become more important than material things.

📖 Ritzer, George. *McDonaldization of Society.* Pine Forge Press, 2004. An enlightening look into how many aspects of our lives, including education, relationships, family, and entertainment, increasingly take on aspects of the fast-food industry. Explains how society is becoming more focused on efficiency, predictability and quantity rather than on quality, authenticity and meaning. Also offers suggestions on how we might resist the "McDonaldization" trend.

📖 Shuman, *Michael H. Going Local: Creating Self Reliant Communities in a Global Age.* Routledge Press, 2000. Shuman has created an essential resource for people wanting to preserve the unique, local character of their communities. He provides persuasive arguments for local self-reliance and then gives wonderful tips for how to make it all happen in your town.

CREATING A BETTER WORLD

You're now ready to take action! We've equipped you with information about the world's problems and a vision of what a better world might look like. If you ever doubt the need for action or find your commitment wavering, reread this chapter.

The rest of the book consists purely of actions. We offer you a broad range of actions to choose from — based on a balance between ease and effectiveness. Match your actions to your vision of a better world so that your unique contribution adds to the canvas we all share. Every action — big or small — is important if it makes for a better world. The world we want, we must create.

Each time a [person] stands up for an ideal, or acts to improve the lot of others, or strikes out against injustice, he [or she] sends forth a tiny ripple of hope. And crossing each other from a million different centers of energy and daring those ripples build a current which can sweep down the mightiest walls of oppression and resistance.

——Robert F. Kennedy

MONEY

Banking
Credit Cards
Saving
Investing

From the time we receive our first allowance as children, we learn the importance and power of money. Some people dedicate their lives to acquiring it; others feel that it is evil and avoid ever thinking about it. Either way, money ends up having power over their lives. Money is not inherently good or evil. It is just another way in which we shape the world around us. Money does not care if we use it to destroy the world or to rebuild it. It merely flows wherever we direct it.

Much of the money that passes through your hands is, at this moment and without your knowledge, aiding in the destruction of many of the things you hold dear in this world. For example, banks and mutual funds often invest in companies that pollute the Earth or violate human rights. This chapter will create possibilities for you to make sure that your money is doing good in the world.

The banking section offers several opportunities for you to support community development in your own community and in economically impoverished areas across the nation, just by opening up a bank account. Credit card options provide simple tools so that you can support social change while you shop. The savings section provides useful tips on how to intelligently manage your money to support your most deeply held values. Finally, the investing section allows you to turn a profit while supporting responsible businesses and community-based development.

BANKING

When you open up an account at any bank, you may think your money sits idly in that account until you need it. At least that's what your monthly statement makes you think. In reality, to make a profit, banks constantly invest your money in all kinds of ventures. They may use your money for:

- funding a strip mine
- backing a union-busting corporation
- extracting petroleum in Burma using forced labor
- creating a factory-style hog lot that dumps thousands of gallons of waste into your local streams

Your money may very well be wreaking havoc on your community and the world without your knowledge. By taking control of your money, you take responsibility for directing its impact on the world.

ACTION: Open an account at a socially responsible bank or credit union

You will sleep better at night if you know that your bank is using your money to promote justice in the world. So how do you begin? Since banks typically invest their money in a wide range of corporations and individuals, you would have to evaluate every one of these entities to determine a bank's level of social responsibility.

Instead of putting your money in large corporate banks, whose overall impact is hard to determine, deposit your money in locally owned banks that have a strong commitment to contribute to their community.

A number of financial institutions, called "community development financial institutions," dedicate themselves to making sure your money helps rather than hurts people. By placing your money in these institutions, you can rest assured that your money will help build new classrooms, renovate low-income neighborhoods, create small businesses and aid needy families in buying their first homes. When you support a financial institution that is truly committed to its community, you are helping that community retain its wealth, instead of having it siphoned off through corporate banks to one of the world's financial centers. You are helping create a strong, self-sufficient economy in your community.

Don't be discouraged by the idea that you have too little money to make a difference. When combined with hundreds of other customers, these small amounts

AREN'T OUT-OF-STATE BANKS A HASSLE?!

If, after doing some homework, you can't find any socially responsible banking institutions in your area, don't worry. Most banking transactions today involve checks or Automated Teller Machines (ATMs), so having an out-of-state bank is not a hassle anymore. The only difference is that you won't be able to use ATMs to deposit your checks. If that's something you need, consider having two accounts: one in-state and one out-of-state.

of money can make a big difference. Initially, to investigate banks is an invest-ment of time, but your choice will have positive consequences every day for years to come. Just think, you'll be helping the world even while you're at home sleeping!

BANKS

The following Community Development Banks operate very much like normal banks, but their business is the permanent, long-term economic development of low- and moderate-income com-munities. Community Development Banks offer all of the services that the giant corporate banks do, including checking and savings accounts, certifi-cates of deposit (CDs), money market accounts, lending and FDIC insured deposits, but they pro-vide one important additional service — a commit-ment to economic justice. Here are some of the best-known Community Development Banks:

SOCIAL RESPONSIBILITY RATINGS FOR BANKS	
A	ALL BANKS & CREDIT UNIONS PROFILED IN THIS CHAPTER
B	(Most Credit Unions)
C	Bank Of America, Wells Fargo, Wachovia, Bank One, Chase, Washington Mutual
D	Capital One, Sun Trust, Compass, National City, South Trust, First USA
F	US Bank, First Union, Citibank

See the Better World Buying Guide in the **Shopping** chapter for data sources.

☆ *Top Choice*

ShoreBank (Chicago, IL/ Cleveland, OH/ Detroit, MI)
(800) 669-7725   💻 www.sbk.com

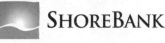

ShoreBank has been dedicated to the South Shore community in Chicago for many years. They use your "development deposits" to reclaim neg-lected buildings, reinvigorate small businesses, and allow people to renovate their homes. ShoreBank also has offices in Detroit, the Upper Peninsula of Michigan, Cleveland and Washington state. They offer a full range of banking and investing services.

ShoreBank Pacific (Ilwaco, WA)
(888) 326-2265   💻 www.eco-bank.com

ShoreBank Pacific is a subsidiary of ShoreBank of Chicago. They promote natural resource stewardship and community development, through their selec-tive lending practices, to small- and medium-sized businesses that want to increase profitability in environmentally responsible ways. They offer checking, saving and money market accounts as well as Certificate of Deposits (CD's).

Albina Community Bank (Portland, OR)
(800) 814-6088   💻 www.albinabank.com

As one of only 55 community development banks in the US, ACB supports local community organizations in a wide variety of ways, including a staff that is deeply committed to volunteering at Portland nonprofits. They offer a wide range of banking options including online banking and a credit/debit card that donates 1% of every purchase to schools.

Elk Horn Bank and Trust (Arkadelphia, AR)
(800) 789-3428 💻 www.ehbt.com
Elk Horn Bank and Trust is a community development bank committed to the economic revitalization of distressed rural communities in southern Arkansas. They use your money to create jobs and support local businesses.

Chittenden Bank (Brattleboro, VT)
(800) 545-2236 💻 www.chittenden.com
Chittenden Bank's Socially Responsible Banking program offers you deposit account options that fund specific lending programs for affordable housing, conservation and agricultural projects, education, downtown revitalization, community facilities and community-based businesses. You know your money is making a difference on a local scale.

City First Bank of DC (Washington, DC)
💻 www.cityfirstbank.com
City First Bank invests in local area nonprofits, small businesses, and affordable housing development throughout the DC area. They offer banking options for individuals as well as businesses and even savings accounts just for kids.

Native American Bank (Browning, MT)
(303) 988-2727 💻 www.nativeamericanbank.com
Native American Bank is owned and operated by a coalition of Native American tribes who invest in their own people, helping Indian businesses raise capital and tribes build vital community infrastructure.

Wainwright Bank (Boston, MA)
(800) 444-2265 💻 www.wainwrightbank.com
Wainwright Bank uses over $140 million to support a variety of projects, including breast cancer research, housing for people living with AIDS, food banks and the protection of wilderness areas.

Community Capital Bank (Brooklyn, NY)
(718) 802-1212 💻 www.communitycapitalbank.com
Community Capital Bank supports community development projects in New York City. Imagine the development that could happen if even one out of every 100 New Yorkers banked here!

Community Bank of the Bay (Oakland, CA)
(510) 271-8400 💻 www.communitybankbay.com
Community Bank of the Bay provides much-needed loans for the development of affordable housing, as well as loans to small businesses and non-profit

organizations. They use your money to create positive social change in the Bay Area and beyond.

Louisville Community Development Bank (LCDB) (Louisville, KY)

(502) 778-7000   www.morethanabank.com

Louisville Community Development Bank's mission is to revitalize 12 inner city neighborhoods of Louisville, Kentucky. They are accomplishing this goal of economic recovery by making targeted loans. In four years, they have made over $23 million in loans that have restored properties and created over 1000 jobs in the community.

University Bank (St. Paul, MN)

(651) 265-5600   www.universitybank.com

University Bank uses its assets to serve economically-challenged communities in the Twin Cities region. It has won numerous awards for its innovative work as a community development leader, and it offers a number of options for people interested in socially responsible banking, including personal checking, savings, and money market accounts.

CREDIT UNIONS

A popular alternative to banks, credit unions are not-for-profit financial institutions with a mission to serve their communities. A credit union collects deposits and loans them to members at low interest rates. Most credit unions have specific membership criteria (usually you must be an employee of a certain organization or a resident of a certain area). Credit unions are an excellent alternative to large corporate banks. They consistently earn excellent ratings from consumers by charging lower fees and having better customer service. The National Credit Union Share Insurance Fund (NCUSIF) protects all federal (and many state) credit union deposits up to $100,000.

Community Development Credit Unions (CDCU) commit to investing in low-income neighborhoods (similar to Community Development Banks). They also provide low-cost financial services to low-income communities. CDCUs accept deposits from individuals and institutions outside of their usual field of membership. It is an amazing feeling to know that they are using your savings to reinvigorate low-income neighborhoods, instead of just padding the pockets of corporate bank CEOs.

☆ *Top Choice*

Alternatives Federal Credit Union

(Ithaca, NY)

(607) 273-4666   www.alternatives.org

Alternatives works to make low-income communities more self-reliant. They base their philosophy on the premise that communities need a supportive financial network to keep their income within their community. Alternatives is dedicated to providing low-cost services to three main groups: 1) low-income families, 2) small business owners and 3) non-profit organizations.

Self-Help Credit Union (Durham, NC)
(800) 476-7428   💻 www.self-help.org

Since 1980, Self-Help Credit Union has financed $240 million worth of loans to assist low-income families (particularly minorities, women, and rural residents) to own homes, build businesses and strengthen community resources. Self-Help's mission stresses that ownership is the key to economic mobility and security.

Permaculture Credit Union (Sante Fe, NM)
(866) 954-3479   💻 www.pcuonline.org

Permaculture Credit Union is dedicated to the following three values: (1) care of the earth, (2) care of people, and (3) reinvestment of surplus to benefit the earth and its inhabitants. It is owned and democratically controlled by the members. One of their many programs includes discounted loans for energy saving upgrades for your home or business.

Opportunities Credit Union (Burlington, VT)
(800) 865-8328   💻 www.oppsvt.org

Opportunities Credit Union has won a number of awards for its outstanding work supporting grassroots community development in Vermont. Their website even highlights individual stories of how their members are making a difference in the lives of real people.

To find a credit union near you contact:
National Credit Union Administration
(703) 518-6300   💻 www.ncua.gov/indexdata.html

Credit Union National Association
(800) 358-5710   💻 www.creditunion.coop/cu_locator/

In Canada:
Search for the nearest credit union at: www.cuets.ca/links.html

☆ *Top Choice*
Citizens Bank of Canada & VanCity
(Vancouver, BC)
(888) 708-7800   💻 www.citizensbank.ca   *Citizens Bank of Canada*
(888) 826-2489   💻 www.vancity.ca

Created by Vancouver City Savings Credit Union (VanCity), the largest credit union in Canada, Citizens Bank provides socially responsible telephone and Internet banking. Before they invest your money in a business, they consider the company's record on human rights, military weapon and tobacco production, the environment and treatment of animals.

ACTION: Write checks that state your values

For as little as $10, Message! Products will send you 200 personalized checks that include a beautiful background design and the logo of one of a number of progressive organizations. Not only are you spreading the message of your group every time you write a check (approximately six people see each check you write), but Message! Products donates a portion of the price of the checks to the organization you choose for your design. Since 1986, they have donated over $2.5 million to these organizations: Sierra Club, PETA, Human Rights Campaign, NOW, National Abortion and Reproductive Rights Action League (NARAL) and many others. These checks work just like the ones that banks issue, but you also get to share your values with the world as you use them.

Message! Products
(800) CHECK-OK   💻 www.messageproducts.com

CREDIT CARDS

Credit cards are an increasingly popular method of making purchases in the US and around the world. Watch out! Credit cards can be handy but they can also lead you down a fast track to debt. Studies have found that people spend significantly more money when they use a credit card than when they pay with cash. And as people spend more, they acquire more debt (and some credit cards charge almost 20% interest). Total credit card debt in the US doubled from 1995 to 2006 and has surpassed $800 billion.[1]

ACTION: Cut up your credit cards

There is a very simple way to avoid credit card debt — get rid of your cards! Start with cutting up all of your department store and gas company cards. You will not only save yourself the stress of having debt, but you will free up your resources for better things that reflect your values. If you think you might want a credit card for travel or emergencies, just keep one multipurpose card (Visa or Mastercard) that you pay off every month. Get rid of all the rest.

ACTION: Donate money while using your credit card

A large number of activist organizations now have agreements with credit card companies. Each time you use your credit card, a small amount of money goes to their organization (or a group of organizations) — at no charge to you. Some of these organizations receive hundreds of thousands of dollars in extra funds each year that help them advance their efforts to make the world better. This is an incredibly easy, no-cost way to help organizations of your choice. Although the individual amounts may be small, they definitely add up. In addition, whoever sees your card also sees your organization's logo — another chance to spread your message. Call up your favorite organization and ask them if they have any contracts with credit card companies.

⭐ *Top Choice*
Working Assets Credit Card
(800) 522-7759 💻 www.workingassets.com/creditcard

Working Assets donates ten cents for each purchase on its credit cards to a pool of non-profit organizations that the cardholders select every year. In 2005, they donated nearly $4 million to progressive organizations such as Greenpeace, Planned Parenthood, Amnesty International, Human Rights Campaign and the ACLU. On top of the donations, you will be supporting Working Assets, one of the most socially responsible corporations in the world.

Salmon Nation Visa Credit Card
Shorebank Pacific
(888) 326-2265 💻 www.eco-bank.com

Shorebank Pacific has partnered with Ecotrust to support a program for sustainable, responsible, bioregional citizenship, starting with the Pacific Northwest. Salmon Nation encourages people to make choices that promote their local communities as well as the natural environment. Not only do your purchases help all of the above, they are processed through the Independent Community Bankers Association rather than a mega-financial institution.

NONPROFIT AFFINITY CREDIT CARDS
MBNA and Chase Bank each offer a number of credit cards that will donate $1/2\%$ of every purchase made to a nonprofit organization of your choice (there is no annual fee). These cards result in millions of dollars every year being donated to nonprofit organizations at no cost to the cardholders.

> Experts estimate that US credit card spending by the year 2008 will exceed $2.6 trillion annually.[2] If just 1% of us make our purchases with an affinity credit card, over $130 million would be generated for animal protection, the environment, and human rights.

MBNA
💻 www.mbna.com/creditcards/enviro_causes.html

Including Defenders Of Wildlife, Humane Society and National Wildlife Federation.

Chase Bank
💻 www.chase.com/pages/chase/pf/creditcards

Including Amnesty International, ASPCA, World Wildlife Fund

In Canada
Citizens Bank Shared Interests VISA
(888) 708-7800 💻 www.citizensbank.ca

Every time you use your Shared Interest VISA, Citizens Bank puts ten cents (Cdn.) into a donations pool to support not-for-profit initiatives for effecting positive social, economic and environmental change. This comes at no cost to you. Card users vote to determine which groups get the donations. Citizens Bank also offers credit cards that raise money for Amnesty International and Oxfam Canada.

SAVING

North Americans are addicted to shopping. It's no wonder, when you consider the amount of advertising companies expose us to on a daily basis. TV and magazines teach us that we should be thinner, wear more stylish clothes and drive faster, fancier cars. It's not surprising that all of us, from time to time, confuse money with happiness. After enough of these purchases, you have a home full of stuff and a heap of debt.

> During the 1980s, Americans saved 9% of their after-tax income. In the 1990s, the savings rate fell to 5%. In 2004, it fell to 1.8%. For 2005, the rate is projected to be negative — meaning that now Americans are habitually spending more than they make.[3]

The first step in escaping from the trap of consumer debt is to confront your urges to meet your needs, solve your problems and enhance your life by buying things you don't need. Once you deal with our cultural obsession with possessions, it will be much easier for you to save your money.

ACTION: Create a budget

Most people look at their bank balance at the end of the month and say, Where did it all go? The first step to financial awareness is to take an honest look at your checkbook and past credit card statements to figure out how much you spend each month. Then compare it to your monthly take-home income. Only then will you know your financial state of affairs. How much are you savings (or going in the hole) every month?

The next step is to determine what you spend your money on. Separate your expenses into categories such as: rent/mortgage, food, car payment, clothing and entertainment. You are now ready to create a budget—a set of goals for controlling your spending (e.g., for next month I will only spend $100 on entertainment). Don't forget to budget the amount of money you want to save every month. Consider having a set amount of money (5-10% of your income) transferred to your savings account to encourage saving.

SAVING MONEY HAS THE FOLLOWING ADVANTAGES FOR YOU AND THE WORLD

- You experience a sense of mental freedom formerly strangled by the shadow of debt.
- You have more liberty to change jobs, work less, or take some time off to spend with your children or travel (to truly break out of the work-and-spend cycle).
- You have the possibility of donating more of your money to organizations that are putting your values into action.
- The fewer products you buy, the more money you save, and the less stress you cause upon the Earth's scarce resources.

☐ ACTION: Reduce your expenses

If you are spending more than you can afford, consider tracking every penny that escapes from your wallet for a month. Then reduce expenses that are not in line with your values. Here are some common areas where we can often find ways to save a little more:

- Reduce or eliminate your cable/satellite TV subscription.
- Get a cheaper cell phone plan (or get rid of it altogether).
- Reduce the features on your phone bill (e.g., caller ID, call waiting).
- Sell your second car (or trade it in for a cheaper car).
- Adjust your thermostat to save on energy bills.
- Reduce your alcohol consumption.
- Reduce how often you go out to eat (you can even split meals when you do).
- Shop less (including eBay and Amazon.com).

⇨ RESOURCE

📖 Dominguez, Joe, and Vicki Robin. *Your Money or Your Life*. Penguin, 1999. This wonderful book helps you gain control of your money so that your spending becomes an expression of your values. It has profoundly changed thousands of people's lives and given them the freedom to escape the bonds of money and enjoy the fruits of frugality.

INVESTING

As the stock market skyrocketed to its peak in 2000, more and more people leaped into the market to make their fortunes. Stories of blue-collar workers making thousands of dollars through online investing filled the news, encouraging everyone with a little extra cash to hop on board and get rich. Naturally, we all want to make as much money as possible through our investments, but have you ever wondered what happens to your money when you invest it? Many people worry about the financial results of their investments, but most forget to analyze the impact of their investments on the world.

Your investments can support:

- the exploitation of workers in crowded sweatshops
- oil companies that destroy indigenous people's land
- chemical manufacturers that pollute the air you breathe

- OR -

- small business development
- environmentally friendly companies
- Bangladeshi women working their way out of poverty

It's your choice. Fortunately, there are several options for investing in ways that lead to a better world.

"Ethical investing," "values-based investing" and "socially responsible investing" are all terms that describe using a "double bottom line" when choosing investment options. Generating a profit is the first bottom line. Making a positive contribution to the world is the second bottom line. For socially responsible investors, making the highest profit regardless of the social and environmental consequences is not a viable option.

Screening is a process by which investors exclude from their portfolios companies that are involved in practices that the investor does not support (negative screens) or include companies that are doing things that the investor thinks are exceptional (positive screens). In this way, many investors are helping to support those corporations that are doing especially positive things for the world (for example, making extensive charitable contributions or having an excellent environmental record). Similarly, investors can withhold their support by excluding companies that act in ways that contradict the investors' values (for example, companies using sweatshop labor or producing nuclear weapons). When you invest in socially responsible corporations, you are using your money to help manifest your values in the world.

Although you can do most investing by yourself, you may want to consider contacting a financial planner in your area who is well versed in socially responsible investing. They can help you make sound financial and ethical decisions (see Investment Resources).

ACTION: Invest in socially responsible stocks

It can be challenging to determine which companies are socially responsible. After a little research, you will quickly come to realize that just as there are no perfect people, so there are no perfect corporations. The point is to do the best you can with the information available. Take into consideration everything you know about a corporation — any boycotts, awards, fines, and whether or not you feel good about the products they make. We've created a couple of lists to help you get started.

The following lists take into account: environmental impact, charity, diversity, working conditions, family benefits, community outreach, and current boycotts by organizations that are working for a better world. Each socially responsible corporation is followed by its corresponding stock symbol in parentheses.

ACTION: Invest in socially responsible mutual funds

A mutual fund company buys stock and/or bonds from many different corporations and government agencies. When you buy a share of a mutual fund, you are in effect getting small amounts of stock

US investors control $2.3 trillion in socially responsible investments (roughly $1 of every $10 professionally managed).[4]

shares and bonds from hundreds of different companies. This diversity of investments lowers the risk to the individual investor.

Much as with individual investors, most socially responsible mutual funds use their own unique screens to keep out corporations engaged in activities that are in opposition to the values of the fund. Many socially responsible investment groups, for example, refrain from investing in tobacco, alcohol, weapons, nuclear power and corporations that are especially polluting or exploitative. Some also exclude companies that conduct animal testing. Many of these funds also seek out companies that promote equal opportunity, create beneficial and safe products, foster good labor relations and are environmentally responsible. Each mutual fund uses different screens, so do some comparison shopping and ask for each fund's prospectus.

Some of the most socially RESPONSIBLE corporations:[5]	**Some of the most socially IRRESPONSIBLE corporations:**	
American Express (AXP)	Pepsi (PBG)	Dupont
Apple Computer (AAPL)	Phillips Van Heusen (PVH)	Enron
AT&T (T)	Pitney Bowes (PBI)	Exxon Mobil
Avon (AVP)	Reebok (RBK)	Federated Dept. Stores
Baxter International (BAX)	SBC Communications (SBC)	General Electric
Cisco Systems (CSCO)	Spectrum Organic (SPOP)	General Motors
Cummins (CMI)	St. Paul Travelers (STA)	Harcout
Cutter & Buck (CBUK)	Sun Microsystems	Hoffman LaRoche
Eastman Kodak (EK)	Timberland (TBL)	Kohl's
Fannie Mae (FNM)		LA Gear
Gaiam (GAIA)	**Some of the most socially IRRESPONSIBLE corporations:**	Marshall's
Green Mountain Coffee (GMCR)	Altria (Philip Morris)	May's
Hain Celestial (HAIN)	Archer Daniels Midland	Mitsubishi
Herman Miller (MLHR)	BASF	Monsanto
Hewlett Packard (HWP)	Bill Blass	Nestle
IBM (IBM)	British American Tobacco	Pillowtex
Intel (INTC)	Calvin Klein	Pfizer
Liz Claiborne (LIZ)	Chevron Texaco	Perry Ellis
Lucent Technologies (LU)	Coca Cola	RJ Reynolds
Mattel (MAT)	Conoco Philips	Royal Caribbean
Motorola (MOT)	Consolidated Stores	Saks Fifth Avenue
New York Times (NYT)	Converse Shoes	Saucony
Northern Trust (NTRS)	Dillard's	Service Merchandise
	Dow Chemical	Stone Container
		TJ Maxx
		Tyson Foods
		Wal-Mart

SOCIAL RESPONSIBILITY IS PROFITABLE!

You're probably thinking, "Sure, investing in socially responsible stocks is great, but I bet you don't make any money." Actually, over the last 10 years, the Domini Social Index (made up of 400 socially responsible stocks) did just as well financially as the S&P 500 — the most representative composite of US stock values.[6]

☆ *Top Choice*

Domini Social Investments
(800) 762-6814 💻 www.domini.com

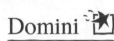

   The Domini 400 (an index of 400 screened companies) is a standard in the ethical investment industry. They are also the leader in using shareholder resolutions to promote ethnic diversity, environmental sustainability, and fair wages and working conditions in the corporate world.

Citizens Funds
(800) 223-7010 💻 www.citizensfunds.com

   Citizens Funds is known for its diversity of fund choices and rigorous social screens. Along with the usual standard social screens they also consider Community Reinvestment Act ratings and the AFL-CIO boycott list.

   For contact information, recent performance, social screens, and investment guidelines for socially responsible mutual funds contact:

Social Investment Forum
(202) 872-5319 💻 www.socialinvest.org

SocialFunds.com
(802) 348-7790 💻 www.socialfunds.com

In Canada:
Ethical Funds
(604) 714-3800 💻 www.ethicalfunds.com

🗒 ACTION: Invest in community development loan funds

Investing in community development loan funds is perhaps the most powerful way to use your money to make the world a better place. Community investment helps support low-income housing development, provides small business loans (often to minorities and women) and creates lasting change in communities that need it most. Investing in community development funds is an especially effective way to fight poverty because:

If you want to invest in mutual funds that focus on women's rights or the environment, then check out the following.

WOMEN'S RIGHTS
Women's Equity Mutual Fund
(800) 385-7003
www.womens-equity.com

ENVIRONMENT
New Alternatives Fund
(800) 423-8383
www.newalternatives fund.com

- The people living in poverty, who know their situation the best, decide how to use the loans to most improve their lives.
- Loan programs for the very poor, when properly administered, teach and reinforce entrepreneurial behavior and self-sufficiency rather than promote dependency. They create lasting change.
- Borrowers demonstrate a remarkable ability to work their way out of poverty.
- Funds spread social change beyond the individual loan recipient by creating jobs, which feed families and fight poverty in general.[7]

Micro-credit lending offers loans as small as $10! In Bangladesh or Latin America, your investment could help a woman buy a sewing machine to start her own business or give a fruit grower the opportunity to purchase his own fruit cart to sell his produce. Without the help of these small loans, people must rent equipment or work for others, perpetuating their poverty.

> Find out more about micro-credit from the Grameen Bank at www.grameen-info.org

Community development loan funds are federally unregulated and uninsured. However, loan funds often use grant money and pre-funded loss reserve to protect your investment, making the risk very minimal. Community investment is a great supplement to other higher-rate investments. A small portion of your savings can make an enormous difference in someone's life.

Here are some Community Development Loan Funds that you can invest in:

☆ *Top Choice*

Calvert Social Investment Foundation

(800) 248-0337   🖳 www.calvertfoundation.org

Calvert Foundation promotes community development and micro-lending throughout the US and the world. They require a minimum $1000 investment and offer returns of 0 to 4%.

Nicaraguan Credit Alternatives Fund (NICA)

(608) 257-7230   🖳 www.wccnica.org

The NICA Fund, a project of the Wisconsin Coordinating Council on Nicaragua, addresses the root causes of poverty by providing low-income Nicaraguans with loans for small business, farming, and cooperatives. This fund is a fantastic opportunity to help people of the second poorest country in the Western hemisphere maintain some control over their own well-being. The fund requires a $2,000 minimum investment for a minimum of two years, and returns range from 0 to 4%.

For information on over 100 community development investments all across the US and world go to: www.communityinvest.org or contact:

National Community Capital Association

(215) 923-4754   💻 www.communitycapital.org

✒ ACTION: Invest your retirement in a socially responsible manner

For the fortunate among us who have a pension, there are some socially responsible alternatives to the traditional investment strategy. TIAA-CREF, a nationwide financial system primarily for employees in higher education, created the Social Choice Account based on customer interest. Also at the beginning of 2001, the $170 billion California Public Employees Retirement System applied human rights, labor, and environmental criteria to their overseas investments.[8] See if, at your work, you can secure your financial future at the same time that you protect future generations. Follow these simple steps:

- Find your pension administrator. Check your pension statement for a phone number.
- Find out if she or he offers a socially responsible alternative. Your administrator should immediately be able to tell you yes or no.
- If the answer is yes, great. Ask to have your pension invested in the alternative plan.
- If there is no socially responsible alternative, say that you would like one and ask to whom you can speak about it.
- Once you've switched your pension, tell your coworkers about it.

⇨ INVESTMENT RESOURCES

📖 Abbey, Deb. *Global Profit and Global Justice: Using Your Money to Change the World.* New Society Publishers, 2004. Learn how to invest and spend your money in a way that creates progressive social change including shareholder advocacy, community investing, and socially responsible investing.
💻 www.realassets.ca

📖 *Co-op America's Financial Planning Handbook.* This inexpensive concise handbook gives you a good introduction to investing, provides socially responsible alternatives, and includes a directory of socially responsible financial planners across the country. It's free with a Co-op America membership. RealMoney newsletter from Co-op America is also a great resource (www.realmoney.org).
(202) 872-5307   💻 www.coopamerica.org

📖 *Co-op America's Guide to Community Investing.* Available free of charge online, The Guide to Community Investing explains the principles behind community investing along with the details of how to get started.
💻 www.coopamerica.org/socialinvesting/communityinvesting/whattoknow/index.cfm

📖 *The Social Investment Forum (SIF)*. The SIF is a national non-profit organization that promotes socially responsible investing. Their website provides contact information for banks, loan funds, and mutual funds. Their guide to socially responsible financial planners is included in Co-op America's Financial Planning Handbook (see Co-op America).
(202) 872-5319　💻 www.socialinvest.org

In Canada:
SocialInvestment.ca
Canada's online Resource for Socially Responsible Investment
💻 www.socialinvestment.ca

SHOPPING

What to Buy
Who to Buy it From
Better World Buying Guide

SHOPPING IS A CHERISHED RITUAL in the United States. A weekly pilgrimage to the local mega-mall has become more common than attending religious services. We often use shopping to meet our emotional needs. If we are happy, we go buy ourselves something to celebrate. If we are sad, we go buy something to make ourselves feel better. If we feel lonely, we go to the mall. If we fall in love, we go buy the person something to show our love. Surprisingly, for all the time we Americans think about and spend shopping, we haven't put much thought at all into how all of these purchases affect the world around us.

Every product on your favorite department store's shelf is made of a collection of natural resources that humans have extracted or harvested from the Earth. These raw materials were then transported, processed, and transported again to the store where we see them on the shelf — all with the integral help of our fellow human beings.

This chapter is about transforming the way you look at shopping. It will help you to consider the social and environmental impacts of the products and services that you buy. It will then be up to you to decide how these social and environmental considerations fit into the other factors that are important to you (price, quality, color, features).

This may sound a little overwhelming, but in fact we've done a lot of the leg work for you to make sure your decision is as simple as possible. The following suggestions will help you use your purchasing power to support your community, the planet, and the businesses that you would like to see flourish — ones that create safe and positive work environments for employees, pay fair wages, nourish their communities, create quality products, and practice environmental sustainability on a daily basis.

ACTION: Resist the urge to go shopping

For some of us, we shop whether we need something or not. Shopping has become entertainment. Resist the urge to go shopping! When you get bored, do something creative instead of going to the store and buying things you don't need. You'll end up saving hundreds of dollars and hours, avoid accumulating more clutter, and give the planet a much-needed breather.

DON'T GET SUCKERED IN BY SALES

Virtually every occasion gets its own sale: We have Father's Day sales, Labor Day sales, after-Christmas sales, 4th of July sales — the list goes on and on. North America is sale crazy. If you get the Sunday newspaper, you receive a huge stack of colorful inserts advertising cheap goods. Sales are clever ploys to get you to buy stuff you don't need. Just because you can get a brand-new Thighmaster for $19.95 doesn't mean you need one!

ACTION: Buy less stuff

Sometimes it seems as if people in our society are in a contest to see who can fill their house with the most stuff. Because our culture trains us to be consumers, we are often unaware of the many, many benefits to being frugal. Remember, everything you own owns you.

When all facets of one person's life are taken into account, it takes almost 120 pounds (55 kilograms) of natural resources per day to maintain the lifestyle of the average American.[1]

Everything you buy you must maintain, store, repair, clean, and perhaps insure. Our stuff quickly becomes a psychological burden. The more you buy, the more money you need, which increases your work time at the expense of your family and friends. Finally, all of our stuff takes natural resources to produce, making everything we buy environmentally costly. Here are a few pointers to help you buy less stuff:

- Fix broken things: Our disposable culture encourages us to replace broken items even when they are relatively easy to fix. Just because you can afford a new lawn mower doesn't mean you shouldn't try to fix your old one.

- Reuse stuff: You can reuse many so-called disposable items, such as paint brushes, sandwich bags and plastic containers.

- Borrow from friends: Borrowing saves resources, money, and time and also helps build community. Check out books, movies and CDs from your local library. Ask your friend if she has a pipe wrench, since you only need it for a day or two.

- Ask yourself, Do I really need it? Advertising makes us feel as if we'll be left out if we don't have the latest gadget or name brand clothing. When it comes down to it, we don't need much of what we buy.

- Take a shopping list: Plan ahead before you shop. Decide exactly what you want before you go; otherwise fancy displays, colorful packaging and salespeople might convince you to buy something you don't need.
- Avoid impulse buys: Companies actually design their stores to encourage impulse buying. Do you really need any of that junk that surrounds you in the check-out line? One powerful technique to avoid impulsively buying big purchases, such as a new stereo, is to wait two weeks before you buy it. If you still really want it, then get it.

ACTION: Treat workers with respect and courtesy

No matter where you shop or what you are buying, be sure to treat the employees (and other customers) with dignity, respect, and friendliness. Being treated like a fellow human being is far superior to being treated like an inanimate object or a subordinate. Show your appreciation when someone goes above and beyond the call of duty. Even though it can be difficult, be sure not to take your anger out on workers for policies and products that they did not create. You can complain about a purchase or policy while treating the other person with respect.

WHAT TO BUY

We grow up buying things unconsciously, never giving a second thought to how our purchases affect the world. There are ten basic questions you can ask yourself about any product before buying it:

1. Can I find it used?
2. Will it last a long time?
3. Is it reusable or at least recyclable?
4. What are the item and its packaging made from?
5. How will I dispose of it?
6. Is it toxic?
7. What conditions do the workers who made it work under?
8. How much will it cost to maintain it?
9. Is it a good value?
10. Will my buying it contribute to a better world?

You probably can't answer every one of these questions about every product. That's OK. The point is to increase your awareness and do your best. You won't become a conscious shopper overnight.

> To get 1 oz (28 g) of gold, you must excavate 30-100 tons of rock and dirt. Cyanide is then used to separate the gold from the surrounding rock.[2] Consider helping the environment by reusing or re-crafting jewelry that has been passed down in your own family. Through a company called Green Karat, you can now even buy wedding bands and jewelry made from certified recycled gold! (www.greenkarat.com)

A GUIDE TO PRODUCT LABELS

LABEL	ISSUE	MEANING	COMMON PRODUCTS
Fair Trade	Human Rights	Livable Wages	Coffee, Tea, Chocolate
Not/Never Tested On Animals	Animal Rights	Cruelty-Free	Body Care Products, Cosmetics
Free-Range	Animal Rights	More Humane Conditions	Beef, Chicken, Eggs
Organic	Environment	Pesticide-Free	Almost Anything
Recycled Content	Environment	Utilizes Material Byproducts	Paper Towels, Toilet Paper, Office Paper
Post-Consumer Content	Environment	Contains Actual Recycled Materials	Paper Towels, Toilet Paper, Office Paper
Biodegradable	Environment	Breaks Down Naturally	Cleaning Products
Chlorine-Free	Environment	Utilizes Less Toxic Alternatives	Cleaning Products
Phosphate Free	Environment	Fish-Friendly	Diswashing and Laundry Detergents
Soy-Based Inks	Environment	Non-Toxic	Packaging, Books

ACTION: Buy used

Buying used products is a great way to lessen the demand for natural resources. Some of the more popular used items include books, compact discs, clothing and cars. But you can also easily find used appliances, computers, bikes, baby clothes, toys and furniture. Check out garage sales, thrift and second hand stores, pawnshops and the classifieds. When you buy a used item you:

- Conserve the energy and resources that would have been used to supply you with a new item.
- Promote a sustainable rather than a throwaway society.
- Retain your money for more fulfilling activities.

Craig's List 💻 www.craigslist.org

Craig's List is the wildly successful internet version of local classified ads. People post (at no charge) what they have or want online along with an email, phone number, or anonymous contact information. You can find just about anything you're looking for very quickly in or around your home town. It keeps dollars in your community, you don't have to pay for tax or shipping, and you usually save something from the landfill to boot!

The Freecycle Network 🖥 www.freecycle.org
Think of Craig's List. Now imagine all of the stuff is free. The Freecycle Network looks to connect those who want to get rid of something with someone from their community who wants it. If you're interested in creating a local network where people help each other just because it's good for the environment AND good for the community, take a look!

eBay 🖥 www.ebay.com
eBay is the popular Internet auction site where any registered user can buy or sell virtually anything. It's likely someone is selling exactly what you're looking for, no matter how obscure. You can register and search for free. eBay is also a great place to get rid of the stuff you no longer need.

TOP FIVE THINGS TO PUT ON YOUR SHOPPING LIST

1. **Compact Fluorescent Light Bulbs**
   less electricity
   saves money
   lasts ten times longer
2. **NiMH Rechargeable Batteries**
   reusable 1000 times
   less toxic
   saves money
3. **Cloth Napkins and Dish Rags**
   less waste
   saves money
   reusable many times
4. **Low-Flow Shower Head**
   less water used
   saves money
5. **Good Quality Shoes**
   fewer resources used
   better labor conditions
   last longer

☐ ACTION: Buy durable and reuseable products

In North America, we demand cheap goods and we get what we pay for. It's so easy to just throw away cheaply-made products because we never have to see them again; our garbage just "disappears." In the long run, it's better to spend a little more money for more durable goods that you can reuse, and therefore don't have to repair or replace all the time. By purchasing reuseable, durable items, you save landfill space, money and natural resources.

It only takes a little research to determine a product's quality. You can find issues of Consumer Reports at your local library that you can use to compare models' reliability and quality.

☐ ACTION: Buy products with minimal packaging

Product packaging sometimes requires more resources than the product itself. Some important questions to ask yourself before you buy are: "What is the packaging made of?" and "What will I do with it when I'm done?"

> Cloth bags aren't just for grocery shopping. Remember to bring them with you whenever you plan to shop.

AVOID	BUY
Disposable razors	Reusable razors
Disposable batteries	Rechargeable batteries
Paper towels/paper napkins	Dishtowels/cloth napkins
Disposable silverware and dishes	Washable dishes and ware
Bottled water	Water filter
Bleached paper coffee filters	Cloth or metal coffee filter
Plastic baggies and wrap	Reusable containers
Aerosol air fresheners	Natural air fresheners
Battery powered watch	Solar or self-winding watch
Disposable cameras	Digital or 35mm camera
Disposable chopsticks	Reusable chopsticks

	PLASTIC TYPE	COMMON ITEMS	ENVIRONMENTAL IMPACT
Better	#1(PETE), #2(HDPE)	Soda Bottles, Plastic Milk Jugs, Shampoos, Bottled Water	Most Easily Recycled
Fair	#5(PP)	Margarine Tubs, Yogurt Containers, Syrup Bottles	Recycling Possible
Poor	#4, #6, #7	Toiletries, Medicinal Products	Landfill-Bound
Worst	#3(PVC)	Shampoos, Mouthwashes	Landfill-Bound, Highly Toxic

PLASTICS

Not only do plastics produce pollution when they are manufactured but, unlike glass and aluminum which can be recycled virtually forever, plastic can usually only be recycled once, if that. Also, while the market for many recycled materials remains robust, recycling plastics currently has very tenuous economic benefits. Avoid plastic items whenever possible. If you are going to buy plastic items, buy things that you will be able to reuse.

Whenever possible, buy products with less packaging (for example, buy in bulk), packaging made from recycled materials, packaging you can recycle, or biodegradable packaging.

WHO TO BUY IT FROM

It is just as important to take into account who produces the items you purchase as the type of item being produced. Different companies manufacturing the same product can have radically different impacts on the environment, workers, businesses and communities. This is where you can shape what kind of world you want to live in with one of the most powerful forces in society: your dollars. If you add up the amount of money you spend on goods and services per year and multiply that by the adult population of the US, you can see what kind of power we have available to change things for the better. Think of every purchase you make as a vote. Instead of voting for government representatives, you are voting for the kinds of companies and business practices that you would like to see succeed. Polluters or environmental pioneers, sweatshops or quality jobs: you choose one or the other with every dollar you spend. Reward companies that make a difference while making a buck, and keep your money out of the hands of those that are sacrificing our quality of life for quick profits.

FAIR TRADE

"Fair Trade" is a term used to distinguish companies and organizations who are committed to paying people in the Third World a living wage for their products while ensuring safe working conditions. Initiated in 1949 by American churches, the Fair Trade movement has grown almost as rapidly as global trade itself. Look for the Fair Trade label on coffee, tea, and chocolate products in particular.
Fair Trade Federation: www.fairtradefederation.org
Transfair: www.transfairusa.org

Look for this Label!

ACTION: Support locally owned independent businesses

When you buy from large corporations, you support the increasing consolidation of wealth and power in the hands of the few. Chain businesses often take those dollars directly away from smaller local businesses that cannot afford to lose the income. By making your purchases at local business, you spread that wealth out to more local people and increase your community's standard of living. Local businesses rely more on local suppliers and service providers, forming a kind of local economic web of interdependence that creates jobs and a thriving community. Every dollar you spend at a local business helps your community maintain its individual character, uniqueness, and diversity while supporting your neighbors in their quest for the good life. Paying in cash, rather than by credit card, can also help local businesses as they are often the ones least able to afford the hefty fees the credit card companies charge them for each and every transaction. Look in the phone book for local alternatives to large corporate chains.

ACTION: Boycott irresponsible companies

Boycotts have traditionally been, and continue to be, one of the most powerful forces for changing corporate behavior. Organizations coordinate people nation- or worldwide to withhold their dollars until the executives agree to listen and

MAJOR BOYCOTTS (2006)

WHO	MAIN REASON
Wal-Mart	Treatment Of Workers
Exxon-Mobil	Largest Contributor To Global Warming
Coca Cola	Unethical Water Privatization
Chevron-Texaco	Toxic Waste Dumping
Altria (Philip Morris, Kraft, Post)	Unethical Business Practices

accommodate the social and/or environmental concerns of their customers. To note some successes: boycotts have helped get General Electric out of the nuclear weapons business, helped save the lives of millions of Third World children, and helped bring an end to apartheid government in South Africa. Keep up to date on the latest boycotts by visiting Ethical Consumer's boycott list (www.ethical consumer.org/boycotts/boycotts.htm). Boycotts often take a lot of time and dedication from organizers and protesters. If you agree with the motivation behind a particular boycott, be sure to avoid purchasing products from that company. Periodically check the status of boycotts to check on the progress of targeted companies.

ACTION: Let companies know how you feel

Whether you notify a company of your dissatisfaction with their business practices or praise them for making positive changes, it is important to let them know that how they run their company matters to you, the customer. If you think that one letter could never really make a difference to a big corporation, consider this: Wal-Mart will consider changing policy with as few as 20 letters from their 70 million customers![3] Here are some recommendations to make your letter powerful.

- Tell them that you will stop/start buying their products because of their behavior.
- Make sure that the letter is addressed to the CEO of the company with copies to newspapers, watchdog groups and government representatives.
- Mention how many other people and organizations share your views and alert the company to the possible effects of a boycott.

ACTION: Shop at home

There are a number of advantages to shopping at home, either through catalogs or on the Internet, rather than driving to a nearby store or mall. It is less time intensive; you are less apt to be taken to impulse buying; salespeople can't pressure you; and you have access to products that you just can't find in your area.

Greater Good

Internet shopping portals are websites that you choose to start from whenever you decide that you're going to shop online. When you link from those sites to your shopping sites, a certain percentage of your purchase price goes to an organization of your choice, without any extra cost to you. They are where you should start when doing all of your online shopping, no matter what you're looking for. By starting your shopping at Greater Good's site, 5 to 15% of what you spend will go to the charity of your choice at no cost to you. (www.greatergood.com)

 ACTION: Buy products from socially responsible companies
Figuring out who are the good guys and the bad guys in the corporate world can be a time-consuming process. What's more, when you finally get it all sorted out, you still have to change your purchasing habits to better reflect your values. We've tried to take out that initial hardship by doing much of the research for you with our Better World Buying Guide. After thorough investigation, cross-comparisons and synthesis, we've created a list of good and bad companies that is both practical and up-to-date.

BETTER WORLD BUYING GUIDE

Our guide rates companies on a relative scale from "A" (the most socially responsible) to "F" (the most socially irresponsible). We've considered research that rates these companies on many issues, including: the environment, animal testing, community involvement, human rights, factory farming, corporate crime, sweatshops, diversity, boycotts and the treatment of both workers and consumers.

Three Ways To Use Our Socially Responsible Better World Buying Guide:
1. Go through each product category and see if you can make product choices that would be more socially conscious than what you are buying now.
2. Pick out at least one product category and commit yourself to buying from an "A" company.
3. Avoid as many products as possible made by companies that received an "F".
   We've used over 20 different sources to rank products and companies. Here are some of the most valuable sources of data:
   - Council on Economic Priorities and *Shopping for a Better World*
   - Multinational Monitor magazine (www.essential.org/monitor)
   - Business Ethics magazine (www.business-ethics.com)
   - Ethical Consumer (www.ethicalconsumer.org)
   - Co-op America (www.coopamerica.org) and *Co-op America Quarterly*

   We consider our list to be the most comprehensively researched and up-to-date list available.

THE BETTER WORLD SHOPPING GUIDE

If you like this guide, but you're looking for a more comprehensive guide to socially and environmentally responsible shopping that you can actually bring with you to the supermarket or mall, consider getting a copy of *The Better World Shopping Guide*. Years of detailed research on evaluating the responsibility of companies has resulted in the most extensive set of ratings available anywhere. For more information, go to www.betterworldshopper.org .

SUPERMARKETS

A	Food Co-ops, Farmers Markets, Whole Foods, WildOats, Trader Joe's
B	Supervalu, A&P, Safeway, Vons
C	Giant Food, Super G, City Markets, Food 4 Less, King Soopers, Krogers, Kwik Shop, Pay Less, Loaf N Jug, Quick Stop, Ralph's
D	Albertson's, Osco, Savon, Lucky's, Thriftway, Winn-Dixie
F	Wal-Mart

RETAIL STORES

A	IKEA, REI
B	Home Depot, LLBean
C	Target, Best Buy, Eddie Bauer, Walgreens, Costco, BJ's
D	JC Penney, Maytag, Rite Aid, K-Mart, Sears
F	Wal-Mart, Sam's Club

WATER

A	Tap / Filtered, Biota, Ethos
B	Trinity, Crystal Geyser, Aquafina, Essentia
C	Fiji, La Croix, Hawaii, Glaceau
D	Crystal Springs, Dannon, Evian, Volvic, Dasani
F	Arrowhead, Calistoga, Perrier, S. Pellegrino, Vittel, Poland Spring, Deer Park, Zephyr Hills, Ozarka

CHOCOLATE

A	Equal Exchange, Endangered Species, Rapunzel, Dagoba, Green & Black's, Newman's Own, Cloud Nine, Tropical Source, Shaman
B	Hershey's, Scharffen Berger
C	Cadbury, Terra Nostra, Chocolove, Whitman's, Russell Stover, Ghirardelli, Lindt, Ovaltine, Droste, Ferrero Rocher
D	Swiss Miss, Dove, Nestle, Perugina
F	Toblerone

CLEANING PRODUCTS

A Seventh Generation, Dr. Bronner's, Earth Friendly, Ecover, Planet, ECOS

B Simple Green, Sunshine Makers, 3M, Colgate-Palmolive, Murphy's Oil

C Proctor & Gamble, Hefty, Dial, SC Johnson, Arm & Hammer, Hefty, Dial

D Chore Boy, Easy-Off, Glass Plus, Jet-Dry, Mop & Glo, Old English, Wizard, Playtex, Sara Lee, Reckitt Benckiser

F Pine Sol, Tilex, S.O.S., Liquid Plumr, Formula 409, Glad, Clorox

CLOTHING

A American Apparel, Patagonia, Lost Arrow, Maggie's Organics, Ecolution, Deva Lifewear,

B Levi Strauss, Timberland, Liz Claiborne, Cutter & Buck, Eileen Fisher, Reebok

C LL Bean, Nordstrum, Nicole Miller, Nike, Target, Gap, Mervyn's, Guess, Ralph Lauren, Limited

D Fruit of the Loom, Kmart, JC Penney, Federated, Calvin Klein, LA Gear, Saks, TJ Maxx, Marshall's, Kohl's

F Wal-Mart, Sam's Club, May's

COFFEE

A Thanksgiving, Song Bird, Café Mam, Caffe Ibis, Equal Exchange, Green Mountain, Adam's, Newman's Own

B Starbucks, Peerless, Peet's, Seattle's Best

C Millstone, Folgers, Continental, Hill Bros, MJB

D Nescafe, Nestle

F Maxwell House, Gevalia, Sanka, General Foods, Yuban

ENERGY BARS

A CLIF, Luna, Alpsnack, BumbleBar

B Larabar, Think, Nutiva, Boomi

C Odwalla, Kashi, Slim Fast

D Powerbar

F Balance

GENERAL FOOD

A Hain, Amy's, Annie's, Horizon, Spectrum, Eden, Cascadian Farm, Barbara's

B General Mills, Quaker, Pepsi, Pillsbury, Colgate-Palmolive

C Campbell's, Kellogg's, Weight Watchers, Johnson & Johnson, Proctor & Gamble

D Nestle, Carnation, Libby's, Coca Cola

F Kraft, Nabisco, Post, Planter's, Oscar Meyer, Knudsen

FOOD

Buying Groceries
Eating
Planting a Garden

As we go through the drive-through at our favorite fast-food joint or pop a frozen dinner into the microwave, we seldom think about where our food came from, how it was produced, and how our demand for it affects the rest of the world. We're usually thinking about taste, price, and convenience. Our fast-paced culture encourages us to eat at fast food chains, shop at one-stop supermarkets, and buy instant meals encased in layers of packaging. Though the familiarity of Burger King and Pizza Hut is sometimes comforting, and supermarkets and prepackaged meals are often convenient, they all have very real downsides that we often overlook. Cities lose some of their individual character when they all have the same restaurants. Prepackaged meals take the creativity out of food and leave behind tremendous waste. Cooking and eating degenerate from enjoyable, sacred experiences to little more than pit stops for maintaining our physical selves. Most of us love to eat, but few of us consider how this love can make our lives more fulfilling and the world a better place.

This chapter will give you some suggestions on how your grocery shopping, your eating habits, and the growing of your own food can make a difference in the world. What we eat is one of our most ingrained habits, and it can be a difficult area to change. Choose to follow only those suggestions that are reasonable for you. As in the rest of the book, gradual change is often longer lasting and thus makes more of a difference in the long run than abrupt change.

BUYING GROCERIES

 ACTION: Buy organic food

Organic foods are available in almost every grocery store, including many of the major chains. You can find everything from organic produce, pasta, and eggs to milk, meat, and herbs. What does the "organic" label mean? In order to earn the US Department of Agriculture (USDA) organic label, producers may use no chemical pesticides, growth-enhancing chemicals, or genetic modification on their crops. Farmers who raise animals organically avoid steroids, hormones, and antibiotics; use organically grown grains as feed; and treat livestock more humanely than do non-organic, corporate feedlots. Organic farmers use renewable resources and work to conserve water and maintain or improve soil quality. Organic food may be more expensive than non-organic. If this is a concern for you, start out by buying a few

organic items that differ little in price from conventional foods. Remember, there are reasons some foods are cheap: employers may pay workers lower wages, chemicals tend to increase crop yields, and organic foods are often not produced in the same massive volumes as non-organic foods. Your budget may allow you to purchase only a few items of organic food, but small changes are what ultimately shift whole industries! Organic foods are the fastest-growing segment of the food industry, and prices are quickly dropping as consumer demand rises.

> **By buying organic foods you:**
> - Lessen cruelty to animals.
> - Avoid health-threatening chemicals.
> - Prevent damaging pesticides from entering the environment.
> - Help maintain soil fertility.
>
> Such a small choice has many positive effects!

To learn more about the certified organic label and organic standards visit www.ams.usda.gov/nop.

 ACTION: Reduce food packaging by buying in bulk

Have you ever bought a box of snacks and discovered that you have to tear through three layers of cellophane and cardboard to get at the food? All of this packaging ends up somewhere, sometimes taking hundreds of years to biodegrade. By purchasing bulk items and those with less packaging, you save energy, resources and landfill space all in one fell swoop. Most grocery stores have a bulk food and spice section and many natural foods stores and co-ops have stations where you can refill your shampoo and soap bottles.

ACTION: Bring your own cloth bags

"Would you like paper or plastic?" What a perplexing question for the environmentally conscious consumer. Hmmm ... paper uses up forests, but plastic comes from petroleum, a non-renewable resource. It's actually a trick question because the real choice is not even listed — the cloth bag. It is reliable, reusable, has sturdy handles, and will even get you a small discount at many stores. Shopping with reusable bags helps to save trees and other natural resources right from the start. Buy a couple of bags and take them wherever you go or leave a few in your trunk so you don't forget them.

ACTION: Buy from local growers and grocers

You may have noticed that it's pretty tough for small, locally owned grocers to stay in business. Supermarket chains can charge less for their food because they sell such a tremendous volume. Small grocers have a tough time competing. Supporting local grocers and farmers offers several advantages over supermarket shopping. First, you are supporting your local economy rather than a multinational corporation. You can see that your purchases are directly benefiting members of your own community. Second, shopping locally enables you to find out more about the food you buy, such as where it comes from and how it is produced. Producers at a farmers' market are more than willing to share how they grew their crops. By educating yourself about your food, you may be able to avoid pesticides and other chemicals large companies often use. Third, local grocers are more likely to stock locally grown food, which cuts down on the tremendous amount of energy wasted and pollution created in the transportation process To find the nearest Farmers' Market, Food Co-op, CSA, or local farm, go online to:

> The food on an average American's dinner plate has traveled 1,400 miles (2,250 kilometers).[1]

Local Harvest: 🖥 www.localharvest.org

Food Cooperatives (Co-ops)

Food cooperatives (co-ops) are nonprofit food businesses owned by their members. Anyone can shop at a co-op, but by becoming a member you get a discount and are allowed to participate in decisions about the future of the organization. Co-ops often sell organic, locally produced, and healthful foods. Food co-ops, though, are much more than just supermarkets. They serve as community hubs for healthy living, environmental awareness, and community-building. Can you say that about your supermarket? To find the food cooperative nearest you, contact:

Co-op Directory Service: 🖥 www.coopdirectory.org/

Farmers' Markets

Farmers' markets are locally run, seasonal, open-air markets that showcase local growers. Many farmers' markets also feature local artists' wares. Farmers' markets help build community by allowing growers and consumers to educate and support each other one-on-one. They support family farmers and allow you to purchase fresh food that hasn't spent weeks in storage or on transport trucks. To find the farmers' market nearest you, contact:

US Department of Agriculture, Agricultural Marketing Service
(202) 720-8998   💻 www.ams.usda.gov/farmersmarkets

Community Supported Agriculture (CSA)

Most people subscribe to at least a couple of magazines. CSA's are basically the same thing except that you are subscribing to fresh fruits and vegetables! On the same day every week you stop by a little downtown store during business hours, and low-and-behold, they have a box of fresh produce for you. This wonderful mix of healthy (often organic) produce comes straight from a local farm to you — no middleman. Your dollars go directly to a family farm, and their harvest comes right to you. Usually you can choose the size of box that best fits your budget and your cooking habits. It's usually quite reasonable if you compare it to buying the same produce from the supermarket, and it's always a wonderful surprise to see the unique mix of fruits and vegetables once a week. To find the CSA nearest you, contact:

Robyn Van En Center for CSA Resources
(717) 264-4141 Ext.3352   💻 www.wilson.edu/csacenter

✄ ACTION: Support socially responsible food companies

Some food companies are trying to make a difference. These companies consistently show their dedication to a clean environment and a just workplace. You can support good companies by buycotting them — consistently choosing to buy their products over others. To find an extensive ranking of companies and how we evaluate them, read the SHOPPING chapter. Use the following short list of food companies and grocery stores to send a message with your dollars; they'll hear you loud and clear.

FOOD COMPANIES		SUPERMARKETS	
The 10 Best	**The 10 Worst**	**The 5 Best**	**The 5 Worst**
Eden Foods	Kraft	"Food Co-ops"	Wal-Mart
Horizon Organic	Nabisco	"Farmers Markets"	Thriftway
Stonyfield Farms	Nestle	Whole Foods	Albertson's
Ben & Jerry's	Carnation	Wild Oats	Lucky's
Amy's Kitchen	Oscar Meyer	Trader Joe's	Winn-Dixie
Annie's Naturals	Knudsen		
Newman's Own	Libby's		
CLIF Bar	Post		
Rapunzel	General Foods		
Cascadian Farms	Dreyer's		

To keep up to date on the best and worst food companies, visit www.betterworldshopper.org.

Fair Trade Coffee

Coffee is one of the most traded commodities in the world and is harvested by some of the poorest workers in the world. As a consumer, you have the power to support these workers by buying coffee that is certified "Fair Trade." By purchasing fair trade coffee you not only enjoy delicious coffee, you ensure that coffee producers receive a living wage and you support small farmers who are often good stewards of the land. Consumer demand is making a difference — over 600 McDonalds restaurants have agreed to exclusively sell fair trade coffee.[2] As consumers demand fairly traded products, the movement will spread to other commodities.

To learn more about fair trade, visit: www.transfairusa.org, the fair trade certification agency for the US.

Equal Exchange ⌨ www.equalexchange.com/coffee
Global Exchange ⌨ www.globalexchange.org/campaigns/fairtrade/coffee

⇨ RESOURCES

📖 Jones, Ellis. *The Better World Shopping Guide.* New Society Publishers, 2006. ⌨ www.betterworldshopper.org

For a simple, pocket-sized book that will help you choose great companies, we strongly recommend our companion book, *The Better World Shopping Guide,* an essential resource for socially responsible shopping. It rates companies on a wide range of criteria, including environmental record, workplace opportunity, ethics awards, community outreach, animal rights, donations to charity, national boycotts and much more. Every company is given an overall grade from A+ to F to let you know what kind of difference they are making in the world so that you can create a better world with every dollar you spend.

EATING

Eating is perhaps the daily ritual we most take for granted. Although changing our eating habits may seem difficult, even small changes will produce significant results. Being conscious of where our food comes from, how it is produced, how it affects our bodies and how it affects the lives of others re-connects us with the world around us.

☞ ACTION: Prepare and eat food with others

Think of how you can make meal time the most meaningful and enjoyable part of your day. Preparing and eating meals with others can be emotionally and spiritually satisfying. Imagine if everyone experienced eating as a sacred activity and a way to build a sense of community with others and a connection with the world around us. Be creative with your meals! Try new recipes and prepare meals without any instructions. Don't forget to turn the TV off so that you can fully enjoy your meal with your friends and family.

Try to avoid using disposable dishes, utensils, and napkins whether you are at home, at work, or on a picnic. Keep a set of silverware with you in your bag, backpack, briefcase, or purse. If you really need to use disposables, try Seventh Generation's line of products made from recycled materials, available at your grocery store.

ACTION: Support locally owned restaurants

When you eat at locally owned, non-chain restaurants, you benefit your community in the same ways as when you buy locally. Have you ever driven cross-country and noticed towns that look strikingly similar to the last 27 you passed: one Burger King, one Bank of America, one Wal-Mart and one Texaco station? Having McDonald's and Taco Bells everywhere around the world eliminates much of the cultural variety that we all value. Over half of the US population lives within a three-minute drive to McDonald's.[3]

Avoiding chain restaurants prevents the "McDonaldization" of the world by preserving the uniqueness of your town. Plus, you may have noticed that many local restaurant owners take more pride in their service and how their food tastes!

ACTION: Eat less fast food

Americans are eating more and more fast food, despite numerous studies that show too much fast food is bad for your health.[4] The American Medical Association reports that obesity, fueled in part by fast food, is one of our top health concerns. The fast food industry has become so powerful that it dictates how other industries do their business. For example, potato growers and chicken farmers produce specially modified spuds and chickens to make the perfect French fry and McNugget. Fast food chains market unhealthy food especially to kids who are even more likely to eat fast food than adults. By eating less fast food you not only improve your health, you oppose an industry that plays a role in environmental destruction, childhood obesity, and the "McDonaldization" of the world — where every town looks the same, with the same stores and restaurants.

RESOURCES

 Supersize Me! Morgan Spurlock, director. 2004 [feature film]. In this award-winning movie, filmmaker Morgan Spurlock undertakes a strange experiment to determine what a month-long McDonalds binge does to the human body. He examines the fast food industry and the marketing of unhealthy food to kids www.supersizeme.com.

Schlosser, Eric. *Fast Food Nation: The Dark Side of the All-American Meal.* Houghton

The "Slow Food" movement advocates slowing down and creating meaningful, pleasurable meals. The movement is based on the principles of environmentally sustainable farming, agricultural diversity, and in opposition to the culture of "fast food." Learn more about this international movement at www.slowfood.com.

Mifflin, 2001. A bestselling, in-depth examination of the fast food industry, including fast food history, meatpacking workers' dangerous jobs and the global impact of a beef-based diet. Schlosser adapted this book into a teen-friendly version titled *Chew On This: Everything You Don't Want to Know About Fast Food.*

ACTION: Eat more fruits, vegetables, whole grains and unprocessed foods

The US Department of Agriculture, National Research Council, the National Cancer Institute and the American Cancer Society all recommend that you eat generous amounts of fruits and vegetables for your health.[5] Plant foods contain fiber, antioxidants, vitamins and minerals, low amounts of fat, and no cholesterol; while meats contain cholesterol, high amounts of fat, no fiber and many artificial and toxic chemicals. Avoid heavily processed foods as they are filled with salt, sugars and fats to replace the flavor that is lost during manufacture. These foods also often contain excess packaging.

ACTION: Eat less meat

If you grew up in a typical American household, you may believe that a meal just isn't a meal unless it's served up with a big piece of meat. For many of us a meat dish is the meal; the bread, salads, and vegetables are just side dishes. Our insistence on eating meat every day, often several times each day, creates problems for the environment, workers, our own health and other people around the world. And due to modern factory farming techniques, it also causes the unnecessary suffering of animals. For one or more of these reasons, millions of people have already reduced the amount of meat they eat.[6] In fact, two out of every three people in the world lead healthy lives eating primarily meatless diets.[7] Once you learn about the environmental, hunger, labor, and health issues surrounding meat, you may want to join them!

To give you an idea of the different impacts each kind of meat has on the world, take a look at the figure on the next page titled "Social and Environmental

TREATING WORKERS FAIRLY

Americans who work in meat-packing and processing plants face some of the poorest working conditions. Most workers can afford little or no health care, yet their repetitive motion, high speed, physically demanding, assembly line jobs injure 1/3 of all workers every year — the highest injury rate of any industry.[22] When these workers can no longer function effectively, they are laid off in lieu of new, healthy workers. This has led to one of the highest turnover rates of any job in the US. Most packing plants are non-union and pay as little as $5 per hour.[23] Hog farms provide particularly dangerous workplace environments. Seventy percent of swine confinement workers suffer from respiratory ailments, such as chronic bronchitis.[24]

Footprint" — a symbolic representation of the relative impacts of each type of food based on environmental damage, resource consumption and worker treatment. As you can see, beef has the most overall negative impact on the world. In fact, reducing your beef consumption may be the single most powerful action you can take in this whole book! Read on to find out why.

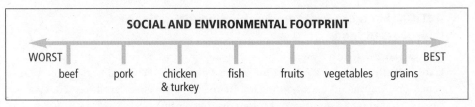

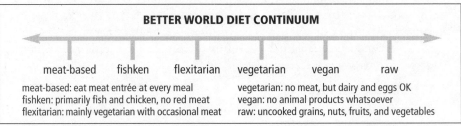

The Environment

By eating less meat you help preserve the environment. Meat production consumes a tremendous amount of natural resources and creates a great deal of waste. In fact, we use about ¹/₄ of the Earth's land to graze cattle.[9] Raising grain for direct human consumption, rather than feeding animals, would require less land, feeding more people with greater efficiency. At the same time, there would be less incentive for the people of Central and South America to create grazing land for cattle by burning down rainforests. Closer to home, cattle grazing has eliminated or severely threatened more plant species in the western US than any other cause and is the number one cause of soil erosion on western public lands.[10] That trend could be slowed or halted if we all lowered our demand for meat.

> Animal agriculture causes 80% of the world's annual deforestation.[8]

Using Our Natural Resources Wisely

Raising livestock for meat is one of the most inefficient uses of land. One acre (0.4 hectares) of land could produce 50,000 pounds (23,000 kilograms) of tomatoes, 40,000 pounds (18,000 kilograms) of potatoes, 30,000 pounds (14,000 kilograms) of carrots or just 250 pounds (100 kilograms) of beef.[11] To produce a year's supply of beef for a family requires over 260 gallons (1,000 liters) of fossil fuel, or approximately one gallon (3.8 liters) of gasoline per pound (500 grams) of grain-fed beef. Finally, it takes up to 10,000 gallons (38,000 liters) of water to produce one pound (500 grams) of beef; to produce one pound of wheat requires 25 gallons (100 liters).[12]

Though not as destructive as beef production, hog and chicken production cause their own environmental problems. Hog waste has become a major source of water pollution in a number of states. In North Carolina alone, 2.5 tons (2.3 metric tons) of hog waste is produced annually for every North Carolinian.[13] Spills have occurred in many states, contaminating our waterways and killing fish. It takes about 420 gallons (2,000 liters) of water to produce a pound (500 grams) of chicken.[14] Farmers also often apply waste from chicken factories to crop fields as a form of fertilizer, which produces similarly destructive results as the runoff ends up as water pollution.[15]

Commercial fishing presents us with a different kind of environmental challenge: the misuse of our marine resources. The UN's Food and Agriculture Organization estimates that, due to wasteful fishing practices, 57 billion pounds (27 billion kilograms) of sea life is caught unintentionally every year and thrown away.[16] The Environmental Defense Fund reports that 13 of the world's 17 major fishing grounds are depleted or in serious decline, due to overfishing.[17]

World Hunger

The Food and Agriculture Organization reports that more than 850 million people go hungry each year.[19] Almost nine million people die from hunger-related causes each year, a majority of them children.[20] Despite these startling statistics, we feed 72% of all grain grown in the world to livestock.[21] In fact, due to the high demand for beef in the First World, agribusiness has transformed much of Central and South America's agricultural land into pastures for raising beef that gets exported to the United States, Australia and Europe. The end result is that the wealthy of the world eat grain fed beef while over a billion people go hungry each day due to a lack of grain.

Health

Many of us have already begun to realize the health benefits of eating less red meat. Diets high in saturated fats and cholesterol have been implicated in numerous medical studies as significantly contributing to a high rate of heart attacks,

EATING SEAFOOD RESPONSIBLY

Synthesizing the latest research done by a number of environmental organizations on responsible commercial fishing practices, we have created a guide to make sure that your seafood choices will help ensure the long-term preservation of sea life.[18]

Audubon's Seafood Guide: www.seafood.audubon.org
Monterey Bay Aquarium: www.mbayaq.org/cr/seafoodwatch.asp
Environmental Defense: www.oceansalive.org/eat.cfm
Blue Ocean Institute: www.blueocean.org/Seafood

BEST TO WORST SEAFOOD	
BEST	Mussels, Clams, Anchovies, Wild Salmon, Pollock, Mackerel, Tilapia, Crawfish, Herring, Sardines, Abalone, Dungeness Crab, Striped Bass, Catfish
GOOD	Oysters, Snow Crab, Stone Crab, Trout, Pacific Cod, Pacific Halibut, Sablefish, Mahi Mahi, Alaskan Halibut,
FAIR	Scallops, Prawns, Squid, Tuna, King Crab, Blue Crab, Imitation Crab, Lingcod, Bluefish, Sturgeon, Lobster, Dogfish
POOR	Shrimp, Eel, Rockfish, Caviar, Swordfish, Flounder, Sole, Sea Bass, Haddock
WORST	Grouper, Orange Roughy, Pacific Roughy, Atlantic Cod, Atlantic Halibut, Monkfish, Marlin, Farmed Salmon, Atlantic Salmon, Snapper, Tilefish, Shark

cancer (such as breast and colon cancer), and strokes.[25] The average US man eating a typical meat-based diet has a 50% chance of dying from heart disease, the number one killer of people living in the US.[26] In addition, the vast majority of factory farms use antibiotics, hormones, and other drugs in beef, pork and chicken production. Each year in the US alone, contaminated chicken kills at least 1,000 people and sickens as many as 80 million others.[27]

Animals

Unfortunately, the image of the small, family farm stocked with a fairly content variety of animals no longer corresponds to the reality of modern livestock conditions. Many animals live in less-than-humane factory farms their entire lives. Most breeding sows are kept in crates for almost their entire lives and 71% of pigs suffer from pneumonia.[28] More than 90% of chickens and eggs are raised on crowded factory farms.[29]

A common myth is that substantial amounts of meat are essential to provide our protein needs. Actually, the average American gets almost twice the amount of protein necessary each day.[30]

Breaking a Pattern

Though there are many compelling reasons to reduce our meat consumption, we may find it difficult to break a pattern we've had since early childhood. The first step might be to not eat meat one day each week or to eat it only for dinner. Remember, it is important to make changes that are right for you. Gradual transformations that you feel comfortable with will likely last. Sudden, drastic changes often lead to frustration and giving up entirely. Think of reducing the meat in your diet as an opportunity rather than as a restriction. You have the chance to explore many new recipes you may not have considered before.

Alternatives

If you want to cut back on your meat but think you'll miss the taste, consider meat alternatives. Soy chicken nuggets, burgers, sausage, bacon, hot pockets, lunchmeat, ground beef, hot dogs, and chicken patties are all readily available in your local market. There are also healthy alternatives to milk, cheese and ice cream that tend to be easier on the planet and taste good, too! Morningstar Farms, Eden Foods, Boca, Rice Dream, Gardenburger and Fantastic Foods are just a few good brands to look for.

> **By eating less meat you:**
> - Help conserve our natural resources.
> - Contribute to the well-being of people in the Third World.
> - Improve your overall health.
> - Lessen cruelty to animals.

To find vegetarian recipes and products, check out these sites:

🖳 www.vegweb.com
🖳 vegetarian.allrecipes.com
🖳 vegkitchen.com

PLANTING A GARDEN

There is only one way to know, without a doubt, where your food comes from and how it is processed — by growing it yourself. You may be thinking that you don't have the time, the space, or even any idea where to begin. Gardening is much easier you think, and with a little creativity you can garden just about anywhere. You can easily turn part of your lawn into a garden, even if it's just a small spot next to your house. Perhaps most importantly, gardening can be a tremendous source of relaxation, pride, fulfillment, and connection with the Earth.

ACTION: Plant an organic garden

You can plant an organic vegetable garden that maintains the integrity of the earth. You get to eat and marvel at the fruits of your labor. Organic gardening reduces your need for expensive and harmful fertilizers and bug killers. By rebuilding your soil with compost, rotating crops, watering early in the morning, and weeding regularly, you can have a healthy, poison-free garden. Ask your local garden center for tips particular to your area. There are many books that can help you with organic gardening. Check out your local independent bookstore or Amazon.com where you can find many of them used.

⇨ RESOURCES

📖 *Organic Gardening* magazine

Their website has helpful gardening, houseplant and landscaping tips, or you can subscribe and learn new techniques every month.

🖳 www.organicgardening.com

◁ Gardens Alive!

Gardens Alive! is a great source for organic gardening supplies (including fertilizers, weed and pest controls and lawn care products).

🖳 www.gardensalive.com

ACTION: Be an urban gardener

If you live in a place without space for a garden, you have several options. First, many cities offer community garden plots. Call your local parks and recreation department. You can share a space (and the work!) with a friend. Second, you might be able to set planters outside your door or near your building. You can grow a few tomatoes or some flowers in a planter. Third, window boxes provide a small area to grow a few green pepper plants or a few onions. Finally, if you don't have the space or resources for these suggestions, try growing a few herbs in small pots. Some fresh basil or garlic tastes great in many dishes. For more information on community and urban gardening, contact:

American Community Gardening Association
(215) 988-8785   www.communitygarden.org

PERSONAL

Extraordinary Living
Emotional Well-Being
Physical Well-Being
Reflection

SOME PEOPLE MAKE THE WORLD a better place simply through their way of being. Think of someone who inspires peace by his or her presence. Imagine a person in your life who makes you smile just by walking in the door. Envision someone with the outlook of a child, free of concerns, encountering the world with a fresh, open mind. These kinds of people touch us in a way we may not fully understand.

In this book, we explore ways to bring your actions in line with your values in each aspect of life. Each of us can also create a personal way of being in the world that makes it a better place for us, our families and our communities. We can make changes in the different spheres of our lives and alter how we experience our lives, moment to moment, hour to hour, and day to day.

The *Personal* chapter encourages you to take action to make your own life extraordinary. Powerful social change begins with powerful individual change. Just think how remarkably different the world would be if more people led fulfilling personal lives. With this in mind, we offer suggestions for transforming your personal consciousness, developing emotional well-being, maintaining physical health and taking time for reflection.

EXTRAORDINARY LIVING

Most of us are mildly content with our lives. Sure, we can imagine some ways life could be better, but overall we get into a comfortable groove and coast along. But what if there was something better? What if certain ways of living could take us beyond our ordinary lives, into a realm of extraordinary possibilities? The actions in this section will empower you to push the limits of your happiness to new heights and make the world a better place simply by your presence.

ACTION: Don't sweat the small stuff

Isn't it crazy how the smallest problems can cause us the greatest frustration? If there's one thing we know for certain, it's that reality is almost never how we expect it to be. In fact, our expectations can cause us a great deal of suffering. We can minimize our suffering by being flexible. Not sweating the small stuff doesn't mean not having any expectations. It simply implies an understanding that reality may not meet our expectations — and that's OK. It means paying attention to our reactions, thinking about them and making a choice to be flexible. Pretty soon it becomes automatic. And remember, as the old cliché goes, almost everything is small stuff.

ACTION: Think and live in color

Perhaps you've had a friend who was extremely unhappy with his job. He agonized over what to do about his dissatisfaction, quickly concluding he could either quit or just stick it out. How many times in our lives do we reduce important decisions or opinions to two options? It's very easy to get stuck at one of two extremes. We've been trained to think in terms of good/bad, right/wrong, black/white. But that's not the way life is! Not only does black and white thinking reduce our own options, it also makes us more judgmental: if I'm right, they must be wrong. Intolerant thinking is evident in many of our society's current conflicts: the abortion debate, affirmative action, gun control, lesbian and gay rights. You name it, people are entrenched at an extreme that dehumanizes the "other side." There are always more than two sides. Try thinking in color. Be open to those who are different than you, explore your options, step outside the norm and avoid the trap of either/or solutions.

ACTION: Live intentionally

Many of us feel powerless to our surroundings. Our lives feel dictated by forces outside our control, like we're being carried on an assembly line through the stages of life. Our mental state becomes dependent upon how our boss or our family treats us, and our behavior becomes dependent on whether our peers praise or criticize us. Life is not a spectator sport. The first step to living with purpose is to gain awareness of one's own life. Take stock of how you are living, then think about how you want to live. To live intentionally means to take personal responsibility for living a life worth living, creating options where there seem to be none and taking a stand to live the life you want to live.

ACTION: Commit to a creative life

Most of us equate creativity with artwork and artists. But creativity applies to all spheres of life, from shopping to family and from food to community. A creative person is able to view ordinary situations in a unique way, create possibilities where there seem to be none, and act outside of the expected or normal realm of action. Creativity is not something some people are born with while others are not. It takes practice. Creative people have to have a commitment to creativity.[1] Take time to explore your creativity in whatever situation you find yourself. Here are a few suggestions:

- Plan a creative party.
- Find a creative way to take a mini-vacation.
- Create your own board game.
- Write your own nursery rhyme, prayer, or riddle.
- Create a way to run all of your errands without using your car.
- Invent a process to teach kids about drugs, sex, or violence.

At least once each week, take time to let your creative energies flow: write, draw, paint, take a dance class, sculpt, play music, cook a new meal, sew — whatever makes your heart sing to the heavens! We are a creative species, meaning we gain fulfillment from bringing our imaginations and skills to life. When you consistently give your creativity an outlet, it will improve your everyday experience. If you don't schedule creative time into your life, chances are you won't take the time.

LIVING OUTSIDE THE BOX

We live in a box. We have an image of how things should be, how we should act, and what is possible and impossible. These images make up the box we live in, the box that limits our possibilities. Consider the American dream: overwork at a job you probably dislike, get rich, buy a bunch of stuff, move into a huge house, have 2.5 kids, retire, and play golf. This dream doesn't allow for much flexibility or individuality, and many of us won't ever be in a position to achieve it.

We generally don't stray too far outside the box society creates for us. Instead, we follow the patterns we've learned from our culture, family, the media and our friends. Often these patterns aren't as fulfilling as living outside the box might be. Check out these examples, then use your creativity to break out of your box.

- Next time you're at the coffee shop, pub, or restaurant, pay for someone else's order.
- After work, greet your partner with a dance instead of hello.
- Go for a walk in the rain without an umbrella.
- Be the most gracious driver on the planet.
- Bike to work in your work clothes, even if you look a bit rumpled when you get there.
- The next time you must give a presentation at work, school, or wherever, focus on making it a totally unique experience.
- Leave an extra large tip for someone who has given you good service.

ACTION: Conquer your fears

Have you ever really thought about what you're afraid of? Not the big fears, such as flying, spiders, or heights, but the little fears that affect you daily. How many times have you wanted to try something new but faltered because you fear failure? Singing in a choir, writing for the local newspaper, taking a dance class — you name it, someone's afraid of it.

Fear prevents many of us from living extraordinary lives. It limits us, keeping us from our full potential. Many of us share common fears such as "I'm not good enough," "People won't like me," "I'm not as good as that person," and "What I do won't make a difference." To live a truly extraordinary life, we must learn to face and manage our fears, because they'll never completely go away. And after you face a fear, you often realize you had nothing to be afraid of.

There will certainly be times when we confront our fears and things won't go our way. If you're not failing once in a while, you're probably not taking the risks necessary to live an extraordinary life! But personal growth and fulfillment require risk, stretching into new territory. So take on your fears and revel in the process.

ACTION: Slow down and live in the moment

Do you write a "to do" list each morning then rush around all day doing your tasks and checking them off? Sometimes we go so fast that we focus more on how many checks we have than on how to experience the day one moment at a time. At the end of the day, we have a list of scratched-off tasks, but we feel sort of empty. Slowing down and doing less is an important key to fulfillment.

Be Present: We spend so much time worrying about the future and thinking about the past that we don't fully experience the present. The measure of a fulfilling life is the quality of experience, not the quantity. Focus on whatever you are doing in the moment. Do one thing at a time. Be present to the people around you — it will improve your experience of whatever you do and make your relationships incredible. Choose a few things to do each day, take your time, and do them well.

Learn to say NO: How many times have you agreed to do something that you knew you really didn't have time for? Perhaps your friend asks you to go shopping or help paint her house on a day you'd rather spend relaxing at home. Many of us have difficulty saying no, and for good reason: we like to help people out and we enjoy being with friends. Too much of a good thing, however, quickly turns fun or helping into an unpleasant burden. Practice saying no to some of the things that take up your time. And don't feel that you always need an excuse! Saying no allows you to put yourself more fully into those activities you choose to do.

ACTION: Own less stuff

We are a nation of people with insatiable desires for stuff — newer cars, faster computers, stylish clothes, better stereos, the latest electronics. Unfortunately, rather than bringing fulfillment, material possessions often create discontent —

you're never happy with what you have. More is always better, right? Wrong. After we meet our needs and have a few comforts, extra purchases can actually become burdens to our existence. Everything you own, owns you. You must maintain it, fix it, insure it, wash it, dust it, and worry about it getting stolen or becoming obsolete. Searching for happiness at the car showroom or in the department store will not bring long-term fulfillment (but it will lead to long-term debt). The acquisition of possessions also keeps our focus on ourselves: what can I get for me? By moderating your desire for material possessions, you liberate your mind from the burdens that come with ownership and free up your energies to live your most deeply held values and make the world a better place.

ACTION: Treat others as humans, not as objects

Do you ever take the opportunity to talk to the cashier at your grocery store? How about the janitor that cleans your workplace? It's amazing how we treat many of the people in our lives as objects rather than as humans. We see the driver of the car in front of us or the people ahead of us in line as obstacles to us getting something done or as people we would rather not interact with. You can counteract these attitudes by smiling or talking to people in your life you normally wouldn't communicate with. Go out of your way to help people, both strangers and friends. Have patience, especially with folks just doing their jobs. The secretary or receptionist of a business you call isn't responsible for the company policies you may disagree with. The telemarketer that calls during dinner is just doing her or his job, too. There's no point in treating these folks poorly. By treating people like humans instead of objects you are making the world a more humane, loving place. A good place to start is with smiling. Have you ever noticed how a smiling, cheerful person can instantly brighten your day? Try smiling at people you meet throughout your day — strangers and friends. Who knows, maybe your good cheer will be the turning point for someone who is having a bad day!

ACTION: Be the change you wish to see in the world

As you read this book, chances are that you are beginning to construct a powerful vision of how the world could be a better place. Most of us imagine a more peace-

WHO ARE YOUR HEROES?

Many people in our lives have a huge effect on us: teachers, family members, friends, leaders. We often unintentionally take these people for granted. Take this opportunity to reflect on some of these folks. Choose ten people who have made a powerful impression on your life. Then think about how each one of them had such an effect on you — what was it about them? Just imagine, you can have the same powerful effect on people in your life! Now that you've recognized these amazing people, tell them how great they are. Call or write them. You will rock their world.

ful, caring and just Earth. You might wish people were more kind, that there was less racism, or that kids received a better education. You can actually be a powerful source of change by living as a citizen of the world you wish to see.

Create ways that you can bring your better world into being. Here are a few examples:

- You wish people had a greater sense of community? Go out of your way to create community where you live.
- You envision a more accepting world? Demonstrate acceptance in your daily life.
- You believe kids should be a higher priority? Make children a huge priority in your life by spending quality time with them.

One of the most powerful ways to create change around you is through patient, personal example. Your powerful example will create change in others; we guarantee it.

ACTION: Live passionately

People that live with passion seem to have a glow about them. They stand out from the crowd. Sometimes we worry so much about failure, what people will think of us, or if we should have done things differently that we live a mediocre life. To live passionately means to go all out once we make a decision and live full steam ahead. If we fail, then we learn something.

To live passionately also means that we dedicate ourselves to ideals that we are passionate about. Decide what you want your life to be about and then create it! Are you about giving unconditional love to children, bringing beauty into the world with your artwork, singing your heart out at Carnegie Hall, or writing a book that you hope will change the world? Whatever you choose (and it may change over time), make it the reason you get up in the morning. You'll know if you get it right, because it'll make you feel truly alive.

ACTION: Expand your circle of compassion

Did you know that more than six million children die of malnutrition every year?[22] Or that many inner city kids attend class in hallways and bathrooms because their school has a classroom shortage? Have you heard that 17 to 70 million animals die each year in unnecessary medical and product tests?[23] It's easy to become so wrapped up in our own lives that we fail to recognize the suffering of other living beings.

It is our privilege to ignore others' suffering. Many of us simply tune out the suffering that goes on around us. It's not that we don't care, it's that we simply feel overwhelmed and helpless. Plus, we've got our own problems to deal with, right?

None of us can give our full attention to all the world's problems. However, tuning out and turning off our compassion is the easy way out. Rather than insulating yourself from the world's struggles, try to learn as much as you can. Really think about and empathize with people. We feel very compassionate toward our family, friends, and pets. What if we expanded this circle of compassion to include strangers, people in other countries, animals, and even the whole planet?

Compassion produces actions that affect the world. If you attempt to empathize with tsunami victims in Thailand, casualties of the Darfur genocide, or earthquake survivors in Iran, you're more likely to send aid than if they were just another news item in the "World" section of the paper. If you develop compassion for women in abusive relationships, perhaps you'll support your local women's shelter with supplies, time, or a donation. If you recognize that the animals that endure cosmetic testing aren't all that different from the animals you keep as pets, maybe you'll buy better cosmetics.

HELP VICTIMS OF NATURAL DISASTERS

In 2005, the tsunami in southeast Asia, earthquake in Pakistan, and Hurricane Katrina in the US showed us all just how devastating natural disasters can be. When a disaster strikes, people need basic necessities, such as food, clothes and shelter. They also usually need medical supplies, mental health support, and a feeling of community to overcome their sense of isolation. You can donate to many organizations that help victims of natural disasters. You could also set up a disaster relief collection through your workplace, religious group, or civic organization. Monetary donations are important, of course, but your time and skills are equally important and sometimes just as necessary for relief. For information on recent natural disasters and links to disaster relief organizations, see www.directrelief.org, contact your local Red Cross, or call (800)HELP-NOW. Often it takes disasters to make us realize that we truly are interdependent members of the global community.

American Red Cross: www.redcross.org
International Committee of the Red Cross: www.icrc.org

DONATE BLOOD

Donating blood is safe, easy, and quick and literally helps save lives. Blood banks are almost always in need of more donors. Learn more and find out where to donate at:

in the US: www.americasblood.org/
in Canada: www.bloodservices.ca

EMOTIONAL WELL-BEING

Do you ever feel burnt out? Not just physically but emotionally? Sometimes we spend so much time meeting our material needs (working, maintaining a household, etc.) and the needs of others that we neglect our emotional needs. In many ways we are fragile creatures. All of us fall out of balance. It is crucial that you look after your emotional well-being for your own sense of peace and for your effectiveness as an unstoppable agent of social change.

☑ ACTION: Forgive yourself

Have you ever met someone who is constantly putting himself/herself down? Perhaps he/she is so stuck in self-guilt and frustration that happiness and fulfillment are the furthest things from his/her mind. We are often our own worst critics.

Constant criticism and guilt are terrible burdens to bear. They stop us, make us less effective, and prevent growth. Guilt never saved anyone. And our self-criticism sets a bad example for others. If we are negative about ourselves, we send the message that others can be, too. Although it benefits us to reflect on and learn from our mistakes, wallowing in self-blame does not. It is when we can transform negative feelings into action that the world is better off.

When we set high ideals for ourselves, it is easy to feel guilty for "not doing enough" to make the world a better place. This can quickly lead us to the "I'm not a saint" trap, stopping us from taking any action because we simply can't live perfect lives. Recognize that you are human and that being human means being less than perfect. Strive towards your ideals, but forgive yourself when you fall short.

☑ ACTION: Manage your stress

Stress prevents us from leading fulfilling lives and creating a better world. Most of us manage to overfill our days with tasks and commitments, both enjoyable and tedious: walk the dog, set up a dental appointment, prepare for a dinner party, stop at the grocery store, meet your friend for lunch, drop off a book at the library, check and answer e-mail and phone messages, ask for time off next weekend, etc. Let's face it: we get stressed out. Stress is our body's response to demands, challenges, and changes. Stress isn't the events we normally think of, such as traffic, nasty coworkers, and work deadlines; it's our reaction to these events. Both "positive" events (marriage, vacation, new job) and "negative" events (illness, divorce, a death in the family) trigger stress. Too much stress has a negative effect on your effectiveness and can lead to serious medical problems, such as ulcers, asthma, heart attacks, and strokes.[4]

How you can manage your stress:

- Decrease or stop using caffeine. Caffeine is a stimulant that creates a stress reaction in the body.

- Laugh! Try to find the humor in any situation — the world is an absurd place.

- Think positively. Positive thinking opens you up to see more opportunities for changing your situation.

- Learn to let go of things outside of your control and recognize when you can make a difference and when you need to step back, take a deep breath and disengage.

- Go away for the weekend. Sometimes we need to physically separate ourselves from our typical surroundings in order to rejuvenate our energy supply.

- Give your time to something or someone you believe in. It can be very therapeutic and re-energizing to give your time to a cause or person you believe in.
- Vent your frustrations. Just telling someone or writing down what's stressing you out can take a huge burden off your shoulders.[5]

A few more stress-relieving actions that we expand on in a later section include regular exercise, getting enough sleep and relaxing and/or meditating. Don't let stress keep you from creating the life you want to live and the world you want to live it in.

ACTION: Seek help when you need it

Sometimes we need a little extra help working through the stresses and struggles of life. Often a trained, impartial professional can help us overcome our troubles and put us back on track towards extraordinary living. If you feel consistently stressed, frustrated, angry, or depressed you might consider counseling, therapy, personal growth seminars, meditation or yoga workshops, or other avenues of healing and growth. Ask your doctor, religious leader, friends, or family members for a referral, or consult your Yellow Pages.

PHYSICAL WELL-BEING

Not satisfied with being the "land of the free," America has become the land of the inactive. Over one-half of us are overweight.[6] Americans are eating more and exercising less than in the past — the perfect combination for increased heart disease and stress, high blood pressure, and diabetes. To be an effective force for making the world a better place, we need to foster a healthy mind, healthy emotions and a healthy body.

ACTION: Exercise regularly

How much time each day do you spend exercising? How much time do you spend watching TV, typing at a computer, or sitting at a desk? Many of us spend far more time sitting than getting our heart rate up. According to the American Medical Association, "More than 60% of American adults do not get the recommended amount of physical activity, and nearly half of American youth are not active on a regular basis."[7] The results of our increasingly sedentary lifestyles include greater risk for heart disease, stroke, cancer and obesity; increased risk for non-insulin dependent diabetes mellitus; and decreased strength and endurance. The AMA recommends that you exercise 30 to 60 minutes each day, four to six times each week, but even 20 minutes three times a week will improve your health.

Hints on maintaining momentum:

- Find someone to exercise with.
- Get rid of your scale — it doesn't measure your commitment to exercising, and a number can't tell you your well-being.

- Keep an exercise journal to monitor your progress.
- Make exercise a priority — schedule it into your day and make it a habit like brushing your teeth.
- Make exercise entertaining. Listen to music or a book on tape. Vary your workout once in a while. Distract yourself with TV if it keeps you going.

THE "NOT-SO-IDEAL" BODY IMAGE

Society creates an ideal body shape that few of us can live up to: the incredibly slender woman and the remarkably muscular man. Corporations use advertising to make us feel ugly so that we buy their products to become "beautiful." Many people, particularly young women, starve themselves in an effort to attain the societal image of perfection. Remember that we make up ideals; they aren't necessarily the best way for us to be. So long as you're healthy, try to be satisfied with your body as it is.

National Eating Disorders Association: www.nationaleatingdisorders.org

 ACTION: Get enough sleep

In our fast-paced world, many of us don't get enough sleep. The average person needs around eight hours of sleep each night but often gets much less. Lack of sleep forces us to function at less than our full potential. How much sleep do you need? John W. Shepard Jr., M.D., of Mayo Clinic's Sleep Disorders Center says, "We define an adequate quantity of sleep as that amount which, when you attain it on a steady basis, produces a full degree of daytime alertness and feeling of well-being the following day."[8] The benefits of enough sleep are huge: it's easier to have a positive outlook, and you'll have increased energy, clearer thinking, and better health. In fact, too much or too little sleep contributes to shorter life expectancy.[9]

 ACTION: Eat healthily

After a long day at work, it's often easier to eat processed, instant foods rather than prepare a nutritious meal. Though this may seem more efficient, it is ultimately counterproductive. Our bodies are our greatest resource. To skimp on food and pollute ourselves with substandard junk is a big mistake in the long run. Your body is, as the saying goes, a temple.

Here are a few basic tips for creating a healthy diet:

- Replace snacks with foods such as raw vegetables, fresh fruit, or a mixture of raisins and nuts.
- Replace coffee, tea, soda, and liquor with fruit juice or water.
- Eat more fresh fruits and vegetables! They help prevent heart disease and certain cancers, lower stress, and boost our immune systems.

- Eat a variety of foods, avoid too many sugars, eat plenty of whole grains, avoid foods high in fat and cholesterol, and stay away from too much salt and sodium.

REFLECTION

In our fast-paced society, we rarely take time to reflect on our lives. We're constantly moving on to the next thing. Reflection gives you time to recognize what you've accomplished and really appreciate what you experienced. It also provides an opportunity for you to grow, express concerns, reconsider your priorities and record interesting and creative ideas.

ACTION: Keep a journal

One of the best ways to reflect is by keeping a journal. Write, draw, or paint whatever is on your mind. Many of us have a preconceived idea of what a journal should be: a special book that you write deep thoughts in every day. But a journal can be whatever you want it to be. Write in it once a day, week, month, or year — whatever's valuable to you. Use a spiral notebook or purchase a hardcover drawing book with blank pages. The journaling process, however you choose to do it, is a very valuable way to reflect on your life.

ACTION: Step out of your comfort zone

Most of us like to be comfortable. We like to feel safe, in control, and unafraid. Unfortunately, comfort rarely creates growth, fulfillment, or a better world. It is often during times of discomfort that we grow the most, and turbulence often creates social change. There is something very powerful about intentionally taking on uncomfortable experiences.

What makes you uncomfortable? Teenagers? Very sick people? Poor neighborhoods? Racism? Often our discomfort is a signal of something we could work on. While we're in our "safe zone," we have little reason to really stretch into something new. Visit a place you normally would be afraid to go, take a class in something that you are nervous about, volunteer with a population that makes you uneasy — whatever will push you into new ground.

ACTION: Examine your stereotypes

Even though we like to think we are completely accepting of people and their differences, our society often teaches us to think poorly of racial and ethnic minorities, women, lesbians, gay men, immigrants, youth, and a host of other groups. Accepting that we have stereotypes is crucial to creating a more tolerant world, where people from diverse backgrounds feel valued and safe. It is not easy to examine our prejudices — it forces us to face our dark side. However, becoming aware of stereotypes is the first step toward challenging them.

ACTION: Reconnect with nature

We are part of a living, breathing planet that sustains our bodies and nourishes our spirits. Most of us feel a need to connect with nature on some level, hence the prevalence of "weekend warriors" who leave the city for the tranquillity and adventure of nature. Appreciating nature means more than going out to play in it, though. Create a meaningful way to reconnect with your natural surroundings. Some suggestions include:

- Sitting on your patio for 15 minutes each evening, listening to the sounds around you
- Taking more hikes
- Connecting with a tree
- Finding a tranquil spot in the woods and practicing being calm
- Appreciating the life that surrounds you when you're in nature. You notice things you wouldn't normally.

ACTION: Reconsider your priorities

If you don't consciously choose to spend time on what's really important to you, the little things will consume your priorities. Make a list of your top priorities and compare it to a list of how you spend your time. You may be surprised to learn that you spend relatively little time on some of your top priorities. Consider focusing your energies on your most important priorities to give them the attention they deserve — strengthening your relationships, reading, exercising, volunteering, enriching your spiritual life, exploring new things, taking a class, spending time outdoors, pursuing hobbies.

ACTION: Write a personal mission statement

If someone asked you what exactly do you stand for, could you tell him? Writing your own personal mission statement can be a powerful way for you to reflect on who you are and who you'd like to be.

- Make a list of your core values.
- Ask yourself how these values tie together.
- Write a statement that encompasses your core being, values, and goals.
- Try to keep it under one page.

Here is an example of a personal mission statement:

I am committed to living a creative, peaceful, compassionate life. Life, to me, is a spiritual journey; I intend to constantly examine my life, stretch into new experiences, and grow personally. There will be highs and lows on this path, but I will try to live an intentional life, staying in the moment and maintaining a peaceful existence. I will never lose sight of my connection with others. I hope that everything I do in some way makes the world a better place. True happiness comes from meaningful connection, and often service, to others.

A personal mission statement gives direction to your life. You can revisit it anytime to reaffirm your sense of purpose, evaluate where you're at now, or change your mission to include new insights.

⇨ PERSONAL RESOURCES

📖 Anderson, Sherry Ruth, and Patricia Hopkins. *The Feminine Face Of God.* Bantam Books, 1991. A book about the spiritual life of women that "shows how many women have redefined traditional beliefs and rediscovered their own unique spiritual heritage."

📖 Cameron, Julia. *The Artist's Way: A Spiritual Path to Higher Creativity.* P. Tarcher, 1992. Composed of a 12-week program of exercises and activities, this book helps you overcome any obstacles that stand between you and a completely creative life. It also links creativity and spirituality in a unique way. If you like this one, consider *Vein of Gold: A Journey to Your Creative Heart* by the same author.

📖 Covey, Stephen. *7 Habits of Highly Effective People: Powerful Lessons in Personal Change.* Fireside, 1990. This book has sold over ten million copies for a reason: it teaches personal effectiveness by encouraging you to see the world in a new way. It will help you live with fairness, dignity, and integrity.

📖 Duerk, Judith. *Circle Of Stones — Woman's Journey To Herself.* InnisFree Press, 1999 [1989]. Myths and stories make this book an exciting journey for women to discover their sacred selves within. A great read, *Circle of Stones* searches for the roots of femininity and the power of women.

📖 Dyer, Wayne. *Power of Intention: Learning to Co-Create Your World Your Way.* Hay House, 2005. Combining insights from psychology and sociology with his vast knowledge of spiritual traditions, Dyer teaches readers to develop inner awareness, reduce stress, and live with intention.

📖 Elgin, Duane. *Voluntary Simplicity: Toward a Way of Life That Is Outwardly Simple,* Inwardly Rich. Quill, 1993 [1981]. This book will help end your enslavement to products and work. It advocates balance, not poverty and connects personal growth to simple living.

📖 Hanh, Thich Nhat. *The Miracle of Mindfulness: A Manual on Meditation.* Beacon Press, 1987 [1975]. Thich Nhat Hanh, an exiled Vietnamese Buddhist monk, offers a guide to meditation that transcends sitting in the lotus position. He offers a variety of interesting activities designed to increase your mindfulness.

📖 Hesse, Herman. *Siddhartha.* Shambala Publishers, 2000. This novel tells the story of Siddhartha's quest for enlightenment. Hesse illustrates the basics of

Buddhist thought in a simple but profound story.

📖 Millman, Dan. *Way of the Peaceful Warrior: A Book That Changes Lives.* Kramer, 1985 [1980]. Dan Millman writes about his days as a college gymnast searching for ultimate happiness. An extremely engaging story with powerful insights applicable to everyday life.

FRIENDS AND FAMILY

Building Strong Relationships
Giving Gifts
Children

MANY FORCES IN TODAY'S WORLD work against strong relationships with our friends and families: consumerism, overworking, individualism and our fast-paced society. Even though our families and friends are the most important people in our lives, these factors often lead us to neglect our relationships and take our loved ones for granted. Ask yourself, "How can I take a more active, intentional role in creating extraordinary relationships?" You'll amaze yourself with the possibilities you create.

One of the most significant ways you can have a positive impact on the world is through your family and friends. With a little effort you can transform your relationships into meaningful connections that provide a nurturing environment for love and personal growth. When supported by loving relationships, you will also create a solid foundation on which to make the world a better place.

Each of us creates what family means for us. Family can mean parents and children, a single parent and children, a couple without children, gay or lesbian couples with or without children, extended family, friends living together, loved ones who live in another state — you name it. Each of us knows who our loved ones are; this chapter is about them.

This chapter addresses several important aspects of relationships, including ways to create strong relationships, gift giving, and raising children. Hopefully it will spark your creativity and help you act toward your family and friends in a way that spreads love and compassion in the world. Imagine a world where everyone committed to creating strong, loving relationships — that's a world we want to live in.

BUILDING STRONG RELATIONSHIPS

Great relationships don't just happen; we have to create them. We all know that certain ways of acting with loved ones strengthen relationships and other ways stymie growth. The following actions are central to the strength of all relationships — friends, siblings, or life partners.

ACTION: Make time for loved ones a priority

It takes time to build strong relationships. You can't create meaningful relationships in the ten minutes between meetings or the hour between errands. It takes effort and it takes commitment. Your boss is never going to get on your case when you neglect your friends and family. You must make your relationships a priority if you want them to prosper.

> Mark a weekly "date night" on your calendar or set aside one weekend a month as a "couple weekend."

Instead of scheduling the items on your to-do list, schedule in your real priorities. If you find that you are neglecting the people who are important in your life, schedule them into your busy life. It's easy to neglect your loved ones when they don't carry much importance on your calendar.

Reunions, parties, and potlucks are great ways to build community, whether they are for extended family or for your college buddies. Everybody loves them but most people don't take the time to plan them. They can be very cheap if you stay at home and have a potluck. Get-togethers can be spontaneous, too. Throw an impromptu barbecue with your neighbors or play an after dinner volleyball game.

ACTION: Check in

Sometimes we get so caught up in the rat race that we forget to check in with the people that we care for. Write a letter, send an e-mail, or pick up the phone. Just ask how they are doing and how their week was. You may even want to schedule a time every week or every month where you catch up with certain people in your life. Open and frequent communication is vital to healthy relationships.

ACTION: Practice deep listening

Have you ever been talking to someone and noticed after a few minutes that she just isn't there with you? Interacting with people whose thoughts are elsewhere is completely annoying. Make sure that you are attentive to your loved ones when you are with them. When you're reading the newspaper, watching TV, being in a hurry, or worrying about what you have to do tomorrow, it detracts from fully experiencing the people you care for. One of the most powerful ways you can show people that you respect and care for them is to listen to them — truly listen to them, whether they are talking about their day at work, what movie they want to see, or cherished memories of a loved one. Deep listening creates a space for people to feel safe and grow.

ACTION: Resolve conflicts collaboratively

Most people learn to deal with conflict in one of two ways:

avoid it at all costs

OR

go for the jugular!

Avoiding conflict at all costs leads to resentment and allows little grievances to grow into huge problems. On the other hand, aggression leads to hot tempers, hurt feelings, and irrational decisions. It doesn't have to be that way. How would your relationships be more fulfilling and productive if you saw conflict as an opportunity for growth? Collaborative conflict resolution engages conflict so that the underlying problems truly get resolved while strengthening the relationship.

WHEN A CONFLICT OCCURS

1. Listen to their side of the story.
   - actually listen (don't just be thinking of what to say next)
   - ask questions to seek understanding
   - restate their point of view in your own words
   - remember the conflict is about an issue, not the person

2. Share your side of the story.
   - seek to be understood, not to blame
   - talk about yourself not about them
   - share feelings

3. Work to find a win-win outcome.
   - create options that would satisfy both people's underlying needs
   - don't just settle for a compromise

ACTION: Give unconditional love and support

Think of a time when someone did something for you, expecting nothing in return, simply because they cared about you. Perhaps your partner surprised you with a lunch date, or perhaps a stranger helped you out when you had car trouble. It's an amazing feeling to know that someone cares enough to make you feel special simply because of who you are, instead of what you do.

Be sure to nourish the personal growth of the people you care for. Encourage them to follow their dreams and spend time developing their interests. Especially when your loved ones are thinking about major life-changing decisions, they need you to love and support them.

ACTION: Share housework and childcare fairly

One of the best ways to keep everyone in your household happy is to share housework and childcare fairly. Despite entering the workforce in increasing numbers, women still spend significantly more time than men on household tasks. On average, working women spend approximately twice as much time as working men on housework and childcare.[1] While men have picked up some of the slack, they still aren't pulling their weight, even if their female partner works the same amount of hours outside the home. When tasks are divided equally, both partners are happier. Openly discussing and equally dividing housework prevents resentment and ensures that everyone has plenty of time to play and relax.

 ACTION: Forgive others

You've probably read stories of people who have visited a prison to forgive their child's murderer. Most of us have difficulty comprehending this level of forgiveness, even when we see that forgiveness helps the distraught parents move on with their lives. Although difficult, the ability to forgive is crucial to emotional well-being.

We're all human beings; others will hurt each one of us many times in our lives. When we enter loving relationships, we open ourselves up to vulnerability, disappointment and hurt. There will undoubtedly be times when others take

THE CRISIS OF MASCULINITY

Unfortunately, the measure of manhood in many cultures lies in how much wealth and status a man can accumulate, how many women he sleeps with, and how tough he is, whether on the basketball court or in the boardroom. Showing emotion (other than anger) or vulnerability are supposedly signs of weakness, femininity, or homosexuality. Men face immense pressure to live up to masculine ideals and to avoid appearing feminine. They "prove" their masculinity by taking risks, acting tough, dominating others, demonstrating sexual prowess and putting pressure on themselves to be the ultimate "provider" for their families. Instead of healthy, confident, loving men, society too often produces frustrated, ultra-competitive, emotionally constipated full-grown boys who feel like they can't measure up. If we are to create a world of happy, fulfilled, compassionate men, a world that is more empowering to women, we have to change the rules.

Ways to subvert the "tough guise":
- Show vulnerability.
- Be a more loving partner.
- Practice deep listening.
- Take a more active, nurturing role in raising kids.
- Resist urges to act tough or to dominate others and teach boys to do likewise.
- Seek ways to cooperate instead of always competing with others.
- Stand up for those who are picked on and ostracized. Speak up when others use sexist and homophobic slurs such as "bitch," "slut," "fag," and "dyke".
- Teach boys to express a full range of emotions (including sadness, happiness, and love).
- Pass on a prestigious promotion or job offer that will require you to spend significantly more time away from your family, friends, community and leisure.
- Speak out against violence, racism, sexism and gay-bashing.
- Boycott videos, websites and magazines that portray women in degrading, demeaning, or abusive ways.
- Encourage women and girls to pursue their educational and career goals.
- Develop meaningful relationships with men and women.

advantage of our vulnerability, causing us pain and anger. Grudges and resentment are difficult burdens to bear. They breed cynicism and distrust and often inhibit personal growth and transformation. Leo Buscaglia writes, "Forgiveness is an act of will ... we either choose to forgive or we do not."[2] Choosing to forgive is a difficult but powerful process. Here are a few suggestions to make it easier:

- Remember all aspects of the relationship, not just the hurtful or negative incidents. It's easy to let the damaging parts of a relationship cloud the good times.
- Put yourself in their shoes. At some point, we've all hurt someone else. How would you want to be treated if you were in the other person's shoes?
- Avoid using forgiveness as a source of power. Don't use your forgiveness to get what you want. If you choose to forgive, then forgive unconditionally.
- Remember what it's like to be forgiven. You are giving the wrong-doer and yourself a tremendous gift, one that can be extremely empowering for everyone involved.

Forgiveness can be hard; that's OK. The price of not forgiving, however, is great.

 RESOURCES

 White Ribbon Campaign. www.whiteribbon.ca.

 Tough Guise: Violence, Media, and the Crisis of Masculinity. Sut Jhally Director, 82 min. Media Education Foundation, 1999 and *Wrestling with Manhood: Boys, Bullying, and Battering.* Sut Jhally Director, 60 min. Media Education Foundation, 2002. These very powerful films uncover how television, movies, and magazines help perpetuate the harmful aspects of masculinity. Check your local public or university library.

GIVING GIFTS

Gift giving is often fun for both the giver and the receiver. Try to think of meaningful ways to express your love that also take into account the well-being of the planet and others around you. Here are a few suggestions for making your gift giving extra special.

ACTION: Get creative with gifts

Instead of buying a ready-made card and present, why not give something that more powerfully shows how much you appreciate the person? Take some time to think about the other person's needs — what would they really appreciate? What would really enhance their life? Show them that they are worthy of your time and energy, not just your money. Try giving of yourself by making a birthday card, writing a song or poem, cleaning the house, or giving your loved one a "coupon" for a back rub or romantic evening together. In other words, put yourself into the gift and think outside the box.

- Go to a bed and breakfast.
- Make a piece of jewelry, pottery, or other handcrafted gift.
- Clean the garage.
- Plan a hike, picnic, or other outing.
- Buy some seeds and plant a flower garden together.

ACTION: Donate money in someone else's name

Eventually, many of us get to the point where we don't need or even want any more stuff. Show that you truly understand your loved one's deepest values by donating money to an organization that is struggling for something that they believe in—instead of buying something that will go straight to the storage closet. Most organizations will send out a small newsletter or magazine on a regular basis throughout the year so that your loved one can see what kind of powerful changes their gift is creating in the world.

Alternative Gifts International
The Alternative Gifts catalog highlights 30 humanitarian projects by which you can honor your loved ones with a donation while empowering people in crisis and protecting the Earth. Examples include: providing solar powered water systems in Honduras, helping female workers in the Maquiladoras (Mexico-US border factories) learn about their rights and their health, and helping provide literacy training in Senegal. Your loved ones receive a gift card in the mail indicating your gift.
   (800) 842-2243   💻 www.altgifts.org

ACTION: Buy socially responsible gifts

Consider buying gifts that are more in line with your values. For example, if you value nonviolence, buy your nephew a toy that encourages cooperation rather competition. Or if you want to prevent eating disorders, buy your niece a stuffed animal, not a Barbie doll. If you are an environmentalist, consider buying someone reusable canvas shopping bags or another gift that will help them lessen their environmental impact. It's tempting to get all our gifts at a superstore such as Wal-Mart or K-Mart, but your shopping dollars are extremely important to locally owned shops and craftspeople. Besides, if you shop locally, you might find something unique! Other gift ideas are:

- creative supplies (paints, drawing pencils, journals, etc.)
- subscription to an alternative magazine (see the MEDIA chapter)
- items made by Third World artisans and workers

Ten Thousand Villages

Ten Thousand Villages is a nonprofit organization that sells handicrafts made by unemployed or under-employed people of the Third World. They promote fair trade (livable prices and wages), reinforce cultural traditions, and support ethical and humane work environments. Contact them to find out where the store nearest to you is located.

    (717) 859-8100   🖥 www.villages.ca

ACTION: Simplify the holidays

Unfortunately, multi-million dollar marketing campaigns have slowly transformed our most cherished holidays into frazzled shopping frenzies. Many of us spend so much time worrying and being anxious that the holidays seem more like a chore than a blessing — not to mention the extra weeks we have to work to pay off our shopping debts. Take time to fully appreciate the meaning of the holidays by slowing down, focusing on what's really important, and cutting back on the amount of money and time you and your family spend in shopping malls. Be creative with your family and find ways to share generosity without giving in to the ploys of Madison Avenue. Simplifying the holidays is a great way to improve your relationships, save the Earth's resources, save some money and frustration, and help halt the commercialization of our most honored times together. Be sure to talk with your family at least a few weeks in advance about your desire to simplify the holidays. Here are some ideas:

- Set dollar limits on gifts.
- Pick names out of a hat so that each person only buys one gift.
- Take some of the money saved on gifts and donate it to a favorite charity (try this at work, too).
- Have each person share a treasured family memory.
- Give of yourself instead of just buying something.

Check out the Center for a New American Dream's "Simplify the Holidays" Campaign for more ideas (www.newdream.org/holiday).

CHILDREN

Many people describe the experience of giving birth and raising children as the most amazing and meaningful experiences in their lives. The responsibilities of child-rearing are also extremely challenging. Much of our children's potential is shaped by their experiences during the first few years of life. The following actions address important issues that parents should consider when raising their children as kind and compassionate members of the human family.

ACTION: Limit your number of children

In 2000, the world's population grew by 78 million. That means the world's population grew by about 2-$\frac{1}{2}$ people every second (that's births minus deaths!).[3] We've got to slow our population growth. The Earth already bends under our collective impact. We can choose to limit our family size to zero, one, or two children. You may think that the "population problem" only exists in China and India, but North Americans use so many resources that an extra North American has a vastly greater environmental effect than does a person born in a developing country.

ACTION: Adopt

Americans adopt approximately 125,000 children each year.[4] Although this seems like a lot of children, many remain without permanent homes. By adopting a child, you provide him or her with a safe, stable home — essential ingredients for a happy, healthy childhood. Adoption is also an ecologically beneficial way to have kids; rather than producing more children and requiring more resources, adoption enables you to support a child already here. After determining your desired family size, consider adopting some or all of your children. If you want three kids, consider having two yourself and adopting one. Adoption is one of the most powerful gifts you can give.

National Adoption Information Clearinghouse (NAIC)
💻 naic.acf.hhs.gov

The Center for Family Building
💻 www.centerforfamily.com

ACTION: Be a foster parent

In any given year there are about 500,000 children in foster care in the US.[5] Children in foster care often have special needs or have been abused or neglected and are especially in need of your help. Adoption agencies usually have information on how you can be a foster parent.

National Foster Parent Association   💻 www.nfpainc.org

ACTION: Share babysitting

In the past, people relied more on friends and neighbors to help with child care. Unfortunately, we often don't know our neighbors well or feel bad about burdening them with our children. Many other parents face these same issues. Why not create a group of friends to share babysitting responsibilities? Start with the groups you already belong to, such as a work or religious community. Announce your idea and pass around a sign-up sheet to see who might be interested. Even if you don't have kids, you can offer to babysit. If you really want to make a difference in someone's life, volunteer to help out new parents, who often can most use your assistance.

☞ ACTION: Spend quality time with children

Our children deserve our time. Some parts of our culture are creating an increasingly hostile environment in which to raise children. Images of violence and excessive consumerism are daily fare for the young in our country, and these images are hard to compete with as parents. The most effective way to raise children is to spend time with them. It shows them that you love them, and it increases the influence you have on their values.

Many adults gripe about children's lack of values. Actually, everyone is teaching your children values: your TV is doing it; their friends are doing it; and you are doing it. If they see you one hour a day and they watch four hours of TV messages — guess whose values are going to win out? It is essential that you play a significant role in the creation of your child's values. When you make your children a priority in your life, it leads them to have a sense of belonging and security that is essential to healthy maturity.

BE A RESPECTFUL SPORTS FAN

You've probably seen news stories about parents at kids' sporting events who belittle and berate young players, shout at other parents, and even start fights with sports referees. As absurd as this sounds, it seems to be a growing trend. Don't be an obnoxious parent at kids' sporting events. Make sure to model good sportsmanship, civility and positivity at any sporting event, especially one involving kids. Emphasize cooperation, hard work, enjoyment, and teamwork rather than domination, aggression and winning at any cost. Show kids how to play hard and do their best while respecting their opponents. Remember, it's just a game!

☞ ACTION: Be a mentor

Whether you have children or not, there are many ways for you to be help kids have fun and grow into responsible, caring young women and men. Consider ways that the neighborhood kids and your nieces and nephews would benefit from your attention — maybe it's a game of basketball or some supportive words when they look upset or down. Mentoring from positive, caring adults is one of the best ways to keep kids out of trouble and help them succeed in school. As you will find your own life enriched as well.

- Volunteer at an after-school program.
- Coach a youth sports team.
- Be a Big Brother or Big Sister. www.bbbsa.org (US), www.bbbsc.ca (Canada).
- Help out at your local Boys or Girls Club. www.bgca.org (US), www.bgc can.com (Canada).

☞ ACTION: Express affection

"I love you" are three of the most powerful words in our language. It's important that family members, both kids and adults, know we love and care about them.

HOST AN EXCHANGE STUDENT

One of the most powerful ways to build dialogue and understanding across cultures is to live with someone from another country. Hosting an exchange student can be hugely rewarding for both the student and you and your family. By hosting an exchange student you are part of a potentially transformative experience for the student.

Center for Cultural Interchange: www.cci-exchange.com/host.htm

American Field Service: www.usa.afs.org

Express your love for each other as much as possible. We all like to hear "I love you." Teaching a child how to love another person through your own example may be the most powerful impact that you can have on them.

 ## ACTION: Discipline children nonviolently

As a parent, there are seemingly endless situations where you want your child to do one thing while they are determined to do another. These situations can be so frustrating that even the most peaceful adults can be driven to yelling and spanking. However, there are alternative ways to discipline children that will help them become responsible, caring members of their families and communities.

Constructive "disciplining" is a patient, principled manner of teaching children the difference between appropriate and inappropriate behavior. It should not be an expression of anger toward our kids. It takes determination, consistency, love, and lots and lots of patience but it can be a powerful tool to teach about your family's core values.

Model for Nonviolent Discipline:

- Continually emphasize the importance of treating others with respect and compassion.
- Explain the reason behind a family rule and how it helps create a safe and healthy environment for everyone to thrive.
- Praise your child's behavior when you see them acting respectfully or responsibly.
- When a child breaks a family rule, immediately identify the broken rule and very briefly explain why the behavior is not acceptable. Remember to focus on the behavior not the child (e.g., say "hitting is not okay" as opposed to "you are a bad boy.")
- To correct consistently inappropriate behavior, present clear consequences for not stopping the behavior ("I need you to come to the door now or you will lose [their favorite toy for one day]"). It is important to stay calm.
- Do not yell. Anger poisons relationships and can spiral into words and actions that one later regrets. If you feel yourself losing control, take a

step back, and gain your composure.

- If the child does not change their behavior, you need to follow through on the consequences. This way the child will learn that behavioral standards are important and that you mean what you say.

- When your child does something more severe (like hitting someone), give them a "time out." This entails pointing out the inappropriate behavior and putting the child alone for a short amount of time (up to one minute per year of age). When the time has expired, ask your child why they got a "time out." Then affectionately excuse them from their "time out."

Remember, we can't expect our children to be perfect. The above principles will teach responsible behavior in a loving manner that leads to a stronger parent-child relationship and will encourage your child's healthy development.

⇨ RESOURCE

📖 Rosenberg, Marshall B. *Raising Children Compassionately: Parenting the Nonviolent Communication Way.* Puddledancer Press, 2004. www.cnvc.org

📖 Neil, Zoe. *Above All Be Kind: Raising a Humane Child in Challenging Times.* New Society Publishers, 2003.

🗒 ACTION: Teach caring and giving

One of the most important values we can instill in our children is the obligation to help others and make a positive contribution to the world. So much of our culture tells our children to do whatever feels good or exciting at the time without thinking of the consequences to themselves or others. Teaching the value of treating others as we would like to be treated goes a long way to building a world that we would all like to live in.

Be creative in encouraging your child to think of others and to give part of their time and money to charitable causes. Volunteer as a family — it's a wonderful way to bond while doing good deeds for others. Children who grow up helping their parents volunteer will likely continue to make service a priority throughout their lives. By teaching your child alternatives to violence and selfishness, you are taking a large step to making the world a more loving, peaceful place. Here are a few suggestions:

- Serve at a soup kitchen.
- Teach children how to oppose bullying.
- Create a holiday gift tree for underprivileged children.
- Donate gifts to your local homeless or women's shelter.
- Make holiday decorations for your local retirement home.
- Do yardwork for the elderly in your neighborhood — for free.
- Participate in any community clean-up programs.

- Go on a litter patrol. Make it even more fun by creating a search team, with a child as team leader.

ACTION: Model flexible gender roles

We teach kids early on what it means to be a boy and what it means to be a girl. Gender differences are especially evident in the division of household labor: women generally clean, cook, do laundry and sew; men typically handle home repairs, heavy yard work, and auto maintenance. Also, our culture teaches that men are the heads of the household and therefore are responsible for important family decisions. Dividing up work and decision making are fine, but doing so on the basis of gender limits our opportunities. Strict gender roles prevent girls and boys from becoming whole people who can express a broad range of emotions and succeed at a broad range of tasks. Consider the following gender-empowering actions:

- Show that it's OK for both women and men to show emotions.
- Trade off on household tasks: scrub the bathroom one week, mow the lawn the next.
- Demonstrate that both men and women can make big decisions.
- Teach boys how to cook and girls how to fix the sink.
- Avoid guiding your kids to gender specific play; encourage them to value and engage in a variety of activities, regardless of gender.

ACTION: Teach an appreciation of diversity

Racism, homophobia, classism, sexism, and religious intolerance cause a great deal of suffering in our world. Kids are not born intolerant; they learn prejudices from adults, the media, and other kids. Going out of your way to teach kids tolerance and even appreciation of differences is a huge step in making the world a better place. They will model and teach what you have taught them — passing on your good lessons. Use real-world examples of racism and other bigotry to discuss how you and your kids can respond when such situations occur in your own lives. Keep in mind that if you don't consciously teach tolerance, children will likely learn and accept negative stereotypes from the media and their peers.

Find ideas for promoting tolerance in your home, school, workplace, and community at www.tolerance.org.

ACTION: Teach the difference between wants and needs

As you are reading this, advertising executives are figuring out how to "brand" your child with images of their products. They spend millions of dollars every year on TV commercials, product placements in movies, cartoon shows based on a product, and other forms of advertising meant to confuse your child about what is really important in life. You can help your child define what is really meaningful (spirituality, friends, family, a clean environment) and what is only fleeting and superficial (the newest toys or fashions). Consider showing your love in more positive ways and only buy gifts on special occasions. Children are extremely observant. Don't wonder why your child demands a new toy every week if you are getting a new outfit every month or a new car every year.

ACTION: Choose childcare that supports your values

Choosing a daycare can be difficult. Several issues concern all parents: safety, cleanliness, stimulating environment, child/caregiver ratio and staff qualifications, for example. In addition to the standard concerns, you may want to consider asking some of the following questions about your childcare provider. Keep in mind that childcare providers are often overworked and underpaid and may have trouble implementing some of these ideas.

- Do they encourage cooperative activities over competitive and/or violent activities?
- Do the supervisors teach sharing?
- Is the daycare "educational?"
- Are children disciplined nonviolently?
- Do the caregivers teach children how to resolve their own conflicts collaboratively?

> Consider choosing your local Boys and Girls Clubs as a childcare option. They offer kids a safe, fun environment with positive role models at a very low cost.

- Does the daycare foster creativity in the children in a variety of ways, or do the kids watch TV?
- How do the caregivers teach other languages, handle gender roles, and encourage cultural activities? Are there children of diverse ethnicity present?
- Does the daycare do its best to reduce, reuse, and recycle? Does the daycare actually teach kids to value the Earth and be environmentally responsible?

ACTION: Limit TV watching

Television is a direct pipeline that delivers gratuitous violence, cheapened sexuality, racial stereotypes, and a barrage of advertisements right into your home. None of us want to believe that TV has a negative effect on us. Unfortunately, experts conclude that television violence increases kids' aggressive behavior. TV viewing also leads to apathy, inactivity,

> The average child watches 20,000 to 40,000 commercials every year.[6]

desensitization to violence, and lack of imagination. An easy way to limit your family's TV watching is to create a TV viewing schedule (yes, all the adults, too). Decide as a family how much Total Tube Time (including shows, movies and video games) each person gets. Keep a log by the TV set for each person to monitor their watching. Encourage your kids to practice selective viewing by checking the TV guide to best use their allotted time. A TV schedule serves several goals:

- You'll find out just how much TV your family wants to watch (it may be a lot).
- You'll see exactly which shows your children like and can reflect on which shows are really worth watching.
- You can compare the actual time you spent watching with your goal and work to cut your time to meet it.
- You won't watch things that aren't important to you just to be watching something.

ACTION: Choose alternatives to being glued to the screen

It is essential for us to teach our children how to spend their time in ways that lead to learning, personal growth, strong friendships, enhanced creativity, and physical health. It takes creativity and discipline to use your time in a productive and positive manner — two skills which television, the primary waster of kids' time, does not teach. TV is addictive, and it encourages you to watch more and more while tuning out the rest of the world.

> 42% of families report that their television is on "most of the time" and 60% have their TV on during meals.[7]

Rarely does watching TV get a kid excited about life or build intimacy between friends or family. Instead of letting your kids lie on the couch all day watching cartoons, engage them in activities which get them actively participating in life. Get them outside — it will not only get them in shape but will help them appreciate our natural environment. Having fun with other family and

SOCIAL ACTIVITIES

Create a family tree, go to parades, play board games or cards, tell stories, enjoy just being together, team work

OUTSIDE ACTIVITIES

Play in the park, play Frisbee, golf, go bowling, go ice-skating, hike, build a snow creature, play basketball, Hacky Sack, fly a kite, play soccer, swim, bike, have a picnic, go sledding, play softball, run relay races, go bird watching, collect leaves, garden, play wiffleball, play croquet, play badminton

EDUCATIONAL ACTIVITIES

Visit museums, go to the public library, go to the theater, visit a planetarium, read, do crossword puzzles, do science experiments

CREATIVE ACTIVITIES

Create art together, play music together, write a poem, draw pictures of each other, color, write a short story, sing, arrange flowers, paint, journal, cook, play with sidewalk chalk, pursue other hobbies friends leads to deeper relationships and a healthier mental state, just as experiencing creative and educational challenges leads to immense personal growth.

ACTION: Talk with your kids about TV

Encourage critical TV viewing in your kids. Kids are in the process of learning about different types of people: men and women, whites and people of color, gay and straight, rich and poor. TV often distorts our perceptions of diversity and fundamentally shapes our ideas about what's really important in life. Consider asking:

> The average US 8-10 year old spends 4 hours and 10 minutes watching TV, over one hour playing video games, and over $^{1}/_{2}$ hour in recreational computer use everyday — that's almost 6 hours spent staring at a screen![8]

- What is the difference between TV and reality?
- What are the stereotypes that TV perpetuates?
- What is the purpose of a commercial?
- How does TV exaggerate some characters' attributes?
- What is the show's message?
- After watching a show with your kids, ask them what they thought of any scenes that could be used as an opportunity to discuss values.

ACTION: Choose alternatives to violent toys and video games

Toy guns, swords, action figures, tanks, and warplanes have filled kids' toy boxes for years. Encourage your children to play with fewer violence-based toys by having a healthy balance of other items around. Stock art supplies, puzzles, building toys such as Lincoln Logs and Tinker Toys, dress-up clothes and sports equipment and make sure they are readily available.

At first glance, violent toys may seem like a "boy issue." Girls, however, engage in their own form of violence when they emulate dolls with impossibly shaped figures. Toys, in fact, play a large role in reinforcing typical girl and boy behavior, which is why making mindful choices is so important.

Most conventional board games teach kids the importance of winning; there can only be one winner and the rest of the players are losers. Pretty depressing, huh? Some games teach kids cooperation rather than competition and encourage helping versus hindering strategies. Some even teach good social skills, such as sharing, being polite, and understanding different points of view.

Video games get more gruesome every year. Watch some current video games and you're likely to see one character rip out the other's spine in a shower of blood. Not only are games violent; they often portray women and minorities in stereotypical and demeaning ways, with women appearing in

> For fun ways for your kids to learn about the environment go to the EPA's Environmental Kids Club at www.epa.gov/kids.

Looking for a good book to read to your children and help them understand different points of view? Dr. Seuss is one of our all-time favorites. *The Sneetches and Other Stories* teaches about racism, *The Butter Battle Book* hints at the absurdity of the arms race, and *The Lorax* has great environmental themes.

skimpy outfits and people of color portrayed as the enemy. There are, however, some games that not only avoid violence and stereotypes but are educational as well. Ask your local computer store about educational games. Before you buy a child a game, make sure you check the game's rating. The Entertainment Software Rating Board provides a useful website that allows you to enter the name of the game and receive a rating reflecting the game's violent and sexual content. You can also find a game's rating on its box along with specific content descriptions such as "animate blood," "drug reference," "mature humor" and "edutainment." The basic rating is on the front of the box while the more detailed rating is on the back.

Ao   = Adults Only, ages 18 and over

M   = Mature, ages 17 and older

T   = Teen, people 13 and older

E 10+ = Everyone 10 and older

E   = Everyone, ages 6 and older

eC   = Early Childhood, may be suitable for ages 3 and older

Entertainment Software Rating Board

    💻 www.esrb.org

⇨ TEACHING POSITIVE PLAY RESOURCES

📣 Family Pastimes. (613) 267-4819, 💻 www.familypastimes.com.
Family Pastimes is an excellent source for friendly and educational games. It is a family-run Canadian company specializing in cooperative games. Contact them for their Catalog of Cooperative Games.

📖 Luvmour, Josette & Ba. *Everyone Wins! Cooperative Games and Activities.* New Society Publishers, revised edition, 2007. This bestseller is a handbook of more than 150 cooperative games. Activities are included for a range of age groups.

📖 Milord, Susan. *The Kids' Nature Book: 365 Indoor/Outdoor Activities and Experiences.* Williamson Publishing, 1997. Set up like a calendar,

GAMES TO AVOID

- Games in which the goal is murder, assassination, or domination.
- Games that glorify gang violence.
- Fighting games.
- Games that objectify women.

LESS VIOLENT GAMES

- Mario and Sonic games type games.
- Racing games.
- Puzzle games.
- Sims games.
- Some sports games.

this book has a season-appropriate activity for every day of the year.

📖 Steffens, Charlie, and Spencer Gorin. *Learning to Play, Playing to Learn: Games and Activities to Teach Sharing, Caring, and Compromise.* Lowell House/ Contemporary Books, 1998. With over 60 entertaining activities, this book teaches how to play without hurting bodies or feelings while fostering cooperation and positive behavior. To order, go to: www.joyin learning.com.

⇨ PARENTING AND CONSUMERISM RESOURCES

💻 Center for a New American Dream. *Tips for Parenting in a Consumer Culture.* www.newdream.org/kids [downloadable guide].

📖 Sherlock, Marie. *Living Simply With Children: A Voluntary Simplicity Guide for Moms, Dads, and Kids Who Want to Reclaim the Bliss of Childhood and the Joy of Parenting.* Three Rivers Press, 2003.

📖 Taylor, Betsy. *What Kids Really Want That Money Can't Buy: Tips For Parenting in a Commercial World.* Warner, 2003.

⇨ OTHER PARENTING RESOURCES

💻 American Psychological Association. *"Raising Children to Resist Violence: What You Can Do."* www.apa.org/pi/pii/raisingchildren.html.

📖 Hill, Linda. *Connecting Kids: Exploring Diversity Together.* New Society Publishers, 2001. Over 200 games and activities teach kids to cherish diversity.

📖 Kivel, Paul. *Boys Will Be Men: Raising Our Sons For Courage, Caring, And Community.* New Society Publishers, 1999. Teaches how to raise boys to be loving and happy while challenging racism, sexism, heterosexism and con-sumerism.

📖 Popov, Linda Kavelin, John Kavelin, and Dan Popov. *The Family Virtues Guide.* New York: Penguin, 1997. A guide to help parents teach 52 virtues (e.g., compassion, honesty, tolerance, perseverance — one for each week) to their children.

COMMUNITY

Neighborhood
Local Community
Community Issues

I T'S IRONIC THAT IN AN AGE of instant global communication, with our cell phones, e-mail, and fax machines, many of us feel more isolated than ever. Virtually all of us want to feel a sense of community — it's comforting, safe, and fulfilling. In fact, community is an essential part of being human. More than just a physical place, a community exists when people care for each other's well-being, share their lives and embrace the ideal of loving others as they wish to be loved. Community is a process by which we open up and begin to embrace others as part of our extended family. Our local communities then become good models for caring about people around the world whom we may never meet — the beginnings of a global community. Community never just happens — we must create it.

Unfortunately, society teaches us to behave in ways that thwart our desire for connection: buy a house in the suburbs as far from neighbors as possible; don't ask your neighbors for favors; drive your own car rather than carpool; and look out for yourself first. We feel that our values as a people are eroding; violence is rising; and our nation is divided.

We've responded to these beliefs in counterproductive ways. Despite our desire for connection, many of us move frequently rather than put down roots, and we take refuge in our homes rather than connect with our neighbors. As a response to fear of crime and perceived decline of social values, many people who actually yearn for community isolate and barricade themselves in protective, exclusive neighborhoods. Our instincts are to withdraw rather than to fully engage the world. Instead of reaching out, we close ourselves off.

But don't despair. Millions of people are showing us how to create the communities we want. Religious groups, communities of color, lesbians and gays,

129

members of the simple living movement and others are being proactive and redefining what community means. Out of necessity, they have created safe, supportive environments in which they thrive. Consider, for a moment, the awesome possibilities for your life and the world when you intentionally create community.

This chapter will inspire you to make your neighborhood and local community better places to live. Its concrete actions and resources will challenge you to make real your dreams of a community where everyone feels a sense of belonging and responsibility toward the common good. It is important to think of community not only as an end goal or a place to exist but also as a process and an ideal to reach. Have an exciting and wonderful journey in creating your world anew!

NEIGHBORHOOD

The creation of community starts at home. The quality of your relationships significantly shapes how you and your neighbors experience your lives. Living in a neighborhood where you can rely on other people and enjoy going outside feels great. There are many things you can do to make your neighborhood into a vibrant and welcoming place. We describe a few below to get you started.

ACTION: Put down roots

Every year, about 42 million of us pack up and move — that's about one out of every six people.[1] The average American moves 11.7 times in a lifetime.[2] Many of us move whenever we find a new job or can afford a bigger, so-called better house. A certain amount of mobility is beneficial (and even unavoidable), but moving every few years reduces the probability of developing meaningful community. It's difficult to justify investing time and effort to connect with a place that you know you'll be leaving soon. Yet putting down roots offers advantages that may outweigh taking a higher-paying job or a larger house in some other community. Long-term friendships and community ties are priceless.

ACTION: Get to know your neighbors

Moving creates a great deal of stress. When new people move into your community, you can help create a sense of belonging by welcoming them. Try to greet new members of your neighborhood within the first week of their arrival. Each day that you wait to introduce yourself decreases the likelihood that you will have the courage to deliver a warm welcome.

A good way to start is to share food. Take over some extra vegetables from your garden, bake some muffins, or invite your new neighbors over for coffee or dinner. This is also a great opportunity to introduce them to other neighbors living around them — maybe you could have a block party. You can even create a list of common services, such as bus schedules, area parks, schools and churches, farmers' markets and/or locally owned grocery stores, a trustworthy mechanic, the nearest cheap movie theater, or good locally owned restaurants, for your new neighbors! Challenge yourself to meet people who may not fit the norm in your neighborhood, such as people of different races, social classes, abilities, ages and backgrounds. Strike up a conversation and start building some real community.

ACTION: Help your neighbors and ask for their help

Imagine waking up on a cold, snowy morning, looking out the window, and seeing that someone has already shoveled your sidewalk. What a great feeling! You can create that feeling in your neighborhood by helping your neighbors when they need a hand. Not only will you help your neighbors out and build community, you'll also find fulfillment that just doesn't come from watching TV or mowing your own lawn. Here are a few suggestions your neighbors will appreciate:

- Shovel snow off their driveway and sidewalk.
- Mow their lawn and feed their pets when they're out of town.
- Take your neighbor to the airport.
- Watch their kids so they can have a nice evening together.
- Help with home repairs and yard work.
- Split the cost of expensive power tools that you can both use.
- If you go to the farmers' market, buy them some produce.
- Borrow from and lend to your neighbors.

Even if you offer your help, you have little control over whether or not your neighbors ask you for help. Although almost everyone is willing to give help, very few people are willing to ask for it. Consider asking your neighbors for their help, to begin the process of establishing a community of people that can count on each other.

ACTION: Organize a neighborhood event

Often our sense of community grows from our participation in events that bring local people together or that benefit the neighborhood as a whole. If your neighborhood lacks these kinds of events, you just might be the person who gets them going. You can begin to revitalize your community. Consider one or more of the following:

- Organize a local litter clean-up walk.
- Coordinate a blockwide garage sale.
- Set up an annual graffiti paint-over day (Check out www.graffiti hurts.org for tips).
- Throw a block party.
- Establish a Neighborhood Watch program (Check out www.nnwi.org).
- Plan a "TV-Turnoff Week" or a "Buy Nothing Day" event (see Resources that follow).

To get started, type up a one-page flyer with a description of the event, a call for some help, and a contact number or e-mail address where people can reach you. Make enough copies so that you can post one on each of your neighbors' doors, and prepare to set up a convenient meeting time to discuss the event. The rest is just a combination of good will and a little sweat.

Keep America Beautiful

Keep America Beautiful is a nonprofit organization dedicated to help-ing people improve their communities, primarily through litter preven-tion, waste reduction (e.g., recycling), and beautification projects. Their online toolbox includes ideas for changing community attitudes, imple-menting local ordinances and empowering neighborhood groups.

    💻 www.kab.org

National Neighborhood Day

The second Sunday in September is National Neighborhood Day, a day to build relationships and improve your community. You can download sam-ple invitations, RSVP, and other materials on their site.

    💻 www.neighborhoodday.org

TV-Turnoff Network's "TV Turnoff Week"

For $15, TV-Turnoff Network will send you a 48-page organizer's kit — com-plete with posters, bumper stickers, alternative activities, articles, essays and much more — to start your own "TV-Turnoff Week" in your community this April. "TV-Turnoff Week" encourages people to dramatically reduce their televi-sion viewing in order to promote healthier and more connected lives, families and communities. Consider encouraging your local school to join in.

    (202) 333-9220   💻 www.tvturnoff.org

Adbusters' "Buy Nothing Day"

Adbusters will send you sample press releases, posters, TV and radio commer-cials, and will connect you with like-minded members of your community to help celebrate "Buy Nothing Day" — an international event on the Friday after Thanksgiving — to publicize the effects of over-consumption on our families, culture, and the planet.

    (604) 736-9401   💻 www.adbusters.org/metas/eco/bnd

Take Back Your Time Day (TBYTD)

TBYTD is organized by individuals and organizations committed to sim-ple living. They use the day to educate the public about the negative impacts of "time poverty" on our physical and mental health, our relation-ships, our communities and on our planet. Created in 2003, TBYTD is celebrated every October 24.

    Find out more at: www.timeday.org.

ACTION: Plant a tree

We owe the air we breathe to the plants and trees around us. Unfortunately, as cities and highways continue to grow, wilderness areas shrink. Planting trees is a fun way to repair some of the damage humans have done to the Earth and to learn how trees grow and thrive. Seedlings make great creative gifts. Go to your local nursery and pick out a tree appropriate to your eco-system.

    American Forests
    (202) 737-1944   💻 www.americanforests.org

LOCAL COMMUNITY

Take time to think about what makes your community unique and special. Is it the food, music, and art? The landscape, parks and wildlife? Is it the old downtown and the local businesses? Is it the opportunities for recreation and local attractions? Is it the schools and community centers? The architecture, history and ethnic diversity? Here are some suggestions for becoming more integrally involved in your community and making it a more spirited, compassionate and beautiful place to live.

ACTION: Participate in community organizations

You don't have to start your own organizations from scratch to create community. There are likely dozens of organizations that already bring people together in positive ways. You can participate or take an active role in maintaining these groups.

- Peace centers
- Civic organizations
- Free clinics
- Service organizations
- Retirement homes
- Boys' and Girls' clubs
- Youth centers
- Churches/synagogues/temples/mosques
- Rape crisis centers/Women's shelters
- YMCA/YWCA/Community recreation centers
- Volunteer fire departments
- City sports leagues

For volunteer opportunities in your area go to www.volunteermatch.org.

ACTION: Volunteer in a soup kitchen, homeless shelter or food pantry

A community is only as strong as its weakest members. Create a strong, caring community by serving those who most need your help, including the homeless and hungry. Food pantries, soup kitchens and homeless shelters always need volunteers and resources. Many businesses and religious and civic groups commit to serving at a soup kitchen or food pantry once each month. Volunteer on your own or get your favorite group to commit with you.

ACTION: Volunteer at your local animal shelter

Expand your circle of compassion to include other species by walking a dog or playing with a cat at your local shelter. It's likely that your underfunded, overworked animal shelter staff does not have enough time to give the animals the love and care they need. You can make a difference in animals' lives and have fun while doing it. Dogs are great icebreakers for communicating with strangers, and working with abused animals can be an incredibly healing experience.

ACTION: Help Habitat for Humanity build homes

Habitat for Humanity, an ecumenical Christian organization, builds community by building homes with people who need assistance in purchasing their own house. The receiving family helps construct the home and pays for much of it through a no-interest mortgage. In this way, Habitat has built over 100,000 homes around the world!

You can help build community by raising money or volunteering at a site. Don't worry — there's a place for you even if you can't hammer a nail. More than likely there is Habitat construction happening in or very near your community. You may want to get your friends, religious group, business, or other groups involved with working or paying for materials.

Habitat for Humanity
(912) 924-6935   💻 www.habitat.org

SENIOR CORPS

Senior Corps is a great way for seniors to stay involved in their communities. Nearly half a million Americans over 55 donate their time to be foster grandparents, companions who help other seniors live independently and volunteers in a variety of community organizations.

Corporation for National Service
(202) 606-5000   💻 www.seniorcorps.org

ACTION: Get involved in your local schools

Ask most people what the long-term solution to their community's problems is and education will likely be at the top of their list. Yet few of us take time to be actively involved in our local school. Getting involved in your local school is an incredibly powerful way to make the world a better place! Engaged adults (not just parents) are crucial to successful schools and to successful students. Contact your local school and ask how you can be of service. They will greatly appreciate your talents. Here are a few possibilities:

- Be a crossing guard.
- Chaperone a field trip.
- Donate money.
- Volunteer.
- Join the Parent Teacher Association.
- Coach a team.
- Participate in after-school activities.

- Attend school plays.
- Serve on the school board.
- Attend sporting events.
- Tutor kids.
- Be a mentor.
- Do a presentation about your career.
- Advise a student group.

ACTION: Decommercialize your schools

Corporations seeking to create brand recognition and brand loyalty at younger ages are now advertising to the captive and impressionable audience of kids in schools. Many companies even develop public relations materials disguised as academic lesson plans, teaching children to consume products they don't need. You can take a stand against corporate sponsorship in your school and keep education from becoming a corporate playground. You'll be protecting kids from corporations whose main motivation is hooking kids on their products for life.

> "If you own this child at an early age, you can own this child for years to come," explained Mike Searles, president of Kids-R-Us, a major children's clothing store.[3]

- Survey the extent of commercialism in your school. Contact Corp Watch at (510) 271-8080 or www.corpwatch.org/ for a step-by-step guide.
- Ask your school to adopt the National PTA guidelines for corporate involvement (www.pta.org/ia_pta_positions_1118175609906.html).
- Share your views by writing a letter to the editor, talking to other parents, or speaking up at a school board meeting.

RESOURCES

The Center for Commercial-Free Public Education

The Center for Commercial-Free Public Education offers great information and actions you can take to decommercialize your school. Their website includes sample press releases, letters to the editor, a resolution against commercialism in schools and many other great resources to assist you.

⌨ www.ibiblio.org/commercialfree

Campaign For A Commercial-Free Childhood

CCFC is a coalition of parents, educators, and health care professionals dedicated to opposing marketing directed towards kids. Their site offers very useful information and tools to help you mount your own campaign against consumerism, violence, sex, and junk food targeted at children.

(617) 278-4172   🖥 www.commercialexploitation.com

✏ ACTION: Create safe schools

Unfortunately, violence in our schools has become all too common. Although school shootings make the news, fistfights and intimidation happen more frequently. Sharp divisions between social cliques lead to verbal harassment, hazing, bullying and feelings of isolation. Differences in social class, race, ethnicity, gender and sexual orientation make certain students especially vulnerable.

Many proactive schools are implementing violence prevention plans. Talk to your local school's principal to make sure your school has such a program. Refer administrators to the following resources and consider offering your help. By starting a violence prevention project, you could literally be saving lives.

As adults, we need to ensure our schools are safe spaces for all students. It seems that the last group it is acceptable to harass and slander is lesbians, gays, bisexuals and transgendered (LGBT) people. Students hear an average of 25 anti-gay slurs each day. LGBT youth have a three-to-seven times higher rate of attempted suicide than other youth.[4] Make certain that your local school is taking action to curb this kind of violence.

➪ VIOLENCE PREVENTION RESOURCES

Teaching Tolerance
The Southern Poverty Law Center's Teaching Tolerance Program is one of the most exciting education-based programs dealing with issues of equality, respect and understanding. They offer a wide variety of free books, magazines, videos and tool kits to educators and educational institutions that request them.
🖥 www.tolerance.org

Center for the Prevention of School Violence (CPSV)   SCHOOL VIOLENCE.
The CPSV provides current school violence research,   LET'S GET IT OUT OF OUR SYSTEM.
manuals for starting a Students Against Violence   Center for the Prevention of School Violence
Everywhere group, educational campaign materials and public awareness ideas.
(800) 299-6054   🖥 www.ncdjjdp.org/cpsv

Parents, Families, and Friends of Lesbians and Gays
(PFLAG)
PFLAG's Safe Schools program offers resources of all kinds. They offer concrete steps you can implement to make your schools a safe place for lesbian, gay, bisexual and transgendered youth.
(202) 467-8180   🖥 www.pflag.org

✏ ACTION: Support local arts and culture

Artists reflect the soul of a community and help celebrate its spirit. Folk musicians who play on the street corner downtown add flavor to the city. Summer arts festivals demonstrate the character of a town. Supporting local arts is often an inexpensive yet meaningful way to connect with members of your community and learn something new. Consider the following actions:

- Go to museums and visit galleries featuring local artists.
- Go to concerts in the park.
- Give money to street musicians.
- Buy artwork from a local artist.
- Attend dance performances, local plays and school productions.

VIRTUAL COMMUNITIES

The next generation of community building is already here, and it's online. Whether it's through internet gaming, blogs, forums or chat rooms, people are connecting from all over the globe through the web. While it's important to be aware of scammers, spammers and product-pushing companies masking as individuals, these virtual arenas are fast becoming a critical form of connecting to people who share interests, locale or past connections. They can also be a great way to organize a group of people to take action on an important issue or even jointly write a book (like this one)!

MySpace: www.myspace.com
Tribe: www.tribe.net
Zaadz: www.zaadz.com (a better world MySpace)

ACTION: Participate in local, county, regional and statewide community events

Attend community celebrations, ethnic festivals, pow-wows, county and state fairs, music and arts festivals, community fundraisers, and street dances. It's a great way to get to know people beyond your immediate area and to discover which issues are important in their community. These events create an opportunity for a community's unique character to emerge. Plus a little creativity and fun is good for the soul!

ACTION: Get involved in your sister city program

Sister city relationships build global community by sharing cultures and ideas, building cooperation, and creating opportunities for sustainable development. Cities in different countries pair up in long-term relationships; people from one city often exchange business and visit others in their sister city. Many cities have sister city relationships with multiple cities in different parts of the world — a great way to form meaningful international relationships. Given the strained relationships between the West and the Middle East, partnering with a city in Iraq, Iran, Syria, or another country in the region would be an especially powerful opportunity. Sister churches are similar. Almost every major religious denomination in the

PEN PALS

Having a pen pal is a great way to make a connection with someone from another culture. Email makes having pen pals easier than ever.

United States has a sister church program, which creates close relationships in the lives of church members across nations. Contact your local churches for more information. To help start a sister city program in your area or to get involved in one that's already established, contact:

> Sister Cities International
> 🖳 www.sister-cities.org
> 🖳 www.supportsistercities.org

Students of the world: This site connects students and teachers from all over the world. It also has educational material about each country, including geography, economy, politics, and climate. A great resource to learn about other nations! 🖳 www.studentsoftheworld.info

COMMUNITY ISSUES

Tired of roads in your neighborhood that are laden with potholes? Sick of a school system that cut your kid's band program? Curious about who decides how much money to allocate for city parks? Find out what decisions your community leaders are making, and let your voice be heard! Local politics has much more of a direct impact on your life than national politics, and you can have more impact at this level, as well.

When most people think of politics, they think of the President and the Congress, but many important decisions are made right at home within your city and county governments. Actually, local governments provide the most important forum for issues such as urban growth, open space protection, education, and transit. Local ordinances and planning have a profound impact on the quality of life in your community. Your involvement in local politics gives you a wide range of opportunities to improve your community for yourself and everyone else.

- Write a letter to the editor.
- Talk to friends and family about livable community issues.
- Collect petitions.
- Attend a city council meeting, school board meeting, or public hearing.

To find out when and where city council or school board meetings are, check the community events listing of your local newspaper or look in the local government section in the phone book and give city hall a call.

ACTION: Stop urban sprawl

If you've ever been in a metropolitan area, you've probably noticed how the city goes on and on and on, consuming surrounding open space and leaving a trail of Wal-Marts and Pizza Huts in its wake. For the past 50 years, development has spread unchecked, leaving us with irresponsible, frustrating urban sprawl. Sprawl destroys open space, increases traffic congestion, adds to pollution, costs taxpayers billions of dollars in subsidies and steals our community's identity. You can fight sprawl by advocating responsible, smart growth that considers the environment and the community before profits. Don't forget that the flip side of stopping sprawl is actively creating a more livable community that people can enjoy for generations to come.

- Join Sierra Club's Stop Sprawl campaign. Find their stopping sprawl tool kit at: www.sierraclub.org/sprawl.

- Attend a city council meeting and demand that policymakers stop unchecked growth.

- Ask your local government to support public transportation rather than build more roads.

> People around the world are wising up to the drawbacks of sprawl. Norway instituted a moratorium on the construction of suburban malls for five years to encourage inner city renovations.[5]

- Support unique local businesses over big cookie-cutter chains.

- Support public parks, open space, and local wildlife.

- Encourage the development of bike paths, pedestrian-only streets, traffic-calming devices, and mixed-use development.

Sprawl Watch Clearinghouse (SWC)

SWC compiles resources and serves as a net-work for grassroots groups fighting sprawl. They feature a list of national organizations and up-to-date information about what's happening in your area.

(202) 332-7000 🖳 www.sprawlwatch.org

Streets for People

Streets for People is a how-to manual people can use to bring traffic calming to their neighborhood. Download it in its electronic form for free.

(212) 629-8080 🖳 www.transalt.org/info/streets4people/index.html

☞ ACTION: Advocate for affordable housing

The lack of affordable housing is one of our biggest challenges. Wages are not keeping up with increasing housing costs. In 1999, the National Low Income Housing Coalition found that in no local jurisdiction in the US could a full-time worker making minimum wage afford the Fair Market Rent for a one-bedroom apartment in her or his community. In fact, in 70 metropolitan areas, minimum wage workers would have to work over 100 hours each week to afford Fair Market Rent in their city![6] By advocating affordable housing in your area, you will join a movement that is dedicated to ensuring economic diversity and the fundamental human right of adequate housing. To find out how to demand affordable housing, check out the resources below.

National Low Income Housing Coalition (NLIHC)

NLIHC educates and organizes people to create affordable housing. Their informative publications influence policy.

(202) 662-1530   🖳 www.nlihc.org

NATIONAL LOW INCOME
HOUSING COALITION/LIHIS

Local and State Affordable Housing Programs

To find affordable housing programs and homeless assistance providers for your state and community, contact the Department of Housing and Urban Development at (202) 708-1112 or www.hud.gov/offices/cpd/ for listings and information. Your state or city office of housing can also be helpful, as can your local Public Housing Authority.

⬛ ACTION: Advocate for a community living wage

Living wage campaigns rest on the premise that hard-working people should be paid enough to support themselves and their families. It's that simple. The income gap between the rich and the poor has soared in the past 20 years, and executive salaries have skyrocketed. In contrast, the average worker in 1998 made 12% less in real wages than in 1973. And for the most vulnerable members of your community, the minimum wage still provides less buying power than it did in the early 1980s. A minimum wage increase would benefit the over ten million families who are trying to get by on meager incomes.[7] Fortunately, community activists are taking matters into their own hands, instead of waiting for Washington to help support poor families. A San Francisco living wage ordinance passed in 2000 guarantees wage increases and benefits for over 21,500 workers who contract with the city. Minimum standards are $9 per hour with a 2-1/2% raise per year; health insurance; and vacation, sick and family leave time.[8] With your support, your community can join 120 cities and counties across the US that have enacted living wage ordinances since 1994.[9]

ACORN

ACORN is a very active coalition of community groups dedicated to creating affordable and livable communities. They also happen to be the major force behind local living wage laws. Local branches in dozens of cities organize people into powerful voices for change.

(202) 547-2500   🖳 www.acorn.org

⬛ ACTION: Advocate for increased school funding

Virtually every politician who runs for office gives lip service to education, yet few take meaningful action towards improving our children's education. Americans consistently place education at the top of their priority lists, and a vast majority of us believe the government needs to increase funding to our schools. Each of us benefits when all kids receive quality education, regardless of whether they're our own kids or not. Money alone won't solve every school's problems, but lack of resources is severely hindering children's educations. Our leaders need to hear loud and clear that repairing dilapidated school buildings and buying textbooks is more important than building a new fleet of fighter planes or giving tax breaks to corporations. When a local bond proposal to fund schools comes up for a vote, make sure to campaign and vote for it. This is a great issue about which to make your voice heard at the local, state, and federal levels of government.

National Education Association (NEA)
The NEA advocates for school funding, better teaching, and fair teaching contracts. They also fight attempts to privatize public schools.
(202) 833-4000   💻 www.nea.org

⇨ COMMUNITY RESOURCES

📖 Shaffer, Carolyn R., and Kristin Anundsen. *Creating Community Anywhere: Finding Support and Connection in a Fragmented World.* G.P. Putnam, 1993. This great how-to manual offers insights on how to create meaningful community and reclaim our connection to something larger than ourselves. It also offers tips on communication and tools applicable to a variety of communities, including your family and friends, your neighborhood and your workplace.

📖 James, Sarah and Torbjörn Lahti. *The Natural Step for Communities: How Cities and Towns can Change to Sustainable Practices.* New Society Publishers, 2004. It provides inspiring examples of communities that have made dramatic changes toward sustainability, and explains how to implement these changes in your own community.

📖 Roseland, Mark. *Toward Sustainable Communities: Resources for Citizens and Their Governments.* Updated and revised edition. New Society Publishers, 2005. Offers practical suggestions and innovative solutions to a range of community problems—including energy efficiency, transportation, land use, housing, waste reduction, recycling, air quality and governance.

📖 Chiras, Dan and Dave Wann. *Superbia! 31 Ways to Create Sustainable Neighborhoods.* New Society Publishers, 2003. A book of practical ideas for remaking suburban and urban neighborhoods to serve people better and to reduce human impact on the environment.

📣 American Independent Business Alliance. www.amiba.net, (406) 582-1255. AMIBA is a national network of local, independent businesses associations that provides a variety of resources to support the creation and growth of IBA's. They offer an IBA startup kit with everything you need to begin in your own community for $20. They will also come and give a professional presentation or workshop in your town to really get things moving.

SPIRITUALITY AND RELIGION

Spiritual Well-Being
Faith In Action
Religious Community
Spiritual and Religious Groups

NO MATTER HOW MUCH our world changes, one factor that stays the same is the
human desire to connect to the eternal, the everlasting, and to something greater
than ourselves, that which many of us call God. Our desire for spiritual wholeness
connects us to all of the human family, to past generations, and to all living beings.
Our search for spiritual truth is the attempt to transcend our own limited consciousness and tap into the energy that ties all life together, providing a oneness to everything
that exists. This spiritual connection is the basis for love, compassion and community.

Unfortunately, throughout much of human history, this thirst to know eternal truths and connect with the divine has often been warped into a desire for
power and absolute knowledge. Practitioners too often use religion to distinguish
between the "good" people and the "bad" people, using dogma to legitimate discrimination and to shield themselves from those who are different. This history
leads some who desire a better world to abandon and even scorn religious people.

Yet religious passion can move peacemakers to put their lives on the line for
social justice. People of faith have formed the backbone of many of the most
powerful and successful movements for peace and justice around the world.
Mahatma Gandhi, Martin Luther King Jr., Rosa Parks, Dorothy Day, Jimmy
Carter, Oscar Romero, Mother Theresa and many others all proclaimed a moral
vision guided by their strong religious faith. Today, spirituality once again unites
many social movements as people of faith come together to fight against AIDS
and global poverty (Jubilee, the One campaign, Bread for the World), war and
violence (Muslim Peace Fellowship, Jewish Peace Fellowship), global warming
(Evangelical Environmental Network, National Religious Partnership for the

Environment) and homelessness (Habitat for Humanity).

At its best, spirituality joins us with others to celebrate that which is most important, that which is much larger than any one of us can express. It allows us to seek wisdom, comfort, and a sense of deep meaning in our daily lives. It also provides avenues for us to help those in need in our communities—those who are grieving the loss of loved ones, those who lack food and shelter. Our desire to deeply connect can be the most powerful force for good.

In this chapter you will learn how your own spiritual journey can be both personally sustaining and a catalyst for making a better world. The chapter includes ways to foster your own spiritual well being, ideas for putting faith into action, and resources for building bridges between religious groups.

SPIRITUAL WELL-BEING

Spiritual growth is a lifelong process of enhancing one's self-awareness and under-standing at a deep level one's place in the world. Cultivating inner peace enhances our daily experiences and enables us to fully experience the joys and wonders of life. This wholeness allows us to live authentic lives that emanate from deep with-in us and prepares us to live balanced lives while making the world a better place.

Despite our many scientific advances and new conveniences, for the most part we're no happier than people fifty years ago. Knowledge alone will not make the world a better place. We need wisdom to guide our knowledge and direct our energies to where they are most needed. Pursuing spiritual well-being prepares us to reorient our lives around the virtues of peace, justice, humility, service, and compassion. These virtues allow us to fully grasp the needs of others and moti-vate us to address our social and environmental challenges.

ACTION: Center yourself

Centering is the practice of mindfulness, a way of paying attention to the moment. It is calming, rejuvenating, and balancing — not some weird religious activity practiced by people who want to escape the world. It's simply an easy way to bring yourself back into balance. Although there is no right way to center yourself, some general principles are helpful:

- Stillness: Choose an area or room where you will be comfortable sitting still and where there's not a lot of activity around you.
- Quiet: If possible, choose a quiet place where you won't be interrupted.
- Deep breathing: Focus on your breathing. Keep your mouth slightly open, breathe in slowly through your nose, hold it for a second or two, then slowly let the breath out through your mouth.
- Affirmation/focus: Some people like to focus on one particular thought or image, such as love, God, or silence. Others repeat a meaningful phrase (mantra) in their heads.

- Emptying the mind: It's nearly impossible to free your mind of all thought, but with practice you can come close. Let your thoughts, any thoughts, come and go as they please. Always return your focus to your breath or mantra.

You can center yourself wherever you are. Some people practice rush hour centering during their commutes. Throughout the day, especially during particularly stressful times, you may want to take brief, calming breaks where you stop what you're doing, close your eyes, and take several deep breaths. Centering time can be one minute or an hour or more. A focused mind and relaxed spirit will substantially improve your day.

ACTION: Foster your spiritual core

Spirituality has always been a vital part of human existence. It deepens our self-awareness, connects us with something outside of ourselves, and gives meaning and direction to our actions. Building a sustained, robust spiritual life takes time and energy and it doesn't just happen by accident. It can be a real challenge to find clarity in the chaos of our daily lives. Taking time to nourish yourself as a spiritual person allows you to look deep within yourself to find out who you are at your core. This awareness can center you in your basic values and serve as an uncontainable force that emanates through all areas of your life. Fostering your spiritual core will embolden you to be who you are meant to be and help you to uncover your fundamental connections to life around you.

- Build a regular time for rest and enjoyment into your busy day.
- Take a hike, focusing specifically on the interconnectedness of life around you.
- Practice prayer, bodywork (e.g., Tai Chi, yoga), and/or meditation.
- Volunteer for a local organization, with the clear intention of making a deep connection with those you help.
- Look for the divine, the sacred, and the humanity in every person.

ASK YOURSELF TIMELESS QUESTIONS

Many questions have been important to humans for eons. These questions form the foundation of our search for wisdom, making them a logical place to start. They give direction, meaning, and motivation to our lives.

- Why is there suffering in the world?
- What is my purpose in life? Why am I here?
- What does it mean to live a "good life"?
- What would I regret if I died today?
- Is there a power greater than us?
- What is my responsibility to my fellow human beings?
- What is my responsibility to animals and the Earth?

- Cherish the wonder and miracle of life.
- Appreciate the cycle of life and death.
- Gather with others and support each other's spiritual quests.
- Turn to a trustworthy person for spiritual guidance and resources.

ACTION: Practice gratitude

It is easy for our daily frustrations to overwhelm our lives — our cell phone runs out of batteries, we wake up feeling ill, the person behind the counter mixes up our food order. While we all encounter significant struggles in our lives, these minor inconveniences and unexpected setbacks derail our well-being because we work under the assumption that we deserve to have our entire day go "just as we planned." Rather than expecting to never be frustrated, try waking up and being grateful for all that you have, whether it's healthy lungs, a good friend, and a job that pays the bills. Starting off in a mindset of gratitude allows us to celebrate the little everyday joys of life and opens up our souls to the needs of others around us. A simple prayer in the morning or before dinner can break us out of our hectic routines and remind us that many in the world go without daily sustenance. Something as simple as "thank you for the food before us, the family beside us, and the love between us" can be very powerful. Other ideas include keeping a "gratitude journal," reminding ourselves at the end of every night the best part of our day, and repeating a grateful mantra when we wake up (e.g., "I'm happy to be alive").

ACTION: Practice religious tolerance

Most would agree that the world's religions share the intention to enhance life and peaceful relations with others. Believing one's faith has all of the answers, is always right, or is the only "true" expression of spirituality, leads down a dangerous road. Fundamentalism tempts us to dismiss or even dehumanize those who hold different beliefs. Deeply-rooted faith can be a source of spiritual comfort and strength, but without tolerance it can lead to close-minded bitterness.

When we think of fundamentalism we typically think of "right wing" Christian denominations or radical Muslims who wish violence on the West. However, fundamentalism can be present all along the political spectrum. Many generally tolerant, progressive people look at religious conservatives with scorn, deriding their supposedly "backward" beliefs. While we should oppose intolerance in any form, including that preached by religious figures, responding with intolerance is no solution. By practicing religious tolerance you open up the possibility of dialogue and understanding. Being truly open to the experiences and beliefs of others does not mean that you need to discard your own deeply-held values. It means to focus on the gifts of others who are different and to celebrate the value of mutual respect.

Action: Learn about other religions and spiritualities

Misinformation, half-truths, and stereotypes make us susceptible to religious intolerance and potentially lead to discrimination or violence. Given the ongoing conflicts in the world, it seems especially essential that Christians and Muslims make a strong effort to learn about and from one another. Both faiths share an emphasis on peace and tolerance that is not reflected in the wars and violence perpetrated by a few. When we take the time to learn about other faiths in depth, we often find we have much in common, a basis for building understanding and cooperation towards our common goals. Understanding and tolerance between religions begins with simply getting to know one another.

- Visit a religious service different from your own.
- Study the sacred texts of other religions.
- Check out Beliefnet and other educational websites.
- Form a pen pal relationship with a person from another faith (see the COMMUNITY chapter).
- Invite people of a different faith over for dinner.
- If you belong to a religious community, try exchanging a few members with another community for one week's service, or hosting a joint celebration, pot luck, or educational event.

Beliefnet
This site offers an abundance of information about a variety of religions, discussions of current events, and summaries of research on religion. A great place to learn about religion, science, politics, health and spirituality.

   🖥 www.beliefnet.org

ACTION: Read a book of wisdom

Sometimes it seems as though each generation attempts to create its own moral system from scratch, as if previous generations had little to offer. In fact, many wise people have pondered significant human questions for thousands of years. We don't have to start over; we can add to their accumulated wisdom.

You don't have to be a follower of a certain religion or belief system to benefit from its teachings. In fact, the commonalties among the world's major faiths are astounding. For example, many faiths address the perils of over-consumption:

Buddhist: "Whoever in this world overcomes his selfish cravings, his sorrows fall away from him, like drops of water from a lotus flower" (Dhammapada, 336).

Islamic: "Poverty is my pride" (Muhammad).

Christian: It is "easier for a camel to go through the eye of a needle than for a rich man to enter the kingdom of God" (Matthew 19:23-24).

Confucian: "Excess and deficiency are equally at fault" (Confucius, XI.15).

Hindu: "That person who lives completely free from desires, without longing ... attains peace" (Bhagavad-Gita, II.71).

Jewish: "Give me neither poverty nor riches" (Proverbs 30:8).

Taoist: "He who knows he has enough is rich" (Tao Te Ching, Chapter 33).

American Indian: "Miserable as we seem in thy eyes, we consider ourselves ... much happier than thou, in this that we are very content with the little that we have" (Micmac chief).

Take the time to read, ponder, and discuss with others some of the ideas in these books:

Baghavad-Gita. The Baghavad-Gita is one of the main Hindu spiritual texts. Written in verse form, it chronicles a discussion between the warrior Arjuna and Krishna, a Hindu deity. "For him who has conquered the mind, the mind is the best of friends; but for one who has failed to do so, his mind will remain the greatest enemy."[1]

Tao Te Ching. Written by Lao-Tzu over 2,500 years ago, the Tao or The Way offers incredibly profound insights into increasing one's spiritual level of being and harmony with the universe. "Nothing in the world is as soft and yielding as water. Yet for dissolving the hard and inflexible, nothing can surpass it. The soft overcomes the hard; the gentle overcomes the rigid. Everyone knows this is true, but few can put it into practice."[2]

Bible. The most sacred book of the Christian faith, the Bible offers a variety of insights in its many verses, including powerful thoughts on love, forgiveness, judgment, greed and faith. "Love your enemies, do good to those who hate you, bless those who curse you, pray for those who mistreat you. If someone strikes you on one cheek, turn to him the other also."[3]

Koran. The Muslim Koran uses lessons and stories of past communities to illustrate great moral teachings on many aspects of life. It discusses law, rights and obligations, and social concerns. "Seest thou one who denies the Judgment (to come)? Then such is the (one) who repulses the orphan, and encourages not the feeding of the indigent. So woe to the worshippers who are neglectful of their prayers, those who (want but) to be seen, but refuse (to supply) (even) neighborly needs."[4]

Torah. As the Jewish holy book, the Torah teaches about the power of tradition, community, compassion, and a deep love of God. "Surely you should divide your bread with the hungry, and bring the poor to your home; when you see the naked, cover him; and do not ignore your kin."[5]

FAITH IN ACTION

While it's easy to fall into the trap of self-absorbed spirituality, true spiritual practice must move beyond feeding our own egos, casting judgment and making ourselves feel superior. "Navel gazing" can lead us to put our own lives at the center of the universe. Our religious communities should never be merely country clubs where we show off our well-behaved and well-dressed children. A truly engaged spirituality engages our inner lives as well as the needs of others across the globe. Rather than being an escape from the world, spirituality can be an avenue to reengage. Truly meaningful spiritual discovery combines both self-awareness and social transformation.

All of the world's major religions call upon their followers to put their faith into action, compelling people to put their lives on the line against tyranny and injustice, help the sick, and shelter the homeless. Faith in peace, kindness, justice and compassion led abolitionists to fight against slavery, Thich Nhat Hanh to promote "engaged Buddhism" in opposition to the Vietnam War, Mother Teresa to work among India's poor, Shirin Ebadi to fight for women and children's rights in Iran, and Archbishop Oscar Romero to stand up to death squads in El Salvador.

Putting one's faith into action means embracing the principle of agape (ah-GAH-pay). Agape is an abundant, overflowing love for all of humanity — not just for our loved ones but for strangers, neighbors, enemies, those of different ethnic groups and nations. It is a form of love that expects nothing in return. It leads to compassionate action not because the recipient "deserves" it but because they are in need.

ACTION: Live your life as a prayer

How would your life change if you lived your life as a prayer? Living out spiritual faith is difficult, particularly with all of the distractions modern society offers. Living your life as a prayer means asking how your faith could influence everyday decisions, big or small, as you set a loving, peaceful, and powerful example for others. It is putting your spiritual hopes and desires for a better world into action, in both simple and profound ways. Throughout the book, we explore ways to integrate different aspects of our life based upon our fundamental values. The same principle applies to spirituality. Ask yourself how you can live out love, peace, forgiveness, mercy, and justice on a daily basis, thus living and being your spirituality. Applying faith to daily decisions can be a powerful way to both change the world and live a spiritual life. Consider these questions:

- How might your faith guide you in purchasing a car? Buying a home? Choosing a bank? Investing your savings?
- How could your faith inform your dinner choices?
- How might your religion encourage you to share your resources?
- What about how you get to work? The type of work you choose?
- Which teachings could you apply to your daily interactions with people?
- If you like, you can view every action in this book as an opportunity to live your life as a prayer.

 ACTION: Feed, clothe, and house the poor

Religious institutions have a long history of reaching out to those in need. Many groups regularly volunteer at soup kitchens, food banks, and homeless shelters. During winter, some churches offer their building to shelters as overflow sleeping space for people who are homeless. Contact your local aid organizations and find out how to get involved. Avoid proselytizing — demonstrate your faith through your actions, not your words. Your efforts will not only help people in need, they will foster spiritual growth in your faith community.

Both of the organizations below offer numerous ways you and your community can get involved.

The ONE Campaign
The One campaign is a coalition of faith-based and anti-poverty groups dedicated to fighting AIDS and hunger.
    💻 www.one.org

Bread for the World
Bread for the World is a Christian organization that lobbies the US government to put resources towards ending hunger worldwide.
    💻 www.bread.org

Bread for the World
Seeking Justice. Ending Hunger.
www.bread.org

ACTION: Reclaim "morality"

Unfortunately, morality now has a very narrow religious and political definition: opposition to gay marriage, abortion, stem cell research, and so called "activist" judges, paired with support for school prayer, the death penalty, and abstinence-only sex education. People of faith have a long history of fighting for a broader set of moral issues: opposing war and violence, helping the poor and oppressed, and reaching out with compassion to those in need. We need to take back the notion of morality, demanding a broader discussion of morality from politicians and religious leaders.

We can speak in moral terms within our communities by asking moral questions:
- Is it moral to give large tax cuts to the wealthiest Americans during a time of war and recovery after Hurricane Katrina?
- Is it moral that 40 million Americans, many of them children, cannot afford health insurance?
- Is it moral that children born to impoverished parents have less access to a good education?
- Is it moral to marginalize people based on their gender, race, or sexual identity?

ACTION: Start a peace and justice group in your spiritual community

Spiritual faith and organized religious groups have played a remarkable role in making the world a better place. The civil rights movement achieved remarkable successes in the 1950s in large part because it built upon the solid foundations of the black church. There are many ways to get your religious community involved. Many people start a peace and justice group within their larger faith community, giving interested members an opportunity to combine their efforts. Here are a few ideas:

- Support a battered women's shelter in your community.
- Conduct a prayer vigil for peace in a public space or outside a government building.
- Plan a Witness for Peace delegation from your temple, mosque, or church (www. witnessforpeace.org).
- Get involved in the Jubilee movement for debt forgiveness (www. jubileeusa.org).
- Sponsor a food, clothing, gift, or blood drive during the holidays.

POLITICAL ISSUES WHERE PEOPLE OF FAITH ARE MAKING A DIFFERENCE	
Debt Forgiveness and HIV/AIDS	The Jubilee movement, The One campaign
Peace and Justice	Ploughshares, Witness for Peace, and Christian Peacemaker Teams
Hunger	Bread for the World, Lutheran World Relief, Mennonite Central Committee
Environmental Issues	Evangelical Environmental Network, Earth Ministry

RELIGIOUS AND SPIRITUAL COMMUNITY

Joining a spiritual community, whether a mosque, temple, synagogue, meditation circle, church, Buddhist study group, or yoga group can be a fulfilling way to cultivate inner peace, build spiritual connections, and work towards a better world. In our increasingly individualistic culture even spirituality can become an isolating, private affair. Participating in a spiritual community allows us to engage on a regular basis with a group of likeminded people, providing a sense of home where we can be inspired, motivated, nurtured and challenged. These communities also ingrain a sense that we are not alone as we experience spiritual challenges related to death, misfortune, or disappointment. Spiritual communities also concentrate and focus the compassion and resources of tens or hundreds of people — a critical mass capable of social transformation.

GANDHI'S SEVEN SOCIAL SINS

Wealth without Work

Pleasure without Conscience

Science without Humanity

Knowledge without Character

Politics without Principle

Commerce without Morality

Worship without Sacrifice

Learn more at gandhiInstitute.org

ACTION: Join a progressive religious group

Learning, communing, meditating, or worshipping together is a very powerful experience. Many of us find comfort and personal growth in spiritual communities. They are often a great way to become involved in community and global issues, from working at a soup kitchen to sending aid to countries devastated by natural disasters.

Most denominations have both conservative and progressive branches. Every sect is home to people with vastly different interpretations of scripture and faith. How do you tell if a community is right for you? You can start by doing a little research, visiting different communities, and gradually asking some simple questions:

- Are women permitted and encouraged to be leaders?
- Are people of all races, social classes, and sexualities welcome?
- Is there a focus on combining spiritual fulfillment and making the world a better place?
- What is the mission statement? What are the core values?
- Is there space for congregants to question the community's beliefs? Is there room for diversity of opinion?

Few spiritual communities will live up to all of these ideals; it's up to you to determine your priorities. Remember that you can be an agent of change in whatever community you choose.

PROGRESSIVE SPIRITUALITY/RELIGION

A progressive religious faith:
- Opposes preemptive war.
- Avoids scapegoating less privileged/powerless groups (e.g., gays/lesbians, the poor, immigrants, single mothers) for societal ills.
- Supports policies that promote a fair distribution of wealth.
- Focuses on social responsibility in addition to personal morality.
- Is open to a variety of viewpoints on social issues.
- Combines worship, meditation and praise with a call to make a real difference in the world.
- Works with members of other spiritual traditions.
- Promotes and works towards some form of the Seven Foundations of a Better World.

ACTION: Join or create a spiritual study group

Religion and spirituality have something to teach us about every issue we struggle with in our world. Your group might apply a spiritual perspective on war, poverty, or the environment. You could read and discuss one of the books listed at the end of this chapter. Some faith groups have even used *The Better World Handbook* as a study tool!

- Teach a class on nonviolent peacemaking or parenting.
- Create a "spirituality and the earth" group to discuss sustainable living.
- Work together on a comparative religion class where you study a variety of faith perspectives.
- Lead a class focusing on scriptural studies of poverty and wealth; try serving fair trade coffee (see the FOOD chapter).
- Lead a study group on the perils of consumerism and the benefits of simple living (www.simpleliving.org).

Fellowship of Reconciliation

FOR is an interfaith organization that has promoted peace and justice for nearly 100 years. Their site contains many articles and resources to keep your study group engaged and busy.

   💻 www.forusa.org

ACTION: Cherish diversity in your spiritual community

Prophets and religious leaders have a history of taking unpopular positions and standing up with marginalized and outcast groups, be they prostitutes, tax collectors, or the sick. While many faiths make a commitment to open their doors to all, some continue to discriminate against women, lesbians and gay men. However, nearly every religious denomination, from Evangelical to Jewish, Catholic to Muslim, Hindu to Presbyterian, has gay-friendly and pro-women organizations. More and more groups are taking a stand for equal rights. By helping create a religious community that cherishes diversity you make a safe space for gays and lesbians, promote equality for women, and set a powerful, loving example for others.

Religious communities often cherish tradition and are slow to change. Thinking you can change beliefs overnight will only end in conflict, bad feelings, and frustration. Start small; talk with others in your community you trust. Like most significant change, this may be a slow process that requires patience and perseverance (and faith!).

Human Rights Campaign

Click on HRC's "Religion and Faith" button for news (and a newsletter), articles, and resources for creating an inclusive spiritual community.

   💻 www.hrc.org

ACTION: Make your religious facility environmentally friendly

One of the simplest ways to follow a spiritual call to honor the earth is to make your religious facility earth-friendly. Many of the ideas from the HOME and WORK chapters are applicable in your religious facility: compact fluorescent lights, Energy Star appliances, recycling, composting, using recycled paper and so on. Consider talking to your facility's building committee about these issues. You could even start an "environmental committee" at your place of worship.

Most spiritual traditions call upon their followers to cherish the earth, and a little effort goes a long way towards living out your faith.

National Religious Partnership for the Environment
NRPE is a coalition of faith groups that offer a religious perspective on the environment and practical ideas toward sustainable living. Visit their site for faith-based environmental handbooks and to learn how you and your community can get involved.

💻 www.nrpe.org

FAIR TRADE COFFEE

If your religious community brews coffee for fellowship time consider using fairly traded coffee. Fair trade coffee is a simple but powerful way to demonstrate your community's commitment to social justice by ensuring that growers receive a livable wage.

💻 www.lwr.org/coffee/getstarted.asp.

FAIR TRADE
CERTIFIED
Look for this Label!

ACTION: Form coalitions with other faiths

Imagine millions of Christians, Jews, Buddhists, and Muslims coming together both for fellowship and to make the world a better place — that would be an unstoppable force! Signs of cooperation are emerging. During the run-up to the invasion of Iraq, diverse religious groups from all over the world united in their opposition to preemptive war. While the Bush administration didn't listen, the anti-war movement formed powerful coalitions among people of many faiths. War isn't the only issue to bring diverse groups together. Many traditionally conservative evangelical leaders are backing a major push to combat global warming, working with progressive leaders and activists despite their other differences.[6] The opportunities for spirituality to be a positive force for change are endless. Reach out to other spiritual groups in your community.

Interfaith Alliance
The Interfaith Alliance brings together people of many faiths to advocate for democracy, tolerance, and civic involvement.

💻 www.interfaithalliance.org

United Religions Initiatives
URI promotes "enduring, daily interfaith cooperation" and create "cultures of peace."  Their Cooperation Circles & Peacebuilding Guides are helpful resources for building bridges between religions.

💻 www.uri.org

Network of Spiritual Progressives
NSP works towards building a spiritual Left, challenging the religious right's "misuse" of religion, and eliminating the anti-religious bias in

liberal culture. Leader Rabbi Michael Lerner is building a movement dedicated to diversity, sustainability, and a values-based economy.

🖳 www.spiritualprogressives.org

☞ ACTION: Resist McDonaldized religion

At their best, religious communities grow and sustain our faith while challenging and inspiring us to live faithful lives. Unfortunately, like many aspects of our society, spirituality often succumbs to "McDonaldization" — we like our religion like we like our fast food: predictable, convenient, comfortable, and immediately satisfying with little effort or sacrifice on our part. "McReligion can easily lose its meaning and compromise its values in the quest to attract and satisfy "customers." Congregants may become "consumers," shopping for the most pleasing faith, stopping by a service to get their fix, and moving on without really putting down spiritual roots.

While every religious community can question consumerist religion, modern mega-churches, some of which house Starbucks coffee shops and can seat 16,000 congregants in a single service,[7] are especially vulnerable to "McDonaldization." While being able to serve more congregants seems like a good idea on the face of it, there are many advantages to smaller religious groups including more interaction with clergy and meaningful relationships with other congregants. Try these ideas:

- Interact with fellow practitioners outside of services.
- Make efforts to create meaningful community such as by taking meals to families.
- Volunteer as a youth leader, worship organizer, or in another role that invests you in the community.
- Choose a religious community where you will be more than just a face in the crowd.
- Take your faith leader out for lunch and get to know her/him.
- Balance feeling good with being spiritually challenged.
- Consider helping "plant" a new congregation rather than expanding your own.

SPIRITUAL AND RELIGIOUS GROUPS

By now you see that dozens of spiritual and religious groups are already fostering spiritual growth, bringing people together and making the world a better place. In this section we profile a few more. There are many ways to use the profiles we list here:

- Find a spiritual community in your area.
- Learn about a specific issue.
- Donate money.
- Gather resources and ideas for your own spiritual community.
- Build connections and community between faiths.

American Friends Service Committee

American Friends Service Committee is a Quaker organization working
for social and economic justice around the world. Members belong to a
variety of faiths, but all believe in the fundamental worth of every
human being. Through relief work, funding, education and lobbying,
AFSC pushes to create a new culture based on peace and justice rather than war
and exploitation. They are involved in almost any progressive cause you can
name. AFSC has a vibrant youth program that brings young people of different
nationalities together for service work.

    1501 Cherry Street, Philadelphia, PA 19102, USA.

    (215) 241-7000   💻 www.afsc.org

Christian Peacemaker Teams (CPT)

Faith compels members of Christian Peacemakers Teams to put their
bodies on the line for peace and justice and to mobilize their communities when they return home. CPT is a faith-based group supported by
the Mennonite Churches, Church of the Brethren, and Friends United
Meeting. Local groups send trained delegates to be a peaceful presence in hot
spots such as Gaza, Iraq, Hebron, Columbia, and Chechnya. CPT accepts invitations from non-violent grassroots organizations for longer stays as well, providing
delegates committed to a three-year service term to emergency situations such as
the Israel/Palestine conflict.

    P.O. Box 6508, Chicago, IL 60680, USA.

    (773) 277-0253   💻 www.cpt.org

The Fellowship of Reconciliation (FOR)

The Fellowship of Reconciliation is the largest and oldest interfaith
organization dedicated to peace and justice. FOR not only pushes for
an end to war, it seeks to create a just and loving world. Members appreciate all
forms of diversity and use nonviolent means to challenge racism, sexism, homophobia, and religious persecution. Programs include demilitarization, peacemak-
er training, education, the lifting of sanctions on Iraq, monitoring human rights
abuses in Latin America, and much more. FOR tactics include nonviolent
demonstrations and direct actions, sending delegations to distress areas, and pressuring political leaders.

    P.O. Box 271, Nyack, NY 10960, USA.

    (914) 358-4601   💻 www.forusa.org

Mennonite Central Committee (MCC)

MCC "strives for peace, justice and the dignity of all people," working
among the poor, the oppressed, and victims of war and natural disasters.

    (717) 859-1151   💻 www.mcc.org

Ploughshares (Canada)

An ecumenical policy agency of the Canadian Council of Churches that works for a more just and peaceful world.

(519) 888-6541 💻 www.ploughshares.ca

Unitarian Universalist Association (UUA)

UUs are known for their tolerance of all religious traditions and work for social justice. Among their programs are promoting equal access to marriage, fighting genocide, and offering disaster relief.

(617) 742-2100 💻 www.uua.org

Progressive Muslim Union of North America

A grassroots organization that promotes "equal status and equal worth of all human beings, regardless of religion, gender, race, ethnicity, or sexual orientation."

(646) 485-1163 💻 www.pmuna.org

Interfaith Center on Corporate Responsibility (ICCR)

ICCR is a coalition of investors, including religious communities, that uses their economic power to encourage socially responsible and environmentally sustainable business practices. Their goals include reversing global warming, eliminating sweatshops, promoting affordable health care and opposing violent video games.

(212) 870-2295 💻 www.iccr.org

Pax Christi

A Catholic peace movement dedicated to opposing racism, working for human rights, and promoting nonviolent peacemaking around the world.

(814) 453-4955 💻 www.paxchristiusa.org

Baptist Peace Fellowship of North America (BPFNA)

BPFNA "gathers, equips, and mobilizes Baptists to build a culture of peace rooted in justice."

(704) 521-6051 💻 www.bpfna.org

School of the America's Watch (SOAW)

Begun by Catholic priest Fr. Roy Bourgeois, SOAW has struggled for over a decade to close the US Army School of the Americas, a facility located in Georgia that trains Latin American soldiers in counterinsurgency, torture and psychological warfare.

(202) 234-3440 💻 www.soaw.org

Evangelical Environmental Network

An evangelical ministry calling attention to global warming, air pollution, and other environmental issues. They publish *Creation Care* magazine and support the www.whatwouldjesusdrive.org campaign to reduce fuel consumption.

(202) 554-1955 💻 www.creationcare.org

Earth Ministry

The goal of Earth Ministry is "To inspire and mobilize the Christian Community to play a leadership role in building a just and sustainable future." The offer news, actions, and resources for individuals, congregations and religious leaders.

(206) 632-2426   www.earthministry.org

Alternatives for Simple Living

A treasure trove of Christian and secular resources on simple living and spiritual, social, and environmental consequences of consumerism. Consider distributing copies of Whose Birthday Is It, Anyway to remind people that Christmas is about much more than just presents.

www.simpleliving.org

Lutherans Concerned — "Reconciling in Christ" program

A "Christian Ministry affirming God's love for people of all sexual orientations and gender identities."

www.lcna.org/ric.shtm

Lutheran World Relief

Fights the underlying causes of poverty and advocates for fair trade, environmental protection, and disaster relief.

(800) LWR-LWR-2   www.lwr.org

Buddhist Peace Fellowship (BPF)

BPF in an international organization that applies the wisdom of Buddhist teachings to solving environmental justice, promoting human rights, and teaching peaceful living. They have a youth program and publish a journal called *Turning Wheel.*

(510) 655-6169   www.bpf.org

Soka Gakkai

A driving force behind the Earth Charter, Soka Gakkai is an international Buddhist organization dedicated to helping members create happy and peaceful lives.

(310) 260-8900   www.sgi-usa.org

Friends Committee on National Legislation (FCNL)

As the lobbying branch of the Quaker faith, FCNL pushes for nuclear disarmament, an end to the weapons trade, justice for Native Americans and reducing oil dependence.

(800) 630-1330   www.fcnl.org

Tikkun Community

Connected with the work of Rabbi Michael Lerner, the Tikkun Community is "an international community of people of many faiths calling for social justice and political freedom in the context of new structures of work, caring communities, and democratic social and economic arrangements."

(510) 644-1200   🖳 www.tikkun.org/community

Indigenous Environmental Network (IEN)

The IEN protects the "circle of life" by promoting environmental education, sustainable lifestyles, and economic justice and opposing environmental racism.

(218) 751-4967   🖳 www.ienearth.org/

Baha'i

A proactively tolerant faith, Baha'i calls for the eliminating all forms of prejudice, closing the gap between the poor and the wealthy, universal education and a sustainable balance between nature and technology.

(800) 22-UNITE   🖳 www.bahai.us

🖳 www.ca.bahai.org/index.en.cfm (Canada)

BAHÁ'Í FAITH

➡️ **RESOURCES**

Magazines

Title: *Sojourners*

Issues: 6 per year   Cost: $30/yr

Web: 🖳 www.sojourners.com

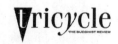

A Christian social justice magazine, *Sojourners* focuses on progressive social issues using the wisdom of the gospels. The authors refuse to separate "personal faith from social justice, prayer from peacemaking, contemplation from action, or spirituality from politics." The religious right is not the only group of Christians who have something to say. Compassion for the poor, persistence for justice, and hope for the future makes *Sojourners* a powerful magazine.

Title: *Tikkun*

Issues: 6 per year   Cost: $29/yr

Web: 🖳 www.tikkun.org

TIKKUN

Tikkun magazine is based on the Jewish principle of tikkun olam — the obligation to be involved in healing and transforming the world. This social justice magazine is deeply rooted in the wisdom of Judaism, while also emphasizing the connectedness of all human beings on the planet regardless of faith. It focuses on creating a world that is ethical, caring, just and ecologically sound. Michael Lerner, a well-known author and rabbi, is the editor.

Title: *Tricycle*

Issues: 6 per year   Cost: $29/yr

Web: 🖳 www.tricycle.com

Ⓥricycle
THE BUDDHIST REVIEW

Tricycle is an international review of all things Buddhist that prides itself on taking a lively, even-handed, non-dogmatic approach. It covers contemporary Buddhist ideas from every major tradition for a primarily Western audience. Whether you are interested in meditation, the Dalai Lama, or a Buddhist review of some of the latest movies to hit the theatres, *Tricycle* is the place to start.

Title: *The Christian Century*
Issues: 26 per year Cost: $49/yr
Web: 💻 www.christiancentury.org
With news stories and editorials about culture, politics, and theology, *The Christian Century* believes that "the Christian faith calls Christians to a profound engagement with the world — an engagement of both head and heart." It combines spiritual connectedness with humor and a good dose of critical thinking and has something to offer anyone with questions for how faith applies in our personal, family, and public lives.

Books

📖 Carter, Jimmy. *Our Endangered Moral Values: America's Moral Crisis.* Simon & Schuster, 2005. Former US president Jimmy Carter shares his insights politics, religion, and the relationship between the two. He warns against the trend towards fundamentalism in both spheres while calling for a progressive morality.

📖 Lerner, Michael. *The Left Hand of God: Taking Back Our Country from the Religious Right.* HarperSanFrancisco, 2006. Rabbi Lerner offers both a historical overview of religious history in the US and ideas for promoting a generous, loving, merciful, and just faith.

📖 Wallis, Jim. *God's Politics: Why the Right Gets It Wrong and the Left Doesn't Get It.* HarperCollins, 2005. Wallis explains how the religious right has promoted a very narrow religious agenda while the secular left too often dismisses the potential power of faith to create a better world. Wallis provides a spiritual response to war, global poverty, racial injustice, and terrorism. You might also want to check out the new edition of Wallis's classic *The Call to Conversion: Why Faith Is Always Personal but Never Private and Faith Works: How to Live Your Beliefs and Ignite Positive Social Change.*

📖 Schut, Michael, ed. *Simpler Living, Compassionate Life: a Christian Perspective.* Living the Good News, 1999. This great resource collects stories, analyses, prayers, and devotions that encourage readers to live a simpler life. Topics include time as a commodity, the role of money in modern life, and how our lifestyles connect with social justice. Includes a useful study guide for prayer and study groups.

Radio

Speaking of Faith with Krista Tippett
💻 speakingoffaith.publicradio.org
SoF is broadcast weekly on public radio stations around the country. Tippett conducts moving and in-depth interviews with influential spiritual and religious figures from around the globe on topics such as religious tolerance, spiritual meaning and personal growth. You can download all broadcasts as podcasts at the program's website.

SPIRITUAL CINEMA CIRCLE

Tired of shallow blockbusters at the movie theatre? Having trouble find-ing inspiring, meaningful movies at the video store? The people behind The Spiritual Cinema Circle think they might have the answer. Think of Netflix, except with hand-picked, award winning movies about spiri-tual and religious themes. For $21/month you get a DVD filled with some of the latest, most thoughtful, deeply moving films from around the world. And, its yours to keep or pass on to anyone you think might also be interested. Reinvent your television watching by using it as a tool for deep reflection.

💻 www.spiritualcinemacircle.com

HOME

Energy
Water
Trash
Lawn and Garden
Your Home

D<small>O YOU REMEMBER</small> your dad constantly reminding you to close the refrigerator or turn off the faucet? Or perhaps you recall your mom telling you to turn down the heat and put on a sweater to save energy. Our homes offer us great opportunities to conserve energy and water, as well as to reduce our trash. Many of us learned early on that conserving resources around our homes is important. Yet as adults our society encourages us to buy bigger and bigger houses that require unimaginable resources to construct and maintain.

In the past, many people settled in one place and lived there for 30 years or more. Their homes became almost sacred places, filled with the stories and memories of a lifetime. In today's highly mobile society, we've given up homes for houses — places in which to store our stuff and return for brief periods of rest between workdays.

The first half of the chapter addresses actions that save water and energy around the home. The rest of the chapter addresses typical home issues, such as recycling and composting, and maintaining a lawn and garden. Finally, we end with some tips on remodeling your current home and choosing where you want to live. Whether you live in an apartment, townhome, condo, or house, you'll learn many easy ways to make your home, and therefore the world, a better place.

ENERGY

Our grandparents knew a time when electricity was a luxury. Today, electricity is so convenient that it is easy to forget it is often produced by the burning of non-renewable, heavily polluting fossil fuels. Most of us are unaware of how generating energy affects the Earth, because to us the power just comes out of a socket in the wall. In our world of coal-fired plants and nuclear reactors, home energy conservation translates into cleaner air, cleaner water, a safeguard against global warming, and the preservation of habitat from strip-mining and drilling — in all, a more sustainable society. And it doesn't hurt that saving energy saves us money, too.

ACTION: Use your appliances efficiently and buy efficient appliances

When you are ready to purchase a new appliance, be sure to consider its impact on the environment. Most major appliances have clearly displayed "Energy Guide" stickers that make it easy to compare individual models' energy efficiency. Consider buying the appliance with the lowest energy usage that meets your needs. Just by installing energy-efficient appliances, you can save over 50% of your energy consumption as compared to standard models.[1] Remember that even if you have to pay extra for the energy-efficient model, it will pay you back every year in reduced energy bills. Before you buy a new appliance, check with your utility company for possible rebates on energy-efficient models.

Here are some easy tips for purchasing energy-efficient appliances and using your current appliances in a more efficient manner.

Heating Systems (The #1 User of Household Energy)

Heating our homes is an extremely energy-intensive endeavor. Efficient natural gas furnaces, pellet wood stoves, and electric space heaters (as a supplement) are great alternatives to inefficient electric furnaces and fireplaces. Ask for "high-efficiency" furnaces that earn an AFUE rating of 90% or higher (compared to the minimum standard of 78% efficient). For heat pumps, an HSPF rating of 7.5 or higher is considered "high efficiency"; the maximum available is 10.0. (6.8 minimum standard).[2]

Tips for use:
- Replace your furnace air filters every season and tune up your furnace annually.

THE ENERGY STAR PROGRAM

By designating the most energy-efficient appliance models as "Energy Stars" the Environmental Protection Agency (EPA) makes it easy for us to purchase energy-saving devices. When you are shopping for a new appliance, look for the Energy Star symbol directly on the item. If you want to make a thorough search for the most efficient appliance, check out the EPA's website. They rate household appliances, furnaces, air conditioners, office equipment, and windows.

💻 www.energystar.gov (888) STAR-YES

- Turn down your heater's thermostat to 65°F (18°C) during the day and 60°F (16°C) at night. Install a programmable thermostat to allow the heat to kick in right before you wake up and just before you come home. Energy savings from programmable thermostats can be 10%.[3]

- Let the sun heat your home. By opening your blinds during the day and closing them at night, you save energy by gaining the sun's warmth and keeping out unpleasant drafts.

Air Conditioners

Every year, the energy used to cool the average air-conditioned home equals about 13% of total household energy use. Fortunately, there are many ways to reduce your cooling energy. Consider alternatives or supplements to central air conditioners to cool your home including: a whole-house ventilating fan, ceiling fans, an evaporative cooler/swamp cooler (in arid climates), or room-size air conditioners (with an EER rating of at least 11). For central air conditioners, seek out Energy Star models with a SEER rating of at least 13 (17 is the highest available, with 10 being the minimum standard).

Tips for use:

- Set the A/C thermostat a little higher (78°F [25°C]) and turn it up even further any time you leave the house for more than a half hour. For each degree below 78°F you use eight percent more energy, and turning up your thermostat by 10-15°F when you're out can save you 5-15% on your energy bills.[4]

- Shut your windows and blinds during the hot parts of the day and open them at night. Night time ventilation is the most effective way to cool your house without using electricity.[5]

- Use heat-producing appliances such as the clothes dryer and oven only during cool parts of the day.

- Install an Energy Star ceiling fan. Ceiling fans use little energy. In hotter climates, they can allow you to raise your thermostat by 4°F (1.5°C).[6]

- Plant shade trees by hot spots, such as southwest-facing windows, or to provide shade for your air conditioning unit.

Water Heaters (The #2 User Of Household Energy)

Heating water consumes enormous amounts of energy. Conserving energy in this area involves reducing our hot water consumption and more efficiently heating the water we use. While buying an especially energy-efficient water heater may cost you a few hundred dollars more than a standard water heater, it will usually pay off the difference within 2-3 years of reduced energy bills.[7] When buying a gas-fired or electric water heater, look for energy-efficient models with an EF rating of at least .63 or .96, respectively. You may also want to consider a tankless on-demand water heater that heats water as you need it. An on-demand model uses 11-28% less energy because it doesn't run when no one is using hot water.[8] You'll also never run out of hot water! Call up any water heater dealer and ask about these energy-saving alternatives. You may even want to consider a solar water heating system. They are considerably more expensive (about $2500), but they pay huge dividends in reduced energy usage.

Tips for use:
- Install a water heater blanket/jacket and insulate the connecting pipes. A water heater blanket ($10-20) can pay for itself in energy savings in one year.[9]
- Turn down your water heater to 120°F (50° C) and even lower when you go on vacation.

Refrigerators (The #3 User of Household Energy)
The energy efficiency of refrigerators varies widely between models and brands — so be sure to compare Energy Guide stickers. The most important eco-tip is to buy the smallest refrigerator that meets your needs. Extra features often increase energy usage, too: a side-by-side refrigerator-freezer uses 10% more energy than a top-bottom model and automatic icemakers increase energy use by 10-20%.[10] Try to avoid running a second refrigerator; as the #3 user of household energy, having two (or more) refrigerators consumes a lot of power. If you purchase a new fridge, get rid of the old one rather than using it in the garage or basement. Older models are much less efficient than newer ones.

Dishwashers
When you are looking for a dishwasher, look for lower levels of water usage (most models use between 8 and 14 gallons [16 and 64 liters] of water each use).

Suggested brands:
Asko (from $700) dishwashers use only 5 gallons (23 liters) of water and save about 65% of the electricity usage of the standard dishwasher.
💻 www.askousa.com

Tips for use:
- Wash full loads.
- Use "light wash," "air dry," and other energy-saving cycles. If your dishwasher is relatively new, it can likely handle even dirty dishes without pre-rinsing — save the water and energy.

Washers and Dryers
Heating water uses 85-90% of the energy consumed during clothes washing.[11] That's why it's important to find models that use less water and allow you to use colder

temperatures. Front-loading washing machines use 30-60% less water and 50-70% less energy than top-loading models.[12] They are sometimes more expensive than conventional models, but over the life of the washer you'll save lots of water and money.

Suggested brands:
Asko, Equator, and Creda can use as little as 13 to 18 gallons (59 to 82 liters) per wash, significantly less than the conventional washer. Dryers with automatic moisture sensors save energy as they prevent the over-drying of clothes.

Tips for use:
- Wash and dry full loads of laundry.
- Wash your clothes in warm or cold water except for highly soiled fabrics. Always rinse in cold water.
- Let the sun dry your clothes (or put them on a drying rack).
- Don't over-dry your clothes.

ENERGY SMART COMPUTING

Here's a checklist of ways you can use your computer to save money and electricity while fighting global warming:
- Set your monitor to turn off after 10 minutes rather than going to a screen saver.
- Switch off your computer when not in use. Most computers use almost as much power when they are being used as when they are not. It will save energy and may lengthen the life of the computer. Very old computers used to suffer when being turned on and off all the time. That is no longer a problem.
- Set your computer to shut down automatically late at night just in case you forget.
- Switch from a standard cathode ray tube (CRT) monitor to a flatter liquid crystal display (LCD) monitor (they typically use over 50% less electricity!).[13]
- Look for an Energy Star certified product when buying your next computer.
- If you have a choice, choose a laptop over a desktop computer ($^3/_4$ less electricity).[14]

American Council for an Energy-Efficient Economy ACEEE)
ACEEE promotes energy efficiency both as a source of economic prosperity and environmental protection. Visit their consumer buying guide to compare brands' energy efficiency.
   www.aceee.org/consumerguide/mostenef.htm

ACTION: Weatherize your home

You can reduce your heating and cooling bills by up to 50% by weatherizing your home.[15]
- Weatherstripping: Install proper weatherstripping and caulking — it's a cinch and very inexpensive. Just check around your windows and doors for energy-wasting drafts. Ask at your local hardware store for tips.

- Insulation: Check with your local utility to determine the proper insulation for your home. The average household could reduce its energy consumption by 20-45% with proper insulation (especially in the attic).[16]
- Energy-efficient windows: Substantially more heat escapes through your windows than through your walls. Double-paned windows are an option for cutting heat loss and your heating bill. Install storm windows in the winter for another great way to conserve heat.

ACTION: Light your home efficiently

Lighting consumes approximately 5-10% of your annual home energy usage.[17] It's no wonder that figure is so high, when a normal (incandescent) 100-watt bulb turned on for 12 hours a day for one year requires 394 pounds (179 kilograms) of coal to be burned.[18] There are two easy steps to remember:

- Turn off your lights when you aren't using them or when you can just let the sun shine in (sunshine is free and naturally renewable).
- Install compact fluorescent light bulbs in your most commonly used lamps and fixtures. Compact fluorescent bulbs are a great alternative because they last 10 times longer and use one-fourth the energy of incandescent bulbs. Compact fluorescent bulbs cost from $3 to $9, but over the life of the bulb, they will save you $45 (mostly from energy savings) and prevent the burning of 300 pounds (136 kilograms) of coal.[19] There are even torchiere lamps available that use compact fluorescent bulbs instead of energy-guzzling halogen bulbs.

ACTION: Contact your local utility company to perform an energy audit

For a nominal fee, your local utility may send someone out to assess the best energy-saving changes that you can make to your home. Look on your utility bill for a contact number. They might even give you a price cut on energy-efficient purchases, such as compact fluorescent bulbs, attic insulation, weatherizing materials, or a water heater jacket.

ACTION: Buy clean power

Many utility companies offer options to buy power produced by renewable energy sources such as solar and wind power. Because alternative energy technology is still relatively new, purchasing green power adds a token fee to your monthly energy bill. However, in time and if enough people contribute, renewable energy will become the norm rather than the exception. Think of the fee as a small donation towards a cleaner, safer future! You can either call your local power company and ask if they provide green options or you can visit the Department of Energy's website and search your state.

Green Power Network

The US Department of Energy's Green Power Network can help you find out how to buy green power in your state.

🖥 www.eere.energy.gov/greenpower

WATER

As with electricity, water is easy to waste because we don't really see where it comes from. Water conservation is an important environmental issue for two main reasons. Saving water (1) helps support wildlife habitat by replenishing local streams and lakes and (2) saves energy that would otherwise have been used to heat and purify the water at your local water treatment plant.

Fortunately, it is quite easy to conserve water at home. To prevent wasting water, try to determine where the water in your home is escaping. The simple act of shutting off your faucet while you are washing your dishes, shaving, or brushing your teeth may seem insignificant, but it quickly adds up to monumental conservation when multiplied by millions of people.

ACTION: Install faucet aerators and low-flow showerheads

Faucet aerators reduce the amount of water you use, while still maintaining the water pressure. They are easy to install and cost less than $10. Most large hardware stores carry them. A faucet aerator can decrease your water consumption from 4 gallons per minute to less than 1 gallon per minute.

Showerheads made before 1994 use up to 6 gallons of water each minute we shower.[20] By using a low-flow showerhead, you will cut your water consumption down to 1 to 2 gallons per minute (a more than 75% reduction), without significantly diminishing water pressure. Some showerheads even have a handy switch to turn off the water while you lather up. An outlay of $25 to retrofit one showerhead and two faucets will save you up to $100 per year on your utility bills and reduce carbon dioxide emissions.[21] Taking showers instead of baths and cutting the length of your showers are also easy ways to save water.

ACTION: Transform your toilet into a water miser

The common household toilet can account for over 25% of a home's indoor water use.[22] A cheap way to reduce the flow in your current toilet is to fill a slim milk jug with water and place it in the toilet tank. This will displace some of the water, reducing the amount required to fill up the tank. Keep adding bottles and jugs until there is just enough water to effectively clean the bowl. Be sure that you don't impede the workings of the toilet's mechanisms. Also, don't use a brick as a displacement device, because it can break apart and can cause plumbing problems. If you want to get fancy, you can purchase a water dam that partitions off part of your tank to reduce water use. Newer toilets use 1.6 gallons of water or less and still keep the bowl nice and clean. Dual flush toilets have two flush settings, one for liquid or light waste (releases 0.8 gallons of water) and one for solid waste (1.6 gallons released). Dual flush toilets cost a bit more up front but use 25-30% less water compared to efficient 1.6 gallon toilets.[23]

 ACTION: Use environmentally friendly cleaners and laundry detergents

If your cleaning cupboard is like most people's, it's filled with myriad sprays, powders, and bottles of all colors and sizes. Chemical companies constantly try to sell us the latest great cleaners, detergents, deodorizers, and stain removers. Unfortunately, cleansers and detergents usually come in a non-recyclable plastic container, expose your family to hazardous chemicals, were tested on animals using horrific methods, and wreak havoc on local lakes and streams. For example, chlorine production and use damages the natural environment possibly more than any other single substance.

CONVENTIONAL PRODUCT	ECO PRODUCT	HOME MADE
Glass cleaner (Windex)	7th Gen glass and surface cleaner	vinegar and water ($^1/_3$ vinegar, $^2/_3$ water) or newspaper
Scrubbing agent (Comet)	Ecover natural cream scrub, Simple Pure Clean scouring powder	baking soda (1 cup) and borax (1/4 cup)
All purpose cleaners/ degreasers (409, Soft Scrub)	Simple Green, 7th Gen citrus cleaner, Ecover degreaser	vinegar and water ($^1/_3$ vinegar, $^2/_3$ water)
Disinfectant (Lysol, Pinesol)	Simple Pure Clean bathroom cleaner	borax (1 tsp), vinegar (3 tbsp), and water (2 cups)
Paper towels (Bounty)	7th Gen paper towels	washable cloth rags
Laundry detergent (Tide, Cheer)	7th Gen laundry soap, Ecover	n/a
Bleach (Clorox)	Ecover or 7th Gen natural non-chlorine bleach	drying clothes in the sun
Fabric Softener (Downy, Snuggle)	7th Gen or Ecover	add $^1/_4$ cup vinegar or $^1/_4$ cup baking soda or borax to final rinse
Toilet bowl cleaner (Lysol, Clorox)	7th Gen mint toilet bowl cleaner, Ecover	baking soda (1 cup) and borax ($^1/_4$ cup)
Stain remover/carpet cleaner (Resolve)	7th Gen carpet cleaner	wash soda (2 tbsp) and warm water (1 cup)
Dish soap (Dawn, Palmolive)	Ecover natural dishwashing liquid	n/a

Note: "7th Gen" = Seventh Generation

Fortunately, there are ways of reducing our dependence on commercial cleaners. It's easy to buy or even make your own non-toxic cleaners, and they have many benefits for the world. Many companies, such as Ecover, Seventh Generation, Bon Ami, Granny's Old Fashioned Products, Seaside Naturals (Simple Pure Clean), Allens Naturally and Ecco Bella, make eco-friendly cleaners and detergents. Look for them at your grocery store, local natural food store, or at their online catalogs. Chlorine-free bleach is also available at any supermarket. In addition, homemade cleaning products take little time to prepare, save you money, reduce hazardous chemical and packaging waste, protect you from harmful chemicals, and often clean just as well as many commercial cleaners.

▷ RESOURCES

Seventh Generation

◀ Most supermarkets carry Seventh Generation's line of cleaning products, though they may be in a separate section from the conventional cleaners. Seventh Generation offers a whole line of non-toxic, biodegradable, vegetable based products that are not tested on animals.
🖥 www.seventhgeneration.com

📖 Berthold-Bond, Annie. *Better Basics for the Home: Simple Solutions for Less Toxic Living.* Three Rivers Press, 1999. This book has everything from non-toxic ways to clean your fireplace and metal items to homemade car wax and furniture polish.

TRASH

The whole concept of throwing away something is really an illusion. You can't throw away anything — you can just relocate it. When we take our garbage out to the curb, we think we wash our hands of it. But it goes from our driveway to an incinerator or a landfill, where someone else has to deal with it. The average American throws away 4.5 pounds (2 kilograms) of waste every day — that's over 1 billion pounds (450 million kilograms) of trash, every day, just in the US.[24]

A number of actions will reduce your contribution to the enormous growth of solid waste and the overconsumption of natural resources in this country. The key to cutting your waste is to better understand what you are throwing away. How could you have prevented even buying what you are throwing away? Can you reuse or recycle it? Can you compost it?

✎ ACTION: Reduce your junk mail

Americans receive almost 4 million tons (3.6 metric tons) of unsolicited junk mail every year — that's about 100 million trees every year — while discarding most of it without even opening it.[25] There are a few easy steps you can take to reduce the amount of junk mail you receive.

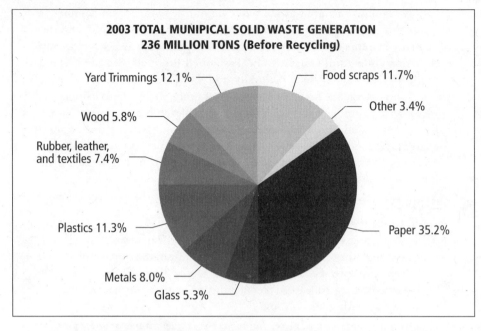

**2003 TOTAL MUNIPICAL SOLID WASTE GENERATION
236 MILLION TONS (Before Recycling)**

Yard Trimmings 12.1%

Food scraps 11.7%

Other 3.4%

Wood 5.8%

Rubber, leather,
and textiles 7.4%

Plastics 11.3%

Paper 35.2%

Metals 8.0%

Glass 5.3%

- Contact companies who send you unwanted mailings and tell them, "Take me off your list." (Use their business reply envelopes!)
- Ask telemarketers, " Please take me off your calling list."
- Obtain every variation of your name, address, and phone number (look at the labels on your junk mail for variations). Send them to the following addresses and ask them, "Remove me from your mailings and telephone lists."

Mail Preference Service
Direct Marketing Association
    P.O. Box 9008, Farmingdale, NY 11735-9008, USA.

Equifax Options
    P.O. Box 740123, Atlanta, GA 30374-0123, USA.
    (800) 556-4711

Trans Union LLC's Name Removal Service
    P.O. Box 97328, Jackson, MS 39288-7328, USA.
    (800) 680-7293

National Do Not Call Registry
    (888) 382-1222   💻 www.donotcall.gov

Telephone Preference Service
    Direct Marketing Association
    P.O. Box 9014, Farmingdale, NY 11735-9014, USA.

In Canada:
Direct Marketing Association
 1 Concord Gate, Suite 607, Don Mills, Ontario M3C 3N6 Canada
 If you want a really easy way to get off of junk mail lists, check out www.newdream.org/junkmail, type in your name and address, and it will generate the letters for you.

ACTION: Recycle

Recycling is a commonsense way of saving resources. It decreases the amount of virgin materials and energy consumed and the amount of pollution created in the production process. Recycling also decreases the amount of landfill space needed to store our garbage. Recycling at home is easy. There are three simple steps to get started:

- Locate a collector or a drop-off site for your recyclables.
- Find out what materials they accept.
- Start recycling!

> For other tips on conserving paper and wood products at home or office, check out www.woodwise.org.

Many neighborhoods have curbside recycling programs in which trash haulers pick up your recyclables and keep them from going to the dump. Check your local Yellow Pages under "Recycling" to see what services are available in your community. If you live in an apartment, consider asking your landlord to expand recycling services.

ACTION: Compost your kitchen scraps and yard waste

Composting is nature's way of recycling organic matter by letting it decay and return to the soil. Think of composting as a recycling bin for your kitchen scraps and yard waste.

Two reasons to compost:

1. It significantly lessens your household waste (by about 30%).[26]
2. It creates a soil additive that helps grow healthy plants and flowers, reducing the need for harsh, petroleum-based chemical fertilizers in your garden. You can also use compost as a mulch.

   All you have to do to start a compost pile is: find a 3-by-3-foot (1-by-1-meter) plot of land and start piling up your leaves, grass clippings and food scraps.

   To aid decomposition and avoid odors: (1) keep an even balance of leaves/ dried grass and food scraps and (2) periodically use a pitchfork or shovel to mix up the pile. Especially in urban areas, many people buy a plastic bin to contain their compost pile. Ask at your local hardware or lawn store for more information.

> Remember the "three Rs" of waste reduction: first Reduce what you use, then Reuse what you can, and finally Recycle what's left over.

⇨ RESOURCES

📢 HowToCompost.org
💻 www.howtocompost.org

📢 Compost Guide
💻 www.compostguide.com

DO COMPOST		DON'T COMPOST	
vegetables and fruit scraps	paper towels	meat	dairy products
flowers and plants	leaves/ grass clippings	bones	weeds
eggshells	straw/ sawdust	fish	infected plants
pasta and bread	fireplace ashes	large amounts of fats (salad dressings)	charcoal
coffee (and filters)/ tea bags			trash

If you use the above tips, it will help produce quality compost and keep the critters away.

🗒 ACTION: Properly dispose of household hazardous waste

Many substances in your home are considered household hazardous wastes. Unfortunately many people just throw these materials in the trash or dump them in the sewer. If improperly disposed of, these materials can poison wildlife or children, pollute your local stream, or injure sanitation workers.

Before disposing of any toxic substances in your home, be sure to call your community disposal site for household toxins. Just look in your Yellow Pages under "Waste Disposal — Hazardous." Hazardous waste drop-off sites usually accept paints, solvents, and other chemicals that you should not throw in the garbage.

Household hazardous waste includes:
- Motor oil, antifreeze, brake fluid, and other auto fluids.
- Pesticides.
- Adhesives and caulk.
- Batteries.
- Chemicals and cleaners.
- Paint, thinner, stripper, varnish and stain.
- Arts and crafts materials .
- Cosmetics
- Weed killer

Earth 911
Earth 911 is a good resource not only for recycling but for all types of hazardous waste disposal. Enter your zip code to find the nearest disposal sites for paint,

batteries, motor oil, and many more household wastes.

    1-877-Earth911   💻 www.earth911.org

LAWN AND GARDEN

Many North Americans enjoy landscaping their yards and tending to flower and vegetable gardens. As you care for your lawn and garden, be sure to also care for our Earth as a whole. There are many actions we can all take to balance our desire for a nice yard with the need to conserve water, energy and toxic chemicals.

ACTION: Xeriscape your lawn and garden

Xeriscaping means that you plant grasses, bushes, and shrubs that will thrive even if they don't receive very much water. This allows you to significantly reduce your household water consumption, especially if you avoid watering during the hottest parts of the day. Ask your local lawn and garden store for the varieties of plants that will work best in your area or search for xeriscape information for your state online.

REDUCE CHEMICAL FERTILIZERS

Americans use over half of a billion pounds (230 million kilograms) of chemical fertilizers on their lawns and gardens every year.[27] It isn't very appealing to think of all that gunk seeping into our groundwater supply. The prevention is to avoid lawn fertilizer and chemical weed killers entirely. Pull weeds by hand, wear golf shoes while you mow to aerate your lawn, and grow grasses and plants natural to the area. If you really think your lawn needs some fertilizer, check into organic fertilizers such as Naturall. Ask your local greenhouse or sod grower for more alternatives.

CFS Specialties, Inc.

CFS Specialties makes 100% organic fertilizers for both lawn and garden.

    (800) 822-6671   💻 www.cfspecial.com

ACTION: Use a manual or electric lawn mower

Manual mowers (reel mowers) are back (actually they never left). The only energy they require is your muscle power — with no air, water, or noise pollution. Current models cut well and are certainly the most ecologically friendly mowers available.

    Believe it or not, you can also buy a mower that plugs into an electrical outlet. Small gasoline engines like those in lawn mowers are extremely inefficient and heavily polluting. In contrast, electric mowers are powered by electricity that has been generated at a power plant which is much more efficient than your lawn mower's little engine. Electric mowers also cut down on noise pollution. These mowers are especially great for folks with smaller lawns. Don't worry, they teach you how to avoid running over the cord (and some electric mowers don't even need a cord).

Clean Air Gardening

If you're looking for an electric or manual mower and can't find one at your local hardware store, Clean Air Gardening is for you. They sell environmentally friendly lawn equipment, compost bins, organic fertilizers, and even electric snow blowers.

(214) 370-0530   💻 www.cleanairgardening.com

ACTION: Don't bag your grass clippings

Buying and using a mulching blade for your lawn mower allows you to leave your grass clippings on your lawn. It will create a nitrogen-rich mulch that decreases the need for water and fertilizer and significantly reduces the amount of yard waste you send to the dump. You can purchase a mulching lawn mower blade at most hardware and department stores for under $10. If you would rather not leave grass on your lawn every cutting, consider bagging every other time.

ACTION: Avoid buying unnecessary power tools

Before you buy that leaf blower, electric edge trimmer, snow blower, or super deluxe giant-sized grill, ask yourself, "For what this costs and the resources it uses, will I really gain that much fulfillment from it?" and "Is there another way I can accomplish what this machine does?" A broom or rake, for example, can generally do whatever a leaf blower can — and you get a little exercise to boot. By avoiding unnecessary power equipment, you save money (purchase price, fuel and maintenance), save space (avoiding clutter), reduce pollution and preserve natural resources.

If, on the other hand, you decide a certain machine will make your life easier, consider purchasing and sharing it with a neighbor. Sharing tools saves money, fosters community and helps reduce clutter. You might store the snow blower while your neighbor keeps a place for the mower.

YOUR HOME

Your home is more than a place to eat and sleep. It has the potential to be a sustainable, spiritual oasis that supports your desire to make a positive contribution to the world. Most of us like having a sense of home — somewhere we feel comfortable, can be ourselves, and experience a sense of belonging. Our choice of a home is such an important decision, because our physical surroundings influence us significantly every day. Take advantage of this opportunity and create a space that increases your energy and intensifies your enjoyment of life while respecting the natural environment.

ACTION: Live close to work

Where we live largely determines how we get to work. If you live less than one mile away from your workplace, your chances of walking or biking to work grow exponentially. Living close to work will prevent pollution and save you time and money, since your commute is shortened.

ACTION: Live in a smaller home

Many of us eventually want to own an enormous dream home to fill with all of our stuff. Unfortunately, they are more difficult to heat and cool, take up more natural space, and require more lumber and plastic to put together.

Also, big homes tend to tie up our time and money; they take longer to clean, require more repairs, and simply cost more to buy. The more money and time our homes demand, the less we have for other things we value, such as volunteering, spending quality time with our families, or giving to worthy causes.

ACTION: Arrange your furniture to encourage conversation

Many people circle their furniture around the TV as if it is a shrine. This leads to a knee-jerk reaction of sitting down and turning on the TV. Your likelihood of reading a book or having a quality conversation increases exponentially if your chair isn't staring right at the boob tube. Consider putting your chairs and couches in an arrangement that fosters communication. At the very least, put the TV in a cabinet or cover it up so it doesn't look so inviting.

> The size of a new house has more than doubled since the 1950s (from 1,000 to 2,349 square feet in 2004 [93 to 181 square meters]) while the size of the average family has decreased.[28]

ACTION: Grow household plants

Plants improve the air quality in your home. They not only take in carbon dioxide and give off oxygen (that's what we breathe), but they also absorb many types of indoor air pollutants. Plants also create a warm living environment. And it is wonderful to be surrounded by living things, instead of exclusively by machines and appliances. Plants also give you the opportunity to be a steward for another living organism, since you get to feed, water, and watch them grow.

ACTION: Sign up with a socially responsible long distance, wireless, and Internet service

Working Assets   🌐 **WORKING ASSETS**®

Imagine if every time you made a long distance call, some of your money went to doctors working in war-torn countries, women's literacy programs in the Third World, or the Educational Fund to End Handgun Violence. Working Assets is a long distance phone company dedicated to social justice and empowerment. They donate 1% of your long distance charges to a variety of nonprofit organizations, from civil rights and environmental groups to peace and economic justice groups. One percent may not sound like much, but since 1985 Working Assets has donated well over $50 million to hundreds of organizations — nearly $4 million in 2005 alone! They offer action alerts about a number of important issues with your phone bill, as well as free calls to your legislators every month, all at very competitive long distance rates. You can also sign up for their wireless plan.

(800) 227-0298   💻   www.workingassets.com

Earth Tones

If you are particularly passionate about the environment, consider Earth Tones, a long distance company similar to Working Assets that gives 100% of its profits to environmental groups. They also offer action alerts and free calls to government officials every month. In addition, Earth Tones has wireless and Internet service.

(888) 327-8486   💻   www.earthtones.com

ACTION: Give away your clutter

Many of us have a room, a basement, or a garage full of stuff that we don't use. Physical clutter not only fills up our homes, it fills up our minds, leading to anxiety and mental clutter. Why have a lot of stuff stored away when other people could be using it right now? Old TVs, clothes, and books will be appreciated by people who are less fortunate.

A few times a year, search through all of your storage space. A good rule to start with is "if you haven't used it in the past 12 months, you probably don't need it." When you give away your extra stuff, you will not only be helping people get quality merchandise at cheap prices but you will help the environment by having your stuff reused.

ACTION: Consciously choose your community

When you consciously choose your community, instead of just happening upon it, your choice can lead to years of benefits. There are a lot of exciting possibilities for creating a living environment that supports strong community building.

Is it important for you to live:

- Near a park for recreation?
- Near bike paths for alternative transportation?
- In an area with a strong sense of community?
- In an area with low levels of traffic?
- In a racially and ethnically diverse neighborhood?

You also might want to consider some of the following non-traditional living environments to build a stronger sense of community.

Shared Housing: Multiple families live in one home. You can rent out unused rooms to family, friends, or strangers. Shared housing is a great way to add some vitality to your house and help pay the bills.

Co-housing: A fast-growing alternative to anonymous suburban life, co-housing combines the privacy of a single family dwelling with the sense of a strong community. Each family has its own unit with private rooms, living space and a small kitchen. Communal spaces include a large kitchen, workshop, office space, children's playroom and garden. Check out The Cohousing Network at: www.cohousing.org for more information.

Intentional Communities: For the true idealists among us, intentional communities are usually formed around shared values such as environmentally sustainable living, vegetarian eating, or a certain spiritual path. Members often share cooking, gardening, and other chores. Check out The Fellowship for Intentional Community at: www.ic.org for more information.

ACTION: Remodel with green materials

Remodeling is an exciting activity for homeowners. As you plan your remodeling, consider your home's impact on the environment. Here are some ideas to get you thinking:

- Use latex (water-based) paint instead of oil-based paint.
- Use adhesives with low levels of Volatile Organic Compounds (VOCs).
- Use second-hand building materials.
- Use recycled products (porches, fences, carpets, and benches can be made from recycled plastic).
- When buying wood, look for labels that indicate environmentally sustainable harvesting methods: Forest Stewardship Council (FSC), Scientific Certification Systems (SCS), or Smartwood.

SOLAR POWER YOUR HOME

Technological advances are making harnessing the power of the sun easier and more cost-effective. Photovoltaic (PV) panels that produce electricity are available from many companies and can be installed on the roof of most homes. You may even be able to receive federal and state tax rebates for producing renewable energy. Check the Database of State Incentives for Renewable Energy (www.dsireusa.org) to find programs in your area. Go on a "solar tour" of homes and buildings in your area. Check out www.ases.org/tour/index.htm for details.

Find Solar
Find Solar can help you locate professional PVP installers in your area.
www.findsolar.com

Ewing, Rex A. and Doug Pratt. *Got Sun? Go Solar: Get Free Renewable Energy to Power Your Grid-Tied Home.* PixyJack Press, 2005. A nice guide to solar-powered living in your current home.

HOME RESOURCES

📖 *Consumer Guide to Home Energy Savings.* American Council for an Energy-Efficient Economy, 1999. Whether you are considering repairs or renovations,

ACEEE's guide to energy savings will get you the information you need on energy efficiency for appliances, insulation, windows, landscaping, lighting and home maintenance. Available for $8.95.

⌨ www.aceee.org (202) 429-0063

Department of Energy's Home Energy Saver

Type in your zip code to find out the most cost-effective, energy-saving home improvement tips for your area.

⌨ http://hes.lbl.gov/

Real Goods

Real Goods is a retailer for all types of environmentally responsible products for the home. Everything from composting toilets and photovoltaic solar cells to energy-efficient appliances are available on their website. Their site is also a great source of information about a number of cutting-edge home technologies. (800) 442-1972 ⌨ www.realgoods.com

Rocky Mountain Institute (RMI)

RMI is a great resource for energy saving tips for the home, energy-efficient cars, and renewable sources of energy for the world. 1739 Snowmass Creek Road, Snowmass, CO 81654-9199, USA.

 (800) 919-2400 ⌨ www.rmi.org

WORK

Workplace Relationships
Socially Responsible Workplace
Finding Good Work

D O YOU LOOK FORWARD to going to work in the morning, or is it a struggle to drag yourself out the door? For some of us, work is nothing more than putting food on the table, while others gain significant meaning from their jobs. The average person who works 40 hours each week for 35 years will work around 70,000 hours in their lifetime. Since we spend so much time working, we ought to consider how we can make our job engaging and fulfilling while actively contributing to a better world.

Somehow work has come to mean a place that keeps you from more enjoyable activities. Many of us are working for the weekend, struggling through a miserable job so that we can afford to escape for a while and play. Unless you consciously choose to pursue fulfilling work, society will likely push you toward monotonous, unsatisfying jobs. Imagine how your life would be different if your job was more than a way to maintain a lifestyle and you were genuinely excited to get to work because you were actively creating a better world each day.

When you integrate your work with your most deeply held values, it becomes a meaningful expression of who you are as a human being. This chapter will empower you with actions that transform your work experience, will help you choose a great job, create an extraordinary place to work, help workers out, and make your workplace socially and environmentally friendly.

ACTION: Limit your work time

Have you ever noticed that when you meet someone, the first question out of your mouth is "What do you do?" This is a very open-ended question. Your new acquaintance could answer, "I garden," "I write poetry," or "I try to be the best parent I can be." The answer, however, is always the person's work.

In our culture, work defines who we are: we are driven to be career focused. Our status and identity often come from our job's prestige and salary rather than from the quality of our relationships and the overall quality of our lives. Consequently, when we're offered a promotion that will increase our status and salary we tend to accept it without hesitation — despite the additional hours, stress, and responsibility.

The average American works 1,966 hours each year. That's 235 hours more than workers in the United Kingdom, 310 more than in France, 392 more than in Germany, and 414 more hours than in Sweden![1] Men worked on average 100 hours more and women 233 hours more per year in 1993 than in 1976. Almost 20% of Americans worked 49 hours or more each week. That's a full extra 8-hour day![2]

Even with the best of intentions, if you don't consciously limit your work time, work will creep in and take over all of your other priorities. How do extra meetings at work or overtime pay compare to your daughter's first soccer game or a special dinner with your significant other? We need to realize that the time we give our friends and family is more valuable than the things we give them.

We realize that many of you may not have the luxury of working less. Rising housing costs and stagnating wages restrict our opportunities to limit work time. However, simpler lifestyles create possibilities for many of us to limit work time and achieve balance between work aspirations and the rest of our lives. Working less will help you lower your stress, improve your health and sleep patterns, improve your relationships, provide time for civic and creative pursuits, and make your life more fulfilling. Consider asking for more vacation time instead of a raise next time around!

ARE YOU A WORKAHOLIC?

Do you regularly work through lunch?	☐ Yes	☐ No
Have your long hours caused strain in your relationships?	☐ Yes	☐ No
Does work interfere with your planned time off?	☐ Yes	☐ No
Do you often think about work outside the office?	☐ Yes	☐ No
Do you work more than 45 hours a week?	☐ Yes	☐ No
Have you given up on your hobbies?	☐ Yes	☐ No
Do you think about work while driving, falling asleep or when others are talking?	☐ Yes	☐ No

If you answered Yes to a majority of these questions, you may want to reconsider your focus on work.

⌨ ACTION: Take your lunch to work

The cost of eating out each day adds up quickly and is often less healthy than making your own lunch. If you bring your lunch from home, you save money, packaging, time and gas (if you drive somewhere for lunch). When you pack your lunch, try to use reusable containers and utensils rather than plastic baggies and silverware. Weather permitting, you can even organize a picnic with your co-workers!

WORKPLACE RELATIONSHIPS

Your experiences in the workplace have an enormous impact on your satisfaction with life. How content you are with your work and your relationships with your coworkers affects your quality of life even more than your salary. If you take time to create some community and a supportive work environment, everyone will experience daily benefits.

⌨ ACTION: Avoid gossip

Nothing creates a hostile work environment more quickly than gossip. Few things feel worse than knowing people are talking about you, and the effects of talking behind people's backs are potentially devastating.

- Don't get reeled in by people who want to gossip. You can remove yourself from the situation or simply listen without adding to the gossip pool.
- Try to resolve conflicts immediately, before gossip and rumors begin, by dealing directly with the other person. You'll save yourself loads of trouble later by dealing with conflict now.
- Stay positive at work. People will have less to gossip about.

⌨ ACTION: Appreciate everyone in your workplace

When we are young, our society teaches us which people deserve respect because of their jobs and which ones do not: doctors, lawyers, and professors are important people, while secretaries, janitors, and manual laborers are not. As adults, we often unintentionally reaffirm this hierarchy in the workplace by giving some people significant respect and treating others almost as if they were invisible. Be respectful of all people in the workplace and thank them when you notice their quality work. This includes the people who clean and maintain your workplace, those who install and fix your equipment, temporary workers, interns, customers, and delivery people. They all make integral contributions to your workplace. Consider taking them out to lunch, telling them how much you appreciate their work, or even giving them a heartfelt gift.

⌨ ACTION: Get to know your coworkers outside of work

Although you may feel that you already spend enough time with your coworkers, consider spending some quality time with them away from work. You'll form more meaningful connections, they'll become more human to you, and working with them will be even more special. We all know what it's like to work in a stressful environment: tempers run short, deadlines make people jumpy, and we get annoyed and angry. Creating a sense of community at work helps us through the stressful times we all encounter. Here are a few suggestions:

- Enter a workplace softball team in your city's league.
- Go to the gym, on a hike, or for a bike ride together.
- Go dancing together.
- Organize a barbecue.

ACTION: Set up a workplace carpool

Carpooling is a great way to reduce your impact on the environment and get to know your coworkers better, and yet over the last 30 years carpooling has significantly declined. Put a sign-up sheet in your break room where people can list their names and addresses. Then determine who lives near each other and divide up driving times. Carpooling will also save you money on gas, parking and maintenance. Carpooling, using public transportation, walking, or biking just one day a week for a year can save around 1,200 miles (1,931 kilometers) of wear on your vehicle and about $570 in driving costs.[3]

> Percentage of people who carpool to work:
> 1980: 20%
> 1990: 13%
> 2003: 9%
>
> Percentage of people who drive alone to work:
> 1980: 64%
> 1990: 73%
> 2003: 79%[4]

Some cities have carpooling services that will send you a list of people in your area who are commuting to a similar location. Vanpooling services charge a monthly fee to pick up a group of people and take them to work (a personalized form of public transit). Call your city government or check out the resources below for more information.

eRideShare.com (USA and Canada)
   www.eRideShare.com

ACTION: Make people from diverse backgrounds feel welcome

In our increasingly global economy, we often find ourselves working with people from other races, regions, countries, and backgrounds. This is an incredible opportunity for us to exchange ideas, cultures, and experiences. Entering a new workplace, however, can be extremely uncomfortable for a person who may be the only member of a certain ethnicity, nationality, or other group. If we truly value diversity and community, we must make sure that people from diverse backgrounds feel welcome. Here are a few suggestions:

This space respects people regardless of gender, race, sexual orientation, social class, ethnicity, age, or ability.

- Invite people to lunch.

- Talk to people; ask them about themselves.
- Have their family over for dinner.
- Offer to show them around town.
- Make a welcome basket.

SOCIALLY RESPONSIBLE WORKPLACE

You not only have the opportunity to create positive and supportive relationships with coworkers but also to help make your workplace more directly benefit your community and the natural environment. It may seem overwhelming to try to change the way your company or organization functions, so just take it one step at a time. First evaluate your own office or department and find manageable changes you can propose or implement. You may even inspire other coworkers who also want to make positive changes.

ACTION: Participate in workplace charitable giving

Many companies offer their employees matching funds when they donate to charities such as the United Way. This is a way to double your impact on the world for free! A number of companies have also started offering to take a specific amount (you decide how much) out of your monthly paycheck automatically and give it directly to the charity or charities of your choice. Ask your company if it has programs like this and if not, would it be willing to start some.

ACTION: Organize around community service

Imagine the good things you and your coworkers could accomplish in your community if you pooled your talents, time, and resources. Some companies actually allow employees paid community service days. The Body Shop, a popular bath and perfume franchise, compensates employees for up to two days of community volunteering each month.[5] Some business leaders are realizing that fostering good community relations improves employee morale and increases profits.[6] Encourage your employer to offer community service incentives.

- Organize a food drive for your community food bank.
- Raise funds to buy winter coats for homeless children.
- Sponsor a local kids' sports team.
- Get involved in the Big Brothers/Big Sisters program (see ORGANIZA-TIONS chapter).

ACTION: Know your rights as an employee

Part of the reason that employers are able to take advantage of employees is that workers are unaware of their rights. To find out the legal ins and outs of your rights as a worker you may want to do your own research on these topics: privacy (can your employer monitor your email, phone calls, and your work? Conduct background checks?), health benefits, overtime pay, sick leave, work standards, safety and equal pay for equal work. When you demand that your employer respect your rights, you are sending a message that she or he must respect the rights of all workers.

Workplace Fairness
Workplace Fairness is a nonprofit organization helping people with "understanding, enforcing, and expanding their rights in the workplace." They assist people who can't afford their own attorney. Contact them if you feel your rights have been violated.
(415) 362-7373   www.workplacefairness.org

 ACTION: Support your fellow employees
The "American Dream" of hard work leading to prosperity is not the reality for millions of people. Many working Americans have forgotten that we're all in this together — blue- and white-collar workers alike need to stick together.

Traditionally, unions have been the main means of uniting workers. Unions played a large role in creating many of the labor standards we take for granted today, including the 40-hour workweek and the minimum wage.

Unions are not a relic of the past. They are still the most effective avenue for millions of people in rich and poor countries to collectively stand up for fair working conditions, hours, and pay. Despite the fact that belonging to a union is economically beneficial for most workers, union memberships have consistently declined in recent decades. In 2000, union workers earned 28% more than their non-union counterparts.[7] Learning about, joining, and supporting unions is an important way to support your fellow workers. You can support your fellow workers by paying attention to strikes, not crossing picket lines, buying union-made products whenever possible, boycotting particularly worker-hostile companies and joining a union.

AFL-CIO
(American Federation of Labor-Congress of Industrial Organizations)
AFL-CIO is a voluntary federation of 66 national and international labor unions. Contact them for information on union organizing and research about economic issues facing average Americans.
 www.afl-cio.org

 ACTION: Confront injustices in the workplace
There is nothing more frustrating than being singled out or harassed because of your sex, age, race, sexual orientation, or ability. Sexual harassment, racial discrimination, and homophobia have been pervasive problems in our society for many years. We have the power to confront injustices where we work; we can create a safe space for each of our coworkers. If you think injustices don't concern you directly, remember that your work environment has a huge impact on you; what affects others affects you.

Common workplace injustices:

- "Gay" jokes.
- Lewd sexual comments/unwanted sexual advances.
- Expecting more from people of color and women.
- Racial/ethnic jokes.
- Inappropriate physical contact.

How you can confront injustices:

- Don't laugh at sexist, racist, and homophobic jokes.
- Offer victims of injustice your support. If you are the victim, seek others' support.
- Tell people who act inappropriately that their actions or words make you uncomfortable. (You don't have to be confrontational, just direct.)
- Document the injustice. This is crucial, even if you presently do not wish to file a complaint.
- Talk to your union representative, if you have one.
- Talk to your employer or someone in human resources.
- File a formal complaint.

National Organization for Women — Women Friendly Workplace Campaign
NOW's campaign against sexual harassment in the workplace offers information about the least women friendly companies and ideas on how you can join the struggle.
   💻 www.now.org/issues/wfw/index.html

 ACTION: Green your workplace

We use a lot of resources at work, especially paper and electricity. Imagine all the resources your workplace uses, and then think of all the other companies out there using just as much if not more. By creatively reducing your workplace's resource use, you will make a huge impact on our environmental well-being. Use your imagination — every little bit helps!

The easiest way to reduce your workplace's impact on the environment is to reduce the resources you require. Send memos by email, turn off unnecessary lighting, print using a smaller font than you normally would, use energy-efficient office machines (look for the Energy Star sticker), and set your printers up to print on both sides if possible. Get your boss on-board by touting how much money the company will save from these changes!

There are many opportunities to reuse materials, as well. Consider reusing the blank side of scrap paper, printing memos on used paper and reusing envelopes/packaging for office mail.

Finally, you can recycle office mail, typing/computer paper, printer cartridges, cardboard and drink containers.

In your break room, make sure to have bins for aluminum cans and plastics. Look up a service in your Yellow Pages under "Recycling Services," and arrange for recycling pickup.

ENVIRONMENTALLY FRIENDLY ACTIONS

- Use paper with recycled content www.greenlinepaper.com.
- Install motion sensor lights and/or compact fluorescent bulbs.
- Use reusable versus disposable dishes.
- Place recycle bins in your break room and near workstations so that everyone has convenient access to them.
- Set all computer monitors on the energy-saving mode. Shut computers down at night.
- Sign your business up with Working Assets Long Distance. Call (800) 789-7022 or visit their website at www.workingassets.com.
- Purchase Energy Star compliant office machines to save energy. Using the Energy Star website, you can compare different products to determine which ones use the least energy when in "sleep" or "off" mode. Visit the website at www.energystar.gov. You can compare computers, monitors, fax machines, copiers, scanners and more.

ACTION: Value people over profits

A nurturing and positive workplace doesn't just happen; you and your coworkers must create it. Everyone's input is important. Good communication is vital to an extraordinary workplace, just as it is in any relationship. You may want to hold check-in meetings several times each year or create a system of anonymous feedback to identify ways to improve well-being — which often boosts productivity.

If you employ or supervise other workers, make sure you take their concerns into account: don't overwork them, put their safety first and try to give them the pay and benefits they deserve. Some of you may face the extremely difficult decision of whether or not to eliminate jobs to boost profits a bit more. Our economy trains us to separate our rational, business selves from our compassionate, humane selves, fostering the belief that we must do everything possible to increase shareholder profits. Do your best to place human concerns before profits.

ACTION: Work to make your company more socially and environmentally responsible

The global economic system too often values profits over people. Too many businesses choose to maximize profits by instigating layoffs, pollution increases, production shortcuts and the overworking of employees. This easy path to short-term profit has immense consequences for our communities and our environment.

Companies constantly change to meet the needs of their customers, employees and the global marketplace. A single person often initiates changes that then catch on with others in the company. Be the person in your company that pushes for more investment in employees and your community, the efficient use of natural resources, and ethical business practices. In many cases, these kinds of changes have helped make companies more profitable, so don't be afraid to bring that up. Encourage your company to join a socially responsible professional organization, such as Businesses for Social Responsibility.

Businesses for Social Responsibility
(415) 984-3200 💻 www.bsr.org

Eldis Corporate Social Responsibility Resource Guide
💻 www.eldis.org/csr/index.htm

FINDING GOOD WORK

Choosing our jobs are some of the most important decisions we will make in our lives. We spend so much time and energy on our work that choosing a fulfilling job that benefits others has a huge effect on the world. Whether you choose a career that requires you to exploit people or to help them will have significant implications for your life and the lives of the people around you. We all have the opportunity to use our skills to make the world a better place. There are even many jobs available where the sole purpose is creating that world.

What are you "called" to do? Discerning your calling requires searching within yourself to determine what you should do with your life. Your calling is where your unique set of talents and passions match with what the world desperately needs. A calling compels you to do something that feeds you emotionally and spiritually while contributing to the lives of others. No job is perfect and striving to live out a calling is tougher for some than others, but finding "good work" is one of the greatest gifts you can give yourself and the world.

ACTION: Choose a fulfilling job

Working at a fulfilling job will transform your experience of life in general. When you work at an unfulfilling job, you're more likely to buy stuff you don't need, be in a foul mood even away from work, take out your frustrations on your friends and family, and generally have a negative outlook on the world. Our work means a lot to us, so choosing work that you are passionate about, that is challenging but not overly stressful, and that you can feel good about will vastly improve your life. Your fulfillment can't help but rub off on your surroundings, thereby making the world a better place.

Perhaps we're making this action sound easier than it is. You've got bills to pay, right? During your working years, you will face many important decisions: Should I take that promotion, which means more money but longer hours? Should I switch to a job that pays less but that I find more fulfilling? Should I accept the transfer to a new city while my kids are in school? How can I manage my career goals and the stress of achieving them? Finding fulfilling work may not always be easy, but with patience, flexibility and commitment you can do it.

Many factors enter into our decisions about work. Just make sure your personal fulfillment and relationships and not money or status are at the top of your list. Keep in mind that working in a fulfilling job can also significantly decrease your living expenses when you no longer have to buy expensive cars, "escape" vacations, or take-out meals every night to try to make up for your dreadful day at work.

ACTION: Use your current job skills to improve the world

Each of us has a unique combination of skills, passions, and ideas that we can contribute to making the world a better place. If you're a nurse, consider volunteering or working at a low-income clinic. If construction is your trade, you might want to supervise a Habitat for Humanity building project. If you're good with computers, there are numerous non-profit organizations that could use your expertise. Accountants and other financial planners also have numerous skills to share. Make a list of your own personal gifts and skills that you can bring to others and then take action.

Teach for America

In 1989, Wendy Kopp, a senior at Princeton University decided it was time to act. Troubled by the inequities in America's educational system, she started Teach for America, a national teacher corps which serves under-privileged school children and gives college graduates one of the most profound experiences of their lives. The program accepts recent graduates with any major for two-year commitments in over a dozen different rural and urban locations. TFA teachers earn regular teacher's salaries, which depend on the area of the country in which they work. To find out more about Teach for America, call: (800) 832-1230 ext. 225, or visit their website at: www.teachforamerica.org.

ACTION: Work for justice

For those of you searching for a career or looking to change careers, there are many opportunities to work with organizations whose sole purpose is to make the world a better place. In many cases, nonprofit organizations need the exact same skills and experience you are now acquiring in your current job. They need computer programmers and promotions experts, administrative staff and public relations folks. You can focus virtually any interest you have into a job that promotes justice.

RESOURCES TO HELP YOU FIND GOOD WORK

Bolles, Richard Nelson. *What Color Is Your Parachute? 2006: A Practical Manual for Job-Hunters and Career-Changers.* Ten Speed Press, 2005. For 30

SOCIALLY RESPONSIBLE PROFESSIONAL ORGANIZATIONS

Concerned individuals in many professions have formed affiliations where they can share information, offer concerns, and support one another's efforts towards social responsibility. There may be such an organization for your line of work. Contact your professional organization or search the Web to learn more. Here are a few examples:

Computer Professionals for Social Responsibility
💻 www.cpsr.org

Businesses for Social Responsibility
💻 www.bsr.org

Physicians for Social Responsibility
💻 www.psr.org

Educators for Social Responsibility
💻 www.esrnational.org

Social Investment Forum
💻 www.socialinvest.org

years *Parachute* has been a useful manual for job hunters and a guide for career changers. Helping people find fulfilling careers has made this book a bestseller. There is a new edition every year, and a regularly updated website at: www.jobhuntersbible.com.

📖 Shabecoff, Alice and, Paul C. Brophy. *A Guide to Careers in Community Development.* Island Press, 2001. This guide introduces the field of community development — the economic, social, and physical revitalization of a community led by members of that community. Professionals, volunteers, and students will find useful information about getting directly involved with community organizing, financing housing, or redeveloping brownfields.

📖 Environmental Careers Organization. *The ECO Guide to Careers that Make a Difference: Environmental Work for a Sustainable World.* Island Press, 2004. This guide not only helps you find a career that will make a difference, it explains the most pressing environmental problems that need tackling. Explores a variety of careers and provides information from both employers and employees.

📖 Hamilton, Leslie. *100 Best Nonprofits to Work For.* ARCO, 2000. If you are looking to make a difference while maintaining your salary, benefits, advancement prospects and job stability, then this is the book for you. Read about the pros and cons of working for some of the greatest nonprofit companies on Earth.

📖 Jansen, Julie. *I Don't Know What I Want, But I Know It's Not This: A Step-By-*

Step Guide to Finding Gratifying Work. Penguin, 2003. This book uses quizzes and questionnaires to help you find meaningful work.

📖 Wetfeet. *Careers in Nonprofits and Government Agencies 2006 Edition: WetFeet Insider Guide.* Wetfeet, Inc., 2005. A small guide that helps you find a nonprofit and get your foot in door. Includes stories from nonprofit employees about what they like and dislike about their work.

Charity Career Village (Canada)

Charity Career Village is a great place to look for jobs with Canadian nonprofits.

💻 www.charityvillage.com/applicant

Community Career Center (CCC)

The CCC lists a variety of community jobs with not-for-profit employers. Search by region, career interests, salary, or job title.

💻 www.nonprofitjobs.org

Environmental Career Opportunities

Environmental Career Opportunities offers a variety of jobs in environmental fields. You can register to receive new job openings or subscribe to their publication.

💻 www.ecojobs.com

Idealist

Idealist posts jobs by state and jobs abroad. Learn useful tips and use their search engine to find numerous nonprofit organizations.

💻 www.idealist.org

Opportunity Knocks

This comprehensive site features job openings at non-profit organizations.

💻 www.opportunityknocks.org

NonProfit Career Network

This site lets you search for full- or part-time work by state. It also has a directory of nonprofits around the country. You can submit your resume so that a nonprofit can find you.

💻 www.nonprofitcareer.com/index.html

➡️ WORKPLACE RESOURCES

📖 Boland, Mary L. *Sexual Harassment in the Workplace: What You Need to Know and What You Can Do.* Sphinx Publishing, 2005. This book not only helps identify sexual harassment, it offers practical suggestions on prevention and plenty of additional resources for further education.

📖 Winfeld, Liz. *Straight Talk About Gays In the Workplace: Creating an Inclusive, Productive Environment for Everyone in Your Organization.* Haworth Press, 2005. Well-researched and containing a list of 101 things to make your workplace more inclusive, this book takes a practical approach to many gay and lesbian issues in the workplace.

📖 Thomas, R. Rooseveldt. *Building on the Promise of Diversity: How We Can Move to the Next Level in Our Workplaces, Our Communities, and Our Society.* AMACOM, 2005. After a brief history of diversity in the US, affirmative action, and the civil rights movement, this book covers the fundamentals of managing diversity in the workplace.

⇨ HELPING WORKERS RESOURCES

Jobs With Justice

Jobs With Justice creates worker coalitions and action campaigns to further workers rights. They offer concrete actions and a variety of educational materials to help you support your fellow workers.

(202) 393-1044   💻 www.jwj.org

The 9 to 5 Job Survival Hotline

9 to 5, National Association of Working Women is a grassroots organization dedicated to helping women work for economic justice. They provide "Action Packets" full of concrete steps anyone can take to close the gender pay gap, challenge sexual harassment and contest unfair/illegal labor practices.

(800) 522-0925   💻 www.9to5.org

Socially Responsible Workplace

Nattrass, Brian, and Mary Altomare. *The Natural Step For Business: Wealth, Ecology, and The Evolutionary Corporation.* New Society Publishers, 1999. Examines how four very successful corporations in Sweden and the United States have shown that a company does not have to choose between profitability and care for the environment.

The Center for Corporate Citizenship at Boston College

The Center's mission is to "engage with companies to redefine business success as creating measurable gains for business and society. The Center achieves results through the power of research, education and member engagement."

💻 www.bcccc.net

Business Ethics magazine

Quarterly publication for those interested in transforming business from the inside. Annual issues on socially responsible investing, 100 Best Corporate Citizens, and business ethics awards highlight the cutting edge of corporate social responsibility.

💻 www.business-ethics.com

MEDIA

Television
Radio
Magazines
Newspapers
Internet

WHAT WE ALLOW CHILDREN to see and do will shape their values and actions as they mature. The same principle is true for adults. The way we think and act in our daily lives is inextricably linked to the information we receive about the world. Unfortunately, many of us are awash in a sea of information about all the crime, war, and disasters in the world. Enough time spent absorbing these messages leaves us feeling frightened of the outside world and powerless to make changes.

Much of what we learn about the world is not from direct experience but from someone else's account of what is going on. Mass media fundamentally shapes our perceptions of the world through the images, sounds and information they deliver to us on a daily basis. The problem is that those who control the media do not necessarily have our best interests in mind when they decide what information is fit to transmit. Profit ultimately determines what we see and hear in the media. If you trust these media corporations as you trust your own mother, then you can skip this chapter. Otherwise, read on.

The media you choose to consult are important, not only because they shape how you think about the world but also because they determine what you are willing to do. You will live a very different life if you spend your free time thinking about how you can contribute to a better world than if you think all day about the lives of the rich and famous.

Here are some aspects of your life that you will gain power over once you more consciously choose your media:

- your mood
- what you think about when you are alone
- what you talk about at parties
- which social issues you consider most important
- what you demand from your political officials
- whether you feel apathetic or empowered
- which avenues you pursue to make the world better
- what solutions (if any) you see to the world's problems
- what stereotypes you have of people you have never met
- what you see as the "good life"

This chapter addresses how the information we receive connects us to the outside world and, more importantly, how we can choose information sources that enrich our own lives and empower us to make a difference. We present alternative options for television, radio, magazines, newspapers, and the Internet that are geared toward social change and suggest actions to help you take responsibility for the media you use. Getting quality information about the world is a vital first step to building a better one.

Mainstream Media

What events are newsworthy? Thousands of interesting and important events occur in the world every day. Which ones should make the news? Understanding how the media decide will help you understand the impact that the media have on our lives. One thing you can be sure of, the news is far from impartial. The values, culture, and economic interests of a news organization significantly influence which events will make it onto the front page or into a newscast.

How many newscasts have you seen that show a violent crime, then politics as usual, then a war, then a celebrity event, then the stock market, then the weather, then the sports, and then empty banter between the anchors? How many times do we have to learn the details of a gruesome murder? Why is a celebrity divorce worth putting on the local news? Why are urgent international issues presented without the necessary historical background? Why are so many shows full of needless violence? The reason is that these stories make money. Bringing in new viewers or readers increases advertising revenues. The most recent "reality-based" show (or any other show for that matter) is on the air because it delivers a captive audience of a certain demographic (age, income, race) to corporations at commercial time.

The advertisements that urge us to buy more and more products are not just harmless, easily ignored messages. Advertising messages surround us and invade our public and private spaces so frequently that we often forget their presence and underestimate the power of their collective impact. For 24 hours a day, seven days a week, advertisers tell us that satisfying each of our fleeting desires is more important than contributing to the welfare of others — an extremely dangerous message, when you consider the ecological, social, and psychological challenges that we face as a global society.

Unfortunately, the pressure to maximize profits often undermines the standards of quality journalism. Investigative reporting becomes a financial liability, as it is comparatively expensive to produce and leaves owners of the news organization open to lawsuits. This insatiable drive to produce cheap news has even led journalists to go directly to corporate and government spin-doctors to acquire their stories. In fact, the public relations industry (PR firms) in America is responsible for a growing portion of the news in today's media, mainly through press releases and advertisements that masquerade as real articles.

Equally disturbing, corporate mergers are rapidly centralizing all aspects of global media production from newspapers to television and from books to movies. Today most of the information we consume on a daily basis comes from fewer than five major corporations.[1] Such a concentration of media power in the hands of a few runs contradictory to the democratic principles that are the foundations of an independent media system.

MAINSTREAM MEDIA	ALTERNATIVE MEDIA
Street Crime	Corporate Crime
Government and Corporate Sources	Independent Sources
US Focus	Local and Global Focus
Tabloid News	Issues of Substance
Commercials	Consumer Protection
Entertainment	Education
How to Invest in the Market	How to Invest in Your Community
Partisan Politics	Effective Political Action
Corporate Mergers	Communities Working Together
Gas Prices	Alternative Energy
Dow Jones	Economic Inequality
Fads and Fashion	Voluntary Simplicity
Corporate Profits	Sweatshop Labor
Voices of the Powerful	Voices of the People
Encourages Passivity	Encourages Action
Military Solutions	Nonviolent Alternatives

Alternative Media

Fortunately, concerned citizens all over the world have developed alternative media organizations to counter the lack of quality choices in the mainstream media. They produce alternative media to provide quality information about our governments, corporations, and communities so that we can live out the potential of a truly democratic society — a society where average people are well informed and actively involved in creating a better world.

ARE YOU A TV ADDICT?

There is one surefire way to tell. Unplug your TV for one full week. This will give you enough time to evaluate the role of television in your life. Try it now. It's just one week. Keep your commitment, and you'll be surprised at what you find.

TELEVISION

The average American will spend almost one-quarter of their waking hours on this Earth watching TV.[2] Watching television has become almost as important as eating and sleeping in our daily rituals. The television has even become the electronic storyteller of our age. It provides us with our news, our entertainment, and increasingly, our link to the rest of humanity. In fact, TV spends more time raising the next generation than we do. The average child spends 900 hours at school and over 1000 hours in front of the TV each year.[3]

Plugging ourselves into the TV changes who we are and how we act as a people. We watch sitcoms instead of telling jokes. We watch romantic movies instead of taking romantic walks. We become friends with TV characters instead of with our neighbors. We watch sports instead of playing them. Many of us just turn on the TV to have some company and some kind of order to quiet our thoughts. Excessive TV watching keeps you from fully participating in life. It creates a world of watchers — not thinkers or doers but merely watchers.

TIRED OF BEING BOMBARDED?

Sometimes it seems like you can't escape TV. You may be out having lunch, enjoying a drink, shopping, or reading and there's a television blaring some inane advertisements or programming at you. Enter "TV-B-Gone"!—the David in the battle with the Goliath of cultural noise. Press the button to shut off just about any TV. Hook it on your keychain and voila! A simple, quick, fun way to reclaim our public space. Check it out at: www.tvbegone.com.

📝 ACTION: Watch less TV

If you are like most people, TV has had a bit of the upper hand for much of your life. In fact, millions of Americans are so addicted to watching television that they actually meet all of the criteria to be categorized as substance abusers!

It is time to renegotiate your relationship with television. For most people the benefits are enormous. Watching less TV will open up time for more constructive activities like: spending quality time with friends and family, catching up on some reading, pursuing hobbies, volunteering, playing music, enjoying nature, exercising, playing with your dog, or just getting outside.

CRITICAL TV VIEWER EXERCISES

- Watch a family member or friend watch TV for 10 minutes. Notice their behavior. Do they remind you of zombies?
- Turn the sound off and watch commercials for 10 minutes. How are the advertisers appealing to your desires?
- Turn the TV off and watch the screen for 10 minutes. How strong is your desire to turn it back on? As you notice your reflection on the screen, consider how we are a reflection of what we see on TV.

Tips For Taking Back Your Life From TV

Set a daily limit on TV watching: A good way to start taking back your power is to actually log how much time you spend in front of the TV in any given week. Once you've done that, consider cutting your TV watching in half.

> **4 hours, 32 minutes** the amount of TV the average American watches each day (the highest amount ever recorded).[4]

Choose what you watch (don't channel surf): Don't let the TV decide what you watch. YOU DECIDE! Consult your TV listings to find programs that you want to watch instead of just flipping through all of the channels. Don't get stuck watching programs that you don't really enjoy because "there's nothing better to do."

Turn off the sound during commercials: Have you ever noticed that the volume increases when the commercials come on? It's just another little trick to get you to buy something. Push the mute button. Then turn and talk to the person sitting next to you (or get up and do something).

Cancel your cable TV / Satellite subscription: You may not realize just how much of your life is spent in front of the television until you experience some time without it. Consider canceling your TV subscription service. You'll be amazed at the amount of time and money you'll save!

ACTION: Watch and support non-commercial television

If there are alternative TV stations in your area, they are wonderful assets to your community. They ensure that a major part of their programming will focus on quality public affairs and artistic productions that benefit your community (in a relatively ad-free environment). Be sure to support these stations financially because they do not rely heavily on corporate donations or advertising revenue to stay in business.

Public Access Television is "run by the citizens for the citizens." Community channels provide an electronic forum to express social and political concerns, as well as the opportunity to share valuable information with friends and neighbors.

> US TV networks broadcast 50% more commercials in 1997 than in 1983.[5]

To find community and public access television stations around the world (and near you) go to: www.openchannel.se.

Public Broadcasting Service (PBS)

Public Television still consistently produces the highest quality TV in town. Be sure to keep up with what's new on public TV, because some of the most powerful, cutting-edge programs are shown on PBS stations.

🖥 www.pbs.org

Look for these great shows on your local PBS station.

Frontline

A mainstay on PBS, "Frontline" is investigative journalism at its best. It gives 60 minutes of coverage to topics that often get 30 seconds on network news. "Frontline" tackles the most important topics of the day in an objective and comprehensive manner.

🖥 www.frontline.org

The NewsHour with Jim Lehrer

Probably the best news show on television, "The NewsHour" covers current events in more depth with less sensationalism. Quality over hype.

🖥 www.pbs.org/newshour

P.O.V.

"Point of View" shows independent documentaries on PBS, highlighting voices that are otherwise marginalized in our society. This show is a great way to catch what the cutting-edge nonfiction filmmakers are up to. "P.O.V." has won just about every major film and broadcasting award for its documentaries.

🖥 www.pov.org

In The Life

This Emmy-nominated public news magazine that airs on over 120 public TV stations provides positive visibility and accurate reporting of both the history and contemporary experiences of the gay and lesbian community.

🖥 www.inthelifetv.org

Alternative TV Networks

Link TV

Link TV is literally a link between US viewers and the rest of the world's media. With a programming line-up specifically chosen to educate, engage, and empower viewers, Link TV is a channel that is laying the foundation for a true global community that celebrates diverse cultures and perspective from around the world.

🖥 www.worldlinktv.org

Free Speech TV (FSTV)

Free Speech TV (FSTV) is available in over seven million American homes across the country, through public-access cable television. FSTV works with progressive organizations to broadcast political, cultural, and environmental issues — all with a focus on social justice. Visit their website to watch programs online or to find out if they have a channel in your area. Call your cable provider and ask for FSTV.

    💻 www.freespeech.org

Current TV

Current TV is a channel that is trying to democratize the production of television itself. Much of the content for the programs are created and produced by viewers themselves as a way to create a dialogue by the people and for the people. Viewers also vote for the programs they like which translates directly into the subsequent line-up of shows. This channel is a very bold experiment in participatory media. Watch, vote, and create.

    💻 www.current.tv

DVR'S, TIVO & THE FUTURE OF TELEVISION

Avid TV watchers now have a simple way to record, organize, watch, pause, and save any program by way of something called a Digital Video Recorder (DVR). This technology transforms TV watching in three ways. First, you choose when to watch your shows so that you don't have to organize your life around a network's changing program schedule; select the programs you want once, and you never have to think about it again. Second, commercials become a thing of the past with a few taps of a button so that viewing not only becomes more time efficient (44 min for a 1 hour show), but you are not forced to watch manipulative advertising. Finally, you can have your DVR automatically record shows that match certain key words like "Martin Luther King," "human rights," or "the environment" (a DVR typically stores from 40-120 hours of programs) so that you don't miss broadcasts of special interest that you may not know about. Try selecting some of the shows we recommend in this chapter! A company called TiVo currently manufactures some of the most popular DVR's on the market.

    www.tivo.com

RADIO

Similar to commercial TV stations, the main purpose of commercial radio is to make a profit. These stations work to expand their audience for the purpose of selling it to advertisers. This means that fluff and immature antics (ala Howard Stern) take precedence over socially useful programming. Public radio stations, in contrast, have the meeting of public needs as their core mission. A type of public radio station called "community radio stations" are an integral part of their communities, are run primarily by volunteers and usually have the most programming diversity on the air.

ACTION: Listen to and support your community and public radio stations

Community and public radio stations tend to broadcast more public affairs programming and more programs that are of interest to progressive listeners. Frequencies between 87 and 92 mHz on the FM dial are almost always reserved for educational, community, and noncommercial use. Why not try browsing?

National Public Radio (NPR)

NPR provides in-depth daily reporting on a wide variety of interesting political, social, and cultural issues. Listen to radio archives and find your local NPR station at: www.npr.org.

 ACTION: Tune in to alternative radio programs

Public and community radio stations offer many of the following alternative radio programs. If your local stations don't offer these great programs, then give 'em a call and request them.

E Town

An hour-long show of diverse, live music, mixed in with interviews of policymakers, authors, and cutting-edge thinkers, includes a short weekly talk with an "E-Chievement Award" winner — an individual who is honored for making a positive contribution in his or her community.

    🖥 www.etown.org

Democracy Now!

A half-hour show from Pacifica Radio, "Democracy Now" deals with hard-hitting political topics you won't hear anywhere else. It features discussions with leading writers, scholars, and activists.

    🖥 www.democracynow.org

Air America

Can't get enough of politics? Looking for talk radio that's not from a conservative perspective? Air America is the country's alternative to the Rush Limbaugh's of the radio world. With shows hosted by Al Franken and Janeane Garaofalo on topics ranging from election fraud to the environment, what more can you ask for?

    🖥 www.airamericaradio.com

> To find non-commercial radio stations from around the globe check out www.gumbopages.com/other-radio.html.

This American Life

Every week, host Ira Glass collects some of the most compelling, unique, human stories you've ever heard and organized them into a one-hour program. Many of these stories are truly transformative and all of them

---

TOP TEN DOCU-MENTARIES LIST

1. The Corporation
2. The Yes Men
3. The Times Of Harvey Milk
4. The Fog Of War
5. Bowling For Columbine
6. Control Room
7. Fahrenheit 9/11
8. Weapons of Mass Deception
9. Why We Fight
10. The Wild Parrots Of Telegraph Hill

bring you closer to your own humanity. The show also has an incredible online listening archive of every show they've produced in the past ten years.

🖥 www.thislife.org

Radio Netherlands

If you are looking for a non-US viewpoint on many global issues, Radio Netherlands is an excellent resource. Their English broadcast service is arguably one of the best in the world, and while it may be difficult to find a local radio station that carries their programming, you can listen online to live programming as well as archives of older broadcasts.

🖥 www.radionetherlands.nl

Alternative Radio

Produced by David Barsamian, "Alternative Radio" offers taped speeches and interviews of many of the most well-known progressive intellectuals and activists in the US.

🖥 www.alternativeradio.org

The Pacifica News Network

"Pacifica" brings you what's happening in the world every day, including issues and viewpoints that the mainstream media just won't cover.

🖥 www.pacifica.org

CounterSpin

Produced weekly by Fairness and Accuracy in Reporting (FAIR), "CounterSpin" uses critical media analysis and well-researched reporting to expose the influence those in power have over mainstream news.

🖥 www.fair.org/counterspin

New Dimensions Radio (NDR)

NDR focuses on bringing the public intimate interviews on a weekly basis with some of the wisest, most creative, innovative figures of our age. NDR is dedicated to empowering people to live a life more connected with themselves, their families, their communities, their spirituality and the planet.

🖥 www.newdimensions.org

MAGAZINES

One of the easiest ways to expand your awareness of current social justice and environmental issues is by reading progressive magazines on a regular basis. We have put together a list of what we think are the best alternative magazines available. Most of them have low-cost subscriptions, but you can also find many of them on the Internet, in your local library, or in nearby independent bookstores. By consciously choosing what kind of news you read, you reclaim control of the thoughts, feelings, and values that the mainstream media marginalizes. It's a great way to keep yourself motivated and focused on making a difference.

ACTION: Read alternative magazines

Where, besides in alternative magazines, are you going to find stories about sweatshop labor, inequality, corporate crime, and actions that allow you to stand up and fight these problems? Many alternative magazines also make it a point to focus on the positive work others are doing around the globe and on progress we're making in those areas.

If you find that you can't afford to subscribe, consider sharing a subscription with a like-minded friend. Be sure to share your alternative magazines with others. Take them to work (especially if there is a waiting room), give them to a friend, or donate them to your local public library.

MENTAL JUNK FOOD

While most of us understand why we can't eat ice cream and potato chips for breakfast, lunch, and dinner, we don't always realize that what we mentally consume is just as important as what we physically consume. There's a lot of attractive, "mental junk food" on display in most magazine racks that should not be the mainstay of our reading diets. *Stuff, FHM, Cosmopolitan, People, The National Enquirer*, and the like may have eye-catching headlines (or neck lines), but they don't facilitate much in the way of critical thinking either and should generally be avoided. Men's magazines in particular often reduce women to little more than sex objects. If you consume mental junk food, make sure to balance out your diet with some of the "nutritious" media in this chapter.

For a comprehensive list of just about every alternative magazine in existence, check out the Alternative Press Index at your local library or online; search it alphabetically or by subject.

💻 www.altpress.org

☆ **Top Pick**

Title: *Ode*
Issues: 10 per year   Cost: $30/yr
Web: www.odemagazine.com

If you want a thoughtful yet accessible magazine that focuses on stories of hope, change, and empowerment from around the world, then *Ode* just may be what you're looking for. Their inspiring stories deal with issues of social justice, the environment, human rights, peace, and community-building in a way that will have you reading it from cover to cover — and be better for it.

General

Title: *Mother Jones*
Issues: 6 per year   Cost: $18/yr
Web: 💻 www.motherjones.com

Mother Jones provides hard-hitting stories in a beautiful layout — what more could you ask for? *Mother Jones* is

known for its investigative reporting and its photo essays on arms dealing, exploitation, inequality and social change activism. It is one of the most engaging magazines on the newsstand. A bonus for web surfers, it is one of the few magazines that publishes its own full web version, so you don't have to miss a story even if you missed the issue.

Title: *YES!*
Issues: 6 per year   Cost: $24/yr
Web: 💻 www.yesmagazine.org

YES! A Journal of Positive Futures "supports people's active engagement in creating a just, sustainable, and compassionate future." *YES!* provides real-world solutions that are being implemented in communities around the globe and in individual lives. Holistic analysis of the world's condition leads this magazine to consider the environmental, economic, political, and spiritual problems and solutions that are before us as a global society. *YES!* will inspire you into action.

Title: *The Nation*
Issues: 50 per year   Cost: $52/yr
Web: 💻 www.thenation.com

One of the oldest, most respected weeklies for progressives, *The Nation* is full of cutting-edge social criticism, intelligently written articles, and political commentary. *The Nation* is considered the mainstay of the Left for political news that is lacking in the corporate media. Art, film and book reviews round out the magazine. How about trading in your *Time* and *Newsweek* for some progressive reporting on Washington politics?

Title: *The Progressive*
Issues: 12 per year   Cost: $32/yr
Web: 💻 www.progressive.org

Lively political and cultural commentary, congressional transcripts and monthly interviews with the most respected figures on the Left make *The Progressive* an informative and engaging read (it's also been around for 90 years). It is a great choice for those looking to keep their finger on the pulse of progressives in America.

Title: *Utne*
Issues: 6 per year   Cost: $20/yr
Web: 💻 www.utne.com

A kind of New Age Reader's Digest for progressives, *Utne* collects articles from the alternative media and creates a very readable bimonthly magazine. The full enjoyment of life, spirituality, ecology, community and alternative health are common topics. *Utne* appeals to a wide variety of tastes in an eye-catching format.

Title: *Co-op America Quarterly*
Issues: 4 per year   Cost: free with $25 membership
Web: 💻 www.coopamerica.org

Co-op America Quarterly focuses on how you can use your buying and investing power to create a socially and environmentally responsible economy. Easy-to-take steps are provided to help end sweatshops, nurture locally owned businesses, and promote community investment. *Co-op America Quarterly* is only one of the excellent publications of Co-op America. With a membership, you also receive the Financial Planning Handbook and the Greenpages directory of socially and environmentally responsible businesses.

Co-op America
COOP AMERICA QUARTERLY

Corporations

Title: *Multinational Monitor*
Issues: 10 per year   Cost: $25/yr
Web: 💻 www.multinationalmonitor.org

MULTINATIONAL
MONITOR

The *Multinational Monitor* "tracks corporate activity, especially in the Third World, focusing on the export of hazardous substances, worker health and safety, labor union issues and the environment." It is the magazine for keeping an eye on some of the most powerful (and destructive) entities on the planet — multinational corporations from McDonald's to Mitsubishi. Each December brings the issue "The Ten Worst Corporations of the Year."

Environment

Title: *E: The Environmental Magazine*
Issues: 6 per year   Cost: $20/yr
Web: 💻 www.emagazine.com

Every issue of *E* highlights articles that show how the natural environment is linked to our health, lifestyles, homes, and economy. The feature stories give great overviews to important topics such as environmental racism, "green" taxes, overconsumption and population growth. In addition, *E* provides many resources for linking with environmental organizations in the field — all in an engaging and eye-catching format.

Title: *Earth Island Journal*
Issues: 4 per year   Cost: $25/yr
Web: 💻 www.earthisland.org

Earth Island Journal

A publication of the late environmentalist David Brower's Earth Island Institute, this magazine addresses issues affecting the conservation, preservation and restoration of the global environment. It analyzes how the actions of governments, corporations and individual citizens affect the sustainability of our planet.

Title: *World Watch*
Issues: 6 per year   Cost: $20/yr
Website: 💻 www.worldwatch.org/mag

WORLD·WATCH
WORKING FOR A SUSTAINABLE FUTURE

World Watch magazine is a product of the highly respected World Watch Institute (which publishes State of the World yearly reports). Its issues usually focus on one or two environmental themes presented in highly researched articles, useful for both policymakers and informed citizens. Common topics are natural resource use, water and air quality, climate change and human health issues.

Title: *Sierra*

Issues: 6 per year   Cost: $15/yr

Web: 🖥 www.sierramagazine.org

Sierra, the official magazine of the Sierra Club, educates and informs readers about the latest wildland conservation issues, environmental legislation, and hidden dangers facing our ecosystems as well as engaging personal essays on experiencing the beauty of nature. Clearly written and filled with beautiful photography, *Sierra* is perfect for anyone who loves the outdoors.

Feminist

Title: *Ms.*

Issues: 6 per year   Cost: $45/yr

Web: 🖥 www.msmagazine.com

Ms.

The major feminist magazine of our day, *Ms.* is one of the few periodicals that you can find on the newsstand without any ads. Every issue has commentary on women's health, work, and the arts. Almost 100 pages of hard-hitting stories address everything from Norplant to working mothers to sweatshops.

Title: *Bust*

Issues: 6 per year   Cost: $20/yr

Web: 🖥 www.bust.com

BUST

If you are looking for something feminist with a large dose of young, hip fun, then pick up a copy of *Bust*. Perhaps the most accessible of contemporary feminist magazines, Bust combines thoughtful irreverence and constructive criticism of mainstream culture.

Gay and Lesbian

Title: **The Advocate**

Issues: 26 per year   Cost: $40/yr

Web: 🖥 www.advocate.com

Advocate

The Advocate is the premiere national news magazine for gays and lesbians. Every issue has commentary on politics, culture, and the arts for the lesbian and gay community. Topics include civil unions, adoption, workplace discrimination and legal protection, and interviews with leading activists and politicians. *The Advocate* is a great resource for keeping informed on the successes and challenges facing the movement for lesbian and gay equality in the US.

International

Title: *Cultural Survival Quarterly*

Issues: 4 per year   Cost: free with $45 membership

Web: 💻 www.cs.org

Cultural Survival Quarterly networks with indigenous groups and researchers to provide you with in-depth articles on the human rights and struggles of endangered cultures around the globe. Each issue focuses on how industrial development, subsistence agriculture and other factors impact indigenous cultures and ways of life. Cultural and economic globalization is creating an intense need for the protection of global diversity. Cultural Survival Quarterly will inform you and inspire you to act for this cause.

Title: *The New Internationalist*
Issues: 11 per year Cost: $36/yr
Web: 💻 www.newint.org

The *New Internationalist* brings you what's happening around the globe, focusing on such issues as economic inequality, pollution, the status of women, globalization and war — especially detailing the condition of the poorest countries. Extremely readable and full of oversized beautiful pictures, this monthly magazine keeps you informed and aware of what's going on from Albania to Zimbabwe.

Media

Title: *Adbusters*
Issues: 4 per year Cost: $20/yr
Web: 💻 www.adbusters.org

The Adbusters Media Foundation is a non-profit group of "Culture Jammers" working to counter the interests of big business that have created our out-of-control consumer culture. *Adbusters* creates "subvertising" and "counter-commercials" that combat the never-ending stream of corporate advertising. The advertisements and articles cleverly combine slick production with a biting social message. This is a fun magazine to read.

Title: *Extra!*
Issues: 6 per year Cost: $19/yr
Web: 💻 www.fair.org

Fairness and Accuracy in Reporting (FAIR) is one of the nation's largest media watchdog organizations and the publisher of *Extra!* Fighting for diversity in media content, *Extra!* combats censorship and media bias with some of the hardest-hitting stories in print. Find out how the stories of the day are often covered in a misleading manner by the corporate media. (Also, listen in to FAIR's weekly radio show, Counterspin, on your local public radio station).

Race

Title: *Color Lines*
Issues: 4 per year Cost: $16/yr
Web: 💻 www.colorlines.com

Color Lines is possibly the best magazine in the country dealing with the politics and issues important to communities of color. Each issue includes commentary on organizing; an in-depth look at diversity in the arts; and creative, insightful analysis of such complex issues as prisons, welfare, educational inequality and environmental justice.

Canadian Magazines
General

Title: *Briarpatch*
Issues: 10 per year   Cost: Can$25/yr.
Web: 💻 www.briarpatchmagazine.com

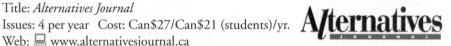

Title: *Canadian Dimension*
Issues: 6 per year   Cost: Can$25/Can$18 (students)/yr.
Web: 💻 www.canadiandimension.com

Title: *THIS MAGAZINE*
Issues: 6 per year   Cost: Can$24/yr.
Web: 💻 www.thismagazine.ca

Environment

Title: *Alternatives Journal*
Issues: 4 per year   Cost: Can$27/Can$21 (students)/yr.
Web: 💻 www.alternativesjournal.ca

Peace

Title: *Peace Magazine*
Issues: 4 per year   Cost: Can$18/yr.
Web: 💻 www.peacemagazine.org

NEWSPAPERS

Newspapers are a mainstay on many North Americans' morning tables. They can be a great way to keep up on current events. Unfortunately with any commercial periodical, advertising eats up a considerable portion of the total space. In fact, advertising demands 60% of the space in the average newspaper.[6]

Action: Read and recycle your local newspaper

Your local newspaper is a great source for finding out about community events and local issues. Local celebrations, concerts, protests and other get-togethers are easy to miss if you don't have an updated community calendar. Keep your eyes open for an alternative local weekly paper. They often contain a listing of community events and more alternative reporting, and they are usually available next to newspaper vending machines for free. Consider only subscribing to the Sunday edition of your paper or reading the news online if you would like to save a tree or two.

ACTION: Write a letter to the editor

Be sure to make your opinions known. The opinion section of the local newspaper is one of the last bastions for public discourse in a world where the average person doesn't have much of a voice. Take advantage of it. A lot of people read this part of the paper. Your letter is more likely to be published if it is concise, well thought out and relates to a recent article or editorial in that newspaper. Most papers accept e-mails as well as typed letters.

INTERNET

With the advent of the Internet, we can communicate with others around the globe in a fraction of a second. The Internet has provided progressives the opportunity to get their message out about the environment, labor struggles, indigenous people's rights and movements for democracy. This type of communication can inform you about the actions and ideas of others around the world and inspire you to act in your community to produce social justice.

 ACTION: Get connected to progressive websites

General News

Common Dreams www.commondreams. org is the most comprehensive news site on the Web, covering issues of interest to progressives. They even provide an extensive list of direct links to related websites of newspapers, magazines, and radio and TV stations.

News for Change www.workingfor change.com is a unique daily news site that focuses specifically on stories of interest to those interested in a better world. Sponsored by Working Assets, this site also makes a point of linking every story to an action that you can take to make a difference around the issue you've just finished reading about.

Straightgoods www.straightgoods.com is "Canada's independent online source of news you can use." A neat website, with loads of great information on a variety of topics.

Activist News

The Independent Media Centre (www.indymedia.org) was founded by a number of independent and alternative media organizations. They dedicated themselves to reporting those stories that may not otherwise be told about grassroots issues of fundamental social change and the activists that are working to make it happen. They offer news from seven Canadian cities in addition to many in the US.

Environmental News

Envirolink (www.envirolink.org) is perhaps the best starting point for finding environmental resources on the Web. This site has everything you can imagine, from the latest environmental news headlines and a comprehensive list of eco-organizations to a powerful search engine for finding all things green.

The Environmental News Network (www.enn.com) is not only a great source of up-to-date news on pressing environmental issues, but it includes in-depth explanations of important environmental topics (alternative energy, global warming) and an engaging format.

ACTION: Join an inspiring email action list

A number of active organizations now have weekly email newsletters that connect you to empowering resources and actions that can help you make even more of a difference. They'll keep you connected to the latest news, actions, ideas and avenues for positive change. This is a great way to stay involved even if you're otherwise very busy. To sign up, just go to the website and fill in your email address in the appropriate box. You should receive your first message almost immediately. Here is a short list of organizations that offer some of the best email newsletters around as well as the link that will take you straight to the appropriate web page to learn more.

Red Jellyfish: www.redjellyfish.com/jellygram-page.html
Care2: www.care2.com/newsletters
Center For A New American Dream: www.newdream.org/make/action
Working Assets: www.actforchange.com
Save Our Environment Action Center: www.saveourenvironment.org

ACTION: Subscribe to some informative podcasts

iPods and other portable digital music players aren't just for music anymore. Audio (and video) podcasts are filling up more and more of these convenient, walk-around devices. Downloading the iTunes software (www.itunes.com) allows you to subscribe to your favorite shows and have them automatically downloaded on your iPod (or computer) every week. No commercials. No schedules. No waiting. Just plug it into your computer for 5 minutes and you're ready for a week of education, ideas and empowerment!

TOP TEN PODCASTS

Democracy Now!
GLRC Environment Report
Living On Earth
On The Media
NOW
P.O.V.
Mother Jones Radio
RadioNation
The Al Franken Show
5 Minutes For a Better
  World

⇨ MEDIA RESOURCES

Adbusters Media Foundation
1243 West 7th Avenue,
Vancouver, BC, Canada, V6H 1B7
(604) 736-9401   💻 www.adbusters.org
Adbusters is on the cutting edge of "jamming"

corporate culture. You have got to see their "uncommericals" on their website. You can even work to get their "uncommercials" on your local TV stations! The "uncommercials" use the master's tools (TV) to take apart the master's house (consumerism) by criticizing the over-watching of TV, ecological destruction, and eating disorders. They also sponsor "Buy Nothing Day," which is an annual event on the Friday after Thanksgiving, to publicize the effects of overconsumption on our culture and the planet.

Center for Media Literacy
P.O. Box 64-1909, Los Angeles, CA 90064, USA
(310) 581-0260   💻 www.medialit.org
Media literacy education teaches critical and analytical viewing skills to people of all ages so they can better understand and navigate our media culture. Print literacy (the ability to read and write) is no longer enough. Media literacy teaches people to ask the right questions: Who created this message? Why? How and why did they choose what to include and what to leave out of this message? How is it intended to influence me?

Hazen, Don, and Julie Winokur, eds. *We the Media.* New Press, 1997. Hazen and Winokur's book uses an engaging format (and excerpts from the most eloquent media critics) to discuss the issues of corporate ownership of the media, media literacy, and the numerous alternative sources of information on TV, radio, and the Web.

Just about anything by Bill Moyers.
Bill Moyers is one of the most profound and influential journalists of our time. He has won more than 30 Emmy Awards for his work making thought-provoking documentaries. He is a prolific writer, and his interviewees include some of our most prominent figures, as well as average people dealing with everyday problems. Whether it's a book, film, or television program, it's hard to go wrong if Bill Moyers is involved in its creation.

📖 Phillips, Peter, and Project Censored. *Censored : the Top 25 Censored Stories of the Year.* Seven Stories Press, 2006. Project Censored is an annual collection of the Top 25 important news stories that were largely neglected by the mainstream media. Examples of past censored stories are: (1) the secret negotiations of the Multilateral Agreement on Investment (MAI), which threatened to restrict a government's ability to stand up to multinational corporations, (2) extensive civilian deaths in the Iraq War, and (3) increasing government secrecy and election fraud.
💻 www.projectcensored.org

POLITICS

Voting
Getting Involved
The Top Ten Issues List

MANY OF US IN THE US are frustrated with politics, and we have some good reasons to be. Misleading campaign ads fill the airwaves. Dubious campaign donations find their way into both parties' coffers. Washington lobbyists, representing everyone but the average American, convince our elected officials to pass legislation in the lobbyists' interest rather than ours. The 2000 election fiasco turned many of us off to the political process, and the 2004 election brewed even more cynicism. It's no wonder so many of us have stopped participating in politics altogether. When we feel that rich and powerful interests drown out our voices, there isn't much incentive to speak up. Half of all eligible American citizens don't even vote for their president![1] That's not much of a democracy.

Yet there are signs of hope. The current state of politics has also created the best opportunity for us to become involved. Americans understand that the system we have isn't working anymore. Stepping up to this challenge, we are beginning to produce long-term political change. The McCain-Feingold campaign finance reform bill has produced modest but important changes, and the Jack Abramoff lobbying scandal is producing further calls for reform. The average person's political power is actually increasing. In a world where most people are content to remain silent, even the smallest of voices becomes a roar. If the 2000 election proved anything, it's that every vote counts (just 537 votes determined who became president). A few votes, first in Florida (2000) and then Ohio (2004) ultimately decided whether the US went to war; and our subsequent policies and the Democratic successes in the 2006 midterm election may ultimately change the nation's course in Iraq. Our engagement in the political process is now more important than ever.

213

In this chapter, you will learn how our political system actually works; how to inform yourself and vote effectively; how to get involved and make a powerful difference in city, state, and national politics; and you will understand the top political issues we face at the turn of the century. When you understand and participate in your government, it will help you feel more engaged and connected to a number of ways in which you can help the world. Ultimately, by taking this on, you can shift the balance of power back to the people, where it belongs.

VOTING

Many people assume that their time to participate in politics comes every four years, in November. In fact, state and national elections happen every two years (during even-numbered years), and local elections for smaller offices can happen in any year. At a minimum, it is important to remember to vote every two years during major elections, the first Tuesday in November.

WHO GETS ON THE BALLOT?

Every other year between January and June, every state holds either a primary or a set of caucuses, where members of the Republican and Democratic parties select their respective party's presidential and congressional candidates. You must be a member of the party to vote at your local primary caucus, but in most cases you can sign up at the door. For third parties, the candidate selection process often occurs at the party's state convention. Each state's results are tallied to determine the parties' presidential candidate. To find out when your primary or caucus meets, call toll free (800) 424-9530 or visit: www.fec.gov. Then go to your local primary or caucus and help determine who your party nominates.

ACTION: Register to vote

To be eligible to vote in most states, you must register to vote (at your current address) at least 30 days prior to an election. This means that every time you change addresses you have to re-register — even if you only move across the street. You can register to vote at your local Department of Motor Vehicles (DMV) or drivers' licensing office, county elections office, or many City/County office buildings. At the DMV, you can register to vote instantly just by getting your new driver's license! Many states also offer registration opportunities at public libraries, post offices, and public high schools and universities.

To get a copy of the National Mail Voter Registration Form, which most states accept, go to the Federal Election Commission's website at: www.fec.gov/votregis/vr.htm.

ACTION: Seek out good information before each election

Every couple of years as we close in on the month of November, campaign strategists barrage us with information, trying to influence how we vote. It comes in

WHERE'S MY POLLING PLACE?

If you are registered to vote, you should receive notification in the mail of the location of your polling place. You may also contact your county election official to find out where you can vote. Look in the "Government" section of the phone book for the "County/ Municipal Clerk," "Supervisor of Elections," or "Board/Commission of Elections."

To find out about voting in Canada, go to Elections Canada (www.elections.ca), where you'll find party information, election results, registration information and more.

the mail, on our doorstep, over the telephone and through the TV. Ninety-nine percent of this information is worse than useless. It's advertising disguised as valid information, but instead of trying to sell us used cars, they are trying to sell us candidates. As citizens in a democracy, it is essential that we fully inform ourselves about the issues and candidates through channels we can trust.

It's not only important to understand where the candidates stand on the issues, but also the other measures on the ballot that may even be more important than who gets elected. We often decide on important issues concerning school funding, abortion, gun control and campaign finance in the voting booth.

> Looking for a good starting point to get a handle on major political issues that includes easy-to-read summaries, how the issues are being framed, graphs and facts? Check out the nonpartisan group Public Agenda Online at: www. publicagenda.org. You won't be disappointed. It is the best site for a nonpartisan exploration of the issues.

Step 1: Contact Project Vote Smart and use FactCheck.org

A bipartisan group of citizens started Project Vote Smart because they were tired of the poor quality of information available to voters. Their excellent website (www.votesmart. org) offers election information that is as well researched and unbiased as you can find anywhere. You can also call them toll free at (888) VOTE-SMART. They can provide you with information on specific candidates, from state legislators up to the president.

FactCheck.org is a nonpartisan watchdog group that monitors political claims in TV ads, speeches, debates and press releases. FactCheck.org can help you see through the exaggerations, distortions, and outright lies politicians and partisan groups use to smear their opponents. They do the homework so you don't have to, carefully dissecting each side's arguments to separate fact from fiction. Not just useful during election time, FactCheck.org analyzes both parties' positions on the most current issues, from social security reform to the war on terror.

💻 www. FactCheck.org

BAD INFORMATION
Unsolicited Mail
TV Ads
Unsolicited Calls

SO-SO INFORMATION
Government Mailed
  Information
TV Debates

GOOD INFORMATION
Project Vote Smart's
  research
Factcheck.org
League of Women Voters
  material
Information from organi-
  zations you respect
Cross-checked research in
  local newspapers

Step 2: Get in touch with your local League of Women Voters

The League of Women Voters is a nonpartisan educational organization that seeks to create informed citizens for a more powerful democracy. Every state and many counties have League of Women Voters chapters that can provide you with information on state and local candidates as well as on ballot issues. They also have a comprehensive website (www.lwv.org) that includes a section for looking up the chapter nearest you.

Step 3: Ask organizations that you respect for information

Be sure to seek out organizations that you know are doing good work in the world, and ask them to send you information on issues and candidates. Almost every organization will have some carefully reasoned positions for you to consider. You don't have to be a member to request this kind of information. Also keep your eyes open for guides put out by organizations you trust that evaluate the candidates' voting records and current stands on the issues. Here are some examples to get you started:

> AFL-CIO: www.aflcio.org/issues/legislativealert/votes
> League of Conservation Voters: www.lcv.org
> Peace Action: www.peace-action.org
> Human Rights Campaign: www.hrc.org

Step 4: Survey local newspapers for election-related material

As the elections near, begin collecting information from your local and statewide newspapers about issues and candidates. Pay special attention on the weekend before election day, which is when many newspapers set aside a large section to deal with the upcoming election. Often newspapers will interview candidates about where they stand on a number of issues, as well as provide arguments for and against upcoming ballot measures. The key is to collect your information from the widest variety of newspaper sources available so that you can truly make informed decisions come election time.

 ACTION: Create your own voting strategy

Voting usually involves imperfect information, limited choices, and striking a balance between being true to your values and being pragmatic. It is important to come up with a voting strategy that you can feel good about. The following

WHAT'S THE ELECTORAL COLLEGE?

The way the electoral college system works in presidential elections mystifies many Americans. Here is a brief explanation.

Every state in the US is worth a certain number of points, based on the number of national legislators that state has in the US Congress. This means that a state is worth 2 points (for its 2 senators), plus 1 point for however many representatives it sends to the US House of Representatives. How many representatives a state has is based on that state's population. So, for example, while California is worth 55 points as of this writing, Colorado is only worth 9 points. Points change every ten years, based on national census information, and that state is allotted more or fewer house representatives accordingly.

When people in a given state cast their votes on election day, all of the votes are tallied, and the presidential candidate with the most votes gets all the electoral points for that state. In the end, the candidate that receives the most points wins.

The flaw in the system is, of course, that it's possible for a candidate to win the popular vote and still lose the electoral vote, and thus the election. Except for three times in the 1800s and in the 2000 election, the winning presidential candidate has always had the most popular votes, as well a majority of the electoral points.

Over the years, many have debated the pros and cons of the electoral college system. To learn more about them and how the system works, go to the following websites:

- www.nara.gov/fedreg/elctcoll
- www.fec.gov/pages/ecmenu2.htm

strategies are just examples to get you started thinking about your own possibilities:

- Consider voting for a major party candidate if the race looks close; otherwise vote for a candidate that more closely matches your values (even if they are from a minor party).

- If you are undecided or can't find enough reliable information about a candidate, vote for the party that best reflects your values.

- Vote for third-party candidates in smaller, local elections where you think they have a better chance of winning.

- Make a note to yourself on how to improve your strategy for the next election, for example "Need to find good research about judges."

- Remember, you can abstain from voting on any particular position or issue, and your ballot will still count.

ACTION: Vote

After you have researched all the referenda, initiatives, and candidates, write down your choices before you go to the polls. That way you don't have to stand there reading the complex wording on the ballots or deciding between city council candidates you don't know much about.

BE PREPARED!

Trying to decide how to vote while you're in the voting booth is stressful and potentially counterproductive. Ballots can be confusing and suddenly discovering you must vote on a state referendum can really throw you off. There are several ways to be prepared before you set foot in your polling place. Registered voters typically receive in the mail a pamphlet listing candidates and ballot issues, referendums, and initiatives. Read this over and then do some research, marking how you'll vote when you've made a decision. Also, most local newspapers print a sample ballot — you can mark your choices and take your "cheat sheet" with you when you vote. Going in prepared makes voting quick and easy.

Be sure to take the opportunity to vote in every election — school board, county, state, and federal. It's easy to forget about local and state elections and pay attention only to the heavily funded and widely publicized federal races. Actually, local and state elections may have more impact on your life. Local candidates decide how to run your schools, how to "reform" welfare, and whether to build bike paths or more roads. Voting is one of the many perks and responsibilities of living in a democracy. It is the first important step in having a say in how your government works.

VOTE FROM HOME

Many people don't realize that you no longer have to even show up to a voting booth on election day to vote. Millions of people every year vote from the comfort of their own homes weeks before election day arrives, using an absentee ballot. Why should you apply for a permanent or ongoing absentee ballot?
- You can vote from home.
- You can vote on a day and a time that work best for you.
- You can take time to really consider your choices.
- You are more likely to vote in every election.

There should be a form for an absentee ballot at the same government offices that keep copies of voter registration forms, or you can find more information by looking up your state on the Project Vote-Smart site: www.vote-smart.org.

 ACTION: Help others vote

Casting your own vote is a powerful act; helping others vote could be the beginning of a movement! There are many ways you can volunteer to help others vote:
- Be a poll monitor to ensure that no one is unfairly denied access to the polls.
- Volunteer for a voter registration drive.
- Help drive people to the polls.
- Participate in a phone bank to call voters.

- Offer your voting research to others.
- Make copies of sample ballots and hand them out to your friends, neighbors, and relatives.

To find out how you can help, contact your state or local party headquarters. You can also find out how to get involved at: www.MoveOn.org, www.Indy voter.org, and www.rockthevote.org.

GETTING INVOLVED

Voting is only the first step in getting involved in politics. The real work comes between elections in organizing, building coalitions, and educating the public on issues you care about. There are a lot of great ways to get more involved in politics. You can:

- Talk to friends and family about important community issues.
- Write letters to the editors of your local newspapers.
- Call or write your elected officials.
- Distribute some literature in your area around election time.
- Register people to vote.
- Assist at the polls.
- Become directly involved in campaigns for people that you believe in.
- Go to a city council meeting and state your desires or concerns.

ACTION: Join a party that reflects your values

Joining a political party is a great way for you to band together with like-minded people to increase your collective voice within our political system. Joining a political party does not mean that you are pledging your unwavering support for every single piece of a party's platform or giving your unquestioning loyalty to each and every candidate they sponsor. It just indicates that you agree with a majority of the issues that the party stands for.

When considering which party to join, you come to a fundamental dilemma. Is it better to change the system from the inside or the outside? Becoming a member of the Republicans or Democrats allows you to work inside the system. It gives you access to more power to make change, but this power usually comes at the cost of having to compromise some of your values. These parties seek to attract such broad coalitions of voters that they may water down issues you care about. You also run the risk of becoming so focused on winning that you lose sight of your values altogether.

Joining a smaller party allows you the ability to work from the outside. Working outside the system lets you hold firmly to your values, but this often comes at the expense of gaining access to the power necessary to change the system. On top of that, there is a danger of spending so much time outside the mainstream that you lose your ability to relate to anyone who is working on the inside. Smaller parties have played an important historical role in US politics, though. Many smaller parties focus on one or two issues that both mainstream parties currently neglect. When the small party gains enough popular support, the Democrats or Republicans usually take on the issue to attract voters back to their party. Smaller parties are also useful for re-energizing disaffected voters.

Democratic Party

The Democratic Party has long been the traditional party of the Left in the US, forming coalitions with labor unions, environmentalists, women's rights groups, and communities of color — although in recent years that position has come into question. There are many who say the Democrats and the Republicans are looking more and more like each other as both parties take in large campaign donations from corporations and other wealthy interest groups, whose interests they are then obliged to serve. Others would argue that the Democratic Party is the only realistic option and that we must work to bring it back into line with its more traditional progressive values.

(202) 863-8000   ▪ www.democrats.org

Republican Party

The Republican Party is committed to a limited role for federal government, a strong military, school vouchers, tax cuts, and traditional family values. Unfortunately the Republicans' economic policies tend to disproportionately benefit wealthy individuals and corporations. The Republican Party also has historically advocated ending legalized abortion and has been hostile toward equality for lesbian and gay Americans. Some signs of hope are the Log Cabin Republicans (lesbian/gay rights) and Republicans for Choice (abortion rights) who are working to change the social conservatism of the party.

(800) 200-1294   ▪ www.rnc.org

Green Party

Perhaps the most exciting third party on the political map, the Green Party is based on ten key values: ecological wisdom, social justice, grassroots democracy, nonviolence, decentralization, community-based economics, feminism, respect for diversity, personal and global responsibility and future sustainability. In the US, local and state Green parties form the backbone of this political party, as volunteers build the party from the grassroots level up. In 2000, their presidential ticket candidate, Ralph Nader, received almost three million votes (for third place).

(303) 543-0672   ▪ www.greenparties.org

New Party

The New Party primarily runs candidates in local elections, and they've been extremely effective at getting them elected. In fact, in the past five years they have won 200 out of their first 300 races! They sit out races that they know they can't win and endorse candidates from other parties that carry similar values. In this way, they never take away votes from other progressive candidates — a strategy that has served them well. Their priorities include campaign finance and other electoral reform, education, public safety, environmentally sustainable economic development and living wages.

(800) 200-1294 💻 www.newparty.org

Natural Law Party

Founded in 1992, the Natural Law Party platform focuses on crime prevention, education that maximizes student potential, preventative health care, mandatory labeling of genetically engineered foods, transition to clean renewable energy sources, increased drug treatment programs and getting big money out of politics. They argue that if we get beyond partisan bickering, we can solve many of our social problems by implementing programs already proven effective.

(800) 200-1294 💻 www.natural-law.org

Libertarian Party

The Libertarian Party is committed to shrinking the role of government down to the protection of individual rights and national defense. They advocate for the protection of civil liberties, such as privacy rights and an end to the drug war that has imprisoned hundreds of thousands of non-violent drug offenders. Unfortunately the Libertarians also call for the elimination of many social services and the social safety net. They oppose any form of government assistance to the poor; social security; public schools; and laws to protect workers, consumers, and the environment. Inequality is not of great concern to them under their economic policies, which put their trust completely in the corporate-run free market to create a better world.

(800) 200-1294 💻 www.lp.org

 ## ACTION: Stay informed

Democracy cannot live up to its full potential without an informed citizenry. Unfortunately, despite ever-greater access to information via cable, satellite, and the Internet, good information is hard to come by. Avoid political scream match shows such as the O'Reilly Factor, Crossfire, and Hannity and Colmes. They teach you almost nothing and even poison the political process with misinformation, political spin, partisan politics, and cynicism. The MEDIA chapter lists many great magazines, TV shows, and radio programs. For the best day-to-day political information, check out these programs:

The News Hour with Jim Lehrer (PBS, weekdays) www.newshour.org. The News Hour provides in depth analysis of current events by the foremost experts.

The NEWS HOUR with Jim Lehrer

All Things Considered (National Public Radio, every afternoon) www.npr.org Tune into your local NPR station while you prepare for dinner or drive home from work to get a recap of the day's news and analysis of pressing issues.

BBC News (PBS, weekday afternoons and late evenings). The BBC newscast gives an international perspective, covering important issues and events that the US media often brushes over.

Washington Week with Gwen Ifill (PBS, Fridays after The News Hour). Washington Week brings together liberal and conservative political and media commentators in a round table format to discuss the latest developments in politics. A nice weekly summary and analysis of political events.

Meet the Press with Tim Russert (NBC, Sunday mornings). Meet the Press has a long tradition of asking politicians the tough but fair questions. No one gets off easy.

The Daily Show with Jon Stewart (Comedy Central, weekdays). The Daily Show features political satire at its finest. Though Jon Stewart and his cast report the "fake news," their incisive commentary also takes politicians to task.

THE BEST OF FRONTLINE

PBS's Frontline produces engaging, informative programs on a variety of subjects. Perfect for showing at a community gathering, in the classroom, or at a "teach in." You can order programs or watch many of them online at: www.pbs.org/wgbh/pages/frontline/view. Most shows have a teacher's guide for educators.

The Last Abortion Clinic (2005)
The Torture Question (2005)
Private Warriors (2005)
Company of Soldiers (2005)
Al Qaeda's New Front (2005)
The Persuaders (2004)
Is Wal-Mart Good for America? (2004)
Rumsfeld's War (2004)
Truth, War, and Consequences (2004)

The American Prospect
12 issues per year, $20/yr
💻 www.prospect.org

If you are a political junkie, *The American Prospect* is the magazine for you. Keep up-to-date on upcoming legislation and pressing political issues including economic inequality, global warming, war and the budget. Their web archive includes important debates over political strategy and policy for creating peace and justice in our world.

Electronic Policy Network (www.epn.org), a project of *American Prospect* magazine, provides in-depth information for progressives on a broad array of topics, ranging from campaign finance reform to criminal justice and poverty.

Speakout.com (www.speakout.com) was started to provide people with quality information about a number of important political issues and to provide avenues for people to speak out about how they feel. In one site, it gives you everything you need to get involved.

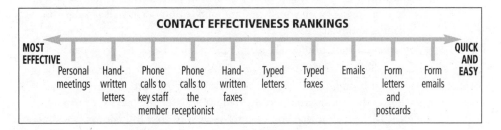
SpeakOut.com

ACTION: Contact your representatives

Legislators hear very little from their constituents on many issues. Thus they may take your letter, call, or email as representative of the view of hundreds or even thousands of voters. Don't ever think that your voice doesn't count — it does. Especially at the local and state level, policymakers pay attention to comments from the public. Legislators often change their minds and votes when even a moderate number of citizens contact them. Remember, it is just as important to support your legislators when they are doing things right as it is to urge them to change when they are headed in the wrong direction. It is best to contact them when they are considering a bill you care about.

Here are some general tips for contacting your representatives:

- If you are concerned with a particular piece of legislation, refer to the legislative bill by both number and title. For example, "I am writing to urge you to support the 'Family Leave Act' (HR.2384, sponsored by Representative Henry Jones), the most important legislation supporting the American family in years."

- Don't worry about not being an expert on an issue. You don't have to be. Your opinion still makes a difference.

- Be courteous and reasonable. Show respect for the policymakers you contact, even when you disagree with them; otherwise they may disregard your message.

- Contact your legislator even if you don't know where they stand on an issue. If you do know that a legislator is doing something right, commend them. If they are doing something wrong, firmly but politely ask them to change their position on the issue.

Tips for Writing Your Representatives

- It's best to be brief, clear, and specific. Do not write more than one page.

CONTACT EFFECTIVENESS RANKINGS

MOST EFFECTIVE ← → QUICK AND EASY

| Personal meetings | Hand-written letters | Phone calls to key staff member | Phone calls to the receptionist | Hand-written faxes | Typed letters | Typed faxes | Emails | Form letters and postcards | Form emails |

Use these addresses to write your Senators and Representatives at the national level:

Your Representative	Your Senator
US House of Representatives	US Senate
House Office Building	Senate Office Building,
Washington, DC 20510, USA.	Washington, DC 20510, USA.

Check out Project Vote Smart (www.vote-smart. org) and type in your zip code to find out contact information for your local, state, and national government representatives.

In Canada, look at Democracy Watch's website (www.dwatch.ca), type in your postal code, and find your MP's contact information.

- State your opinion and your specific request within the first few sentences. Give reasons to back up your opinion in your own words.

- Speak in terms of your values, not just your opinion about a law or policy. Values often resonate more deeply than simple demands.

- Hand-write your letter if possible. That is the only way your representative knows that it truly comes from an individual. If you must type the letter, add a P.S. that is handwritten.

- Make the letter as personal as possible, using your own words.

- At the end of your letter, make a specific request and ask the policy-maker to state her or his position on a specific issue.

- If you want to have your letter read by the top people and receive an original reply, ask a question that is too specific to be covered by a general response form letter. If you do at first receive a form letter that does not respond to your particular question, call or write again and ask politely that they do so.

Tips for Calling Your Representatives

- Begin your call with something like, "Hi, this is Bob Carlson from Little Rock, Arkansas, and I'm calling about X." In this way you let the person know exactly what you're calling about. You also make it clear that you are a constituent.

- Most people who call will only be able to talk to a receptionist. Ask to speak with the staff member in charge of your particular issue. If you have to, leave a message with your name and phone number as well as what you are calling about.

- Before ending any phone call, make sure to ask for a written response.

- It is usually quite difficult to get to talk to your legislator personally on the phone (although you'll have more luck with your state legislators than national). If you feel very strongly about an issue, be persistent in your efforts. Make it clear that you wish to speak with your legislator personally and that you are willing to call back for as long as it takes. When you finally get to speak to your legislator, it is important to be quick and to the point about your issue.

You can call the US Capitol switchboard, (202) 224-3121, and the operator will connect you directly to your Senator's or Representative's office. To contact your state legislators, check out: www.vote-smart.org.

If you want to go straight to the top with your opinions, leave a message on the White House comment line, from 9 a.m. to 5 p.m. EST, seven days a week, at (202) 456-1111. The President is given a summary every day of how many people called in about each issue. Only about 2,000 people call in on any given day![2]

Tips for Meeting with Your Representative

A personal meeting with your legislators shows both that an issue is very important to you and that you are very politically active. They will learn that you are someone they would prefer to have on their side rather than against them.

EXAMPLE LETTER

Representative Mark Udall
US House of Representatives
Washington, DC 20510, USA.

Dear Representative Udall:

There is a bill moving through Congress, called the "Taxpayer Relief Act" (HR 1725, sponsored by Representative Sam Smith), which is completely misguided in its approach. Taxpayers do not need an extra few hundred dollars when the US has such a large deficit, social security is running out, and our schools are some of the least developed in the industrialized world. I am writing to strongly encourage you to vote against this destructive piece of legislation. The money could be better spent on improving education, a top priority for most Americans, including myself. Please send a written reply explaining your position. I look forward to your response. Thank you.

Sincerely,
(Signature)
Jane Smith
123 W Elm Street,
Boulder, CO 80305, USA.

Remember, at the state and federal level the representative will most likely not read your letter. One of his/her staff people will read it, tabulate your letter, and tell the representative that X number of his/her constituents feel this way about Issue Y.

Having trouble getting started? 20/20 Vision provides its members with monthly action notices, full of facts about a pressing environmental or peace issue and tips for contacting an elected official. Their timely action notices guarantee that your voice is heard at the most pressing moment in the legislative process. Your energy goes directly where it will have the most impact. Call them at (800) 669-1782, or go to: www.2020vision.org.

20/20 VISION™

Actforchange.com is another amazing site that allows you to instantly send your representatives your opinion on a variety of issues. If you want to make your voice heard, but feel that you need to know more about the issues first, this is the site for you. Visit them at: www.actforchange.com.

Although it takes more time and effort than any other option, it is also the most effective of your contact options.

- Call to schedule an appointment with your legislator. If he/she is not able to meet with you, plan a meeting with the key staff member or legislative assistant in charge of the type of issue you are concerned about.

- Pick one issue. Be prepared to talk about why this issue is important to you and everyone. You don't need to be an expert, just somewhat informed and very concerned.

- Find out what your legislator's stand is on your issue so that you understand how much you are asking him or her to move from it.

- If you have time, consider creating a packet of materials that you can hand your legislator that provides more information about the issue. This could include newspaper clippings, fact sheets, editorials and your own contact information.

- Tell the legislator what you would like him/her to do and give your reasons why. Be specific and share with her/him the values behind your request. Do you want him/her to vote for a bill, co-sponsor it, or take a public leadership role on the issue?

- Before leaving, thank the legislator for his/her time and patience.

ACTION: Speak powerfully

Conservatives have spent decades refining their language in order to better sell their proposals to the public while many liberals and progressives have been on the defensive, playing to the middle rather than staking out a true vision. How we talk about issues greatly impacts whether people will support our cause. For example, the elimination of the estate tax had no political traction for almost ten years until conservatives began calling it the "death tax." Suddenly, people who stood to gain nothing (the tax effects mainly million dollar inheritances) by repealing the estate tax began to vehemently support conservative efforts to abolish it. Those of us who want to make the world a better place have deeply-held values, yet we need to learn how to communicate our values more effectively. Many of us are uncomfortable talking about them, as if only religious conservatives hold values. It's time to stand up and speak clearly about ethical economics, honest democracy, a culture of hope, rehumanizing politics, and practical idealism.

The Rockridge Institute
The Rockridge Institute is a nonpartisan group dedicated to building a progressive vision, helping progressives better articulate their values and reframing the public debate. They offer advice on speaking about current events and practical manuals on how to create and talk about progressive policies.

    💻 www.rockridgeinstitute.org

THE TOP TEN ISSUES LIST

ONE: Campaign finance reform

Well, the people have finally won one of the battles in the war for clean and honest government. The Bipartisan Campaign Reform Act of 2002, better known as

---

THE SEVEN THINGS YOU SHOULD KNOW ABOUT MONEY AND POLITICS

1. Both the Republicans and the Democrats have been moving further to the Right, mostly for the benefit of people in positions of power, at the expense of the average citizen. In fact, on some issues, it is difficult to distinguish between the two parties.

2. Corporations and wealthy interest groups have made both parties dependent on their help, and thus they have a powerful influence on how our political representatives behave.

3. Political parties need corporations and wealthy interest groups, because there is no other way to get the large amounts of money needed to win an election.

4. Politicians need large amounts of money, because running political ad campaigns is incredibly expensive — especially television ads, which are some of the most effective at influencing voters.

5. There is such a powerful correlation between how much a candidate spends on advertising and how many votes he/she gets, it is almost impossible to win without big money.

6. Campaign contributions are like drugs: corporations and wealthy interest groups are like the dealers and our political representatives like the addicts. The average citizen cannot come up with enough drugs to get the addict high and thus has little influence on the addict.

7. Some people blame the addicts (our representatives) for the problem, when the real issue is how to curb the addiction.

SIGNS OF HOPE

MoveOn.org — this grassroots online organization shows us the power of using the Internet to mobilize people and resources and the media to spread a progressive message.

McCain-Feingold campaign finance reform — though far from perfect, this legislation at least brought renewed attention to the problem of money and corruption in politics.

Protests for peace — During her vigil at President Bush's ranch, Cindy Sheehan, mother of slain US soldier Casey Sheehan, showed us that one person's powerful witness could make a difference.

Women leaders elected around the world — Chile, Germany, Finland, Liberia and other countries elected their female heads of state.

Gay rights — many countries, including Finland, Canada, New Zealand, Portugal, Germany, Spain, and the Netherlands, have legalized either same sex civil unions or marriage. In 2003, the US Supreme Court ruled sodomy laws unconstitutional.

ANWR — Thanks to pressure from concerned citizens, the Senate continues to reject attempts to legalize oil drilling in the Arctic National Wildlife Refuge.

Global warming — despite resistance from the US, many nations are taking the threat of global warming very seriously, agreeing to reinforce the Kyoto Protocol's goals to reduce emissions.

War — In the 2006 US Congressional elections, voters elected Democratic majorities in both houses of Congress for the first time in years, in large part to express their opposition to the Republicans' handling of the war in Iraq.

the McCain-Feingold Law, outlawed "soft money" (unlimited contributions to political parties) and restricted "issue ads" near an election. But unfortunately it raised individual contribution limits from $1,000 to $2,000. Big-money lobbyists also follow up their campaign contributions with increased access to our leaders. Each year, candidates break campaign contribution records, and each year our government representatives become more beholden to the people who fund them. Campaign spending is now in the billions, and many elite donors give to both the Democrats and Republicans in the same races so that they can ensure that no matter who wins, they always win. It is time to take our government back!

To educate yourself and take action on this issue, contact:

Public Campaign

(202) 293-0222   www.publicampaign.org

TWO: Global trade agreements

Trade agreements are immensely important because they set the rules for the global economy. Corporate interests have dominated trade negotiations so corporate profits have taken precedence over labor standards, environmental protection, and any other social considerations. As widespread public protests trade meetings indicate, however, corporate leaders and government officials no longer monopolize interest in global trade. Trade agreements will increasingly become battlegrounds for labor unions, environmentalists, advocates for the global poor and those worried about local sovereignty.

To educate yourself and take action on this issue, contact:

Public Citizen's Global Trade Watch

(202) 588-1000   www.citizen.org

THREE: Prisons

The US incarcerates a higher percentage of its citizens than any other country in the world. In 2000, over 2 million people called US prisons "home."[3] Prison construction is one of the fastest-growing industries in the US. Further, the increase in profit-driven corporate prisons threatens our values of fair and humane treatment of prisoners.

Despite widely acknowledged statistics showing that the national crime rate (including violent crime) has been going down for years, politicians continue to be rewarded for appearing tough on crime. Since few dollars end up focused on reintegration and rehabilitation, the prison system has become merely a place to lock up our societal problems and hope they go away. Collectively, we have the opportunity to create a safer and more humane society by limiting the growth of the prison industry and by implementing effective crime prevention and treatment programs.

To educate yourself and take action on this issue, contact:

The Center on Juvenile and Criminal Justice

(415) 621-5661   www.cjcj.org

FOUR: Reproductive health

Reproductive health is essential to the economic, political, and social empowerment of women around the globe. The ability to be physically healthy and to exercise control over one's fertility is an essential component of individual freedom. Unfortunately, access to family planning methods, sexual health information, and abortion services can be quite scarce and/or too expensive for much of the world's population. Even in the US, many health insurance plans do not cover the costs of birth control. While many of us are preoccupied defending the Roe v. Wade decision, states enact laws making it increasingly difficult for women to access safe and legal abortion. With concerted effort, we can empower the world's women by helping to ensure healthy, planned pregnancies and quality sexual and prenatal health.

To educate yourself and take action on this issue, contact:

NARAL (National Abortion and Reproductive Rights Action League)

(877) 968-3324   www.naral.org

FIVE: Global warming

Human-caused warming of the planet threatens our future. As the temperature of our atmosphere increases, changes in climate have a significant impact on agricultural yields, habitat integrity, and vulnerable coastal populations around the globe. Unfortunately, many powerful constituencies, including the automobile and oil industries, oppose a decisive global transition from fossil fuels to cleaner sources of energy. This very serious threat to humanity may yet lead to the creation of a more healthy and sustainable society, where factories, transit systems and communities function in balance with the natural environment — if we are up to the challenge.

To educate yourself and take action on this issue, contact:

Union of Concerned Scientists

(617) 547-5552   💻 www.ucsusa.org

SIX: Racial inequality

Despite the historical advances made in providing equal opportunities for minorities, our society still faces the challenge of overwhelming racial inequality. The impacts of historical racism live on in our schools, neighborhoods, churches and workplaces. The cumulative impacts of past discrimination, added to current discrimination, creates significant inequalities that affect income, education, home ownership, treatment by the police and courts, entry to corporate America, and access to the halls of government for people of color. We need to demand a more inclusive society where each and every person, regardless of their race or ethnicity, has educational and occupational opportunities.

To educate yourself and take action on this issue, contact:

National Association for the Advancement of Colored People (NAACP)

(410) 602-6969   💻 www.naacp.org

SEVEN: Health care

The US is the only industrialized country in the world that does not have universal health insurance. The existence of excessive medical costs and over 40 million uninsured has made the medical system a nightmare for many. The increasing administrative pressure to generate profits in the health care system is squeezing both patients and doctors. Denial of treatment and fights with insurance companies have become commonplace for many Americans. In the richest country in the world, doctors should not have to choose between the health of their patients and the pressure to cut costs. And patients should not have to choose between paying their skyrocketing health insurance premiums or paying their rent. It is high time that the US public demanded health care as a basic component of living.

To educate yourself and take action on this issue, contact:

Physicians for a National Health Program

(312) 554-0382   💻 www.pnhp.org

EIGHT: Militarism

In a time when the US claims to be the only superpower left standing, we behave as if the whole world is on the brink of starting a war against us. The US spends as much money on the military as the next 30 nations combined.[4] It is time that we start to build bridges globally with all nations, instead of constantly preparing for war. A peaceful world will not come about through fearing each other. It will only come as citizens around the world stand up to their governments and demand alternatives to militarism. The enormous economic savings of a peace-based economy would also create the opportunity for us to fight disease and poverty, and to bring justice to millions around the world.

To educate yourself and take action on this issue, contact:
Center for Defense Information
(202) 332-0600   www.cdi.org

NINE: Lesbian and gay rights

Sometimes progress can be measured by the backlash it creates. Decades of increasing acceptance of lesbians, gays, bisexuals, and transgendered people have produced a backlash resulting in "Defense of Marriage" amendments to state constitutions. Hate-motivated crimes against gays and lesbians are far too common in the US and abroad. In the corporate world, more and more companies are allowing employees to share benefits with their same-sex partners; however, the vast majority still does not. In 2004, only 15 states had laws banning discrimination on the basis of sexual orientation. However, those states account for 47% of the US population![5] Until lesbians and gays have equal rights and protections as individuals, couples and parents our society is not truly free. As a global society, we now have the opportunity to stand up and support equal rights and to nurture all loving relationships.

To educate yourself and take action on this issue, contact:
National Gay and Lesbian Task Force
(202) 393-5177   www.thetaskforce.org

TEN: Fair taxation

From 2002-2004, many state governments experienced severe budget crises. Overall they had to close $200 billion in budget gaps with tax increases and cuts in programs to help the poor. During the same period, federal tax cuts to the richest 1% of Americans (those who make more than $337,000 per year) amounted to $197 billion.[6] What's wrong with this picture? Many wealthy corporations and individuals do their best to avoid their tax obligations. From the 1940's to 2003, corporations' share of federal tax revenues fell from 33% to 7%.[7] It's no wonder that the US Treasury Department says the problem of corporate tax evasion is "unacceptable and growing".[8]

Beware of proposals to "flatten" or "simplify" the tax structure. Although they may look very appealing at first, they are often just tools to decrease the share that the wealthy have to pay! The most recent boondoggle of the American public is the drive to repeal the estate tax. Less than 1% of all Americans are affected at all by this tax in their lifetime. It only applies to those who have wealth of $2 million or more.[9] A grassroots movement is needed to create a fair tax structure that encourages investment in inner cities, wealth creation among the poor and renewable energy development.

To educate yourself and take action on this issue, contact:

United for a Fair Economy

(202) 588-1000   💻 www.faireconomy.org

⇨ RESOURCES

📖 Lakoff, George. *Don't Think of an Elephant: Know Your Values and Frame the Debate.* Chelsea Green, 2004. George Lakoff explains how conservatives think, how they done a better job getting out their message, and how progressives can reinsert our values into the political debate. You can also check out his DVD, How Democrats and Progressives Can Win.

📖 Hazen, Don and Lakshmi Chaudhry, eds. *Start Making Sense: Turning the Lessons of Election 2004 into Winning Progressive Politics.* Chelsea Green, 2005. A great anthology of analyses about what went wrong and what we can build on from the 2004 election.

📖 MoveOn. *MoveOn's 50 Ways to Love Your Country: How to Find Your Political Voice and Become a Catalyst for Change.* Inner Ocean Publishing, 2004. Filled with ideas from emailing politicians and mobilizing under-represented voters to responding to biased reporting and volunteering for a campaign, this book offers practical opportunities to getting involved in politics.

📖 The Daily Show with Jon Stewart Presents: *America (The Book): A Citizen's Guide to Democracy Inaction.* Warner Books, 2004. A parody of a high school history textbook with a tongue-in-cheek attitude and a penetrating analysis of politics and the media.

TRANSPORTATION

Walking
Bicycling
Public Transit
Automobiles

ROAD RAGE AND TRAFFIC JAMS have become routine experiences for millions of us as we join countless commuters in a daily ritual of bumper-to-bumper mayhem. North Americans love their cars and are stuck in the habit of always driving, whether they are traveling ½ mile or 2,000 miles. Even when bicycling might get us to our destination just as fast as driving, we hop in the car. Our dependence upon the internal combustion engine is a major cause of global warming, air pollution, oil spills, traffic congestion, high taxes for road construction and maintenance, accidents, and international conflicts to secure scarce oil resources that are scheduled to peak in the next few years. It also contributes to the exploitation of impoverished communities, such as those in Nigeria and Burma, during the extraction of petroleum.

In this chapter, you will learn about transportation options that can maximize your personal well-being while minimizing your environmental impact. The key to becoming transportation "literate" is to be fluent with all forms of transportation so that you can choose at any given time which one is best for you, your family, your community, and the world.

ACTION: Use the slowest form of transportation that is practical

Using slow transportation goes against much of what our society stands for — efficiency, speed, and the notion that time is money. We seem to be in a hurry even in our leisure time. Unfortunately our focus on maximizing the quantity of our daily experiences has led us to lose focus on the quality of our experiences.

The slower your form of transportation, the more connected you feel to your surroundings. You have time to more fully appreciate the beauty of your environment and your community — the character of architecture, the uniqueness of local people, the smell of flowers, the mischievous nature of a squirrel. You live in the present, ready to fully experience whatever happens. When you are moving too fast, you can't even register individual human faces.

WALKING

 ACTION: Go on a daily walk

A walk is a wonderful way to take a breather from your fast-paced life and get to know your community. It's ironic that we hop in the car to travel six blocks, then go home and exercise on the stairmaster for an hour. Walking is free, healthy and produces no pollution. You will learn more about your local businesses, find shortcuts through wooded areas or interesting neighborhoods, and stop and talk with people that you know.

How many of us walk to work:[1]	
1960:	10%
1980:	6%
1997:	4%
2003:	3%

Walking is also a great form of meditation. It can create a serene place for you to think about your day and to consider what's important to you. Any errands that take you within a mile (1.6 kilometers) of your home afford a perfect opportunity for you to use your walking shoes and give the atmosphere a break. Consider picking up litter along the way!

BICYCLING

Biking is an exciting way to get around town and to get some exercise. Free parking, no fuel costs, low maintenance costs, no pollution, the wind blowing through your hair — what more could you ask for? Quick parking and easy shortcuts can also make biking more versatile than driving. Trips of less than three miles (5 kilometers) provide a great opportunity for you to get out on your bike, because it will probably take 15 or 20 minutes at most.

Bicyclists around the globe are taking back the streets from cars in organized "critical mass" rides. To find out more, check out: www.critical-mass.org

 ACTION: Use your bike for commuting and errands

Biking is a great way to get to work and do errands, especially if you live within a few miles of your destination. In high traffic areas, bike paths often allow cyclists to move faster than car traffic. Just put a backpack on and you're ready to go.

You may even want to transform your bicycle into a sport utility vehicle by purchasing a bike rack, some panniers, and a cargo cart that you can pull behind you. Biking to work once a week would be a great start.

Make some time to find out if your community has any designated bike paths. This is a great way to bike — it's safer, has less pollution and no stop lights!

Contact your city government or local bicycle shop to see what resources they have for bikers. Some cities even publish a map of designated bike paths, as well as the safest streets that have bike lanes.

ELECTRIC BICYCLES

Electric bicycles are normal bikes that have a built-in electric motor. Some move the bicycle without any assistance on your part while others require a little pedaling on your part and then give you that extra push up the hill during your commute. That by itself may get you out of your car for good. Electric bikes can propel you 10-25 mph (16-40 kph) under normal conditions. You can either buy a bike with the system installed or install it yourself on your current bike. For those who are looking for a bit more speed, electric scooters and motorcycles are also available.

Learn more at The Electric Bikes Page (www.electric-bikes.com).

PUBLIC TRANSIT

Our sprawling highway system has taken its toll on the number of people who use public transit. In 1960, 13% of Americans took public transit to work. That number dropped to 5% by 1990 and to 4% by 2003.[2] However, public transit is making a comeback in some American cities. Subways, cross-town buses, and light rail lines are great ways to get around town. It's also a great way to experience the diversity of our American cities, while knowing that you are doing your part to clean up the environment.

ACTION: Use public transit for commuting and errands

Taking public transit to work in the morning can be a wonderful experience. You can take a nap, read, or talk with a friend without worrying about traffic. You also save wear and tear on your car and money for gas and parking. Make sure to talk with your employer about discounts on bus fares. Some cities encourage businesses to give incentives to workers who use public transportation because they are doing good for their communities. To learn more about public transit and to find which routes are convenient for you, contact your local transit authority — look in your phone book under "Transportation" in the "Government" pages.

ACTION: Take a bus

A bus is like a carpool for up to 80 people. What a great way to save gasoline and cut pollution! The next time you have to travel to the next city, consider taking the bus instead of driving your car by yourself. It is also one of the cheapest ways to travel. Greyhound serves over 2,600 destinations in the US as well as areas of Canada and Mexico.

(800) 231-2222   💻 www.greyhound.com

ACTION: Take a train

Join the train enthusiasts by taking Amtrak the next time you are traveling cross-country. Trains have big comfy seats suitable for long trips, and they are a great way to experience the beauty of our country while avoiding crazy airports. Observation cars allow you to spread out and enjoy the views.

SOCIAL RESPONSIBILITY RATINGS FOR AIRLINES	
A	American
B	Southwest, Delta, British Airways
C	United, Alaska Air, US Air
D	Continental
F	Northwest, Korean Air

See the Better World Buying Guide in the **Shopping** chapter for data sources.

If you ride coach, you can create a nice community in your car. It's even better to travel with a group of family and friends, because there are plenty of opportunities to walk around, play cards and talk! The trip itself becomes an enjoyable part of your vacation.

(800) USA-RAIL   💻 www.amtrak.com

AUTOMOBILES

North Americans sure love their cars. We spend an average of one hour every day in our cars. Although driving is incredibly polluting, cars are extremely convenient when you are hauling large loads or making several quick stops. (You can only fit so many bags of groceries on your handlebars.) Since few of us will give up our cars completely, the goal is to become a responsible user of our automobiles — using them only when other modes of transport just won't do, and then driving them in a manner that reduces their environmental impact.

Driving Your Car

ACTION: Set concrete goals for reducing driving

Every gallon of gas that you conserve means less oil that has to be extracted and refined, fewer oil spills, and less air and water pollution. Take account of your odometer so that you can monitor how much you drive. Set a goal to reduce your driving. If you drive an average of 200 miles (320 kilometers) per week, cut it by 25% to 150 miles (240 kilometers).

Consider combining trips so that you save gasoline. Since you're already out on the roads, why not stop by the grocery store for your groceries and the hardware store for your garden tools? It's important to limit the number of car trips you take, because cars pollute the most during the first couple minutes when they are cold.

PUT SOME BUMPER STICKERS ON YOUR CAR

Especially in rush-hour traffic, bumper stickers are a great opportunity to get people to think about what's important to you. They often spark good conversations between drivers and passengers. If you can't find any good ones locally, just call Northern Sun and request a free catalog of progressive t-shirts, bumper stickers, buttons, posters, and more.

(800) 258-8579   💻 www.northernsun.com

THE TRUE COSTS OF CAR CULTURE

According to the Union of Concerned Scientists, "personal use of cars and light trucks (including pickups and SUVs) is the single most damaging consumer behavior."[3]

Automobile driving is a major cause of:

1. Global Warming: Carbon dioxide emissions from autos are the largest contributor to global warming.

2. Air Pollution: Automobiles produce nitrogen oxides, sulfur dioxide, hydrocarbons, carbon monoxide, and particulate matter that contribute to smog and respiratory illnesses.

3. Water Pollution: Automobile manufacturing, gas and oil production, road runoff of fuel, oil, and antifreeze, underground gasoline storage tanks and marine oil spills all pollute our water.

4. Habitat Destruction: Oil drilling, metals mining and road construction all damage wildlife habitat.

5. International Conflict: Nations compete over oil reserves. The US currently imports 48% of its oil — the highest levels ever.[4] Many analysts tie this oil dependency to the hundreds of billions we have spent on Persian Gulf wars.

ACTION: Be a considerate driver

Don't give in to road rage. Not only is it safer to be a considerate driver, it also results in less stress and gives you the opportunity to brighten someone's day when you let them change lanes or pull in ahead of you. Also, be sure to watch out for pedestrians and cyclists when you're out on the streets. They are the real troopers out there using sustainable transportation, so treat them with respect and share the road.

ACTION: Maintain your car in good running condition

A poorly maintained car uses more gas, emits more pollutants, and costs you big money in repairs. Check your owner's manual for maintenance specifics. You should also keep track of any maintenance or repair work that is done on your car in a logbook. All of the following tips will extend the life of your car.

- Check your air pressure monthly (5-10% increase in fuel efficiency).
- Get your oil changed 2-4 times per year (dramatically extends the life of the car).
- Check your fluid levels 2-4 times per year (dramatically extends the life of the car).
- Get your tires rotated twice yearly. It will even out the wear and extend the life of your tires.
- Change your air filter yearly (extends life of the heater and A/C).

ACTION: Drive moderately

Driving like a bat out of hell is not only a public nuisance but is bad for the environment. Rabbit starts and brake slamming waste gas and cause excessive wear to many car parts. Accelerate gradually and anticipate stops instead.

Cars run most efficiently at around 45 miles per hour (70 kilometers per hour), so the faster you drive, the lower your fuel efficiency. Driving at 70 miles per hour (110 kilometers per hour) uses 20% more gas than driving at 55 miles per hour (90 kilometers per hour).[6]

AN ECO-FRIENDLY AAA?

AAA (American Automobile Association) is known for its 24-hour roadside assistance, travel discounts, and free maps. What's not as well known is that the  organization also includes a powerful lobby that fights any law that requires increased fuel efficiency. Enter the BWC (Better World Club). Think of it as AAA for those of us that care about the environment. Their rates and benefits are almost exactly the same except that BWC donates directly to environmental causes and hooks you up to all kinds of eco-friendly travel resources and discounts. It's even endorsed by the hosts of public radio's Car Talk, Tom and Ray Magliozzi. What more could you ask for?

www.betterworldclub.com

ACTION: Carpool

A carpool is a great way to help protect the environment. Whether you are driving to work or driving to a football game, carpooling is more fun, saves money on parking, and makes you feel like you are using your car responsibly.

Percentage of people who carpool to work:		Percentage of people who drive alone to work:[7]	
1980:	20%	1980:	64%
1990:	13%	1990:	73%
2003:	9%	2003:	79%

ACTION: Fuel up responsibly

When you are at the pump remember three main rules:

1. Don't top off the gas tank. When the gas pump automatically shuts off, don't keep pumping. If you top off the gas tank, you allow more fumes to escape and often spill some on the ground. Then as you drive, gasoline expands and spills out on the road, which causes ground level ozone (leading to smog).

2. Buy the lowest octane that your owner's manual recommends. The higher the octane the more oil is necessary to produce the gasoline (and you don't get any better mileage).[8]

3. Buy gas from a socially and environmentally responsible gas station. Oil companies are, in general, not the most socially conscious corporations on the planet. Their drilling, processing, refining, and transportation are usually very environmentally destructive. Many have been implicated by human rights groups as being closely involved with exceptionally repressive Third World governments. It's important not to reward the worst oil companies with your dollars. Use the following list to help you choose better stations to gas up at.

SOCIAL RESPONSIBILITY RATINGS FOR GASOLINE	
A	Sunoco, BP, Amoco Arco
B	Marathon, Ashland Super America, Citgo, 7-Eleven, Valero, Beacon
C	Total, Hess, Shell, Costco
D	Conoco, Phillips, 76, Jet Coastal, Chevron, Texaco
F	Exxon, Mobil

Choosing a Car

For most North Americans, aside from our homes, our car is the most expensive purchase we will make. We consider many factors when buying a car, including size, model, color and make. We also need to consider the impact our car will have on the world over its lifetime.

BIGGER ISN'T BETTER

Larger vehicles are currently in vogue. In 1980, only 17% of new auto purchases were light trucks (SUVs, vans, and pickups). By 2000, over 50% of new car buys were these kind of vehicles.[10] The bigger the car, the more it will pollute, and the more it will cost in gas and repairs. The average light truck (SUVs, vans, and pick-ups) gets 21 miles per gallon (8 kilometers per liter) as compared to 29 miles per gallon (12 kilometers per liter) for the average car.[11] That's almost 40% lower fuel efficiency! Unfortunately, light trucks not only burn more fuel, they also have significantly dirtier emissions. Also keep in mind that more powerful engines named "Turbo" "V8" or "HEMI" mean one thing—more fuel. In general, buy the smallest vehicle that meets your needs (and remember that you can always rent or borrow a SUV/truck when you need to move your aunt's furniture). Need more convincing? Check out Car Talk's very thoughtful "Live Larger, Drive Smaller" website. It should help persuade even the most ardent SUV enthusiasts — www.cartalk.com/content/features/suv.

ACTION: Buy a used car

Buying a used car allows you to reuse a car (preserving resources necessary to build a new car), and it saves you significant amounts of money. Remember that a car loses a significant portion of its value immediately after you drive it off the lot. Also, the more expensive the car, the bigger your loan and the more you will pay in interest to the bank. A five-year $20,000 loan at 9% will cost you almost $5,000 in interest.[9]

Reliability is also an important environmental issue. The more parts that break, the more parts are thrown into landfills, requiring the manufacture of new cars. Also cars that are not running at full capacity have a lower than average fuel efficiency.

Consider checking out the Consumer Reports Used Car Guide at your local library for guidelines on how to find a reliable used car. (See www.consumer reports.org.)

CLEANING UP AFTER YOURSELF

Our mothers always teach us to clean up after ourselves around the house. Why should we not do the same for our cars? The average car emits around 10,000 pounds (4,500 kilograms) of CO_2 each year, which is a major contributor to global warming. Now there is a way to clean even that up. An organization called TerraPass allows you to purchase a combination of carbon offsets and renewable energy that will remove exactly what your car puts out every year. On their site, you can calculate exactly how much CO_2 you are adding, and for as little as $30, remove it all. They even give you a sticker to place in your window to remind you that you are technically driving emission free for the year. Highly researched and third party verified, TerraPass empowers everyone to stop global warming.

www.terrapass.com

 ## ACTION: Choose a low emission, fuel-efficient car

The car you buy is one of the most important environmental choices that you will ever make — partly because of the environmentally destructive nature of the automobile but also because it will have an impact on the environment for as long as you drive it. There are two main factors to consider when assessing the environmental impact of an automobile: (1) fuel efficiency and (2) tailpipe emissions.

It is important to drive a car that gets at least 30 miles per gallon (12 kilometers per liter). Each 0.1 mile per gallon (0.2 kilometer per liter) improvement in the US car fleet saves 12 million gallons (55 million liters) of gas annually.[12] Gas mileage largely correlates with the size of a vehicle. Subcompacts and compacts always get better gas mileage than do sport utility vehicles and minivans. If you do choose a larger vehicle, make sure that you get the model with the best fuel efficiency in its class. To compare fuel efficiency by model, go to: www.fueleconomy.gov.

CHOOSE THE CAR THAT MAKES THE MOST SENSE		
	2006 TOYOTA PRIUS	**2006 DODGE RAM 1500**
MPG	55	10
Tank Of Gas	$24	$78
Miles On A Full Tank	589	315
Lifetime Fuel Cost*	$6,818	$37,500
Overall Crash Test Rating	4 /5 Stars	4.5/5 Stars
Lifetime Greenhouse Gases**	35 tons	183 tons
Lifetime Toxic Emissions***	349 lbs	1398 lbs

*   Based on an average vehicle lifetime of 10 years, $2.50 per gallon, 15,000 mi/yr
**   Incl. CO_2, nitrous oxide & methane
*** Incl. carbon monoxide, smog producing organics, formaldehyde & particulates

Automobile emissions are one of the primary causes of global warming and air pollution. Carbon dioxide, a primary greenhouse gas, is a common byproduct of internal combustion engines. Also, as you drive, your tailpipe spews out sulfur oxides and nitrous oxides, which cause acid rain and smog. Diesel engines often significantly surpass gasoline engines for fuel efficiency. Unfortunately, that's not the whole story. Current diesel cars pollute 20 times as much nitrous oxide and 10-20 times as much particulate matter (which cause the majority of deaths from air pollution).[13] To compare tailpipe emissions by model, go to: www.epa.gov/autoemissions.

The internal combustion engine is a technological dinosaur. It is inefficient, highly polluting and loud. It will still be around long enough for you to say your farewells, but there are now many more environmentally friendly technologies that are being used to power automobiles:

Biodiesel

Recently, there has been a strong upsurge in the popularity of biodiesel fuel. Biodiesel is fuel made from 20-100% plant-based materials such as soybeans or corn that will work in many diesel-powered vehicles with little to no mechanical modifications. The advantages are that biodiesel burns cleaner than diesel, is made with renewable resources (in part or in whole) rather than from petroleum (a fast-dwindling resource), and decreases our addiction to foreign sources of oil. Public facilities are sprouting up all over the country where you can

FUEL CELL VEHICLES

Fuel cell vehicles use hydrogen, methanol or natural gas to produce electricity in your car and an electric motor to propel it. Upcoming fuel cell technology may have as much impact on our society as the advent of the light bulb.[15] The fuel cell vehicle of the future promises to be 98% to 100% percent cleaner than today's cars.[16]

fuel up your diesel car with biodiesel. For more information, check out www.biodiesel.org.

SOCIAL RESPONSIBILITY RATINGS FOR CAR MAKERS	
A	Toyota, Lexus, Scion
B	Ford, Jaguar, Land Rover, Lincoln, Mercury, Mini, Volvo
C	Volkswagon, Subaru, Chrysler, Dodge, Jeep, Mercedes, Honda, Acura, Mazda, Porsche
D	Audi, BMW, Isuzu, Suzuki, Hyundai, Kia, Infiniti, Nissan
F	Buick, Cadillac, Chevrolet, GMC, Hummer, Pontiac, Saab, Saturn, Mitsubishi

See the Better World Shopping Guide in the **Shopping** chapter for data sources.

Hybrid Cars

Hybrid vehicles combine a highly efficient gasoline engine with a battery-powered electric motor to propel the car. Their success over electric vehicles is due, in part, to the fact that they never have to be plugged in. Owners just fill them up at gas stations along with everyone else. These vehicles cut CO_2 emissions in half and other pollutants by as much as 90%, when compared to standard gasoline engines.[14] They have the potential to get 70 to 80 miles per gallon (28 to 32 kilometers per liter) of gasoline, without the range limitations of standard electric vehicles. While hybrid vehicles first achieved popularity with the Toyota Prius and Honda Insight, many vehicle models are now available in a hybrid form including the Honda Civic/Accord, Ford Escape, Toyota Camry/Highlander and Mercury Mariner.

WHAT KIND OF CAR SHOULD I BUY?

Ultimately, you have to make a decision that combines your values with your specific needs and budget. We can, however, provide some simple rules that you should consider when buying your car:
1. Get the smallest class of car that will meet your needs.
2. Get the most fuel efficient model available in that class.
3. Buy from a socially responsible car company. (See "Social Responsibility Ratings for Car Makers.")

	MAKE/MODEL	MPG	CLEAN AIR	PRICE (MSRP)
TOP CHOICE:	Toyota Prius (H)	55	9.5 /10	$22,000
RUNNER UPS:	Honda Insight (H)	56	9 /10	$22,000
	Honda Civic (H)	50	9.5 /10	$22,000
	Ford Escape (H)	33	9.5 /10	$27,000
HONORABLE MENTIONS:	Honda Civic	33	7/10	$18,000
	Toyota Corolla	33	7/10	$15,000

(H) = Hybrid Vehicle

⇨ BICYCLES RESOURCES

League of American Bicyclists

The League of American Bicyclists (LAB) is working on improving conditions for cycling throughout the country by influencing transportation policy and legislation, identifying and designating Bicycle Friendly Communities, and sponsoring National Bike Month and Bike-to-Work Day.
(202) 822-1333   💻 www.bikeleague.org

Rails-to-Trails Conservancy (RTC)

Since 1996, RTC has converted over 7,000 miles (11,200 kilometers) of abandoned railroad track corridors to pedestrian and bicycle paths. Contact them for information about how to accomplish this in your community.
(202) 797-5400   💻 www.railtrails.org

⇨ AUTOMOBILE RESOURCES

📖 Decicco, John, ed., Jim Kliesch, and Martin Thomas. *ACEEE's Green Book: The Environmental Guide to Cars and Trucks.* American Council for an Energy Efficient Economy. [Published annually.] Put out yearly by the American Council for an Energy Efficient Economy, this book gives a 'green' rating from 1 to 100 for every new model car, based on emissions and fuel economy. It includes listings for alternative fuel cars as well. www.greenercars.com

📖 Alvord, Katie. *Divorce Your Car: Ending the Love Affair with the Automobile.* New Society Publishers, 2000. This insightful book tells the story of the advent of car culture, the social and environmental consequences in an automobile addicted society, and myriad reasons and methods to escape your car.

📖 Consumer Reports *New Car Buying Guide, Used Car Buying Guide.* Published annually. Put out by the editors of Consumer Reports magazine, these books give the highest quality information available on what you should know for purchasing a car that meets your exact needs. Best known for their reliability ratings for every model of car by year, Consumers Union gives us an island of reason and common sense in a sea of advertising.

TRAVEL

**Where to Go
Where to Stay
What to Do
Extraordinary Travel**

TOURISM HAS BECOME a major part of the global economy and an especially important source of income for many developing countries. In fact, it is one of the largest industries in the world, employing over 230 million people and producing more than 10% of the world's gross national product![1] Many Americans travel to take a breather from our stressed-out, fast-paced world and to enjoy life a little more fully. There are many other great reasons to travel throughout the US and around the world, as well:

- to better understand and appreciate other cultures and people
- to experience the amazing diversity of geography and wildlife
- to spend time with your loved ones
- to take time to reconsider your priorities in life
- to recharge your batteries

There is no better way to build understanding across cultures and communities than to actually experience other people's way of life. Traveling can be an intense learning experience about how people outside of your own community live. And breaking down barriers goes a long way towards making the world a better place.

It is important to remember that our travels have huge effects both on other people and on our natural environment. Whether you are interested in exploring the Himalayas, the Amazonian rainforest, or your local state park, there are easy steps you can take to ensure that your travels have a positive impact on you, the people you meet, and the natural environment.

In this chapter, you will learn about opportunities for exciting and educational travel that supports the cultures, economies, and environments that you experience. Tips on where to go, where to stay, what to do, and how to make your trip extraordinary will help your travels reflect your values. When you add concern about the environment and other human beings to your traveling, it can transform your vacation into an adventure far beyond what you've come to expect.

Before you leave on your trip don't forget to....
- Stop your newspaper delivery.
- Ask a neighbor to collect your mail and water your houseplants.
- Turn down your water heater, furnace, and air conditioner.
- Unplug unnecessary appliances or switch off their power strips.

WHERE TO GO

We all know the common destinations for American travelers: Disneyland, Disney World, Las Vegas, or a shopping spree in the nearest big city. Put some extra thought into choosing your travel destination, instead of accepting the pre-packaged vacation experiences that often drain your pocketbook and leave you exhausted. Think about what you want from a vacation: a sense of relaxation and calm, connection with nature, beautiful vistas, excitement, action, quality time with loved ones, an experience of new cultures, or new learning opportunities. Consider how your next vacation might better reflect your most deeply held values.

ACTION: Explore your own backyard

It's easy to forget that in every community, including your own, there are many cultural landmarks and natural settings that you can explore and enjoy. Staying close to home will not only save money, gasoline, and vacation time, it will make you feel closer to your community and your natural environment. State parks, museums, and local celebrations and fairs provide great opportunities for you to get away and have some fun. Buy a travel book that includes your local area for interesting ideas on nearby destinations, and pay attention to event announcements in your local paper. What you've overlooked or forgotten about may surprise you.

ACTION: Experience nature

Vacation time is a great time to connect with the living environment all around us. Hiking within the serenity of wilderness, feeling the crashing of ocean waves, or observing playful wildlife are great alternatives to the frantic, overly scheduled vacations that have become common for most Americans. You will actually return rested and ready to take on new challenges back home, while having enhanced your appreciation of the natural environment.

Hiking and camping are great ways to relax and enjoy the outdoors. Inexpensive or used camping gear is easy to find. You can even rent gear if you just want to give it a try. Without the conveniences of home — such as a microwave and television — you will focus more on enjoying the scenery and your loved ones.

When you are hiking or camping, consider these easy tips to protect the habitats you encounter:

- Stay on established and designated trails.
- Never touch, harass, or disturb wildlife.
- Whenever possible, use existing campsites.
- Choose a durable campsite (not on delicate wildflowers).
- Take only pictures; leave only footprints (take all litter with you; leave rocks and plants where they are).

☐ ACTION: Visit state and national parks

The 378 state and national parks that we have here in the US provide wonderful educational, cultural, and recreational opportunities for people of all ages (often at an inexpensive price). Beautiful ecological reserves, ancient Native American artifacts, and local historical landmarks make up one of the most extraordinary park systems in the world. Go out and experience it for yourself.

National Park Service
(202) 208-6843   🖥 www.nps.gov

> **IS YOUR SKI AREA GREEN?**
>
> Ski Area Citizens has created an essential online resource that ranks ski areas from all over the Western US based on their environmental responsibility. The rankings are updated annually with simple grades from A to F as well as detailed data on why each ski area has received its particular score.
>
> 🖥 www.skiareacitizens.com

HUMBOLDT REDWOODS STATE PARK (HUMBOLDT, CA)

Ancient redwoods and sequoias are the oldest living creatures on the planet, some reaching up to 2000 years old. They are also the tallest, some having grown over 360 feet (110 meters) tall (taller than the Statue of Liberty!). The Redwoods State Park in Humboldt County is the largest old-growth redwood preserve in the world. The awe you will experience at being in the presence of these majestic creatures is indescribable. Admission is free in most of the park's areas. There are fees for camping.

(707) 946-2409
🖥 www.humboldtredwoods.org

☐ ACTION: Travel off-season and to unknown places

Some of our most famous parks, such as Yellowstone and Rocky Mountain National Parks, receive millions of visitors every year. If you can, schedule your travel outside of the peak travel times (which differ, depending on the country or area of the US). If you travel during the off-season, it lessens the social and environmental impacts a region must endure at one time. You will also encounter fewer crowds, have less stress and pay cheaper prices during your visit. Contact your destination beforehand to find out when their visitor traffic is low. Avoiding the most common destinations is also a great strategy for an incredible vacation. Many lesser-known sites around the world are just as beautiful and enjoyable as the famous ones.

FIVE POWERFUL MUSEUMS

US Holocaust Memorial Museum (Washington, DC)

The Holocaust Memorial Museum in Washington, DC provides us with a meaningful education on the Nazi Holocaust. It is a powerful call to remember those who suffered and inspires us to contemplate the moral implications of our choices and responsibilities as citizens. The museum offers exhibitions for adults and children and includes the designated national memorial to victims of the Holocaust. Admission is free, but assigned times are required to space out visits.

(202) 488-0400   💻 www.ushmm.org

National Civil Rights Museum (NCRM) (Memphis, TN)

The NCRM houses the first and only comprehensive overview of the civil rights movement in exhibit form. Its mission is to provide an understanding of the civil rights movement and its impact on human rights movements worldwide. Located in the Lorraine Motel, the site of Martin Luther King Jr.'s assassination, a visit to this museum may well be one of the most moving experiences you could have on a vacation.

(901) 521-9699   💻 www.civilrightsmuseum.org

Smithsonian Institution Museums (Washington, DC)

The Smithsonian Institution maintains a collection of 16 incredible museums and galleries most of which are located on or near the National Mall in Washington, DC. Museums include the National Museum of African Art, the National Air and Space Museum and the National Museum of Natural History. Admission is free to most of the museums.

(202) 357-2700   💻 www.si.edu

National Museum of the American Indian (New York)

The National Museum of the American Indian works with indigenous Western peoples to protect, foster, and share their unique cultures with the rest of the world. It gives us the opportunity to educate ourselves about Native life and history in interesting and creative ways. An additional branch of the museum is located on the National Mall in Washington, DC. Admission is free.

(212) 668-6624   💻 www.si.edu/nmai

National Women's Hall of Fame (Seneca Falls, NY)

Long considered the birthplace of women's rights, Seneca Falls is now home to the National Women's Hall of Fame as well as the Women's Rights National Historical Park. The Hall is a tribute to some of the greatest women in American history, including Jane Addams, Harriet Tubman and Rachel Carson. Admission runs $2-$3 per person.

(315) 568-8060   💻 www.greatwomen.org

WHERE TO STAY

Whether you are traveling abroad or staying near home, there are a lot of great alternatives to the high-rise hotel with sterile hallways and free cable. Think about where you could stay on your trip that would have a positive impact on the local economy and create the most meaningful experience for you.

ACTION: Stay with the locals

One great way to get to know an area is to stay with the people who live there. They are a great source of knowledge and provide the best way to learn about the local culture. By staying at a local host's home you will experience unforgettable hospitality. Sometimes its easy to overlook family connection, distant friends, or even a friend of a friend that would be happy to be a host for a short time. In this way, your travels can provide an opportunity to reaffirm old, or establish new, relationships as well as provide a new experience.

SERVAS International
SERVAS works to build understanding, tolerance, and world peace through a network of hosts around the world who are prepared to open their doors to travelers for a two-to-three-day stay. Good for both domestic and international travel. It costs $65 per year to register as a traveler.

(212) 267-0252   www.servas.org

> ### TIP HOTEL CLEANING STAFF
> While you may not have much interaction with the people who clean your hotel room, they play an essential, and often over-looked, role in making your stay comfortable. These are generally not highly paid positions. Consider leaving a tip of $1 per day. Even a thank you note or small gift is often very much appreciated.

ACTION: Stay in a hostel

When you're on a tight budget, finding cheap lodging is a must. Prices usually don't get much cheaper than a hostel. Hostels come in all shapes and sizes and are scattered around almost every country imaginable (including the US). Most offer clean, dormitory-style rooms (some even have a few private rooms), a shower and possibly some food. Best of all, people from all over the world stay in hostels, giving you a great opportunity to make a variety of friends who share your passion for traveling.

Hostelling International
(202) 783-6161   www.hiayh.org
Hostels.com
www.hostels.com

ACTION: Stay at a bed & breakfast

The B and B experience is the polar opposite of staying in a big chain hotel. Each B and B is unique and is usually run by a local family in a large, old home with an interesting history. While it may cost a little more, often you will wake up to a home-cooked breakfast and a chance to meet a few fellow travelers, as well as learn about the area from your knowledgeable hosts. Best of all, your money stays in the hands of the locals and promotes a more meaningful, human travel experience. Check out these resources to find a B and B in the areas you're interested in visiting.

BBOnline

(615) 868-1946 🖳 www.bbonline.com

Bed and Breakfast.com
🖳 www.bedandbreakfast.com

✏ ACTION: Exchange your home

Do what?! Yes, you read right. You can trade houses with someone in another country. Hotels can be expensive, both for folks traveling here and for us when we go abroad. They can also prevent us from really experiencing our destination. If you want to get a feel for the local way of life, living in a neighborhood through home exchange might be for you. You can cook your own meals, sightsee at your leisure and feel more at home. In the meantime, foreign travelers will enjoy your home while you're gone.

⇨ HOME EXCHANGE RESOURCES

The following websites include both a wide variety of countries to choose from and detailed information on each home and family.
🖳 www.homeexchange.com
🖳 www.homexchange.com

WHAT TO DO

Socially responsible travel is more meaningful, because it combines your passion for travel with your interest in preserving the environment, supporting local cultures and nurturing local economies. A number of actions can ensure that your trip is both rewarding for you and helpful to your host community.

✏ ACTION: Connect with the locals

You may have noticed that no matter what incredible sights you see, what museums

---

TRAVEL TIPS

- Consider not working the day before and after your trip. You will more fully enjoy your vacation and adjust more easily to being home.
- Slow down and be flexible. Many Americans lead such hurried daily lives that they schedule their vacations as if it were three-day business meetings. Make sure to leave flexibility in your schedule so that you can enjoy unexpected events.

you visit, or what entertainment you take in while on vacation, your best memories are often of the people you meet. Having a discussion with someone from a different place and being open to what they have to teach can be a great learning experience, and it's a way of appreciating the people who opened up their community for your enjoyment. You may even consider studying up on the local history and culture (and even the language) as a show of respect. These connections that we make with people from different backgrounds help us build bridges across our differences and ultimately create a more humane world.

Here are some other tips for connecting with the locals:

- Walk around town instead of driving.
- Visit local neighborhoods.
- Seek out unique experiences that reflect the local culture, instead of just hitting the normal tourist sites and eating at McDonald's.

> **ETHICAL TRAVELER**
>
> www.ethicaltraveler.com With guidelines for ethical travel and a list of the world's best ethical travel spots, this site offers advice for trips that benefits you, the earth, and your local hosts. Tsunami relief and protecting old growth forests are just two of their campaigns for human rights and environmental sustainability.

HELP PREVENT TOURISM FROM DESTROYING LOCAL CULTURE

You've probably noticed travel advertisements that show a beautiful couple frolicking on a white sand beach with their five star, state of the art resort behind them. The exotic images seem to suggest that although the resort is in a Third World country, guests will have all the comforts of home and more — a virtual paradise. Developing countries often cater to what they believe Western tourists want. Corporations from industrialized countries attempt to create a paradise for Westerners, often at the expense of local businesses, culture, and the environment. Before you schedule a cruise or take a pre-packaged resort vacation, consider the impact that our demands for paradise have on local workers, the environment, and indigenous culture. Consider taking a more alternative vacation instead of something pre-packaged, where you get to know local people, explore the many aspects of their culture and experience the unique natural beauty that surrounds them.

ACTION: Limit your vacation trinkets

Many of us get overwhelmed on vacation and buy carloads of T-shirts, stuffed animals, mugs, and other assorted souvenirs. The workers who produce our cheap vacation trinkets often work in poor conditions. Consider the usefulness of a souvenir before you buy it. Often pictures are the best souvenirs for capturing the essence of our travel experiences.

ACTION: Support local economies

Tourism has given a significant boost to the economies of many struggling communities and developing nations. Even though tourism brings millions of dollars to impoverished countries, corporate hotels and resorts siphon off much of the wealth in such a way that the host community actually gains little wealth. To keep your tourism dollars in the hands of those who need them and to avoid feeding the corporate beast, buy from local merchants whenever you can. The principle of supporting local economies applies whether you are driving through Nebraska or canoeing in the Amazon.

> When traveling abroad, be sure to avoid buying products made from endangered plants and animals. Also avoid genuine local artifacts, such as relics from archeological digs.

When we're traveling, it's easy to stop for meals at fast food chains and to shop at large corporate retailers that exist in every town. They're familiar, convenient, and cheap. However, we can do more to support local economies by seeking out local diners and stores — the food and service are generally better, and we're helping Mom and Pop stay in business. For a real treat, find out which locally grown fruits and vegetables are in season and purchase them directly from the growers at roadside stands or farmers' markets.

If you need someone to show you around, particularly in a foreign country, find a local guide. You will not only be contributing to the economic well-being of the community, but you will have an opportunity to learn directly about the area and culture from a local.

ACTION: Use alternative transportation

Get out of the car on your vacation! It is definitely worth your time to learn about the transit options in the areas where you are traveling. Many places in the US and around the world have excellent rail, subway, and bus systems that may make the automobile obsolete. Walking around town is also a much better way to get to know the geography and the people firsthand while avoiding the traffic and parking hassles that come with the automobile. Above all, it is only courteous to reduce the amount of pollution you leave behind at the place that treated you to a wonderful vacation.

> *Ross:* While traveling in the American Southwest, I wanted to purchase a small Navajo rug. I had the opportunity to buy one from many tourist shops that buy from local people, raise the prices, and sell the rugs for a profit. However, wanting to support the native people, I waited to buy a beautiful rug straight from a Navajo woman on the reservation. My money went directly to their economy (which needed it) rather than to the hands of a dealer. With this choice, I was able to make a small contribution to the Navajo traditional way, as well as bring home a cherished reminder of my journey.

EXTRAORDINARY TRAVEL

Traveling can be so much more than getting away from it all. Imagine going on a spiritual retreat, backpacking through extraordinary wilderness areas, taking an educational trip to learn about social injustice, or volunteering in another country. If you want a traveling experience that will really expand your mind, you must begin to reshape your fundamental ideas about travel itself. We have detailed five amazing opportunities for the traveler who is ready for the experience of a lifetime: (1) study abroad (2) reality tours, (3) eco-journeys, (4) volunteer travel and (5) personal growth vacations.

ACTION: Study abroad

One of most exciting and least expensive ways to travel is to study abroad. Picture visiting Mexico City's greatest museums as part of your art class or curling up with a good book near an ancient Buddhist temple in Thailand. When you study abroad, it is a wonderful opportunity to learn about another part of the globe while earning course credit. Here are some of the leading programs:

Council on International Educational Exchange (CIEE)

Council *International Study Programs*
CIEE: Council on International Educational Exchange

CIEE is a non-profit group that provides college and high school level educational programs for both students and teachers. CIEE offers work exchange and voluntary service programs, as well as discount travel services for students, teachers and young people. CIEE puts out a good magazine called *Student Travels,* available on most college campuses or directly from CIEE.

(888) COUNCIL   www.ciee.org

American Field Service (AFS)

AFS is a non-profit exchange organization that sends people to over 55 countries. It focuses more on high school students, teachers and administrators than do other international exchange programs, claiming to "help people develop the knowledge, skills and understanding needed to create a more just and peaceful world." Its emphasis on diversity, tolerance and global citizenship make it an excellent choice.

(800) AFS-INFO   www.afs.org

National Student Exchange (NSE)

NSE is a great program for college students who want to participate in an exchange but aren't interested in leaving the States. US universities from all parts of the country participate in a national exchange, where students can attend another university for a semester or year while paying their home university's tuition. It's fun, relatively cheap and you get to live in another part of the country.

(800) 735-1989   www.nse.org

ACTION: Take a reality tour

A "reality tour" is an opportunity to travel across the planet and learn first-hand about war, poverty, globalization, sustainable agriculture, and other forces that are shaping our future. Reality tours are a great way to move beyond the mainstream media's portrayal of global issues and experience them for yourself. Another advantage of reality tours is that you will be able to travel with others who are committed to social justice and environmental sustainability.

Global Exchange

Now you have an opportunity to visit GLOBAL EXCHANGE and learn about the another country's history and current situation from the people themselves. You may choose to meet with community leaders in Cuba, Haiti, South Africa, or Ireland and learn about military atrocities, sustainable farming, or exciting breakthroughs in the fair trade movement. Global Exchange's Reality Tours take groups abroad to visit people and places you would never encounter during your normal travels.

(800) 497-1994 💻 www.globalexchange.org/tours

Witness For Peace

For almost 20 years, Witness for Peace **⟨⟩WitnessforPeace** has been sending groups of average US citizens to Mexico, Central America, and the Caribbean to see firsthand the impacts of uncontrolled globalization on Third World people. In addition, participants experience what it's like to work for justice abroad at the grassroots level. The trips typically last one to two weeks and are offered throughout the year.

(202) 588-1471 💻 www.witnessforpeace.org

ACTION: Take an eco-tour

Many of us like to spend our vacations exploring the wonders of our natural world: crystalline caves, old-growth forests, rugged badlands, or painted deserts — we love them all. Generally, tourism affects nature less than other types of development, such as logging, mining, or real estate; however, poorly managed tourism can result in long-term ecological damage.

Eco-tourism works on the assumption that traveling should contribute to the long-term preservation of entire ecosystems. Governments and business people are realizing that tourists love visiting wilderness areas, so by supporting eco-

---

By supporting environmentally responsible tourism, you are:
- Encouraging local landowners to develop tourist facilities with less environmental impact.
- Promoting environmental awareness, education and the protection of natural resources.
- Spending money that supports local projects in agriculture, water supplies, tree farms and others.
- Providing economic incentive to stop wildlife poaching and protect natural areas.

tourism, you are stating that wilderness areas here and around the world deserve protection and are valuable beyond their uses as raw materials. Your vacation may become an adventure that raises your awareness about our fragile environment.

Sierra Club Outings

Sierra Club volunteers lead outings that contribute to the overall conservation and environmental goals of the club. Most of their trips are wilderness trips. They expect participants to help with chores and other necessary work. Sierra Club outings are also a great way to learn about eco-friendly travel and camping tips.

(415) 977-5630   💻 www.sierraclub.org/outings

World Wildlife Fund (WWF)

WWF's tours like to feature the wondrous wildlife that surrounds us all. Visits to WWF-funded conservation projects are also a part of many of their trips. On most trips, a WWF staff member accompanies you throughout, while local guides, guest speakers, and other experts complement the staff.

(888) 993-8687   💻 www.worldwildlife.org

⇨ ECO–TOURISM RESOURCES

Sustainable Travel International (STI)

STI provides consumers a useful online resource for finding eco-tours across the globe. They have their own Eco-Certification Program as well as a reliable carbon offset program (to offset the impact of your air travel). If you want to help people and the planet while you travel, start your trip by going to STI's web site.
💻 www.sustainabletravel.com

The Eco-tourism Society

This non-profit organization works to promote eco-tourism through education and networking. They publish fact sheets, books, and newsletters, educating the public about the benefits of eco-travel.
802-447-2121   💻 www.ecotourism.org

WARNING

A word of caution: eco-tourism has become so popular that some places may falsely claim eco-friendly tourism. It's best to ask a lot of questions and try to check a company's references before signing on. Some important questions include:

- How long has the company been in business? Often businesses that have been around for a while have earned the necessary customer support by living up to their claims.
- Does the company offer locally owned accommodations such as hotels, restaurants and guided tours?
- How has the company affected the locals' lives?
- Does the company contribute directly to conservation efforts?

ACTION: Combine service and travel

Have you ever considered volunteering during your travels? What? Work while on vacation? Imagine the best vacation you've ever taken. It might have been relaxing, adventurous, or just new and exciting. Now imagine a time when you really helped someone out, someone you may not have even known, expecting nothing in return. Picture their appreciation and how you made a difference in their lives. You can create these feelings for yourself and others on a regular basis! Today, there are many opportunities for you to combine the fun of traveling with the powerful experience of satisfaction that you get from volunteering. Traveling is a privilege and a luxury for most in the world. By using your vacation time to volunteer you make incredible connections with people and help them out with your labor or expertise.

> Ross: Working with children at an orphanage in the forests of Guatemala transformed my life. Experiencing first hand the problems of the Developing World made me reflect on my life and my role in helping to make the world a better place.

Volunteer experiences help build understanding, compassion, and hope—important keys to creating a more humane world. When you serve, in the US or abroad, you expose yourself to other ways of life. Perhaps more importantly, you eventually come home and share your experiences with others. Volunteering can create tremendous changes within you; through your experiences, you can also create tremendous change in others.

Short-Term Volunteering

Many organizations lead volunteer travel excursions around the globe for periods of time as short as one week. These short-term volunteer trips can be a great way to travel abroad, get to know the locals, and make a difference in other people's lives.

Global Citizens Network (GCN)

Global Citizens Network offers a variety of service trips around the world, where volunteers immerse themselves in the daily life of the community. Trips last one, two, or three weeks, depending on the site, and a trained GCN team leader leads each team. The team works on projects initiated by people in the local community. Such projects could include setting up a library, teaching business skills, building a health clinic, or planting trees to reforest a village.

Global Citizens Network

(800) 644-9292   🖥 www.globalcitizens.org

United Planet (UP)

UP provides volunteer opportunities for short-term (1-12 weeks) or long-term "quests" in 50 nations around the globe. UP programs focus on building cross-cultural understanding through service. Opportunities include doing HIV/AIDS education, providing medical care, and child and elder care. UP also has an ambassador program for high school and college students to encourage inter-cultural appreciation.

800-292-2316   💻 www.unitedplanet.org

Habitat for Humanity International

Habitat is an ecumenical Christian organization composed of volunteers that help families build affordable housing — don't worry, extensive construction skills are not required. One- to three-week trips to US or international destinations will teach you about the local culture, poverty, and social empowerment in ways that you will never forget.

(912) 924-6935   💻 www.habitat.org

Long-Term Volunteering

If you are really looking for the best way to experience another culture, you need to live with its people for an extended period of time. Ever since President Kennedy helped initiate the Peace Corps, it and many other organizations have sent people around the world to help people in developing countries. There are many opportunities for longer-term commitments abroad and at home, so that you can find the group that best suits your needs and interests. Many churches also provide the opportunity for long-term global service.

The Peace Corps

Founded in 1961, the Peace Corps has sent over 160,000 Americans to other countries to fight "hunger, disease, illiteracy, poverty, and lack of opportunity." Volunteers from agriculture, business, education, health, engineering, urban planning, environmental education, and other fields help Third World countries face the challenges of development. The Peace Corps offers 77 possible destinations, including countries in Africa, Asia, the Pacific, Central and South America, the Caribbean, Central and Eastern Europe and the former Soviet Union. Volunteers sign on for a two-year stay, receive a monthly stipend to cover living expenses, and take up to two weeks vacation per year.

(800) 424-8580   💻 www.peacecorps.gov

Ellis: In 1993 I joined the Peace Corps. I signed up right out of college, feeling as if I needed to get my hands dirty and make a difference in the world after reading so many books that just talked about it. They placed me in the Environmental Education Program in the southern region of Panama, despite my having no knowledge of Spanish. I ended up teaching, making movies, organizing environmental groups, putting on conferences, writing a book, editing a newsletter, speaking on national television (all in Spanish, mind you) — things I never dreamed I'd do. More importantly, though, the people there were so kind that I learned a real generosity of spirit. It seems that as much as I had to teach, the people always had twice as much to teach me.

Voluntary Service Overseas (VSO)

VSO is Canada's version of the Peace Corps. They send volunteers for two-year stays in developing countries around the world. They need people from a variety of professions, including teachers, health workers, computer technicians, business people, natural resource development workers and more. Volunteers work in a variety of programs, including health, poverty and AIDS projects. VSO pays a small stipend for living expenses, travel expenses, health and medical coverage, and a "resettling" grant when you return home.

Sharing skills • Changing lives

(888) 876-2911   💻 www.vsocanada.org

Americorps

Each year, more than 40,000 members serve with Americorps programs in every state in the nation. You can tutor kids, build new homes, restore parks and coastlines, help communities hit by natural disasters, and take on many other challenges, either in your community or far away from home. For your service, you will garner valuable skills, a living allowance, an education award to help pay for college, and the satisfaction of having made a difference.

(800) 942-2677   💻 www.americorps.org

⇨ VOLUNTEER TRAVEL RESOURCES

📖 Giese, Filomena, and Marilyn Borchardt, eds. *Alternatives to the Peace Corps: A Directory of Third World and US Volunteer Opportunities.* Food First Books, 1999. A small book, offering information on voluntary service organizations, technical service programs, work brigades, study tours, and alternative travel in the Third World. It also includes a reference section, resources about jobs in development, and a brief critique of the Peace Corps.

📖 McMillon, Bill. *Volunteer Vacations: Short-term Adventures That Will Benefit You and Others.* Chicago Review Press, 1999. A fantastic source for journeys in the US and abroad. The book details many different adventures, indexing them by cost, length, location, season and project type. It also lists many other resources including agencies, directories and periodicals.

🗒 ACTION: Take a personal growth vacation

Most vacations help us relax and get away from it all, but some end up being life-changing experiences. Have you ever taken a vacation or been on a retreat that left you feeling exhilarated, emotionally uplifted, or ready to take on the world? We all need time to recharge our batteries, particularly when we're committed to making the world a better place. If you want to supercharge your batteries, consider the following possibilities:

- Yoga retreats.
- Women's groups.
- Zen meditation weekends.
- Outward Bound programs.
- Spiritual workshops.
- Catholic monasteries.

⇨ RESOURCE

📖 Lederman, Ellen. *Vacations That Can Change Your Life: Adventures, Retreats and Workshops for the Mind, Body and Spirit.* Sourcebooks Trade, 1998. Ellen Lederman details several types of vacations, including holistic, spiritual, healing and health, self-improvement and learning vacations. She includes cost ranges and contact information for each program.

⇨ TRAVEL RESOURCES

📖 Lonely Planet Guidebooks. Lonely Planet guidebooks have been a great resource for travelers for over 20 years. They have a book for almost any destination you can imagine, in the US or abroad. Each tells you everything you need to know, including background information, transportation options, medical concerns, lodging possibilities, maps, common phrases and the best sites. They also publish walking guides and phrase-books. Their authors are generally sensitive to the concerns of travelers who are socially and environmentally responsible. Look for these guides at your local library or bookstore.
(800) 275-8555   💻 www.lonelyplanet.com

Transitions Abroad Magazine. *Transitions Abroad* is full of practical information on affordable alternatives to mass tourism: living, working, studying, or vacationing alongside the people of the host country.
(800) 293-0373   💻 www.TransitionsAbroad.com

Better World Club
The Better World Club is one of the most useful organizations for environmentally concerned travelers to come along in years. Not only do they provide a great alternative to an AAA (American Auto Association) membership, they can help you access green car rentals, hotels, vacation packages and carbon offsets.
💻 www.betterworldclub.com

ORGANIZATIONS

Getting Involved
Giving
Finding Organizations
Amazing Organizations
The Best of the Rest

H AVE YOU EVER FELT ALONE in your desire to make the world a better place? Ever wonder if what you do really makes a difference? Have no fear. You don't have to do it all by yourself. There are literally millions of people working all over the globe to bring peace and justice to this world. Groups of organized, forward-looking people with a deep-seated desire for justice and equality have always been the most important catalysts for bringing about a better world.

- The labor movement fought for and won the eight-hour workday, safer working conditions, and paid vacations.
- The populist movement demanded and won the right to public education and instituted the progressive income tax to fight historic levels of economic inequality.
- The suffrage movement helped gain the right to vote for women.
- The civil rights movement helped dismantle the legalized segregation of blacks on buses, at lunch counters, and in schools.
- Lesbian and gay activists have fought for cultural acceptance and legal equality and have transformed Americans' views on sexual orientation.
- Environmentalists ignited a global movement that has preserved endangered habitats such as the Arctic National Wildlife Reserve and generated respect for our natural world.

By joining together with our neighbors and other like-minded citizens, we create the potential for significant positive social change in our communities and around the world. Successful acts of cooperation and solidarity create momentum that empowers our communities and propels our vision of justice into the future.

On February 15, 2003, after Colin Powell made it clear in his presentation to the United Nations that the US was going to invade Iraq due to irrefutable evidence of weapons of mass destruction (WMD's) in that country, an estimated 10-30 million people in 800 cities across the globe took to the streets to protest the Bush Administration's decision to go to war. Never in the history of the planet have so many people in such a diversity of countries around the world united on such a scale to speak with one voice for peace.

Public demonstrations not only send a loud message to powerholders but they also inspire their participants. As one woman said of her experiences at a demonstration, "I came unprepared for the beautiful and unconditional solidarity between people. As I experienced the outpouring of love, concern, food and support from thousands of strangers, I felt as if I was experiencing true community for the first time....We are powerful people and we have the ability to take the beautiful solidarity we created in the streets and bring it into our daily lives."[1]

Every day, people like you confront injustice, sometimes very publicly and other times very much behind the scenes. While working in concert with others, the individual and the group can nurture and inspire each other. With this synergy, we increase the possibility for more profound and long lasting social change. Your single voice becomes a deafening roar, and your single action becomes part of a social movement when you join with others to build a better world.

This chapter will help you to support and get involved with causes you believe in and to identify specific local, national, and international organizations that are working to transform your ideals into reality. Now is our time to stand up and make a difference.

GETTING INVOLVED

There are many ways to get involved with organizations that you care about. Each level of involvement is crucial to a group's success. Consider, for a moment, how creating an effective social justice organization requires many of the same elements that go into a good theatrical play. A collaboration of everyone from the set designers to the lighting crew and actors makes a fantastic play. Likewise, everyone from the people who send in a check to those who carry picket signs to folks who talk with government officials make a social change organization run.

Many of us participate by becoming a donating member of an organization. If you want to give more, consider any special talents, skills, or interests that you have and figure out how you could be useful to an organization you care about. Are you good at promotions? Are you media savvy? Have you done research on a specific issue? Do you perform music? Do you know how to raise money? Can you design eye-catching posters? Do you like speaking in public? Perhaps you are simply very passionate about your cause. There is always a place for you — regardless of the amount of time or money you have!

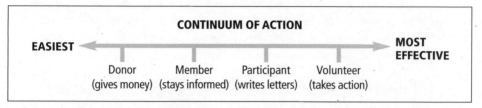

ACTION: Join an organization you care about

When you join an organization, you become the committed audience for the social change "actors." Without the audience to purchase tickets and appreciate what's being created, the play would not survive. The audience not only helps financially support the production of the play but it generates word of mouth interest for other prospective audience members and helps to inspire the actors in their work.

The easiest way to support an organization is to become a member. This usually involves sending a small donation and keeping informed of the group's work. Members often wait in the wings to become involved when the organization most needs their efforts.

ACTION: Participate in an organization you care about

Consider getting out and showing your support for the organizations you care about. Just by attending a lecture, meeting, or fundraiser or by participating in a demonstration, you can really lift the spirits of the more involved members of that organization. Your participation is a quick, easy, and fulfilling way to show your appreciation for what the group does. And it helps educate your community about issues you care about. Ask the organization to keep you informed of any events in your area. And if it's a demonstration, don't forget your picket sign.

ACTION: Volunteer for an organization you care about

Many of us would like to support the great work of organizations that reflect our values — if we just had enough time. Getting involved in an organization may seem like an overwhelming commitment, but remember that involvement is not an all or nothing endeavor. Figure out how much commitment is sustainable for you and then just go get involved — even if it's only a few hours a month! You may think that the last thing you need is another commitment — that if you just had more free time and fewer obligations you would be happier. Ironically, we're often happiest and most fulfilled when we're helping someone else out. Becoming involved can enrich your life as you get to know other like-minded people and spend your time contributing to a better world.

A play is not possible without the efforts of the people behind the scenes. Time spent preparing the set, costumes, and programs is necessary for a successful performance. The supporting cast of an organization attends events and meetings and puts in the sustained effort that keeps a group going by answering the phones, passing out literature, and fundraising. The work of the supporting cast and stage crew set up the groundwork for the organization to be successful on a daily basis. Don't worry, you don't have to spend 20 hours a week volunteering. Donate whatever amount of time works for you.

TIPS FOR MAKING AN ORGANIZATION MORE EFFECTIVE

- Make new people feel welcome. Make sure you introduce a new person to everyone in your group. Nametags are a great way to help new folks fit in. Asking everyone, "What compels you to be here?" is often a great way for members to share their passions.
- Have fun and build community within your group. One of the biggest myths about social change is that it's all work and no play. Be sure to take time to build strong relationships by having fun and even scheduling recreational time outside of your organizational work.
- Make everyone feel involved and important. One of the best ways to keep members involved is to make sure that they feel they're making a contribution to the group. Rotate meeting facilitators, share responsibilities and give everyone concrete tasks.
- Start and end gatherings in an inspiring way. Too many long meetings end with members feeling drained and overwhelmed. Use your creativity to send people off inspired to fulfill their commitments to your organization. Start gatherings with a ritual, end meetings with a cheer and tie social change to personal growth.
- Set concrete, attainable goals. When you begin recognizing and challenging injustice it's easy to want to take on the whole world at once. Trying to change everything overnight only produces frustration. Set short-term, attainable goals in addition to your long-term vision.
- Be open to setbacks; learn from mistakes. No one ever said social change was easy. If you commit to living out your passions, you're bound to make mistakes and encounter setbacks. Make time periodically to review your accomplishments and discuss setbacks. Build reflection time into your organization and examine ways to improve.
- Celebrate your successes. After your organization makes progress, it's easy to just jump right into pursuing your next goal. If you take time to acknowledge your hard work and celebrate your successes, then you will ensure that members stick around for the next campaign.
- Form coalitions with like-minded groups. Don't be afraid to call upon potential allies when your group needs help. Often different organizations' goals overlap enough that pooling resources and supporting one another makes complete sense.
- Be creative. Creativity is the soul of social change. For any issue that comes up, you can ask your group, "How can we be creative about this?" Fundraising, recruiting, demonstrations, and community education all require creativity. If you have the intention to be creative, your group will be dynamic and effective.

THE TOP FIVE BOOKS FOR THE NEW ACTIVIST

1. *An Action A Day Keeps Global Capitalism Away* — Mike Hudema (Between the Lines, 2004)
2. *Grassroots: a Field Guide for Feminist Activism* — Jennifer Baumgardner and Amy Richards (Farrar, Straus & Giroux, 2005)
3. *Organizing for Social Change: A Manual for Activists* — Kim Bobo et. al. (Seven Locks, 2001)
4. *Take It Personally: How To Make Conscious Choices To Change The World* — Anita Roddick (Weiser, 2001)
5. *The Activist's Handbook: A Primer* — Randy Shaw (University of California, 2001)

⇨ ORGANIZING RESOURCES

　📖　Bobo, Kim, Jackie Kendall, and Steve Max. *Organizing for Social Change: A Manual for Activists in the 1990s.* Seven Locks Press, 1996. A great sourcebook for the fundamentals of social change: planning and facilitating meetings, recruiting, fundraising, using the media, public speaking and networking with unions and religious organizations.

　📖　Kaner, Sam. *Facilitator's Guide to Participatory Decision-Making.* New Society Publishers, 1996. This book explains how to create a group where everyone feels involved and committed by encouraging full participation, promoting full understanding, and building inclusive, sustainable agreements within your group.

GIVING

A contribution to social change organizations is a great way for you to create positive change with your money. In our society we tend to think negatively of money's power — an "Everyone has their price" way of thinking. Donating some of your money to amazing organizations is one way you can control the power of money.

✍ ACTION: Donate money based on your values

Americans are generous people, with almost 90% of households contributing to nonprofits and charities they support. Yet each household on average donates only about 3.4% of household income yearly[2] and households making less than $25,000 actually give a higher percentage (4.2%) of their income than households earning over $100,000 (2.7%).[3] Consider budgeting a percentage of your income, whether it's one, three, five, or even ten percent. When you donate money to something that you believe in, you are helping to make your values real in the world. Your donation becomes an investment in positive social change. For example, if you give some of your earnings to Amnesty International, the time you spend at work suddenly becomes time working for human rights, regardless of your job. Don't worry if you don't have much money — every dollar counts.

You can even automatically deposit a certain percentage of your income into a separate "giving account" if that will inspire you to reach your giving goals.

☐ ACTION: Set up a giving budget

Many people consider creating a monthly spending budget, but very few consider that their charitable contributions are worth budgeting. On January 1st every year, make up a list of your values. Then find organizations that are working to make those values real in the world. Don't let your giving be dictated by who sends you a request in the mail, either. Do some research to find the best organizations and the ones that best represent your ideals. The last step is to set up dates and the dollar amounts that you plan to send to those organizations. A giving budget keeps your charitable giving at the forefront of your mind throughout the year so that it doesn't take a back seat to all of the other ways you want to spend your money.

GIVING BUDGET			
VALUES & GROUPS	**MONEY BUDGETED**	**DATE TO GIVE**	**ACTUAL**
Environment			
Sierra Club	$55	April	
Local enviro group	$60	Feb	Feb 3rd $60
Assisting the Poor			
Habitat for Humanity	$100	Jan	Jan 25th $120
Local Homeless Shelter	$50	Mar	
Social Justice			
National Gay and Lesbian Task Force	$90	Sept	
NAACP	$70	Jun	
Faith/Religious Group			
Church, Mosque,			
Temple, etc.	$80	Monthly	
Sustainable Culture			
Center for a New American Dream	$100	Dec	
Public Media			
PBS Ch.12	$40	Oct	

☐ ACTION: Put an organization in your will

A gift that you make to an organization through your will is a great way to keep supporting great causes into the future. Your vision for a better world can live on even after you have passed. Just contact an organization that you care about and ask them for more information.

⇨ RESOURCES

Guide Star

Guide Star is an online searchable database of nonprofits that allows you to find and compare organizations to which you are considering donating time or money. It provides a wealth of information on just about every nonprofit you can think of, including mission statements, programs, financial reports, goals and accomplishments, areas served, and contact information.

(757) 229-4631   💻 www.guidestar.org

FINDING ORGANIZATIONS

There is at least one organization committed to fighting for almost any issue that you can imagine, and it may even be right in your own community. With just a little research, you will find the organizations that best fit your values and desire for involvement.

Are you interested in an organization that:

• has a local, state, national, or global focus?
• has a lot of opportunities for direct involvement from members?
• is focused on legal, political, or social issues?
• works with children, adults, or the elderly?

☑ ACTION: Support organizations that create long-term social change

Be sure to seek out organizations that address the root causes of social and environmental problems, in addition to ones that meet your community's immediate needs. For example, although giving money to your local homeless shelter has an immediate impact on people's lives, giving to the National Low Income Housing Coalition will help eliminate the need for homeless shelters. Donating money to a developing country suffering from famine is important, but so is giving to a group such as Oxfam that helps develop self-sufficient, sustainable economic growth in local economies. Other groups creating long-lasting social change focus on nonviolent conflict resolution, community development and empowerment, local businesses, and getting money out of politics. Think about a group's potential for long-term social change as you decide which ones to support.

☑ ACTION: Support local organizations

Although supporting national and global social justice organizations is important, it is just as important to help out groups in your own community. When you support local organizations, you have the opportunity to more tangibly experience the positive results of the money you donate and the time you volunteer.

Also when you get involved locally, you become part of a tight community of people who share your values and commitment, which can make your experience even more fulfilling.

⇨ RESOURCES

IGC is the largest community of progressive activist organizations on the Internet. IGC's four subgroups (PeaceNet, EcoNet, WomensNet and Anti-RacismNet) provide everything from job listings and headline news to events calendars and extensive listings of social change organizations.

💻 www.igc.org

AMAZING ORGANIZATIONS

We've compiled a short list and briefly described some of the most powerful social change organizations in the world. We have selected organizations that are both accessible to a wide number of people and doing good work in a number of very important areas. You can find a more comprehensive list, "The Best of the Rest," directly after.

Animal Rights
Humane Society of the United States (HSUS)
2100 L Street, NW, Washington, DC 20037, USA.
(202) 452-1100   💻 www.hsus.org

Working primarily through legislation and education, HSUS is a massive animal protection organization with a variety of programs. Pet overpopulation, animal sheltering, circus cruelty, dissection, fur, animal research, factory farming and wildlife are just some of their concerns. HSUS continually monitors legislation at the state and federal levels, including the Endangered Species Act. They also work closely with animal shelters to provide healthy environments for animals.

People for the Ethical Treatment of Animals (PETA)
501 Front Street, Norfolk, VA 23510, USA.
(757) 622-PETA   💻 www.peta.org

With over 700,000 members, PETA is the world's largest animal rights group. Founded in 1980, PETA is dedicated to establishing and protecting the rights of all animals. PETA operates under the simple philosophy that animals are not ours to eat, wear, experiment on, or use for entertainment. Using nonviolent direct action, research, education, legislation, investigation, animal rescue and celebrity supporters, PETA focuses its efforts on factory farms, the fur trade, laboratories and the entertainment industry. Members receive an informative newsletter, *Animal Times,* which includes actions and campaign updates.

Community

Association of Community Organizations for Reform Now (ACORN)

2-4 Nevins Street, Second Floor, Brooklyn, NY 11217-1010, USA.

(718) 246-7900   ▣ www.acorn.org

Formed by a group of welfare mothers, ACORN is a coalition of community groups dedicated to standing up for the poor and powerless.
Living wages, jobs, affordable housing, better schools and environmental
justice are among ACORN's many struggles. Community members lead
this grassroots group in filing lawsuits, lobbying, organizing petitions and
nonviolent direct actions such as sit-ins and marches.

Big Brothers Big Sisters of America (BBBSA)

230 North 13th Street, Philadelphia, PA 19107, USA.

(215) 567-7000   ▣ www.bbbsa.org

Since 1904, BBBSA has created powerful relation-
ships between millions of kids and positive adults. This unique mentoring
program links "Littles" one on one with "Bigs." Bigs and Littles usually get
together several times each month for sporting events, a trip to the park, visiting a museum, or just to hang out and talk. Research shows that BBBSA is
one of the most effective programs at reducing delinquency, drug use, school
absence and violence. Indeed, there is perhaps no better way to positively
affect a child's life than through individual mentorship.

Boys & Girls Clubs of America (B & GCA)

1275 Peachtree Street, NE, Atlanta, GA 30309-
3506, USA.

(404) 487-5700   ▣ www.bgca.org

Boys & Girls Clubs have provided a safe, empowering place for more than three
million kids to spend their free time. Clubs encourage kids to develop their
athletic, artistic, and scholastic abilities to their full potential. Gang prevention,
alcohol/drug prevention, health education, and leadership development are just
a few of the amazing programs clubs offer. The Chronicle of Philanthropy
ranked B&GCA the number one youth organization five years in a row. The
clubs serve many inner city youth from low income and single parent households, making them an excellent investment in these kids' futures.

Habitat for Humanity International

121 Habitat Street, Americus, GA 31709-3498, USA.

(229) 924-6935   ▣ www.habitat.org

Since 1976, Habitat volunteers have built more than 100,000 houses for families
around the world. Habitat is a nonprofit ecumenical Christian organization
that brings together families in need, volunteer labor and donated materials
to eliminate homelessness and poverty housing. The receiving families help

build their homes and then buy them with no-interest, affordable financing.
To find your local affiliate, check their website or give them a call.

Economic Justice
Co-op America

1612 K Street, NW, Suite 600, Washington, DC 20006, USA.
 (800) 58-GREEN   💻 www.coopamerica.org

Co-op America offers a wide range of phenomenal services
and information for businesses and individuals who want their money to
make the world a better place. Co-op America helps you support local environmentally friendly businesses, invest in socially responsible companies, and make
informed decisions on how you save and spend your money. Membership
includes the *Co-op America Quarterly* magazine, National Green Pages and a
financial planning handbook. Learn how to live sustainably!

United for a Fair Economy (UFE)

29 Winter Street, Second Floor, Boston, MA 02108, USA.
(617) 423-2148   💻 www.faireconomy.org

United for a Fair Economy works to narrow the growing gap between the rich
and the rest of us. They report that the wealthiest 1% of the population controls more wealth than the bottom 95%. Through education and policy
campaigns, UFE hopes to create a fairer economy where families need not
struggle just to get by. UFE can teach you how to educate and organize your
community about both local and global economic disparity. Their publications and workshops will rock your world.

Environment
Greenpeace

702 H Street, NW, Washington, DC 20001, USA.
(800) 326-0959   💻 www.greenpeace.org/usa

GREENPEACE

Greenpeace uses a variety of nonviolent direct action tactics to raise awareness
and protect the environment, including blocking ships filled with genetically engineered corn, observing whaling vessels, and hanging protest banners
on toxic refineries. Greenpeace is an independent organization that refuses
donations from governments, companies and political parties. Instead it
relies completely on donations from its 2.5 million supporters. Toxic waste,
genetic engineering, climate issues and forests are among the many issues
Greenpeace takes on.

Sierra Club

85 Second Street, Second Floor, San Francisco CA, 94105, USA.
(415) 977-5500   💻 www.sierraclub.org

For over 100 years, Sierra Club has lobbied at the local, state and national levels
for environmental reform and wilderness protection. In 2000, Sierra Club

challenged factory farm pollution, urban sprawl, logging in national forests and wildland destruction. Chapters in every state promote local issues and involvement; members can even attend locally sponsored Sierra Club Outings, retreats, hikes, and other events. Members also receive the superb *Sierra* magazine.

World Wildlife Fund (WWF)
1250 Twenty-Fourth Street, NW, Washington, DC 20090-7180, USA.
(202) 293-4800   💻 www.worldwildlife.org
World Wildlife Fund is the largest independent conservation organization in the world with almost 5 million members in 100 countries. WWF works with governments, corporations, landowners, and local citizens to preserve wildlife habitat and endangered species; and to address global threats such as climate change, forest destruction and ocean degradation.

Gay and Lesbian
Human Rights Campaign (HRC)
1640 Rhode Island Avenue, NW, Washington, DC 20036-3278, USA.
(800) 777-4723   💻 www.hrc.org
Human Rights Campaign's fundamental mission is equal rights and safety for gays and lesbians. Their full-time lobbying team is the largest working for gay and lesbian issues, such as eliminating workplace discrimination, demanding protection under federal hate crime laws, fighting for AIDS-related and other health issues, blocking anti-gay legislation and electing open-minded politicians. HRC lobbies, educates the public, recruits and organizes volunteers, takes part in elections and conducts training and outreach at the local level.

National Gay and Lesbian Task Force (NGLTF)
1325 Massachusetts Avenue, NW, Suite 600, Washington, DC 20005, USA.
(202) 393-5177   💻 www.thetaskforce.org
Since 1973, NGLTF has struggled for lesbian, bisexual, transgender, and gay rights at the local state, and national levels. It provides vital information, funding and resources for grassroots organizations. Key NGLTF issues include fighting Radical Right anti-gay legislation, ending job discrimination and demanding improved government action on the AIDS crisis. They also create publications and organizing materials.

Human Rights
Amnesty International (AI)
5 Penn Plaza, 14th Floor, New York, NY 10001, USA.
(212) 807-8400   💻 www.amnesty.org
The world's largest human rights organization, Amnesty International

puts pressure on countries to abide by the Universal Declaration of Human Rights. AI works to free prisoners of conscience; ensure fair and prompt trials for political prisoners; abolish the death penalty, torture, and other degrading treatment; and end 'disappearances' and extrajudicial executions. They use a variety of tactics, including "Urgent Actions," or letter campaigns on behalf of political prisoners; lobbying, investigating and exposing human rights violations; and promoting youth activism.

Human Rights Watch (HRW)

350 Fifth Avenue, 34th Floor, New York, NY 10118-3299, USA.
(212) 290-4700   🖳 www.hrw.org
Human Rights Watch exposes government abuses and human rights
   violators in the international community. Using the influence of
the US government, World Bank, United Nations, Tokyo, and the European Union, HRW pressures countries to abide by international human rights law. They interview victims and witnesses directly and meet with a variety of government, church, labor and local human rights leaders. By publishing reports and holding perpetrators accountable, HRW creates a more humane world.

International
Global Exchange (GX)

2017 Mission Street, #303, San Francisco, California 94110, USA.
(415) 255-7296   🖳 www.globalexchange.org
Global Exchange is "a non-profit research, GLOBAL 🔆 EXCHANGE
   education, and action center dedicated
to promoting people-to-people ties around the world." They educate Americans to injustices, urging governments to support humane, fair, and sustainable development; and promote Reality Tours, a program that takes people to struggling countries. GX craft stores and online shopping are part of a growing international fair trade movement, offering goods created under fair labor standards. Their books, videos and speakers educate grassroots organizations about political and economic rights.

Oxfam

26 West Street, Boston MA 02111, USA.
(800) 77-OXFAM   🖳 www.oxfamamerica.org

Oxfam builds partnerships with poor communities around the world, helping them become self-sufficient for the long term. Oxfam works to alleviate the root causes of poverty and hunger, end social injustice and improve health programs. They also support community activism, encourage governments to adopt long-term development plans and promote education around social justice issues. Their 11 branches worldwide have earned enormous respect for helping local grassroots groups help their people rather than dictating programs.

United Nations Children Fund (UNICEF)

3 United Nations Plaza, New York, NY 10017, USA.

(212) 326-7000   💻 www.unicef.org

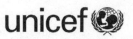

UNICEF struggles for the protection of children's rights and basic needs and tries to expand kids' opportunities to reach their full potential. As the only UN organization exclusively focused on children, it helps fund health care, education, safe water, and sanitary sewage conditions through programs in 161 countries. UNICEF advocates raising the minimum military age, eliminating child sex trafficking, and increasing child immunization.

Peace

Peace Action

1100 Wayne Avenue, Suite 1020, Silver Spring, MD 20910, USA.

(301) 565-4050   💻 www.peace-action.org

Formerly SANE/FREEZE, Peace Action is the nation's largest grassroots peace and justice organization, with a membership of 55,000, 27 state affiliates, and over 100 local chapters. Through national and grassroots citizens' action they promote global nuclear disarmament, significant military budget reductions and the ending of the international arms trade. Peace Action also produces voter guides to educate the public on candidates' voting history and current stands on peace and human rights. They also promote campus organizing through the Student Peace Action Network.

War Resisters League (WRL)

339 Lafayette Street, New York, NY 10012, USA.

(212) 228-0450   💻 www.warresisters.org

Beginning in 1923, members of the War Resistors League have insisted that war is a crime against all humanity, and that resisting war is a top priority for making the world better. WRL uses education, lobbying, nonviolent direct action, and demonstrations to "work for peace within a framework of social justice." They support war tax resistance, publish *Nonviolent Activist* magazine, and use their Youthpeace program to create a culture of peace by resisting war toys and military recruiting.

Witness for Peace (WFP)

3628 12th Street, NE, First Floor, Washington, DC 20017, USA.

(202) 547-6112   💻 www.witnessforpeace.org

Witness For Peace is a politically independent, grassroots organization that raises awareness about injustice in the Americas through letter writing campaigns, publications, nonviolent direct actions, and speaking tours. WFP has sent over 7,000 US citizens to Central and South America, Cuba, Mexico and Haiti. The delegations' goals include education, exposure to alternative economies and cultures, and creating momentum for advocacy campaigns at home. Their current "Stop the War Against the Poor" campaign challenges US-sponsored terrorism and economic exploitation in the Americas and the Caribbean.

Political Action
Global Response (GR)
P.O. Box 7490, Boulder, CO 80306, USA.

(303) 444-0306   www.globalresponse.org

GR focuses the energy of its members on corporations and governments who are destroying the earth and abusing the rights of its people. Targeted letter-writing campaigns unleash the power of average citizens to shine the light of truth upon global injustices. Campaigns often focus on the connection between environmental destruction and indigenous peoples' rights in the developing world. Their Young Environmentalist Actions (YEA) program for kids brings these campaigns to schools and families. Since their first campaign in 1990, GR has been successful in over 40% of their campaigns!

20/20 Vision
8403 Colesville Road, Suite 860, Silver Spring, MD 20910, USA.

(301) 587-1782   www.2020vision.org

20/20 Vision's mission is to make grassroots political action easy for busy people who care about peace and environmental issues. Members receive information each month on how they can make the most difference in 20 minutes. 20/20 provides up-to-date research and timely action notices for contacting your legislators. They campaign on issues of air and water pollution, military waste, campaign finance reform, and arms control. 20/20 offers you a unique way to stay informed and politically active from month to month. Voice your opinion!

Public Interest
Public Citizen (PC)
1600 20th Street, NW, Washington, DC 20009, USA.

(202) 588-1000   www.citizen.org

Public Citizen is the ultimate Washington watchdog, working on consumers' behalf. Since Ralph Nader founded the organization in 1971, they have fought for safer drugs and medical products, fair trade, a cleaner environment, and a more democratic government. The Congress Watch branch lobbies and monitors lawmakers to protect public safety and end corporate welfare. The Global Trade Watch branch works for government and corporate accountability. PC helps you protect your own rights as a citizen.

Public Interest Research Groups (PIRG)
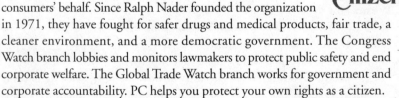
[your state] PIRG, c/o National Association of State PIRGs
3435 Wilshire Boulevard, Suite 385, Los Angeles, CA 90010, USA.

(213) 251-3680   💻 www.pirg.org

State PIRGs work in 26 states to protect their citizens' interests. They fight for greater democracy, the environment, and consumer safety. The PIRG website offers a Congressional scorecard system, where you can evaluate your lawmakers' voting records on public interest issues. They also have action alerts explaining simple actions you can take to make a difference. Visit their website to learn how your safety, rights and your own backyard are threatened in your own state. Then take action!

Race and Ethnicity

National Association for the Advancement of Colored People (NAACP)

4805 Mt. Hope Drive, Baltimore, MD 21215, USA.

(877) NAACP-98   💻 www.naacp.org

The NAACP's main goal is "to ensure the political, educational, social, and economic equality of minority group citizens of the United States." Over 2,200 branches of the NAACP press for change, using nonviolent strategies including petitions, court struggles, voter organizing, demonstrations, and press releases. As the largest US civil rights organization, the NAACP uses its resources to create stay-in-school programs, economic development and health care outreach.

National Council on La Raza (NCLR)

Raul Yzaguirre Building, 1126 16th Street, NW, Washington, DC 20036, USA.

(202) 785-1670   💻 www.nclr.org

NCLR
NATIONAL COUNCIL OF LA RAZA

National Council on La Raza seeks to eliminate poverty and discrimination and provide opportunities to Hispanic Americans. Their research and advocacy branch provides Hispanics a powerful voice in national policy decisions. Their community support branch assists local groups in economic development, local governance, and resource management. Health care, immigration, housing, education and welfare are just a few of NCLR's many issues. Their blend of national policy goals and local development is especially crucial as the number of Hispanic working poor grows.

Native American Rights Fund (NARF)

1506 Broadway, Boulder, CO 80302-6296, USA.

(303) 447-8760   💻 www.narf.org

Native American Rights Fund

Native American Rights Fund provides "legal representation and technical assistance to Indian tribes, organizations, and individuals nationwide." Their goals include protecting human rights, tribal resources, and tribal existence. By educating Native Americans and the public about Indian rights, NARF seeks to hold the government accountable for its actions. NARF monitors court cases, legislative action, and activist campaigns, sending updates to concerned individuals and issuing press releases to inform the public.

Simplicity

Center for a New American Dream (CNAD)

6930 Carroll Ave., Suite 900, Takoma Park, MD 20912, USA.
(877) 68-DREAM   💻 www.newdream.org
The motto "More fun, less stuff" reflects CNAD's dedication
to "reduce and shift consumption to enhance quality of life and protect the environment." Debt, bankruptcy, overworking, neglected relationships, and environmental degradation are all consequences of our insatiable desire to buy more and more stuff. CNAD's educational campaigns, such as "Kids and Commercialism" and "Simplify the Holidays," have reached millions of people overwhelmed by materialism. Their newsletter *"Enough!"* provides you with amazing information about what you can do to create a culture of simplicity.

Violence

The Brady Campaign to Prevent Gun Violence (TBC)

1225 Eye Street, NW, Suite 1100, Washington, DC 20005, USA.
(202) 898-0792   💻 www.bradycampaign.org
The Brady Campaign pushes for more sensible gun laws at
every level of government. Thanks to their hard work, legislators have passed an assault weapon ban, child access prevention laws, and waiting periods and background checks on handgun purchases. TBC also monitors enforcement of current laws and resists making concealed weapon permits easier to obtain. The Brady Center to Prevent Gun Violence is the educational and research branch of TBC, where a variety of professional researchers work against the spread of gun violence in the US.

V-Day

388 Market St, Suite 400, San Francisco, CA 94111, USA.
   💻 www.vday.org
V-Day is a group dedicated to ending violence against women and girls around the world, including rape, battery, incest, sexual slavery and female genital mutilation. Best known for producing "The Vagina Monologues" to help raise awareness and funds around these issues, this organization builds powerful networks to end violence in myriad countries.

Women's Rights

National Abortion and Reproductive Rights Action League (NARAL)

1156 15th Street, NW, Suite 700, Washington, DC 20005, USA.
(202) 973-3000   💻 www.naral.org
NARAL's mission is "Securing and Protecting Safe, Legal Abortion and Making Abortion Less Necessary — Not More Difficult or Dangerous." Although

the majority of Americans are pro-choice, a very vocal minority continues the fight to eliminate a woman's right to choose. Through public education, lobbying, public policy research, and grassroots organizing, NARAL resists anti-choice violence and campaigns designed to restrict abortion rights. It promotes pregnancy prevention programs and reproductive healthcare.

National Organization for Women (NOW)
1100 H Street, NW, 3rd Floor, Washington, D.C. 20005, USA.
(202) 628-8669   💻 www.now.org
For over 30 years, NOW members have struggled for women's rights.
   Their campaigns include ending violence against women; supporting abortion rights; advocating for rape, harassment and abuse survivors;
   ending racism, sexism and homophobia; and electing feminist legislators at every
   level of government. Their tactics include massive marches, lobbying, educa-
   tion/conferences, litigation, organizing and nonviolent civil disobedience.

Planned Parenthood Federation of America
434 West 33rd Street, New York, NY 10001, USA.
(212) 541-7800   💻 www.plannedparent-
hood.org

Planned Parenthood is a national organization dedicated to sexual and reproductive health. Their mission is to provide comprehensive reproductive health
   care services, empowering sexuality education, and advocacy for public policies that ensure reproductive health, freedom, and research. Planned
   Parenthood provides reproductive health care to over 5 million women,
   men, and teenagers annually at over 850 health centers.

THE BEST OF THE REST

Here is a list of more incredible organizations working to build a better world on a daily basis. Be sure to contact them to find out more about each organization.

Activism
Student Environmental Action
Coalition
   www.seac.org
United Students Against Sweatshops
   www.studentsagainstsweatshops.org
Ruckus Society
   www.ruckus.org

Animal Rights
EarthSave
   www.earthsave.org

Farm Animal Reform Movement
   www.farmusa.org
In Defense of Animals
   www.idausa.org
Vegetarian Resource Group
   www.vrg.org

Community
Center for Community Change
   www.communitychange.org
Institute for Community Economics
   www.iceclt.org

Institute for Local Self-Reliance
www.ilsr.org

South West Organizing Project
www.swop.net

Economic Justice

Jobs with Justice (see resources in
WORK chapter)
www.jwj.org

National Labor Committee
www.nlcnet.org

Environment

Community Coalition for
Environmental Justice
www.ccej.org

Rainforest Action Network (RAN)
www.ran.org

Earth First!
www.earthfirst.org

GrassRoots Recycling Network
www.grrn.org

Indigenous Environmental Network
www.ienearth.org

National Resource Defense Council
www.nrdc.org

Sea Shepherd
www.seashepherd.org

Union of Concerned Scientists
www.ucsusa.org

The Wilderness Society
www.wilderness.org

Population Connection
www.populationconnection.org

Gay and Lesbian

ACT UP
www.actupny.org

Gay and Lesbian Alliance against
Defamation (GLAAD)
www.glaad.org

Parents and Friends of Lesbians And
Gays (PFLAG)
www.pflag.org

Homelessness

National Coalition for the Homeless
www.nationalhomeless.org

Human Rights

American Civil Liberties Union
www.aclu.org

Disability Rights Education and
Defense Fund
www.dredf.org

National Coalition to Abolish the
Death Penalty
www.ncadp.org

Prison Activists Resource Center
www.prisonactivist.org

International

50 Years is Enough
www.50years.org

FINCA (Foundation for
International Community Assistance)
www.villagebanking.org

International Development Exchange
www.idex.org

International Forum on
Globalization
www.ifg.org

Jubilee USA Network
www.jubileeusa.org

ONE: The Campaign to Make
Poverty History
www.one.org

Voices in the Wilderness
www.vitw.org

Military

Center for Defense Information
www.cdi.org

Peace

The Carter Center
www.cartercenter.org

Peace Brigades International
www.peacebrigades.org

School of the Americas Watch
www.soaw.org

Politics

Common Cause
www.commoncause.org

League of Independent Voters
www.indyvoter.org

League of Women Voters
www.lwv.org

MoveOn.org
www.moveon.org

Project Vote Smart
www.vote-smart.org

Public Campaign
www.publicampaign.org

Public Interest

Center for Science in the Public
Interest
www.cspinet.org

Race and Ethnicity

Anti-Defamation League
www.adl.org

Center for Third World Organizing
www.ctwo.org

Cultural Survival
www.cs.org

First Nations Development Institute
www.firstnations.org

Southern Poverty Law Center
www.splcenter.org

Simplicity

Center for Commercial-Free Public
Education

www.commercialfree.org

Commercial Alert
www.commercialalert.org

Northwest Earth Institute
www.nwei.org

Seeds of Simplicity
www.seedsofsimplicity.org

Women's Rights

9 to 5 National Association of
Working Women
www.9to5.org

Feminist Majority Foundation
www.feminist.org

MADRE
www.madre.org

National Organization of Men
against Sexism
www.nomas.org

IN CANADA

Activist

Web Networks Community
community.web.ca

Links to hundreds of Canadian
activist organizations.

Economic

The Council of Canadians
www.canadians.org

Ecumenical Coalition for Economic
Justice
www.ecej.org

Halifax Initiative
www.halifaxinitiative.org

Environment

GreenOntario
www.greenontario.org

Sierra Club of Canada
www.sierraclub.ca

THE TOP TEN ACTIONS
FOR A BETTER WORLD

IF YOU'VE READ THE WHOLE BOOK and said, "Wow! What a great book!" but haven't really taken any actions, you may be feeling overwhelmed. Here's a short-list of the ten most powerful actions for a better world that you can tear out and put on your refrigerator:

1. Buy products from socially responsible companies (SHOPPING).

2. Buy a low emission, fuel efficient car (TRANSPORTATION).

3. Eat less meat (FOOD).

4. Open an account at a socially responsible bank or credit union (MONEY).

5. Conserve energy and water (HOME).

6. Buy less stuff (SHOPPING).

7. Limit your work time (WORK).

8. Get to know your neighbors (FRIENDS & FAMILY).

9. Watch less TV (MEDIA).

10. Join an organization you care about (ORGANIZATIONS).

NOTES

SEVEN FOUNDATIONS
OF A BETTER WORLD

1. Shaohua Chen and Martin Ravallion. "How Have the World's Poorest Fared Since the Early 1980's?" World Bank Policy Research Working Paper 3341, June 2004.
2. United Nations Development Programme. *The 2005 Human Development Report.* Oxford University Press, 2005, p. 4.
3. Ibid.
4. Jens Martins. *A Compendium of Inequality: The Human Development Report 2005.* FES Dialogue on Globalization, 2005, p. 3.
5. UN Food and Agriculture Organization (FAO), *The State of Food Insecurity in the World 2004.* United Nations, 2004.
6. United Nations Development Programme. *The 1999 Human Development Report.* Oxford University Press, 1999.
7. UN World Food Programme. "Paying the Price of Hunger." United Nations, May 18, 2004.
8. Business Week annual CEO pay surveys, Bureau of Labor Statistics, "Average Weekly Earnings of Production Workers, Total Private Sector" Series ID: EEU00500004 [online]. [cited May 23, 2006]. www.faireconomy.org/research/CEO_Pay_charts.html.
9. AFL-CIO. "Executive Paywatch" [online]. [cited June 8, 2006]. www.aflcio.org/corporatewatch/paywatch/ceou/database.cfm?tkr=YHOO&pg=1.
10. Edward N. Wolff. "Changes in Household Wealth in the 1980s and 1990s in the US." The Levy Economics Institute, Working Paper # 407, 2004.
11. Ibid.
12. Ibid.
13. US Bureau of the Census. Income, Poverty, and Health Insurance Coverage in the United States: 2004, Report P60-229, August 2005 [online]. [cited May 23, 2006].Tables B-1 and B-2, pp. 46-57. www.census.gov/prod/2005pubs/p60-229.pdf.
14. National Center For Children In Poverty. "Low-Income Children in the United States (2004)" [online]. [cited May 23, 2006]. www.nccp.org/pub_cpf04.html.
15. Lawrence Mishel, Jared Bernstein, and Sylvia Allegretto. *State of Working America 2004/2005.* ILR Press, 2004, p. 16.
16. CIA World Fact Book. "Rank Order – Life expectancy at birth" [online]. [cited May 23, 2006]. www.cia.gov/cia/publications/factbook/rankorder/2102rank.html.
17. Jorn Madslien. "Debt relief hopes bring out the critics" [online]. [cited May 23, 2006]. BBC News, June 29, 2005. news.bbc.co.uk/2/hi/business/4619189.stm.
18. Jubilee USA Network. "Why Drop The Debt?" [online]. [cited May 23, 2006]. www.jubileeusa.org/jubilee.cgi?path=/learn_more&page=why_drop_the_debt.html.
19. Larry Rohter. "Brazil, IMF At Odds Over $22 Billion in Social Programs." Denver Post, (February 21, 2000), p. A4.
20. Marie Michael. "Food or Debt: the Jubilee 2000 Movement." *Dollars and Sense,* July/August 2000.
21. Megan Rowling. "Nicaragua." *Z Magazine,* January 2001.
22. Oxfam International. *Rigged Rules and Double Standards: Trade, Globalization, and the Fight Against Poverty.* Oxfam [2002, p. 3. www.make tradefair.com/assets/english/report_english.pdf.
23. Oxfam International. *Rigged Rules and Double Standards: Trade, Globalization, and the Fight Against Poverty.* Oxfam, 2002. www.maketrade fair.com/assets/english/report_english.pdf.
24. Co-op America. *Guide to Ending Sweatshops.* 5th edition, Co-op America, 2004, p. 6.
25. Human Rights Watch. "Tainted Harvest: Child Labor and Obstacles to Organizing on Ecuador's Banana Plantations" [online]. [cited May 23, 2006]. HRW, 2002. www.hrw.org/reports/2002/ecuador.
26. Co-op America. *Guide to Ending Sweatshops.* 5th edition, Co-op America, 2004, pp. 6-7. See www.sweatshops.org.
27. Barry Yeoman. "Silence in the Fields." *Mother Jones,* January/February 2001.
28. United Nations Development Programme. *Human Development Report 2004.* UN, 2004, pp.168-171.
29. Martin Wroe. "An Irresistible Force." *Sojourners,* May/June 2000.
30. Debt Aids Trade Africa (DATA). "DATA reaction to IMF-World Bank debt cancellation deal" [online]. [cited February 6, 2006]. www.data.org/archives/000745.php.
31. Jeffrey Sachs. *The End of Poverty.* Penguin Press, 2005, p. 218.
32. Ibid., p. 302.
33. Ibid., pp. 304-6.
34. The Fair Trade Federation. "2005 Executive Summary." *Fair Trade Trends in North American and the Pacific Rim* [online]. [cited May 23, 2006]. FTF, 2005, p. 1. www.fairtradefederation.org/research/trends/2005/index.htm.
35. Transfair USA. "2004 Annual Report." Transfair USA, 2005, pp. 4-5.
36. Fair Trade Federation. "Fair Trade Coffee and Food Products" [online]. [cited February 6, 2006]. www.fairtradefederation.org/memcof.html.
37. Edward Epstein. "Stark Wants Government To Serve Fair Trade Coffee" [online]. [cited May 23, 2006]. *San Francisco Chronicle,* July 29, 2003. www.globalexchange.org/campaigns/fairtrade/coffee/901.html.
38. Transfair USA. "The Fair Trade Beat." [online]. [cited February 3, 2006]. Winter 2006. www.transfairusa.org/content/email/ftbeat_winter_06.htm.

39. Transfair USA. "2004 Annual Report." Transfair USA, 2005, p. 3.
40. ACORN'S Living Wage Resource Center. "The Living Wage Movement: Building Power in our Workplaces and Neighborhoods" [online]. [cited February 1, 2006]. www.livingwagecampaign. org/index.php?id=2071.
41. Co-op America. *Guide to Ending Sweatshops.* 5th edition, Co-op America, 2004, p. 4.
42. "CIW Ends Boycott, Gets Taco Bell to Meet All Demands." *Oxfam Exchange,* Spring/Summer 2005.
43. United Students Against Sweatshops. "Affiliates" [online]. [cited June 8, 2006]. www.students againstsweatshops.org/about/affiliates.php.
44. Liza Featherstone, "The New Student Movement," The Nation, May 15, 2000.
45. CDFI Coalition. "Directory of Community Development Financial Institutions"[online]. [cited 1999]. www.cdfi.org.
46. South Shore Bank. "Fast Facts" [online]. [cited April 4, 2006]. www.sbk.com.
47. Grameen Bank. "Grameen Bank Monthly Update in US$: December 2005" [online]. [cited May 23, 2006]. www.grameen-info.org/bank/December 05US$.htm.
48. Eric Hobsbawm. *The Age of Extremes: A History of the World 1914-1991.* Vintage Books, 1994, pp. 26, 49.
49. Ibid., p. 49.
50. Howard Zinn. *The Zinn Reader.* Seven Stories Press, 1997, p. 260.
51. United Nations Development Programme, *Human Development Report 2000.* Oxford University Press, 2000, p. 36.
52. BBC News. "Q&A: Peace in Sudan" [online]. [cited March 10, 2006]. news.bbc.co.uk/1/hi/world/africa/3211002.stm.
53. "Nuclear Weapon." *Wikipedia* [online]. [cited March 10, 2006]. en.wikipedia.org/wiki/Nuclear_warheads.
54. BBC News. "Iraq Body Count: War Dead Figures" [online]. [cited March 20, 2006]. news.bbc.co.uk/1/hi/world/middle_east/4525412.stm.
55. William Shawcross. *Deliver Us From Evil.* Touchstone, 2000, chapter 5.
56. BBC News. "Rwanda Slaughter 'Could Have Been Prevented'" [online]. [cited June 8, 2006]. news.bbc. co.uk/2/hi/africa/308542.stm. Also see: Alison Des Forges. *Leave None to Tell the Story: Genocide in Rwanda.* Human Rights Watch, 1999. www.hrw.org/reports/1999/rwanda.
57. Jeevan Vasagar and Ewen MacAskill. "180,000 Die from Hunger in Darfur" [online]. [cited May 23, 2006]. Guardian, March 16, 2005. www.guardian.co.uk/sudan/story/0,14658,1438471,00.html; Kofi Annan. "Billions of Promises to Keep" [op-ed]. *New York Times,* April 13, 2005.
58. Center for Defense Information. "The World's Nuclear Arsenals" [online]. [cited May 23, 2006]. www.cdi.org/issues/nukef&f/database/nukearsenals.cfm, updated February 4, 2003; Federation of American Scientists. "Nuclear Weapons Programs" [online]. [cited May 23, 2006]. www.fas.org/ nuke/guide/dprk/nuke/index.html, updated June 9, 2003.

59. Center for Defense Information. "The World's Nuclear Arsenals" [online]. [cited May 23, 2006]. www.cdi.org/issues/nukef&f/database/nukearsenals. cfm, updated February 4, 2003; Alliance for Nuclear Accountability. "Stockpile Stewardship" [online]. [cited May 23, 2006]. Spring 2005. www.ananuclear.org/FactSheetsDCD05/SPS05DCD.pdf.
60. Elisabeth Skons, Catalina Perdomo, Sam Perlo-Freeman and Petter Stalenheim. "Military Expenditures." *SPIRI Yearbook 2004,* Stockholm International Peace Research Institute, June 9, 2004, chapter 10.
61. Richard F. Grimmett. "Conventional Arms Transfers to Developing Nations, 1997-2004, Report for Congress." US Congressional Research Service, August 29, 2005.
62. Christopher Hellman. "Last of the Big Time Spenders" [online]. [cited May 23, 2006]. Center for Defense Information, updated February 3, 2003. www.cdi.org/issues/wme/spendersfy04.html.
63. Anup Shah. "High Military Expenditure In Some Places" [online]. [cited May 23, 2006]. Global Issues.Org. www.globalissues.org/Geopolitics/Arms Trade/Spending.asp, updated March 27, 2006.
64. Anup Shah. "The Arms Trade is Big Business" [online]. [cited May 23, 2006]. Global Issues.Org, updated January 28, 2006. www.globalissues. org/Geopolitics/ArmsTrade/BigBusiness.asp.
65. Chalmers Johnson. *Blowback: the Costs and Consequences of American Empire.* Henry Holt, 2000, p. 36.; Richard Wolffe. "Technology Brings Power with Few Constraints." *Financial Times.* February 18, 2002, p. 4.
66. Christopher Hitchens. "Rogue Nation USA". *Mother Jones.* May/June 2001.
67. P. Tjaden and N. Thoennes. "Extent, nature, and consequences of intimate partner violence: findings from the National Violence Against Women Survey." [online] [cited September 15, 2005]. US Department of Justice, Publication No. NCJ 181867, 2000. www.ojp.usdoj.gov/nij/pubs-sum/181867.htm.
68. Sharon LaFraniere. "Entrenched Epidemic: Wife Beatings in Africa." *New York Times,* August 11, 2005.
69. Chicago Associated Press. "Kids' Doctors Call on TV Biz." *The Hollywood Reporter,* June 9-11, 1995.
70. The American Psychological Association. "Children and Television Violence"[online]. [cited July 18, 2001]. www.helping.apa.org/family/kidtvviol.html.
71. National Center for Injury Prevention and Control. *Injury Mortality Reports,* as reported by Brady Campaign to Prevent Gun Violence, "Firearm Facts." [online]. [cited May 23, 2006]. June 2005. www.bradycampaign.org/facts/fact sheets/pdf/firearm_facts.pdf.
72. Amnesty International. "Facts and Figures on the Death Penalty" [online]. [cited May 23, 2006]. web.amnesty.org/pages/deathpenalty-facts-eng.
73. Ibid.

74. Richard C. Dieter. "Innocence and the Crisis in the American Death Penalty" [online]. [cited May 23, 2006]. Death Penalty Information Center, 2004. www.deathpenaltyinfo.org/article.php?scid=45&did=1149.

75. BBC News. "'Million' March Against War" [online]. [cited May 23, 2006]. February 16, 2003. www.news.bbc.co.uk/1/hi/uk/2765041.stm.

76. United Nations Development Programme, United Nations Environment Programme, World Bank, and World Resource Institute. *World Resources 2000-2001 People and Ecosystems: The Fraying Web of Life.* World Resources Institute, 2000.

77. Jonathan Loh and Mathis Wackernagel. *Living Planet Report 2004.* World Wildlife Fund, United Nations Environmental Programme-World Conservation Monitoring Centre, 2004, p. 2.

78. CNN. "Study Says Most Ancient Forests Gone" [online]. [cited May 23, 2006]. March 4,1997. www.cnn.com/EARTH/9703/04/vanishing.forest/index.html.

79. Food and Agriculture Organization (FAO). *Agriculture: Towards 2015/30, Technical Interim Report.* United Nations, 2000.

80. United Nations Development Programme. *Global Environmental Outlook-3.* Earthscan Publications, 2002, p. 94.

81. The World Conservation Union (IUCN) and Species Survival Commission (SSC). "Species Extinction" [online] [cited May 23, 2006]. 2004. www.iucn.org/themes/Ssc/red_list_2004/Extinction_media_brief_2004.pdf.

82. Food and Agriculture Organization (FAO). *The State of World Fisheries and Aquaculture 2004.* United Nations, 2004, pp. 24, 32.

83. Lester Brown. *Plan B 2.0: Rescuing A Planet Under Stress And A Civilization In Trouble.* W.W. Norton, 2006, p. 42.

84. Ibid., chapter 2.

85 John C. Ryan and Alan Thein Durning. *Stuff: The Secret Lives of Everyday Things.* Northwest Environment Watch, 1997. Based on M. Wackernagel and W. Rees. *Our Ecological Footprint: Reducing Human Impact on the Earth.* New Society Publishers, 1996.

86. International Energy Agency (IEA). *Energy Balances of OECD Countries (2003 Edition)* and *Energy Balances of non-OECD Countries (2003 Edition).* Organization for Economic Cooperation and Development (OECD), 2004; Population Division of the Department of Economic and Social Affairs of the United Nations Secretariat. *World Population Prospects: The 2002 Revision.* Dataset on CD-ROM. United Nations, 2004.

87. Alan Durning. "Asking How Much Is Enough" in Lester Brown et al., *State of the World 1991.* W.W. Norton, 1991.

88. Authors calculations based on data from: Global Footprint Network. "Humanity's Footprint: 1961-2002" [online]. [cited June 8, 2006]. www.footprintnetwork.org/gfn_sub.php?content=global_footprint.

89. Harvard School of Public Health. "Air Pollution Deadlier Than Previously Thought" [online]. [cited May 23, 2006]. Press release, March 2, 2000. www.hsph.harvard.edu/press/releases/press03022000.html.

90. World Health Organization (WHO). "Fact Sheet 187: Air Pollution" [online] Revised September 2000. www.who.int/mediacentre/factsheets/fs187en.

91. United Nations Development Programme. *Global Environmental Outlook-3.* Earthscan Publications, 2002, p. 221.

92. Ibid., pp. 210-232.

93. United Nations Development Programme. *Global Environmental Outlook-3.* Earthscan Publications, 2002, p. 153. Based on World Commission on Water. *World's Rivers in Crisis — Some Are Dying; Others Could Die.* World Water Council, 1999.

94. Douglas Frantz (New York Times). "Cruising Outside Pollution Laws." *Denver Post,* January 3, 1999.

95. Intergovernmental Panel on Climate Change (IPCC), *Climate Change 2001: The Scientific Basis. Contribution of Working Group I to the Third Assessment Report of the Intergovernmental Panel on Climate Change.* Cambridge University Press, 2001.

96. Lester Brown. *Plan B 2.0: Rescuing A Planet Under Stress And A Civilization In Trouble.* W.W. Norton, 2006, p. 64.

97. Intergovernmental Panel on Climate Change (IPCC). *Climate Change 2001: The Scientific Basis. Contribution of Working Group I to the Third Assessment Report of the Intergovernmental Panel on Climate Change.* Cambridge University Press, 2001.

98. US Bureau of the Census. *Statistical Abstract of the United States: 2005.* US Government Printing Office, 2005, table 1332 [Source: Organization for Economic Cooperation and Development, *Environmental Data Compendium,* 2002].

99. National Highway Traffic and Safety Administration (NHTSA). "CAFE Overview — Frequently Asked Questions" [online]. [cited April 5, 2006]. www.nhtsa.gov/cars/rules/CAFE/overview.htm.

100. US Census Bureau. International Data Base [online]. [cited February 7, 2006]. www.census.gov/main/www/popclock.html.

101. UN Department of Economic and Social Affairs. *World Population Prospects: The 2004 Revision.* United Nations, 2005, p.1.

102. Dave Tilford. "Turning Down the Heat." *In Balance,* Summer 2005, no. 32.

103. J.D. Power and Associates. "Sales of Hybrid Electric Vehicles Expected To Grow 268 Percent By 2012". [online]. [cited May 24, 2006]. Press release, January 4, 2006. www.jdpa.com/news/releases/pressrelease.asp?ID=2006001&search=1.

104. Lester Brown. *Plan B 2.0: Rescuing A Planet Under Stress And A Civilization In Trouble.* W.W. Norton, 2006, p. 187.

105. Ibid., p. 194, compiled from Paul Maycock. "PV News Annual Market Survey Results." *Photovoltaic News,* April 2005.

106. Harry Dunphy (Associated Press), "Report Finds World in Ecological Decline," Daily Camera, January 14, 2001.

107. "Indicators." *YES! a journal of positive futures,* Winter 1999/2000.

108. Vote Solar. "The San Francisco Story" [online]. [cited February 6, 2006]. www.votesolar.org/sf.html.

109. Lester Brown, *Plan B 2.0: Rescuing A Planet Under Stress And A Civilization In Trouble.* W.W. Norton, 2006, p. 229.

110. Bette K. Fishbein, John R. Ehrenfeld, and John E. Young. *Extended Producer Responsibility: a materials policy for the 21st century.* Inform, 2000, p. 244.

111. Beverly Thorpe and Iza Kruszewska. "Strategies To Promote Clean Production" [online]. [cited May 24, 2006]. January 1999. www.svtc. org/cleancc/pubs/strat.htm.

112. Sam Cole. "Zero Waste — On the Move Around the World." *Eco-Cycle Times,* Fall/Winter 2000.

113. Jennifer Bogo. "Like a Virgin: A Grassroots Group Pressures Coke to Use Recycled Plastic." *E! The Environmental Magazine,* January/February 2001; City of Toronto Press Release. "Task Force 2010 Seeks Made-in-Toronto Solutions for Waste." January 29, 2001.

114. USAID. "Bangladesh's Emerging Success Story In Population And Family Planning" [online]. April 1996 www.usaid.gov.

115. Gene B. Sperling. "Toward Universal Education." *Foreign Affairs,* September/October 2001, pp. 7-13.

116. Roger Highfield. "Antarctic Ozone Hole Shrinking." *The Telegraph* (U.K.), December 22, 2002.

117. United Nations Development Programme. *Global Environmental Outlook-3.* Earthscan Publications, 2002, pp. 211, 230.

118. Federal Election Commission. "National Voter Turnout in Federal Elections: 1960–2004" [online]. [cited March 10, 2006]. www.info please.com/ipa/A0781453.html.

119. International Institute for Democracy and Electoral Assistance. "Voter Turnout: A Global Survey. Turnout in the World: Country by country performance." {online]. [cited April 5, 2006]. www.idea.int/vt/survey/voter_turnout2.cfm.

120. The Century Foundation, Common Cause Education Fund, and Leadership Conference on Civil Rights. "Voting In 2004: A Report To The Nation On America's Election Process" [Conference Proceedings]. December 7, 2004, Washington, D.C.

121. Keith Meatto. "Donation Inflation." *Mother Jones,* July/August 2000.

122. Larry Makinson. *Speaking Freely: Washington Insiders Talk About Money In Politics.* Center for Responsive Politics, 2003.

123. Public Campaign. "Why Fat Cats Are Purring about Congressional Reforms" [online]. [cited July 10, 2000]. www.publicampaign.org/fatcat 2.html.

124. Center for Responsive Politics [online]. [cited March 1, 2005]. www.opensecrets.org.

125. Center for Responsive Politics. "Business-Labor-Ideology Split in PAC, Soft & Individual Donations to Candidates and Parties" [online]. [cited March 2, 2006]. www.opensecrets.org/big picture/blio.asp?Cycle=2004&display=Pacs.

126. Center for Responsive Politics. "2004 Presidential Election" [online]. [cited March 2, 2006]. www.opensecrets.org/presidential/index.asp?grap h=receipts.

127. Buy Blue.Org. Company profiles based on data released by the Federal Election Commission [online]. [cited April 6, 2006]. www.buy blue.org.

128. Ibid.

129. Common Cause. "527 Groups" [online]. [cited March 3, 2006]. www.commoncause.org/site/ pp.asp?c=dkLNK1MQIwG&b=201162.

130. Mark Memmott and Jim Drinkard. "Election Ad Battle Smashes Record in 2004." *USA Today,* November 25, 2004.

131. Leonard Sussman and Karen Deutsch Karlekar. *Survey of Press Freedom 2002.* Freedom House, 2001.

132. Ben Bagdikian. *The New Media Monopoly.* Beacon Press, 2004.

133. Mike Budd, Steve Craig, and Clay Steinman, *Consuming Environments: Television and Commercial Culture.* Rutgers University Press, 1999.

134. Dan Smith. *The Penguin State of the World Atlas.* Penguin, 2003, p. 12.

135. Public Campaign. "First Gubernatorial Clean Money Candidate Clears Vermont Threshold" [online], Press release, June 14, 2000. www.pub licampaign.org.

136. Public Campaign. "Record Number Of 'Clean' Candidates Elected In Maine and Arizona System Also Takes Hold in North Carolina" [online]. [cited May 24, 2006]. Press release, November 5, 2004. www.publicampaign.org/pressroom/press releases/release2004/release_11_05_04.htm.

137. The Century Foundation, Common Cause Education Fund, and Leadership Conference on Civil Rights. "Voting In 2004: A Report To The Nation On America's Election Process" [Conference Proceedings]. December 7, 2004, Washington, D.C.

138. United Nations Development Programme. *Human Development Report: 2000.* Oxford University Press, 2000, p. 4.; UN Millennium Project. *Taking Action: Achieving Gender Equality and Empowering Women.* Task Force on Education and Gender Equality. Earthscan, 2005.

139. Nafis Sadik and United Nations Population Fund. *The State of World Population Report 2000: Lives Together, Worlds Apart — Men and Women in a Time of Change.* United Nations Population Fund, 2000.

140. Ibid.

141. UN Population Fund. "Press Summary" [online]. [cited May 29, 2006]. *State of World Population 2005: The Promise of Equality: Gender Equality, Reproductive Health & the MDG's.* UN, 2005. www.unfpa.org/swp/2005/presskit/summary.htm.

142. Inter-Parliamentary Union. "Women in National Parliaments" [online]. [cited May 29, 2006]. www. ipu.org/wmn-e/world.htm, updated January 31, 2006.

143. UN Population Fund. "Press Summary" [online]. [cited May 29, 2006]. *State of World Population 2005: The Promise of Equality: Gender Equality, Reproductive Health & the MDG's.* UN, 2005. www.unfpa.org/swp/2005/presskit/summary.htm.

144. International Women's Health Coalition [online]. [cited May 20, 2000]. www.iwhc.org/help. html.

145. Nafis Sadik and United Nations Population Fund. *The State of World Population Report 2000: Lives Together, Worlds Apart — Men and Women in a Time of Change.* United Nations Population Fund, 2000.

146. National Abortion Rights Action League. "Abortion" [online]. [cited March 17, 2006]. www.prochoiceamerica.org/issues/abortion.

147. Inter-Parliamentary Union. "Women in National Parliaments" [online]. [cited May 29, 2006]. www.ipu.org/wmn-e/world.htm, updated on January 31, 2006.

148. James Heintz, Nancy Folbre, et al. *The Ultimate Field Guide to the US Economy: A Compact and Irreverent Guide to Economic Life in America.* New Press, 2000, p. 58.

149. US Census Bureau. *Income, Poverty, and Health Insurance Coverage in the US: 2004* [online]. [cited May 29, 2006]. US Government Printing Office, 2005, Table 3, p.10. www.census.gov/hhes/www/poverty/poverty04.html.

150. Associated Press. "Study Says White Families' Wealth Advantage has Grown." New York Times. October 18, 2004, p. A13.

151. US Census Bureau. "Current Population Survey 2005 Annual Social and Economic Supplement" [online]. [cited May 29, 2006]. Detailed Poverty Tables, Table POV05, March 2005. www.pubdb3.census.gov/macro/032005/pov/new05_100_05.htm and www.pubdb3.census.gov/macro/032005/pov/new05_100_16.htm.

152. Jennifer Kerr. "ACLU Sues California Over Schools." Associated Press, May 19, 2000.

153. Danielle Knight. "Controversy Swirls Around Mercury Shipment from US to India." InterPress Service, January 25, 2001.

154. Robert Bryce. "Toxic Trade Imbalance." *Mother Jones,* January/February 2001.

155. Jim Motavalli. "Toxic Targets: Polluters that Dump on Communities of Color are Finally Being Brought to Justice." *E! The Environmental Magazine,* July/August 1998.

156. Dan Smith. *The Penguin State of the World Atlas.* Penguin, 2003, pp. 62-3. Data from a survey conducted by the International Lesbian and Gay Rights Association www.ilga.org.

157. Associated Press. "Dubai Police Raid Mass Gay Wedding." November 26, 2005.

158. Defense Of Marriage Act Watch. Marriage Amendment Summary. [online]. [cited March 17, 2006]. www.domawatch.org/about/amendment summary.html.

159. World Health Organization. "World Health Organization Assesses The World's Health Systems." Press release, June 21, 2000. www.who.int/inf-pr-2000/en/pr2000-44.html.

160. United Nations Development Programme. *Human Development Report 2004.* UN, 2004, pp. 168-171.

161. Laura Dely. "Aiding and Abetting an Epidemic." *Sojourners,* November/December 1999; United Nations Development Programme. *Human Development Report 2004.* UN, 2004, p. 171.

162. Lester R. Brown. "Challenges of the New Century." In *State of the World 2000.* W.W. Norton, 2000; United Nations Development Programme. *Human Development Report 2004.* UN, 2004, p. 170.

163. US Census Bureau. *Income, Poverty, and Health Insurance Coverage in the US: 2004.* [online]. [cited May 29, 2006]. US Government Printing Office, 2005, Figure 5, p.17. www.census.gov/hhes/www/poverty/poverty04.html.

164. Raja Mishra. "US Health Care System Ranked 37th." *The Boston Globe,* June 21, 2000.

165. Analysis of US Department of Justice Data in Jason Ziedenberg and Vincent Schiraldi. *The Punishing Decade: Prison and Jail Estimates at the Millennium.* Justice Policy Institute, May 2000.

166. Ibid.

167. Michael J. Sniffen. "Murder rate hits 40-year low; all major crime rates down." Associated Press. October 17, 2005.

168. Information is taken from various pages on ACORN's website www.acorn.org [cited February 15, 2006].

169. United Nations Development Programme. *Human Development Report 2001.* Oxford University Press, 2001.

170. Ilene R. Prusher (Christian Science Monitor). "Kuwati Women Seek Vote." *Colorado Daily,* August 9, 2000.

171. US Census Bureau. *Income, Poverty, and Health Insurance Coverage in the US: 2004.* [online]. [cited May 29, 2006]. US Government Printing Office, 2005, Figure 2, p. 7. www.census.gov/hhes/www/poverty/poverty04.html.

172. V-Day. "About V-Day" [on-line]. [cited June 8, 2006]. www.vday.org/contents/vday/aboutvday.

173. "Same-Sex Marriage" *Wikipedia* [online]. [cited February 23, 2006]. www.en.wikipedia.org/wiki/Same-sex_marriage.

174. National Gay and Lesbian Task Force. 2005. "Glass Nearly Half Full: Analysis Shows 47% of U.S. Population Now Protected From Discrimination Based on Sexual Orientation" [online]. [cited May 29, 2006]. Press Release, January 25, 2005. www.thetaskforce.org/media/release.cfm?releaseID=782.

175. Jeffrey Sachs. "A New Map of the World." *The Economist,* June 22, 2000.

176. United Nations Population Fund. "Press Summary" [online]. [cited May 29, 2006]. *State of World Population 2005: The Promise of Equality: Gender Equality, Reproductive Health & the MDG's.* www.unfpa.org/swp/2005/presskit/summary.htm; Lester Brown. *Plan B 2.0: Rescuing A Planet Under Stress And A Civilization In Trouble.* W.W. Norton, 2006, p. 127.

177. United Nations Population Fund. "Press Summary" [online]. [cited February 18, 2006]. *State of World Population 2005: The Promise of Equality: Gender Equality, Reproductive Health & the MDG's.* www.unfpa.org/swp/2005/presskit/summary.htm.

178. Adrienne Germain. "Making Progress: An International Agenda to Secure and Advance Sexual and Reproductive Rights and Health." Speech at *HIV/AIDS and Reproductive Health: Everybody's Business* conference, October 25, 2005.

179. Lester Brown. *Plan B 2.0: Rescuing A Planet Under Stress And A Civilization In Trouble.* W.W. Norton, 2006, p. 133.

180. Ibid., p. 140.

181. United Nations Development Programme. *The 1999 Human Development Report.* Oxford University Press, 1999.

182. United Nations Development Programme. *The Human Development Report: 1998.* Oxford University Press, 1998.

183. Ibid.

184. *Ad and the Ego.* Sut Jhally, Director. California Newsreel, 1996. [documentary film].

185. Fairness and Accuracy in Reporting (FAIR). "In the Soup at The View: ABC allows corporate sponsor to buy talkshow content" [online]. [cited May 30, 2006]. Action Alert, November 20, 2000. www.fair.org/index.php?page=1708.

186. Juliet Schor. *Born to Buy.* Scribner, 2004, p. 76.

187. "Dealing for Dollars," *Austin American-Statesman,* May 17, 2000; American Council for an Energy-Efficient Economy. "The Meanest Vehicles for the Environment 2006" [online]. [cited May 30, 2006]. www.greenercars.com/ 12mean.html.

188. Lynette Lamb. "Shielding Our Little Consumers." *The Lutheran,* May 2000.

189. Melissa Dittmann. "Protecting Children from Advertising" *Monitor of Psychology.* Volume 35, No. 6 (June 2004), p. 58.

190. Martin Lindstrom. *Brandchild.* Kogan Page, 2003.

191. Kaiser Family Foundation. *Kids and Media @ the Millennium.* Kaiser Family Foundation, 1999.

192. Juliet Schor. *Born to Buy.* Scribner, 2004, p. 19.

193. David Leonhardt and Kathleen Kerwin. "Hey Kid, Buy This: Is Madison Avenue Taking 'Get 'em While They're Young' Too Far?," *Business Week,* June 30, 1997; Michael Jacobson and Laurie Ann Mazur. *Marketing Madness.* Westview Press, 1995.

194. Jeffrey D. Stanger and Natalia Gridina. "Media In The Home 1999: The Fourth Annual Survey of Parents and Children" [online]. [cited May 30, 2006]. Annenberg Public Policy Center, 1999. www.annenbergpublicpolicycenter.org/05_media _developing_child/mediasurvey/survey5.pdf.

195. Thom Marshall. "Gloria Shoulda Had a Coke and a Smile." *Houston Chronicle,* March 29, 1998, p. A37.

196. Tim Dickinson. "'E' is for E-Commerce." *Mother Jones,* May/June 2000.

197. Channel One Network, *Teen Fact Book: 1997-1998.*

198. Cara DeGette. "To Ensure Revenue, Coke Is It; Schools Urged to Boost Sales." *Denver Post,* November 22, 1998, p. B-01.

199. Mary Sutter. "Marketers Boost Pope's Visit to Mexico With Tie-ins." *Advertising Age,* January 25, 1999.

200. The Harwood Group. "Yearning for Balance: Views of Americans on Consumption, Materialism, and the Environment." Merck Family Fund, 1995.

201. Marshall Glickman. *The Mindful Money Guide.* Ballantine Wellspring, 1999, p. 188.

202. Leigh Eric Schmidt. *Consumer Rites: The Buying And Selling Of American Holidays.* Princeton University Press, 1995, p. 292.

203. Melissa Dittmann. "Consumerism: APA Task Force Recommendations" [online]. [cited May 30, 2006]. *Monitor of Psychology.* Volume 35, No. 6 (June 2004), p. 59. www.apa.org/monitor/ jun04/apatask.html.

204. Amy Saltzman. "When Less is More." *US News & World Report 1998 Career Guide,* October 27, 1997.

205. Gerald Celente. *Trends 2000: How To Prepare For And Profit From The Changes Of The 21st Century.* Warner Books, 1997.

206. Juliet Schor. *The Overspent American.* Harper-Perennial, 1998, p. 114.

207. Marilyn Berlin Snell. "Riders of the World, Unite." *Sierra,* January/February 2001.

208. "Indicators." *YES! A Journal Of Positive Futures,* Winter 1999/2000.

209. David Engwicht. *Street Reclaiming: Creating Livable Streets and Vibrant Communities.* New Society Publishers, 1999.

210. Christopher Gunn and Hazel Dayton Gunn. *Reclaiming Capital: Democratic Initiatives and Community Development.* Cornell University Press, 1991, p. 28.

211. Richard Moe and Carter Wilkie. *Changing Places: Rebuilding Community In The Age Of Sprawl.* Henry Holt 1997.

MONEY

1. Federal Reserve. "Consumer Credit" [online]. [cited May 30, 2006]. Federal Reserve Statistical Release: G19. March 7, 2006. www.federalreserve. gov/releases/G19/.

2. US Department of Commerce. *Statistical Abstract of the United States: 2006.* US Government Printing Office, 2006, Table 1175, p. 776.

3. Tom Abate. "Americans Saving Less Than Nothing." *San Francisco Chronicle,* January 8, 2006.

4. Social Investment Forum. "US Socially Responsible Investment Assets Grew Faster Than Rest Of Investment World Over Last Decade." [online]. [cited May 30, 2006]. Press release, January 24, 2006. www.socialinvestmentforum. org/Areas/News/2005Trends.htm.

5. For an explanation of the criteria we used to create these lists see the Shopping Guide in the SHOPPING chapter.

6. Domini Social Investments. "Prospectus: Domini Social Equity Fund." [online]. November 30, 2005. www.domini.com/Prospectus/index.htm.

7. Grameen Foundation USA. "Information on Microcredit" [online]. [cited May 20, 2000]. www.grameenfoundation.org/microcredit.html.

8. Laura Daly. "Aiding and Abetting an Epidemic." *Sojourners*, November/December 1999.

SHOPPING

1. John C. Ryan and Alan Durning. *Stuff: The Secret Lives of Everyday Things.* Northwest Environment Watch, 1997, pp. 4-5.

2. Jane Perlez and Kirk Johnson. "Behind Gold's Glitter: Torn Lands and Pointed Questions." *New York Times*, October 24, 2005.

3. Joel Makower. *The Green Consumer Supermarket Guide.* Penguin, 1991, p. 169.

FOOD

1. Co-op America. *National Green Pages.* Co-op America, 1999.

2. "TransFair USA Joins Oxfam in Welcoming McDonald's Rollout of Fair Trade Certified (TM) Coffee" [online]. [cited March 2, 2006]. TransFair USA press release, October 31, 2005. www.transfairusa.org/content/about/pr_051031.php.

3. Jeremy Rifkin. *Beyond Beef: The Rise and Fall of the Cattle Culture.* Dutton, 1992, p. 267.

4. Rosalie Bliss. "Grabbing a Quick Bite Nabs More Calories" [online]. [cited February 2, 2006]. USDA Agricultural Research Service, May 21, 2004. www.ars.usda.gov/is/pr/2004/040521.htm.

5. US Department of Agriculture. "Dietary Guidelines for Americans 2005 Executive Summary" [online]. [cited June 1, 2006]. www.health.gov/dietaryguidelines/dga2005/document/html/executivesummary.htm.; Lee W. Wattenburg. "Inhibition of Carcinogens by Minor Dietary Constituents." *Cancer Research*, 52, no. 7, April 1, 1995.

6. Vegetarian Resource Group — Roper Poll. "How Many Vegetarians Are There?" *Vegetarian Journal*, 16, no. 5, September/October 1997.

7. Jeremy Rifkin. *Beyond Beef: The Rise and Fall of the Cattle Culture.* Dutton, 1992.

8. H.W. Kindall and David Pimentell. "Constraints on the Expansion of the Global Food Supply." *Ambio*, 23, no. 3, 1994.

9. *Beyond Beef,* p. 153.

10. Joanne Stepaniak and Virginia Messina. *The Vegan Sourcebook.* Lowell House, 1998.

11. Norine Dworkin. "22 Reasons to Go Vegetarian Right Now." *Vegetarian Times*, April 1999, p. 91.

12. Based on research by David Pimentel as cited in: Cornell University. "End Irrigation Subsidies and Reward Conservation" [online]. Press release, January 20, 1997. www.news.cornell.edu/releases/Jan97/water.hrs.html.

13. Hog Watch. "Factory Hog Farming: The Big Picture" [online]. [cited June 21, 2000]. www.hogwatch.org.

14 Based on research by David Pimentel as cited in: Cornell University. "End Irrigation Subsidies and Reward Conservation" [online]. Press release, January 20, 1997. www.news.cornell.edu/releases/Jan97/water.hrs.html.

15. Derek M. Brown. "How The Meat Industry Destroys Waterways." *Good Medicine,* 8, no. 1, Winter 1999.

16. Tom Knudson. "Part Two: Waste on Grand Scale Loots Sea." *Sacramento Bee,* December 11, 1995.

17. Environmental Defense Fund. *Annual Report.* 1997.

18. Audubon Society. "Audubon's National Seafood Wallet Card" [online]. [cited May 25, 2006]. Released May 2004. seafood.audubon.org .

19. UN Food and Agriculture Organization (FAO), *The State of Food Insecurity in the World 2004.* United Nations, 2004.

20. United Nations Development Programme. *The 1999 Human Development Report.* Oxford University Press, 1999.

21. David Pimentel. "Livestock Production: Energy Inputs and the Environment." In *Canadian Society of Animal Science: Proceedings of the 47th Annual Meeting,* edited by Scott and Xin Zhao, Montreal, Quebec, July 1997, pp. 16-26.

22. Christopher D. Cook. "Hog-Tied: Migrant Workers Find Themselves Trapped on the Pork Assembly Line." *The Progressive,* September 1999.

23. Stephen J. Hedgers. "The New Jungle." *US News & World Report,* 121, no. 12, September 23, 1996.

24. Humane Farming Association. "A Look Inside the Pork Industry." [online]. [cited May 17, 2000]. 1990. www.hfa.org.

25. R.L. Phillips. "The Role of Lifestyle and Dietary Habits on Risk of Cancer Among Seventh Day Adventists." *Cancer Research,* 35, 1990, pp. 3513-3522.

26. John Robbins. *Diet for A New America.* Stillpoint, 1987.

27. Richard Behar and Michael Kramer. "Something Smells Foul." Time, October 17, 1994.

28. Erik Marcus. *Vegan: The New Ethics of Eating.* McBooks Press, 1998.

29. Jim Mason. "Fowling the Waters." *E! Magazine,* September/October 1995.

30. Physicians Committee for Responsible Medicine. "The Protein Myth." [online]. [cited June 5, 2006]. www.pcrm.org/health/veginfo/vsk/protein_myth.html .

PERSONAL

1. We owe our understanding of creativity to the incredible mentorship of Jim Downton.

2. UNICEF. "Malnutrition: Causes" [online]. [cited March 4, 2000]. The State of the Worlds Children 1998. www.unicef.org/sowc98/fs01.htm.

3. Barbara F. Orlans. "Data on Animal Experimentation in the United States: What They Do and Do Not Show." *Perspectives in Biology and Medicine,* 37 no. 2., Winter 1994.

4. Arnot Ogden Medical Center [online]. [cited October 20, 2000]. www.aomc.org (link expired).

5. Ibid.

6. Report issued by the National Center for Health Statistics, presented by Katherine Flegal at the October 1996 meeting of the North American Association for the Study of Obesity.

7. American Medical Association [online]. [cited May 16, 2000]. www.ama-assn.org/insight/gen_hlth/fitness/fitness.htm (link expired).

8. Mayo Clinic [online]. [cited May 16, 2000]. www.mayohealth.org/mayo/9610/htm/ sleep.htm (link expired).

9. J.H. Peter, T. Penzel, T. Podszus, and P. von Wichert, eds. *Sleep and Health Risk.* Springer-Verlag, 1991, p. 555.

FRIENDS AND FAMILY

1. Labor Department Study cited in Edmund Andrews. "Survey Confirms It: Women Out-juggle Men." *New York Times,* September 15, 2004.

2. Leo Buscaglia. Love. Fawcett Books, 1996.

3. Zero Population Growth Population Education Program. *Countdown to 6,000,000,000.* ZPG, 1999.

4. National Adoption Information Clearing House. "Statistics – General – How Many Children Were Adopted in 2000 and 2001" [online]. [cited June 2, 2006]. www.naic.acf.hhs.gov/profess/admin/ stats/index.cfm.

5. Adoption and Foster Care Analysis and Reporting System. Report 2001.

6. Michael F. Jacobson and Lauri Ann Mazur. *Marketing Madness.* Westview Press, 1995, p. 22.

7. Kaiser Family Foundation. *Kids and the Media at the Milennium.* Menlo Park, CA, 1999.

8. Ibid.

COMMUNITY

1. US Census Bureau Public Information Office. May 15, 2000.

2. US Census Bureau. Geographical Mobility March 1992 to March 1993.

3. Judann Pollack. "Foods Targeting Children Aren't Just Child's Play." *Advertising Age,* March 1, 1999.

4. Parents, Families, and Friends of Lesbians and Gays [online]. [cited July 15, 2001]. www.pflag. org/schools/educators.htm (link expired).

5. "Indicators." *Yes! Magazine,* Summer 1999.

6. National Low Income Housing Coalition. "Out of Reach" [online]. [cited June 5, 2006]. 1999 Report. www.nlihc.org/oor99/index.htm .

7. Economic Policy Institute. America's Well-Targeted Raise. September 1997.

8. Kathleen Haley. "Innovative Living Wage Law in Sam Francisco." *Business Ethics,* September/October 2000; "Compass'. *Utne Reader,* November/December 2000.

9. ACORN's Living Wage Resource Center. "The Living Wage Movement: Building Power in Our Workplaces and Neighborhoods" [online] [cited February 1, 2006] www.livingwagecampaign.org/ index.php?id=2071.

SPIRITUALITY AND RELIGION

1. His Divine Grace A. C. Baktivedanta Swami Prabhupada. *Baghavad-Gita As It Is.* International Society for Krishna Consciousness, 1972.

2. Stephen Mitchell. *Tao Te Ching: A New English Version.* HarperPerennial, 1988, verse 78.

3. Robert G. Hoerber, editor. *The Concordia Self-Study Bible.* Concordia Publishing House, 1990, Luke 6:27-29.

4. Amatal Rahman Omar, translator. *The Holy Quaran.* Noor Foundation International, 1997, Chapter 107:1-7.

5. Nosson Sherman, translator. *The Chumash: The Artscroll Series.* Mesorah Publications, 2000, Isaiah 58:7.

6. Laurie Goodstein. "Evangelical Leaders Join Global Warming Initiative." *New York Times,* February 8, 2006.

7. Kris Axtman. "The Rise of the American Megachurch" [online]. [cited June 5, 2006]. *Christian Science Monitor,* December 30, 2003. www.csmonitor.com/2003/1230/p01s04-ussc.html.

HOME

1. Donald Lotter. *Earthscore: A Personal Environmental Audit and Guide.* Morning Sun Press, 1993.

2. "Home Energy Brief #4, Space Heating" [online]. [cited June 6, 2006]. Rocky Mountain Institute, 2004. www.rmi.org/sitepages/pid171.php#LibH shldEnEff.

3. US Department of Energy. "Energy Savers: Programmable Thermostats" [online]. [cited June 6, 2006]. www.eere.energy.gov/consumer/tips/ thermostats.html.

4. "Home Energy Brief #3, Space Cooling" [online]. [cited June 6, 2006]. Rocky Mountain Institute, 2004, p.6. www.rmi.org/sitepages/pid171.php# LibHshldEnEff.

5. Ibid.

6. Ibid.

7. "Home Energy Brief #5: Water Heating" [online]. [cited June 19, 2006]. Rocky Mountain Institute, 2004, p. 6. www.rmi.org/sitepages/pid171.php# LibHshldEnEff.

8. Ibid., p. 3.

9. American Council for an Energy-Efficient Economy (ACEEE). "Home Energy Checklist for Action" [online]. [cited February 7, 2006]. www.aceee.org/consumerguide/chklst.htm.

10. "Home Energy Brief #8: Kitchen Appliances" [online]. [cited June 19, 2006]. Rocky Mountain Institute, 2004, p. 2. www.rmi.org/sitepages/pid 171.php#LibHshldEnEff.

11. "Home Energy Brief #6: Cleaning Appliances" [online]. [cited June 6, 2006]. Rocky Mountain Institute, 2004, p.1. www.rmi.org/sitepages/pid 171.php#LibHshldEnEff.

12. Ibid., p.2.

13. "Home Energy Brief #7: Electronics" [online]. [cited June 19, 2006]. Rocky Mountain Institute, 2004, p. 2. www.rmi.org/sitepages/pid171.php# LibHshldEnEff.

14. U.S. Department of Energy. "Estimating Appliance and Home Electronic Energy Use" [online]. [cited June 19, 2006]. www.eere.energy. gov/consumer/your_home/appliances/index.cfm/ mytopic=10040.

15. Diana Barnett & W.D. Browning. *A Primer on Sustainable Building.* Rocky Mountain Institute, 2004, p. 39.

16. "Home Energy Brief #4, Space Heating" [online]. [cited June 6, 2006]. Rocky Mountain Institute 2004. www.rmi.org/sitepages/pid171.php# LibH shldEnEff.

17. A. Wilson, J. Thorne & J. Morrill. *Consumer Guide to Home Energy, 8th ed.* American Council for an Energy-Efficient Economy (ACEEE), 2003.

18. Diane MacEachern. Save the Planet. Dell, 1995, p. 19.

19. Umoja Edwards. "The Five Bulb Challenge." *Real Money,* Winter 2000; Michael Brower and Warren Leon. *The Consumer's Guide to Effective Environmental Choices: Practical Advice from the Union of Concerned Scientists.* Three Rivers Press, 1999, p. 106.

20. Sue Hassol. "Home Energy Brief #4: Water Heating." Rocky Mountain Institute, 1994; "Home Energy Brief #5: Water Heating" [online]. [cited June 19, 2006]. Rocky Mountain Institute, 2004, p. 1. www.rmi.org/sitepages/pid171.php#LibHshldEnEff.

21. Sue Hassol. "Home Energy Brief #4: Water Heating." Rocky Mountain Institute, 1994.

22. James P. Heaney, Len Wright, and David Sample. "Sustainable Urban Water Management." In James P. Heaney, Robert Pitt, and Richard Field, editors. *Innovative Urban Wet-Weather Flow Management Systems.* U.S. Environmental Protection Agency, EPA/600/R-99/029, 1998, p. 3-10.

23. John Koeller. "Dual-Flush Toilet Fixtures-Field Studies and Water Savings" [online]. [cited June 20, 2006]. P.E. Koeller and Company, 2003. www.cuwcc.org/Uploads/product/Dual_Flush_Fixture_Studies_03-12-17.pdf.

24. US Environmental Protection Agency. "Basic Facts: Municipal Solid Waste (MSW)" [online]. [cited February 16, 2006]. www.epa.gov/epaoswer/non-hw/muncpl/facts.htm.

25. Ohio EPA, Office of Pollution Prevention. "Junk Mail Reduction" [online]. [cited February 16, 2006]. www.epa.state.oh.us/opp/consumer/junkmail.html.

26. Harmonious Technologies. *Backyard Composting.* Harmonious Press, 1997, p. 7.

27. Diane MacEachern. *Save the Planet.* Dell, 1995, p. 67.

28. National Association of Homebuilders. "Characteristics of New Single-Family Homes (1987-2004)" [online]. [cited February 16, 2006]. www.nahb.org/generic.aspx?genericContentID=374.

WORK

1. Phineas Baxandall and Marc Breslow. "Does Inequality Cause Overwork?" *Dollars and Sense,* 221, January/February 1999.

2. Philip L. Rones, Randy E. Ilg, and Jennifer M. Gardner. "Trends in the hours of work since the mid-1970s." *Monthly Labor Review,* April 1997.

3. "It All Adds Up to Cleaner Air Fact Sheet" [online]. [cited March 30, 2006]. 2003 data compiled for the Federal Highway Administration. www.italladdsup.gov/pdfs/fall/2005Fall_ConsumerFactSheet.doc.

4. US Department of Transportation (DOT). "Commuting Alternatives in the US: Recent Trends and a Look to the Future." 1994; US DOT. *Transportation Statistics Annual Report.* November 2005, p. 73

5. Joel Makower. *Beyond the Bottom Line: Putting Social Responsibility to Work for Your Business and the World.* Touchstone Books, 1995, p. 235.

6. Ibid., p. 227.

7. US Department of Labor. "Employment, Hours, and Earnings" [online]. [cited January 7, 2001] www.bls.gov/ces.

MEDIA

1. Ben Bagdikian. *The New Media Monopoly.* Beacon Press, 2004.

2. TV-Turnoff Network. "Facts and Figures about our TV Habit" [online]. [cited March 4, 2001]. www.tvturnoff.org/images/facts&figs/factsheets/FactsFigs.pdf.

3. Benjamin Barber, *Harper's,* November 1993, p. 41; Nielsen Media Research, 2000. In TV-Turnoff Network. "Facts and Figures about our TV Habit" [online]. [cited March 4, 2001]. www.tvturnoff.org/images/facts&figs/factsheets/FactsFigs.pdf.

4. Nielsen Media Research. "Nielsen Reports Americans Watch TV at Record Levels" [online]. [cited June 20, 2006]. Press release, September 29, 2005. www.nielsenmedia.com/newsreleases/2005/AvgHoursMinutes92905.pdf

5. Robert McChesney. *Corporate Media and the Threat to Democracy.* New York: Seven Stories Press, 1997, p. 29.

6. Michael Jacobsen and Laurie Ann Mazur. *Marketing Madness.* Westview Press, 1995.

POLITICS

1. Federal Election Commission. "National Voter Turnout in Federal Elections: 1960–2004" [online]. [cited March 10, 2006]. www.infoplease.com/ipa/A0781453.html.

2. 20/20 Vision [online]. [cited February 20, 2000]. www.2020vision.org/admin.html.

3. Jason Ziedenberg and Vincent Schiraldi. *The Punishing Decade: Prison and Jail Estimates at the Millennium.* Justice Policy Institute, analysis of US Department of Justice Data, May 2000.

4. Center for Arms Control and Non-Proliferation. "US Military Spending vs. the World" [online]. [cited June 8, 2006]. February 6, 2006 www.armscontrolcenter.org/archives/002244.php.

5. National Gay and Lesbian Task Force. "Glass Nearly Half Full" [online]. [cited June 8, 2006]. Press Release, January 25, 2005. www.thetaskforce.org/media/release.cfm?releaseID=782.

6. United for a Fair Economy. "Shifty Tax Cuts: How They Move the Tax Burden off the Rich and onto Everyone Else" [online]. [cited June 8, 2006]. April 20, 2004, p. 4. www.faireconomy.org/Taxes/HTMLReports/Shifty_Tax_Cuts.html.

7. Donald L. Barlett and James B. Steele. *America: Who Really Pays the Taxes.* Touchstone, 1994, p. 140; Congressional Budget Office. "The Budget Outlook: Fiscal Years 2005 to 2014." January 2004, Table F-3.

8. Tim Dickinson. "Tax-Free Inc." *Mother Jones,* March/April 2000.

9.   United For a Fair Economy. "Estate Tax Action Center" [online]. [cited April 1, 2006]. www.faireconomy.org/estatetax/index.html.

TRANSPORTATION

1.   US Department of Transportation (DOT). "Commuting Alternatives in the US: Recent Trends and a Look to the Future." 1994; US DOT. Transportation Statistics Annual Report. 1997; US DOT. *Transportation Statistics Annual Report.* 2005, p. 73.
2.   US Department of Transportation (DOT). "Commuting Alternatives in the US: Recent Trends and a Look to the Future." 1994; US DOT. *Transportation Statistics Annual Report.* 2005, p. 73.
3.   Michael Brower and The Union of Concerned Scientists. *The Consumer's Guide to Effective Environmental Choices.* Three Rivers Press, 1999, p. 86.
4.   US Department of Transportation, "Long-Distance Travel and Freight." Transportation, Statistics Annual Report, 1998, p. 107.
5.   Mark Shenk. "Oil Rises to 7-Week High on Forecast of Gasoline Supply Decline." March 28, 2006. www.Bloomberg.com.
6.   Gary Branson. *The Complete Guide to Recycling at Home.* Betterway, 1991, p. 82.
7.   US Department of Transportation (DOT). "Commuting Alternatives in the US: Recent Trends and a Look to the Future." 1994; US DOT. *Transportation Statistics Annual Report.* 2005, p. 73.
8.   Joel Makover. *The Green Commuter.* National Press, 1992, p. 68.
9.   Editors of Consumer Reports. *1999 Used Car Buying Guide.*
10. Michael Brower and the Union of Concerned Scientists. *The Consumer's Guide to Effective Environmental Choices.* Three Rivers Press, 1999, p. 90; "Support Cleaner Cars for Cleaner Air." 20/20 Vision, May 2000.
11. Michael Brower and the Union of Concerned Scientists. *The Consumer's Guide to Effective Environmental Choices.* Three Rivers Press, 1999, p. 90.

12. Joel Makower. *The Green Commuter.* National Press, 1992, p. 35.
13. Union of Concerned Scientists. "Biodiesel: FAQ" [online]. [cited June 9, 2006]. Last updated September 28, 2005. www.ucsusa.org/clean_vehicles/big_rig_cleanup/biodiesel.html.
14. "Environmental Commitment" [online]. [cited July 15, 2001]. www.toyota.com/ecologic.
15. Jim Motavalli. "Your Next Car?" *Sierra,* July/August, 1999.
16. Jason Mark. "Zeroing Out Pollution: The Promise of Fuel Cell Cars." Union of Concerned Scientists, 1996.

TRAVEL

1.   Accenture. "Global Travel and Tourism Exceed US$6 Trillion in 2005; Strong Performance Expected in 2006" [online]. [cited June 22, 2006]. News release, March 6 2006. www.accenture.com/xd/xd.asp?it=enweb&xd=_dyn%5Cdynamicpressrelease_962.xml.

ORGANIZATIONS

1.   A. Miranda. "Solidarity." In *Voices from the WTO: an anthology of writing by the people who shut down the World Trade Organization in Seattle 1999,* edited by Stephanie Guilloud. Evergreen State College Bookstore, 2000, p. 73.
2.   Independent Sector. "Giving and Volunteering in the United States – Key Findings" [online]. [viewed March 31, 2006]. 2001. www.independentsector.org/programs/research/GV01main.html.
3.   Rebecca Gardyn. "Generosity and Income: For Americans, Those Who Earn the Least Money Tend to Give the Most Away" [online]. [cited March 31, 2006]. *American Demographics,* December 1, 2002. www.findarticles.com/p/articles/mi_m4021/is_11_24/ai_95309979.

ACTION CHECKLIST

MONEY

BANKING
- ❏ Open an account at a socially responsible bank or credit union
- ❏ Write checks that state your values

CREDIT CARDS
- ❏ Cut up your credit cards
- ❏ Donate money while using your credit card

SAVING
- ❏ Create a budget
- ❏ Reduce your expenses

INVESTING
- ❏ Invest in socially responsible stocks
- ❏ Invest in socially responsible mutual funds
- ❏ Invest in community development loan funds
- ❏ Invest your retirement in a socially responsible manner

SHOPPING
- ❏ Resist the urge to go shopping
- ❏ Buy less stuff
- ❏ Treat workers with respect and courtesy

WHAT TO BUY
- ❏ Buy used
- ❏ Buy durable and reuseable products
- ❏ Buy products with minimal packaging

WHO TO BUY IT FROM
- ❏ Support locally-owned independent businesses
- ❏ Boycott irresponsible companies
- ❏ Let companies know how your feel
- ❏ Shop at home
- ❏ Buy products from socially responsible companies

BUYING GUIDE

FOOD

BUYING GROCERIES
- ❏ Buy organic food
- ❏ Reduce food packaging by buying in bulk
- ❏ Bring your own cloth bags
- ❏ Buy from local growers and grocers
- ❏ Support socially responsible food companies

EATING
- ❏ Prepare and eat food with others
- ❏ Support locally owned restaurants
- ❏ Eat less fast food
- ❏ Eat more fruits, vegetables, whole grains, and unprocessed foods
- ❏ Eat less meat

PLANTING A GARDEN
- ❏ Plant an organic garden
- ❏ Be an urban gardener

PERSONAL

EXTRAORDINARY LIVING
- ❏ Don't sweat the small stuff
- ❏ Think and live in color
- ❏ Live intentionally
- ❏ Commit to a creative life
- ❏ Conquer your fears
- ❏ Slow down and live in the moment
- ❏ Own less stuff
- ❏ Treat others as humans, not objects
- ❏ Be the change you wish to see in the world
- ❏ Live passionately
- ❏ Expand your circle of compassion

EMOTIONAL WELL BEING
- ❏ Forgive yourself
- ❏ Manage your stress
- ❏ Seek help when you need it

PHYSICAL WELL BEING
- ❏ Exercise regularly
- ❏ Get enough sleep
- ❏ Eat healthily

REFLECTION
- ❏ Keep a journal
- ❏ Step out of your comfort zone
- ❏ Examine your stereotypes
- ❏ Reconnect with nature
- ❏ Reconsider your priorities
- ❏ Write a personal mission statement

FRIENDS AND FAMILY

BUILDING STRONG RELATIONSHIPS
- ❏ Make time for loved ones a priority
- ❏ Check in
- ❏ Practice deep listening
- ❏ Resolve conflicts collaboratively
- ❏ Give unconditional love and support
- ❏ Share housework and childcare fairly
- ❏ Forgive others

GIVING GIFTS
- ❏ Get creative with gifts
- ❏ Donate money in someone else's name
- ❏ Buy socially responsible gifts
- ❏ Simplify the holidays

CHILDREN
- ❏ Limit your number of children
- ❏ Adopt
- ❏ Be a foster parent
- ❏ Share babysitting
- ❏ Spend quality time with children
- ❏ Be a mentor
- ❏ Express affection
- ❏ Discipline children nonviolently
- ❏ Teach caring and giving
- ❏ Model flexible gender roles
- ❏ Teach an appreciation of diversity
- ❏ Teach the difference between wants and needs

- ❏ Choose childcare that supports your values
- ❏ Limit TV watching
- ❏ Choose alternatives to being glued to the screen
- ❏ Talk with your kids about TV
- ❏ Choose alternatives to violent toys and video games

COMMUNITY

NEIGHBORHOOD
- ❏ Put down roots
- ❏ Get to know your neighbors
- ❏ Help your neighbors and ask for their help
- ❏ Organize a neighborhood event
- ❏ Plant a tree

LOCAL COMMUNITY
- ❏ Participate in community organizations
- ❏ Volunteer in a soup kitchen, homeless shelter, or food pantry
- ❏ Volunteer at your local animal shelter
- ❏ Help Habitat For Humanity build homes
- ❏ Get involved in your local schools
- ❏ Decommercialize your schools
- ❏ Create safe schools
- ❏ Support local arts and culture
- ❏ Participate in local, county, regional and statewide community events
- ❏ Get involved in your sister city program

COMMUNITY ISSUES
- ❏ Stop urban sprawl
- ❏ Advocate for affordable housing
- ❏ Advocate for a community living wage
- ❏ Advocate for increased school funding

SPIRITUALITY AND RELIGION

SPIRITUAL WELL-BEING
- ❏ Center yourself
- ❏ Foster your spiritual core
- ❏ Practice gratitude
- ❏ Practice religious tolerance
- ❏ Learn about other religions and spiritualities
- ❏ Read a book of wisdom

FAITH IN ACTION
- ❏ Live your life as a prayer
- ❏ Feed, clothe and house the poor
- ❏ Reclaim "morality"
- ❏ Start a peace and justice group in your spiritual community

RELIGIOUS AND SPIRITUAL COMMUNITY
- ❏ Join a progressive religious group
- ❏ Join or create a spiritual study group
- ❏ Cherish diversity in your spiritual community
- ❏ Make your religious facility environmentally friendly
- ❏ Form coalitions with other faiths
- ❏ Resist McDonaldized religion

HOME

ENERGY
- ❏ Use your appliances efficiently and buy efficient appliances
- ❏ Weatherize your home
- ❏ Light your home efficiently
- ❏ Contact your local utility company to perform an energy audit
- ❏ Buy clean power

WATER
- ❏ Install faucet aerators and low-flow showerheads
- ❏ Transform your toilet into a water miser
- ❏ Use environmentally friendly cleaners and laundry detergents

TRASH
- ❏ Reduce your junk mail
- ❏ Recycle
- ❏ Compost your kitchen scraps and yard waste
- ❏ Properly dispose of household hazardous waste

LAWN & GARDEN
- ❏ Xeriscape your lawn and garden
- ❏ Use a manual or electric lawn mower
- ❏ Don't bag your grass clippings
- ❏ Avoid buying unnecessary power tools

YOUR HOME
- ❏ Live close to work
- ❏ Live in a smaller home
- ❏ Arrange your furniture to encourage conversation
- ❏ Grow household plants
- ❏ Sign up with a socially responsible long distance, wireless and Internet service
- ❏ Give away your clutter
- ❏ Consciously choose your community
- ❏ Remodel with green materials

WORK
- ❏ Limit your work time
- ❏ Take your lunch to work

WORKPLACE RELATIONSHIPS
- ❏ Avoid gossip
- ❏ Appreciate everyone in your workplace
- ❏ Get to know your coworkers outside of work
- ❏ Set up a workplace carpool
- ❏ Make people from diverse backgrounds feel welcome

SOCIALLY RESPONSIBLE WORKPLACE
- ❏ Participate in workplace charitable giving
- ❏ Organize around community service
- ❏ Know your rights as an employee
- ❏ Support your fellow employees
- ❏ Confront injustices in the workplace
- ❏ Green your workplace
- ❏ Value people over profit
- ❏ Work to make your company more socially and environmentally responsible

FINDING GOOD WORK
- ❏ Choose a fulfilling job
- ❏ Use your current job skills to improve the world
- ❏ Work for justice

MEDIA

TELEVISION
- ❏ Watch less TV
- ❏ Watch and support non-commercial television

RADIO
- ❏ Listen to and support your community and public radio stations
- ❏ Tune in to alternative radio programs

MAGAZINES
- ❏ Read alternative magazines

NEWSPAPERS
- ❏ Read and recycle your local newspaper
- ❏ Write a letter to the editor

INTERNET
- ❏ Get connected to progressive web sites
- ❏ Join an inspiring email action list
- ❏ Subscribe to some informative podcasts

POLITICS

VOTING
- ❏ Register to vote
- ❏ Seek out good information before each election
- ❏ Create your own voting strategy
- ❏ Vote
- ❏ Help others vote

GETTING INVOLVED
- ❏ Join a party that reflects your values
- ❏ Stay informed
- ❏ Contact your representatives
- ❏ Speak powerfully

TRANSPORTATION

- ❏ Use the slowest form of transportation that is practical

WALKING
- ❏ Go on a daily walk

BICYCLING
- ❏ Use your bike for commuting and errands

PUBLIC TRANSIT
- ❏ Use public transit for commuting and errands
- ❏ Take a bus
- ❏ Take a train

AUTOMOBILES
- ❏ Set concrete goals for reducing driving
- ❏ Be a considerate driver

- ❏ Maintain your car in good running condition
- ❏ Drive moderately
- ❏ Carpool
- ❏ Fuel up responsibly
- ❏ Buy a used car
- ❏ Choose a low emission, fuel-efficient car

TRAVEL

WHERE TO GO
- ❏ Explore your own backyard
- ❏ Experience nature
- ❏ Visit state and national parks
- ❏ Travel off-season to unknown places

WHERE TO STAY
- ❏ Stay with the locals
- ❏ Stay in a hostel
- ❏ Stay at a bed & breakfast
- ❏ Exchange your home

WHAT TO DO
- ❏ Connect with the locals
- ❏ Limit your vacation trinkets
- ❏ Support local economies
- ❏ Use alternative transportation

EXTRAORDINARY TRAVEL
- ❏ Study abroad
- ❏ Take a reality tour
- ❏ Take an eco-tour
- ❏ Combine service and travel
- ❏ Take a personal growth vacation

ORGANIZATIONS

GETTING INVOLVED
- ❏ Join an organization you care about
- ❏ Participate in an organization you care about
- ❏ Volunteer for an organization you care about

GIVING
- ❏ Donate money based on your values
- ❏ Set up a giving budget
- ❏ Put an organization in your will

FINDING ORGANIZATIONS
- ❏ Support organizations that create long-term social change
- ❏ Support local organizations

INDEX

ABOUT THE AUTHORS

ELLIS JONES, PH.D., currently teaches in the department of sociology at the University of California, Davis and is the founder of The Better World Network, a nonprofit dedicated to the democratization of activism to create a more just and sustainable world. Ellis leads workshops around the country on global social responsibility and the translation of lofty ideals about saving the world into sustainable, effective, everyday actions. His other works include *The Better World Shopping Guide: Every Dollar Makes A Difference* (New Society Publishers, 2006).

ROSS HAENFLER, PH.D., is a sociology professor at the University of Mississippi where he teaches Social Movements, Political Sociology, and Men and Masculinities. His book *Straight Edge: Clean Living Youth, Hardcore Punk, and Social Change* (Rutgers, 2006) is the first in-depth study of the straight edge scene. As a member of the Mennonite Church, Ross has been part of many social movements. He loves hiking and backpacking, vegetarian cooking and listening to many kinds of music.

BRETT JOHNSON, PH.D., is a sociology professor at Luther College. He teaches courses in the areas of social conflict, social movements, environmental studies, research methods, statistics and political economy. He has most extensively studied the US Voluntary Simplicity movement. He loves singing and playing acoustic guitar. He lives in Decorah, Iowa with his wife, Jen, and their children, Ben and Katie.

If you have enjoyed *The Better World Handbook* you might also enjoy other

BOOKS TO BUILD A NEW SOCIETY

Our books provide positive solutions for people who want to make a difference. We specialize in:

**Environment and Justice • Conscientious Commerce
Sustainable Living • Ecological Design and Planning
Natural Building & Appropriate Technology • New Forestry
Educational and Parenting Resources • Nonviolence
Progressive Leadership • Resistance and Community**

New Society Publishers

ENVIRONMENTAL BENEFITS STATEMENT

New Society Publishers has chosen to produce this book on Enviro 100, recycled paper made with **100% post consumer waste**, processed chlorine free, and old growth free.

For every 5,000 books printed, New Society saves the following resources:[1]

32	Trees
2,881	Pounds of Solid Waste
3,170	Gallons of Water
4,135	Kilowatt Hours of Electricity
5,237	Pounds of Greenhouse Gases
23	Pounds of HAPs, VOCs, and AOX Combined
8	Cubic Yards of Landfill Space

[1]Environmental benefits are calculated based on research done by the Environmental Defense Fund and other members of the Paper Task Force who study the environmental impacts of the paper industry.

For a full list of NSP's titles, please call 1-800-567-6772 *or check out our website at:*

www.newsociety.com

NEW SOCIETY PUBLISHERS